Blvd. Peripherique

Porte de
gnancourt
Blvd. Ney
Porte de
la Chapelle
Porte
d'Aubervi
Blvd.
Porte
iéral Leclerc
ive

D0126600

e Ordener
Blvd. Ornano
Rue de la Chapelle
Rue Riquet
Rue de Crimée
Pantin

Rue Custine
Place
du Terte
Rue Marx
Dormoy
Rue de Flandre
Ave. Jean Jaurés

Sacré-
Coeur
Blvd. de la Chapelle
Rue du Faubourg St-
Denis
Rue du Faubourg St-Martin
Rue Manin
Parc des
Buttes-
Chaumont
Rue General
Bresnet
Blvd. Sérurier

Blvd. de Clichy
Blvd. Barbés
Gare du
Nord
Rue de Belleville
Porte
des Lilas

e de
teaudun
La Fayette
Gare de
l'Est
Rue de Strasbourg
Ave. Claude
Vellefaux
Blvd. de la Villette
Rue des Pyrénées
Ave. Gambetta

d. Montmartre
Rue d' Hauteville
Blvd. de Magenta
Rue de Faubourg du Temple
Blvd. de Belleville
Blvd. Mortier

ibliothèque
itionale
Rue Réaumur
Blvd. St-Martin
Ave. de la République
Ave.Gambetta
Rue Belgrand

des Petits Champs
alais
oyal
Rue de Turbigo
Blvd. du
Temple
Ave. Parmentier
Rue du Chemin-Vert
Cimetière du
Père-Lachaise
Blvd. Davout

du Louvre
Les Halles
Garden
Archives
Nationales
Rue du Temple
Blvd. Beaumarchais
Rue Richard Lenoir
Blvd. Voltaire
Blvd. de
Ménilmontant

Pont-
Neuf
Rue de Sébastopol
Rue Beaubourg
Rue Rambuteau
Picasso
Museum
Rue St-Antoine
Ave. Philippe
Auguste
Rue d'Auron
Rue des Pyrénées
Blvd. Peripherique

Palais de
Justice
Ste.-
Chapelle
Tour
St.-Jacques
Place de
Vosges

St.-Germain
onne
ais du
embourg
Notre-
Dame
Place de
la Bastille
Rue St-Antoine
Place de
la Nation
Cours de
Vincennes
Ave. du Dr. Netter
Blvd. Soult

Michel
Rue Gay
Lussac
Rue Monge
Panthéon
Rue Henri IV
Rue Bourdon
Blvd. de la Bastille
Ledru Rollin
Ave. Daumesnil
Blvd. Diderot
Rue de Charenton
Ave. de
St.-Mandé
Rue de Picpus
Ave. du
Gen. Bizot
Blvd. Soult
Porte
Dorée

Rue Claude
Bernard
Rue Mouffetard
Jardin
de Paris
Quai St.-Bernard
Quai de la Rapée
Gare de
Lyon
Blvd. de Bercy
Blvd. de Reuilly

M. de Port Royal
Rue de l'Hôpital
Gare
d'Austerlitz
Velodrome
D'Hiver
Quai de Bercy
Bois de
Vincennes

serervatoire
Paris
d. Argo
Ave. des Gobelins
Blvd. St-Marcel
De l'Hôpital
Quai d'Austerlitz
Rue de Paris

St.-Jacques
tre
pitalier
Anne
d'Alésia
Blvd. Vincent Auriol
Place
d'Italie
Seine
Blvd. Poniatowski

Rue Bobillot
Rue de Tolbiac

de
tsouris
Blvd.
Kellermann
Ave. d'Ivry
Ave. de Choisy
Ave. d'Italie
Blvd. Masséna
Porte
d'Ivry
Blvd. Peripherique

ersitaire
Porte
d'Italie

3

Orientation

At first glance, Paris' broad expanse looks like one great tangle of medieval streets. Don't be dismayed, however, for there's logic in the layout that, once grasped, makes Paris as easy to navigate as your average college campus. Tall buildings are forbidden (the Montparnasse Tower was a temporary aesthetic lapse on the part of former president Georges Pompidou), and the reference points provided by the major monuments (Eiffel Tower, Panthéon, Arc de Triomphe, etc.) and the Seine river make locating yourself and your destination reassuringly easy. Part of the logic is that the city is subdivided into 20 numbered *arrondissements* (quarters). Starting from the first arrondissement (the area around the Louvre), they spiral outward like the compartments of a snail's shell to the city limits.

Since each arrondissement has its own distinct class and character, Paris feels less like a monstrous metropolis than a score of small towns. The seven walks in this book—from "The Islands" on page 10 to "Montmartre" on page 166 —offer you a diverse array of Parisian neighborhoods and sights to visit and savor. The system of axes that cuts through the city, connecting landmarks and generally giving the city shape, is also a splendid means of orientation. The most obvious axis runs in a straight line from La Defénse in the west, eastward through the Arc de Triomphe, down the Champs-Elysées to the Louvre, continuing all the way to the Bastille.

On roads perpendicular to the Seine, the street addresses begin at the river and increase as you move inland. With your back to the Seine (on either bank), the even numbers will be on the right, the odds on the left. Streets running parallel to the Seine are numbered from east to west, the direction the river flows. If the street is on an island, with the Seine all around, a No. 1 address is to the south, closest to Rome. Be aware that even and odd street addresses often don't correspond; No. 42 may be across the street from No. 85, not No. 43 as you might expect.

While this overall understanding of Paris is helpful, it won't change the fact that the streets are labyrinthine. The basic—and essential—tool for threading your way through this maze is the *Paris par Arrondissement,* a pocket-size book of maps sold at newsstands and bookstores throughout Paris and at some specialty travel bookstores in the United States. It contains a map of each arrondissement, as well as métro and bus-route maps. Every thoroughfare in the city, from Rue de l'Abbaye to the Boulevard de la Zone, is listed alphabetically in the front of the book, with its arrondissement, letter/number map coordinates, and the nearest métro station. Be sure to check carefully whether the street you need is designated *rue* (street), *boulevard,* or *avenue.*

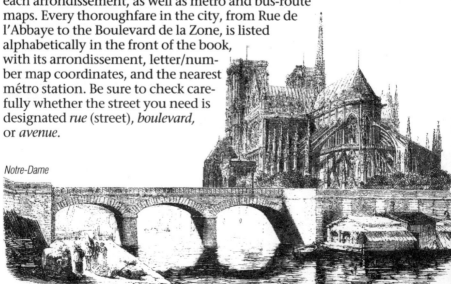

Notre-Dame

Arrival and Departure
Airports

There are two main airports in Paris: **Roissy-Charles de Gaulle** (16 miles or 25.75 kilometers to the north) and **Orly** (about the same distance to the south). They can be reached from the center of the city by bus or taxi in about 45 minutes, barring any major traffic snarls. Trains and the métro also provide 45-minute service, except during peak commute hours when there may be significant delays. Play it safe by allowing about an hour and a half to reach your destination. The buses and trains leave approximately every 15 minutes.

From **Roissy-Charles de Gaulle** airport, a shuttle bus will take you to the **RER** (Réseau Express Régional) train, which runs south through the **Gare du Nord** and the **Luxembourg** métro stations. There is also a bus that takes passengers to the **Porte Maillot** (on the métro line **Pont-de-Neuilly/Château-de-Vincennes**).

From **Orly** airport, the **Orly Rail** will take you to the **Gare d'Orsay, Gare St.-Michel,** and **Gare d'Austerlitz** stations. The bus from Orly will take you to the **Invalides Air Terminal** located in the center of Paris. From there, you can take the métro or bus to your destination.

Roissy-Charles de Gaulle Airport
Airlines:

Air France ... 800.237.2747 (US); 45.35.61.61 (Paris)	
Delta	800.221.1212; 47.68.92.92
Lufthansa	800.645.3880; 42.65.37.35
Northwest	800.225.2525; 42.66.90.00
TWA	800.221.2000; 48.62.21.31
UTA (owned by Air France)	800.237.2747; 45.35.61.61

General Information:

Airport Information	48.62.12.12
Airport Security	48.62.31.22
Customs and Immigration	48.62.35.35
Lost and Found	48.62.39.48, 48.62.52.87
Lost/Damaged Baggage	48.62.20.85, 48.62.52.89
Medical Emergencies	48.62.28.00, 48.62.53.32

Rental Cars:

Avis	48.62.34.34, 48.62.59.59
Eurorent	48.62.40.77, 48.62.57.66
Hertz	48.62.29.00

Orientation

Orly Airport
Airlines:

American	800.433.7300; 42.89.05.22
Delta	800.221.1212; 47.68.92.92
United	800.241.6522; 48.97.82.82

General Information:

Airport Information	49.75.52.52
Airport Security	49.75.43.04
Customs	45.00.29.79
Lost and Found	49.75.34.10, 49.75.42.34
Paging	49.75.00.86, 49.75.01.35
Parking	49.75.56.50

Rental Cars:

Avis	49.75.44.91, 49.75.44.97
Budget	46.75.01.07
Eurorent	49.75.90.83

Getting around Town
Autos

If you've got a suicide wish, hire a car and drive around the Arc de Triomphe a few times. But be forewarned: the most civilized Parisian becomes a homicidal maniac on the road—stoplights are ignored and one-way streets simply imply a challenge. Any vehicle entering from the right has the right of way. And if you think driving is tough, wait until you try to park the car (your best bet is to find an underground parking lot). *Bonne chance.*

Bicycles

Two wheels can be more fun—not to mention more hazardous—than four. The energetic and adventurous can rent bicycles from **Paris Vélo** (4 Rue du Fer-à-Moulin, 43.37.59.22) or **La Maison du Vélo** (8 Rue de Belzunce, 42.81.24.72).

If you're planning day trips outside Paris, however, you may want to wait until you get to Chantilly, Fontainebleau, Versailles, or other destinations and rent a bike for the day at the local train station. You can

rent a bike from the RER stations in Noisiel-le-Luzard, Vincennes, St.-Germain-en-Laye, Courcelle Vallée de Chevreuse, or Vallée de la Marne. Paris is surrounded with beautiful, flat countryside that's perfect for bicycling. During the summer, cycling trips outside Paris are sponsored by the **Bicy-Club de France** (8 Place de la Porte Champerret, 47.66.55.92). For general cycling information, contact the **Fédération Française de Cyclotourisme** (8 Rue Jean-Marie-Jégo, 45.80.30.21).

Boat Tours

On a late summer afternoon, nothing surpasses an hour touring the Seine river in a *bateau mouche* (a small passenger steamer), especially if you take along some creamy goat cheese, a fresh baguette, and a bottle of cool St.-Joseph. Take a seat at the rear of the boat out of range of the irritating tape-recorded commentary, then put your feet up and watch the sun set over the City of Light. Or try a more luxurious option—booking one of the expensive candlelit dinner cruises. Rides lasting between one and three hours (the lunch and illuminated-dinner cruises) are avail-

5

able from **Bateaux Mouches** (Embarcadère du Pont de l'Alma, Rive Droite, 42.25.96.10); **Bateaux Parisiens** (Port de La Bourdonnais, 47.05.50.00); and **Vedettes du Pont-Neuf** (Square du Vert-Galant, 46.33.98.38).

Buses

Riding the métro may be the quickest and easiest way to get around town, but buses are a far more pleasant means of transportation in Paris. The tourist office on the Champs-Elysées has selected more than a dozen get-acquainted bus routes for tourists, and it provides maps and trilingual commentary on the sights along the way. The **No. 24** bus, for example, makes a marvelous circuit of Paris. It crosses the Seine four times and passes Place de

Orientation

la Concorde, the National Assembly, the Louvre, Pont-Neuf, Notre-Dame, Ile St.-Louis, Place St.-Michel, goes down Boulevard St.-Germain, then turns back past the Jardin des Plantes and the Musée d'Orsay—all for just a few francs. The **No. 30, 48, 82,** and **95** routes are equally enjoyable.

Maps of the bus system are usually pasted on the walls of bus shelters. When planning a sight-seeing excursion, remember that bus service is limited in the evenings and on Sundays. Bus tickets may be purchased from all métro stations, or you may buy a single ticket on the bus. You must punch in your ticket in the machine beside the driver when you board. Bus rides of more than four or five stops may cost an extra ticket unless you have a pass. (For discount ticket information, see "Métro" at right).

If observing the city through the windows of a climate-controlled, double-deck tour bus is your idea of an ultimate sight-seeing experience, climb aboard one of the coaches at **Cityrama** (3 Rue des Pyramides, 42.60.30.14, or 21 Rue de la Paix, 47.42.06.47) or **Paris Vision** (214 Rue de Rivoli, 42.60.31.25). They both offer tours (in several languages) past all the main attractions, as well as separate tours to **Versailles, Malmaison, Chantilly, Chartres, Fontainebleau, Mont St.-Michel,** the **Loire Valley,** and **Barbizon.** Night tours journey to the **Moulin Rouge, Lido,** and **Folies Bergère,** and a special **Paris X** tour will take you to various striptease and sex shows (they aim to please).

Car Rental Agencies

If you dare to drive, the main car rental agencies are: **Avis** (5 Rue Bixio, 45.50.32.31, or 60 Rue de Ponthieu, 43.59.03.83); **Hertz** (92 Rue St.-Lazare, 42.80.35.45, or Invalides Air Terminal, 45.51.20.37); and **Europcar** (48 Rue de Berri, 45.63.04.27, or 30.43.82.82). Europcar offers a nonresident discount, but you must make your reservations 24 hours before arriving to France, and there is a minimum rental period of three days and a maximum of 99 days. Be sure to take out car insurance if you aren't covered by your own auto insurance agency.

Maps

For navigating the city's streets, Parisians carry a map of the métro in their heads and a *Paris par*

Arrondissement guide in their pockets. Sold at most newsstands and bookshops, this little book lists every street in Paris, with indexed references to maps of each of the city's 20 *arrondissements* (quarters). Don't leave home without it.

Métro

It's one of the oldest—and best—subway systems in Europe. The first line, designed by engineer Fulgence Bienvenue, opened on 19 July 1900 between Maillot and Vincennes. In the early 1900s the station entrances were covered with exotic Art Nouveau masterpieces designed by Hector Guimard. These days, the motif of the system has become the yellow- and brown-striped ticket of the **RATP** (Réseau Autonome du Transport Parisien), which is everywhere on promotional purses, cigarette lighters, and costume jewelry cheaper than Yves Saint Laurent's designs and just as trendy.

Nearly 120 miles of rail snake beneath the streets of Paris, connecting about 300 stations. Aboveground, you're never too far away from a métro stop, and for the cost of a single ticket you can ride all day anywhere within the system, which operates between 5AM to about 12:45AM (each train pulls into its final destination at 1:15AM). Hang onto your ticket: occasionally a *contrôleur* in a blue uniform boards the train to check tickets.

Getting lost in Paris takes some effort. Métro maps are everywhere—inside and outside the stations. And the métro lines are named for the stations at which they end. Simply follow the signs for the terminus in the direction you are headed. If, for example, you want to go from the Louvre to Concorde, take the line marked *Direction Neuilly.* To transfer from one line to another, look for an orange-and-white *correspondence* sign on the station platform. Each station has a map of the neighborhood surrounding it, so you can get your bearings before you emerge aboveground.

When purchasing tickets, it's cheaper to buy a *carnet* (a book of tickets) of ten, which cuts the price of a single ticket in half. Also available are three- and five-day tourist passes, which are valid for both the métro and the bus. A *Formule 1* pass is valid for one day, and a *carte orange* is good for a month and requires a photograph.

Slip the magnetized ticket into the slot by the turnstile, retrieve it when it pops up, and pass through. Remember that when getting on and off the métro you must open the car door yourself; it closes automatically behind you.

A métro ticket also allows you to use the RER rail system (an express métro) within Paris, but study its route before you board because it is primarily for the suburbs, and the stops within the city are few and far between. Always hang onto your tickets; you may need them to get in and out of the station.

Taxis

Most of the time, the city's 15,000 taxis are clustered at *tête de stations* (taxi stations)—except, of course, when you really need one. While it may be more convenient to just hail a cab, it is not an acceptable practice in Paris, and the taxis will not stop in the middle of the street to accept passengers. Your best bet is to locate a tête de station and wait for the next taxi with its roof light on bright (a dim light means the cab is occupied). Even then drivers may not pick you up, because if you're not going in their direction, *tant pis* (tough luck). Bluff some understanding of the city and tell drivers the main street or métro station closest to your destination; given that guidance, they may not take you out of your way. Taxis aren't usually expensive, but the rates increase at night (between 10PM and 6:30AM), on Sundays, and if you're picked up at a train station, hotel, or outside the city. If you need to be somewhere at a specific time (including the airport), phone ahead for a cab; the meter starts running the moment the cabdriver receives the call, but the dispatcher will tell you how long it will take for a cab to arrive (it's usually less than ten minutes). Tip the driver 10 to 15 percent. For a taxi, call 49.36.10.10; 47.46.11.11; 47.39.47.39; or 49.00.05.55.

Trains

In Paris you can't simply jump into a taxi and cry *"A la gare!"* (To the station!). It may be a dramatic gesture, but it would be incomplete. Paris has six train stations, each one serving different regions of France. The destinations available at the stations are as follows: **Gare d'Austerlitz** for southwest France, Spain, and Portugal; **Gare de l'Est** for eastern France, Luxembourg, Switzerland, southern Germany, Austria, and Hungary; **Gare de Lyon** for south and southeastern France, Switzerland, Italy, and Greece; **Gare Montparnasse** for western France (including Versailles), Chartres, and Brittany; **Gare du Nord** for northern France, Belgium, the Netherlands, Scandinavia, the former Soviet Union, northern Germany, and Britain; and **Gare St.-Lazare** for northwestern France, Normandy, and Le Havre, a port where ships depart for Britain and the Americas. Within each station, there are two types of

trains: *banlieue,* for riding to the suburbs, and *grandes lignes* for long distances. Before boarding either train, you must punch *(compostez)* your ticket in one of the orange machines in the station or else the conductor might charge you the price of another ticket. For general train information for all stations, call 45.82.50.50.

Walking in Paris

Whether promenading along the broad boulevards or threading through intimate medieval neighborhoods, the best way to discover Paris is on your own two feet. As you will learn on the seven walks in this book (pages 10 through 193), walking yields the joy of noticing the little things—the grace notes, embellishments, and architectural details that define the

feel and texture of Paris. But walking can be a somewhat perilous proposition: on the street you're fair game for distracted car drivers, and on the sidewalk you're likely to tread on what dogs have left behind (every third Parisian owns a dog, and someone in city hall has calculated that the average pedestrian sets foot in canine droppings every 286th step. As a result, ever-vigilant squads of sanitation workers on motorcycles sweep and vacuum the sidewalks of Paris constantly).

For those who like to walk with direction, **Bonne Journée** offers several walking tours. The two- to three-hour walks, led by English-speaking guides, include a moveable feast that traces the haunts of Ernest Hemingway and his fellow expatriates during the 1920s, the history of crime in the city, and a walk that explores where the French Revolution was plotted on the Left Bank. For the less history-minded, owner and ex-New Yorker Laurie Lesser-Chamberlain offers shopping tours. For more information, contact **Bonne Journée** at 37 Rue Andre Antoine, 75018 Paris, 46.06.24.17.

FYI

Banks

Banks are generally open from 9AM to 4:30PM, but they close at midday the day before a holiday. They will display a sign reading CHANGE if they exchange foreign currency. For the best exchange rates, try **American Express** (11 Rue Scribe) and **Thomas Cook and Son** (2 Place de la Madeleine), which are open on Saturday. If you're stuck with a fistful of dollars and the banks are closed, you can also change money at these train stations: **Gare d'Austerlitz** (until 5PM), **Gare de l'Est** (until 7PM), **Gare St.-Lazare** (until 8PM), and **Gare de Lyon** (until 11PM).

Cafés

As noble a French institution as the Académie Française, cafés serve light meals and a variety of beverages throughout the day. Try a *créme* (strong coffee with hot, frothy milk) in the morning, and in the afternoon you might switch to *vin rouge, un demi* (a 25-centiliter draft beer), or a *citron pressé* (fresh lemonade). Drinks are cheaper at the *zinc* (bar), and coffee is more expensive after 10PM, but by then

you'll probably have moved on to cognac, Armagnac, brandy, or perhaps *eau de vie.*

Cinema

Parisians are film fanatics. Each week more than 300 films are shown in the city and are all listed along with their show times in the weekly publications *Pariscope* and *L'Officiel des Spectacles.* The *v.o. (version originale)* after a film title means it's in its original language, with French subtitles, while *v.f. (version française)* means it's dubbed in French. If you arrive in time for the *séance* (cinema previews), you'll see the ads, which are sometimes risqué, usually silly, and often themselves worth the price of admission. Once in the movie theater, be prepared to surrender a franc to the usher, who may do no more than tear your ticket and gesture toward an empty seat. You might resent this scam less if you go to the movies on Monday, when ticket prices are uniformly reduced by 30 percent.

Climate

Chances are that fabled Paris in the springtime will be soggy. The city logs more rainy days a year than

London, so equip yourself with an umbrella or trench coat. Winters are cold and damp, and summers can be as cool and dry as the martinis at the Ritz bar. The average temperature ranges from 38°F in January to 64°F in July. May and September are the best times for finding decent weather and fewer tourists. August, when many Parisians leave the city, can be quite hot.

Emergencies

For round-the-clock medical house calls, call **SOS Medecins**, 43.37.77.77. The **American Hospital** is just outside Paris (63 Ave Victor-Hugo, Neuilly-sur-Seine, 46.41.25.25), and most of the physicians speak English.

Orientation

Emergency Phone Numbers

Police Department	17
Fire Department	18
Poison Center	40.37.04.04
Burn Center	42.34.17.58
Telephone Information	12

Entertainment

"Everything that exists elsewhere exists in Paris," said Victor Hugo in *Les Misérables*. So it goes for the array of entertainment options available—as a spectator or a participant. For a daily recording (in English) of exhibitions and concerts, call 47.20.88.98.

There are two kiosks that sell half-price tickets to about 120 events in Paris, including plays, concerts, ballets, and operas on the day of the performance. One is in the **Châtelet-Les Halles** métro station and the other is at the **Place de la Madeleine**.

Hotels

Hotel reservations are essential in Paris not only in the summer months but also during the heavy convention and trade-show months of March and October. A free brochure from the tourist office charting room availability throughout the year is available through the Office de Tourisme de Paris, 127 Avenue des Champs-Elysées, 75008 Paris; 47.23.61.72.

Museums

Most Parisian museums tend to stay open late one night a week and are open on Sunday, but many are *fermé* (closed) on Tuesday. If you're planning on some serious museum-hopping, buy a *carte* pass, which gains you reduced admission to more than 60 Parisian museums and monuments. You can buy a pass that's valid for one, three, or five days. They are sold in major métro stations and at most of the participating attractions.

Pharmacies

In Paris, all pharmacies are marked by a neon green cross on the front of the building. When the cross is lit, it means the pharmacy is open for business. Although many pharmacists speak English, at the following places you will be certain to get English prescriptions translated and filled with equivalent medicines: **British and American Pharmacy** (1 Rue Auber, 47.42.49.40); **Pharmacie Anglaise** (62 Ave des Champs-Elysées, 43.59.22.52); and **Pharmacie Swann** (6 Rue de Castiglione, 42.60.72.96).

Post Offices

Post offices are marked **PTT** and are open from 8AM to 7PM on weekdays and 8AM to noon on Saturdays. The main post office at 52 Rue du Louvre is open 24 hours a day. If you want to buy stamps, make sure you're in the correct line and not wasting your time queuing up at the window where Parisians pay their gas and telephone bills. Stamps are also sold at *tabacs* (tobacco shops), hotels, and some newsstands.

Publications

Two English-language standbys will keep you abreast of world events and Parisian happenings: *The International Herald Tribune* (a felicitous child of the *Washington Post* and *The New York Times*) appears at newsstands every morning, and *Passion,* a periodical along the lines of the *Village Voice* is published every six weeks. The French dailies in Paris are *Le Monde, Le Figaro*, and *Libération*.

For weekly listings of exhibitions, movies, concerts, plays, discos, and restaurants, pick up a copy of *Pariscope* or *L'Officiel des Spectacles*, which both come out on Wednesday. They are on sale for a few francs at newsstands, and although they're written in French, they are not impossible to decipher if you do not speak the language.

Radio Stations

The only English-language radio station in Paris is the European News Service (ENS), a cable station that broadcasts into 30 major hotels. If you have a very strong receiver, however, you may be able to pick up the BBC or even Voice of America.

Restaurants

To dine at a particularly popular restaurant such as Taillevent or Lucas-Carton, you might have to book reservations months in advance, but in most cases advance notice of one week, or even a day or two, should suffice. In many restaurants you can order à la carte or choose a less expensive fixed-priced menu, which often includes the day's special. The fancier restaurants usually offer a *dégustation* (sampler) of the chef's specialities. If the wine list puzzles you, ask the waiter or the sommelier for advice; and remember, the quality of the wine does not necessarily increase with the price. Cleverly, a 15-percent service charge is almost always included in the bill, so, even if you are served shoddily, the server gets a tip. Therefore, in Paris and throughout France, a supplementary tip is not necessary, though you may leave an additional five percent for *service extraordinaire*.

Shopping

When the going gets tough, the tough go shopping in Paris. Perhaps no other city in the world enjoys such a reputation as a shoppers' mecca. Haute couture, jewelry, perfume, and gourmet delights are all here. The smaller shops are likely to be closed Monday and don't open their doors the rest of the week until 10AM. Most stay open until

6:30PM. While August is still the *fermeture annuelle,* when many Parisians flee the city on holiday and leave countless shops and restaurants closed in their wake, more and more stores and restaurants are staying open. Also, annual closing times may vary from one year to the next.

For those indefatigable shoppers interested in tours, bilingual guides offer four tours (each about four hours long) weekday afternoons and Saturday mornings. Stroll the Left Bank or the Marais, peruse the flea markets, or go whole hog with the VIP Tour—a private tour for you and a few of your closest friends. For more information, contact **Chic Promenade** at 21bis Rue Voltaire, 43.48.85.04.

Street Smarts

Pickpockets flock to tourists like fruitflies to bananas, and the busy métro lines, such as Pont-de-Neuilly to Château-de-Vincennes, are their natural habitat. In crowds, watch your money pouch, keep the clasp of your purse against your body, and don't put your wallet in your back pocket, especially if it bulges. Beware of bands of children—sometimes they possess a sleight of hand Fagin would have envied. Don't wear the right jewelry in the wrong places (like on the métro or at Montmartre), don't leave possessions unattended, and if you see trouble coming, try to avoid it.

Telephones

Phone booths adorn half the street corners in Paris, but it's a minor miracle to find one that works. Many operate only with special phone cards, which are sold at post offices. For phones in cafés, you may have to purchase a *jeton* (phone

token) at the bar. Save your international calls for the post office or your hotel. For calls outside Paris, dial 16 for the provinces, 191 for the United States and Canada, and 1944 for the United Kingdom.

Toilets

You can usually walk into any café and use the toilet, though in some cases you must tip the *gardienne* (keeper) a couple of francs. Such a facility may be a hole or a throne, with or without toilet paper. Your alternative is using the beige automatic toilets in the streets. For a franc, these clever contraptions automatically let you in and out and disinfect themselves between visits. Warning: don't let young children into the automatic toilets

alone; they're not strong enough to push open the doors to get out.

VAT Refunds

Included in the purchase price of many items is a VAT (value-added tax) that may be more than 20 percent of the price. To reclaim it, ask for the VAT refund forms when you make your purchase and be prepared to produce the item and the forms at the airport *détaxe* (refund) desk.

Visas/Passports

In July 1989 France and the United States reached a bilateral accord removing tourist visa requirements between the two countries. Passports are always required when traveling abroad.

How To Read This Guide

PARIS ACCESS® is arranged by neighborhood so you can see at a glance where you are and what is around you. The numbers next to the entries in the following chapters correspond to the numbers on the maps. The paragraphs are color-coded according to the kind of place described:

Restaurants/Nightlife: Red   **Hotels:** Blue

Shops/ 🌿Outdoors: Green   **Sights/Culture:** Black

Rating the Restaurants and Hotels

The restaurant ratings take into account the service, atmosphere, and uniqueness of the restaurant. An expensive restaurant doesn't necessarily ensure an enjoyable evening; however, a small, relatively unknown spot could have good food, professional service, and a lovely atmosphere. Therefore, on a purely subjective basis, stars are used to judge the overall dining value (see star ratings above). Keep in mind that the chefs and owners sometimes change, which can drastically affect the quality of a restaurant. The ratings in this book are based on information available at press time.

The price ratings, as categorized at right, apply to restaurants and hotels. These figures describe general price-range relationships between other restaurants or hotels; they do not represent specific rates.

★ Good	$ The price is right
★★ Very good	$$ Reasonable
★★★ Excellent	$$$ Expensive
★★★★ Extraordinary	$$$$ A month's pay

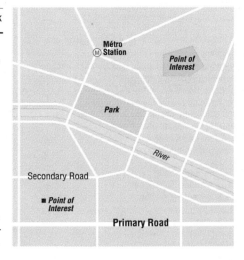

Métro
Ⓜ Station

Point of Interest

Park

River

Secondary Road

■ Point of Interest

Primary Road

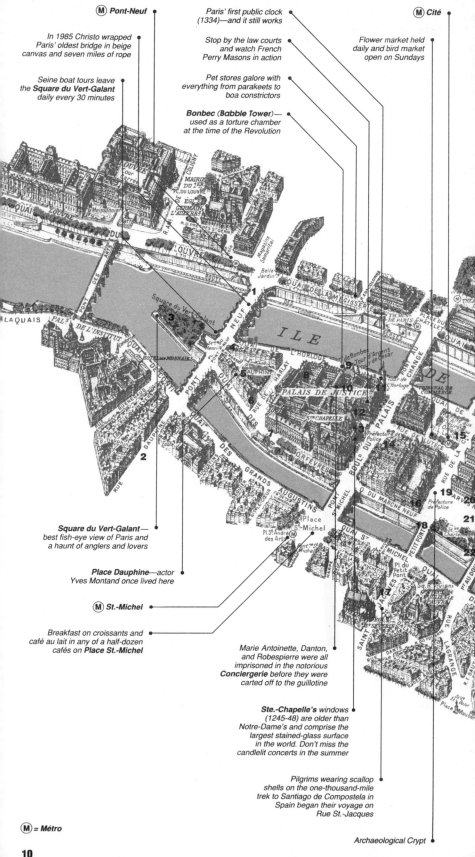

M Pont-Neuf

In 1985 Christo wrapped Paris' oldest bridge in beige canvas and seven miles of rope

Seine boat tours leave the **Square du Vert-Galant** daily every 30 minutes

Paris' first public clock (1334)—and it still works

Stop by the law courts and watch French Perry Masons in action

Pet stores galore with everything from parakeets to boa constrictors

Bonbec (Babble Tower)— used as a torture chamber at the time of the Revolution

M Cité

Flower market held daily and bird market open on Sundays

Square du Vert-Galant— best fish-eye view of Paris and a haunt of anglers and lovers

Place Dauphine—actor Yves Montand once lived here

M St.-Michel

Breakfast on croissants and café au lait in any of a half-dozen cafés on **Place St.-Michel**

Marie Antoinette, Danton, and Robespierre were all imprisoned in the notorious **Conciergerie** before they were carted off to the guillotine

Ste.-Chapelle's windows (1245-48) are older than Notre-Dame's and comprise the largest stained-glass surface in the world. Don't miss the candlelit concerts in the summer

Pilgrims wearing scallop shells on the one-thousand-mile trek to Santiago de Compostela in Spain began their voyage on Rue St.-Jacques

M = Métro

Archaeological Crypt

10

The Islands:
Ile de la Cité & Ile St.-Louis

At the heart of Paris are two islands: the sloop-shaped **Ile de la Cité**, which cradles **Notre-Dame** in its stern, and the **Ile St.-Louis**, which follows in the wake. Although the islands have no grand hotels, banks, major restaurants, theaters, or designer shops, they do possess two gems of Gothic architecture (Notre-Dame and **Ste.-Chapelle**), a world-famous prison, an elegant 17th-century subdivision, some of the city's most beautiful private mansions, the nation's law courts and police headquarters, an Art Nouveau métro station, a flower and bird market, 15 bridges, and one too many souvenir shops selling miniature Napoléon busts and I Love Paris bumper stickers.

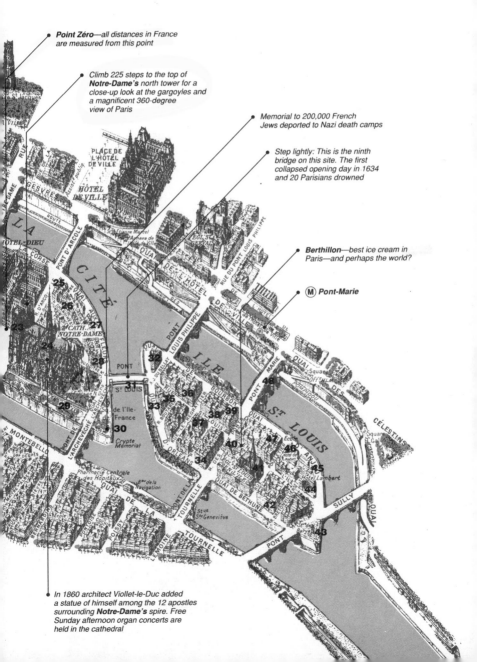

Point Zéro—all distances in France are measured from this point

Climb 225 steps to the top of **Notre-Dame's** north tower for a close-up look at the gargoyles and a magnificent 360-degree view of Paris

Memorial to 200,000 French Jews deported to Nazi death camps

Step lightly: This is the ninth bridge on this site. The first collapsed opening day in 1634 and 20 Parisians drowned

Berthillon—best ice cream in Paris—and perhaps the world?

(M) **Pont-Marie**

In 1860 architect Viollet-le-Duc added a statue of himself among the 12 apostles surrounding **Notre-Dame's** spire. Free Sunday afternoon organ concerts are held in the cathedral

The following sites represent more of a wander through the islands than a walk. If you tour this area on a Sunday, the added attractions include **Notre-Dame's** morning Mass (10:30AM) and late-afternoon organ concerts, the bird market at **Place Louis-Lépine,** and free admission to the **Hôtel Lauzun,** one of the most opulent 17th-century town houses in Paris. If visiting the **Ile St.-Louis** galleries and boutiques and the **Palais de Justice** is more your style, a weekday would be a better time to visit. Your walk might begin with a stop at a pastry shop to purchase croissants en route to a boat tour up the Seine (tour boats leave from the Pont-Neuf). Then, after visiting the flower market and Notre-Dame, have lunch at a tea salon on the Ile St.-Louis before strolling down to the Hôtel Lauzun. Top off the walk with a candlelit concert in **Ste.-Chapelle,** followed by dinner at the exceedingly fancy **L'Orangerie** or the more plebian all-you-can-eat **Nos Ancêtres Les Gaulois.**

Ile de la Cité

The Cité, the birthplace of Paris founded by the Parisii in the third century BC and overtaken by the Romans in 52 BC, survived attacks by Germans, barbarians, flood, and famine, but succumbed to a Frenchman, **Baron Georges-Eugène Haussmann,** Napoléon III's prefect (1853-1870), who ordered the Cité's *hygienizing.* Haussmann destroyed 90 streets and most of the medieval and Louis XIII homes. In their place, he constructed four architecturally dull buildings (Hôtel-Dieu Hospital, Préfecture de Police, Tribunal of Commerce, and Palais de Justice) and increased by six times the size of the square in front of Notre-Dame.

1 Pont-Neuf Despite its name (New Bridge), the Pont-Neuf was completed in 1607 and is the city's oldest and most famous bridge, and the first in Paris to be constructed without houses on top of it. Crossing the Seine with 12 broad arches at the river's widest point, the city's grandest bridge incorporates a series of turrets for street vendors, jugglers, and acrobats. The bridge became such a well-traveled thoroughfare that, legend held, it was impossible to cross without encountering a monk, a prostitute, and a white horse. One of

the most notorious Pont-Neuf charlatans was the **Great Jean Thomas,** who in 1715 set up a stall on the bridge to peddle bottles of an odorous elixir called Solar Balm. As part of an inventive advertising campaign, he hawked his wares dressed in a scarlet suit, a hat of peacock feathers, and a string of human teeth hung around his neck.

The Pont-Neuf was completed under **Henri IV.** The popular Henri of Navarre, who is remembered best for promising the peasants in his kingdom "a chicken in every pot," inaugurated the city's first pedestrian bridge by galloping his charger across it. The bronze equestrian statue of **Henrici Magni** at the bridge's center is an 1818 replacement; the original, erected two centuries earlier by the king's wife, **Marie de Médici,** was melted down to make cannons during the Revolution. The cornices overlooking the river have a carved frieze of grimacing caricatures, perhaps of King Henri's ministers and courtiers. Designed by **Androuet du Cerceau,** the bridge was painted by **Turner,** rhapsodized by poets, and, in 1985, wrapped by Bulgarian artist **Christo** in acres of beige canvas and more than seven miles of rope.
♦ Métro: Pont-Neuf

2 Rue Dauphine The construction of the Pont-Neuf channeled traffic over to the Left Bank. When **Henri IV's** request to put a highway through a monastery's vegetable gardens was denied, he snapped: "I will open the new road with cannonballs!" Rue Dauphine was built and named after his son. ♦ Métro: Pont-Neuf

3 Square du Vert-Galant Borrowing **Henri IV's** nickname ("Merry Monarch" and "Gay Old Dog"), this cobblestoned spit of land lush with chestnut trees may be reached by steps behind the king's statue. A haunt of anglers by day and of lovers on warm summer nights, the square affords the best fish-eye view of Paris. Departing from here are one-hour boat tours of the Seine offered by **Les Vedettes du Pont-Neuf.** ♦ Tours: daily every 30 minutes 10AM-noon, 1:30-6:30PM, 9-10:30PM. May-15 Oct: "Lights of Paris" boat tours begin departing at 9PM. Métro: Pont-Neuf. 46.33.98.38, 43.29.86.19

Pont-Neuf

4 Taverne Henri IV ★★$ Named after the king in bronze across the street, this reasonably priced bistro serves delicious charcuterie, regional cheeses, and goose rillettes and is well stocked with Bordeaux and Burgundy. ◆ M-F 11:30AM-9:30PM; closed 15 Aug-15 Sep. 13 Place du Pont-Neuf. No credit cards. Métro: Pont-Neuf. 43.54.27.90

5 Place Dauphine Once the royal garden, this tranquil triangle of stone and redbrick town houses dates from 1607 and takes its name from **Henri IV's** son, the princely Dauphin who became **Louis XIII.** The square was one of Henri IV's first city-planning projects in the 16th century and regrettably lost its third side with the expansion of the **Palais de Justice.** Surrealist poet **André Breton** (1896-1966) called it "one of the most secluded places I know." ◆ Métro: Pont-Neuf

5 Hôtel Henry IV $ The wallpaper is peeling, the rooms are tiny, and the showers and bathrooms are in the hall, but that's a minor price for a room with a view of one of the prettiest squares in Paris and a daily rate that costs less than a decent bottle of wine. Very popular and only 22 rooms, so reserve well in advance. ◆ 25 Place Dauphine. Métro: Pont-Neuf. 43.54.44.53

5 La Rose de France ★$$ This tiny restaurant with an outdoor terrace specializes in tasty *côtelettes d'agneau*, lamb chops with *herbes de Provence*, curried monkfish stew, and *filet de boeuf en croute*. ◆ M-F noon-2PM, 7-10PM; closed the last three weeks of Aug and Christmas through New Year's Day. 24 Place Dauphine. Métro: Pont-Neuf. 43.54.10.12

5 Fanny Tea ★★$ On a misty afternoon, this is the coziest of niches where you can scribble in a journal or peruse the volume of French poetry that is left on each table. Fanny offers scented teas served in Victorian pewter pots and a symphony of delicious tarts, ranging from salmon to apple, with outdoor service in the summertime. ◆ W-F 1-7PM; Sa-Su 3:30-8PM; closed 14 July-Aug, two weeks during Christmas, one week at Easter. 20 Place Dauphine. Métro: Pont-Neuf. 43.25.83.67

5 Le Caveau du Palais ★★$$ A comfortable restaurant (illustrated above) wedged between the Quai des Orfèvres and the Place Dauphine. Sample the terrine of veal sweetbreads with pistachios, fricassee of calf's kidneys and sweetbreads with honey, sole and monkfish with fresh mint, and *chocolat marquise*. ◆ M-Sa 12:15-2:30PM, 7:15-10:30PM, June-Sep; M-F 12:15-2:30PM, 7:15-10:30PM, Oct-May. 19 Place Dauphine. Métro: Pont-Neuf. 43.26.04.28, 43.26.81.84

5 Le Bar du Caveau ★$ Managed by Le Caveau du Palais next door, this wine bar serves light lunches: charcuterie, country cheese, and a variety of Bordeaux and Beaujolais. ◆ M-F 8:30AM-8PM. 19 Place Dauphine. Métro: Pont-Neuf. 43.54.45.95

6 Chez Paul ★★$ Long marble tables and cloth napkins as big as dish towels dominate this spot. Try the pike dumplings or the veal in puff pastry stuffed with mushrooms. During the summer months don't miss the wild strawberries. ◆ W-Su 12:15-2:15PM, 7:30-10:20PM; closed Aug. 15 Place Dauphine (52 Quai des Orfèvres). Métro: Pont-Neuf. 43.54.21.48

7 Quai des Orfèvres The Goldsmiths Quay is the Scotland Yard of Paris. PJ stands for "police judiciare" or detective force. The famous member of the PJ in the detective sto-

ries of the late **Georges Simenon** is, incidentally, not Parisian; Inspector Maigret comes from Belgium. ◆ Métros: Pont-Neuf, St.-Michel

8 Palais de la Cité This massive interlocking structure has been occupied by the French government since 52 BC, first as the palace of Roman prefects, later as the Gothic palace of the first 12 kings of France. In the 13th century it was the residence of **Saint Louis** (Louis IX), who lived in the upper chambers (now the First Civil Court). The king meted out justice beneath a tree in the courtyard. All that remains of the original palace is the breathtaking **Ste.-Chapelle** and the gloomy **Conciergerie,** one of history's most hideous and brutal prisons. Most of the site was covered by the **Palais de Justice,** built after the great fire of 1776. ◆ Métros: Pont-Neuf, St.-Michel

9 Tours de Bonbec, d'Argent, and de César Along the Quai de l'Horloge side of the old palace is a set of round, imposing towers. The first is Tour de Bonbec, nicknamed the "babbler" because it was used as a torture chamber during the Reign of Terror, a period of brutal purges following the Revolution. Next are the Tour d'Argent, where the royal treasure was once kept and where the famous restaurant across the river got its name; and the Tour de César, two steepled gate towers beside the entrance to the Conciergerie. ◆ Métros: Cité, Pont-Neuf

10 La Conciergerie Following the bloody mob revolt led by **Etienne Marcel** in 1358, young **King Charles V** moved the royal residence to the Marais but left behind the royal dungeon and supreme court in the charge of the concierge (*Comte des Cierges* or Count of Candles), the king's caretaker. The guest list included distinguished criminals such as **Ravaillac,** the fanatic who murdered popular Henri IV and was imprisoned and tortured here before his execution.

During the Revolution, the Tribunal commandeered the palace and administered its own ruthless form of justice. The Conciergerie became the antechamber to the guillotine during the Reign of Terror between January 1793 and July 1794. About 2,600 Parisians were condemned to death, among them **Charlotte Corday,** who had stabbed **Marat** in his bath, and, perhaps the best remembered inmate, **Marie Antoinette,** the Austrian queen who had reputedly scoffed at the starving French masses with the phrase: "Let them eat cake." Shortly after the Tribunal executed her husband, **King Louis XVI,** she was held here in a tiny cell from August until October 1793, when the tumbrils delivered her to the guillotine. Royalty were not the only victims; no one in a position of authority was safe. Revolutionary **Danton,** who had ordered the execution of 22 people, was in turn condemned to death by citizen **Robespierre,** who later was sent to the guillotine by a panel of judges, the

The Islands

Thermidor Convention. At the end of the terror, the Tribunal's own public prosecutor, **Fouquier-Tinville,** was dragged off to the gallows shouting "I am the ax! You don't execute the ax!"

Put yourself in the shoes of Marie Antoinette as she walked down Rue de Paris (which once led to the quarters of an executioner during the terror known as **Monsieur de Paris**) with footsteps echoing off the vaulted ceiling. She was jailed in dank cell number VI; in the cell next door, both Danton and Robespierre were held on death row, and, in the adjoining chapel, the 22 condemned Girondins heard Mass before their execution. All these rooms, as well as the *salle de la derniere toilette,* from which prisoners were led to the block, have recently been restored.

On your way out, duck into the magnificent medieval vaults of the four-aisled **Salle des Gens d'Armes** (Hall of the Men-at-Arms), frequently used these days for classical concerts, theater, and wine tastings. The spiral staircase at the far end of the hall is worth a peek. Waltz through the 14th-century kitchen that served some 3,000 guests and had walk-in ovens large enough to roast a pair of oxen. The souvenir shop near the exit sells replicas of Revolutionary playing cards that replace kings, queens, and jacks with humbly clothed men and women personifying common virtues such as Industry and Justice. The original deck (1793) by **Jaume** and **Dugorc** is kept in the Bibliothèque Nationale. ◆ Daily 9:30AM-6PM, Apr-Sep; M-Sa 10AM-5PM, Oct-Mar; closed holidays. Guided tours available in the Conciergerie. 1 Quai de l'Horloge. Métro: Cité

11 Tour de l'Horloge This tower was the site of the city's first public clock (1334). Today's more Baroque version is set in a constellation of golden *fleurs-de-lis* and flanked by angels, rams, and royal shields. Until the French Revolution, the clock signaled royal births and deaths by pealing nonstop for three days. ◆ Quai de l'Horloge (Blvd du Palais). Métro: Cité

12 Palais de Justice (Law Courts) Behind the lusciously gilded Louis XVI railing and portal gates on the Boulevard du Palais is the main entrance to the Palais de Justice and the **Cour du Mai** (the May Courtyard was named for the trees from the royal forest planted over the centuries by the court clerks each spring, but don't bother looking for them; they were toppled centuries ago). This courtyard was the last stop for the condemned before leaving by wooden carts, or tumbrils, for the gallows in the **Place de la Concorde.** Look above the door at the top of the grand marble steps for the words *Liberté, Egalité, Fraternité.*

Inside and to the right in the lobby (**Salle des Pas-Perdus,** literally "the Room of the Wasted Steps") is the amusing statue of **Berryer,** a 19th-century barrister. To his right sits a sculpted muse with her foot on a turtle, a candid jab at the speed of the legal process. Behind the door to the left is the gorgeous blue-and-gold **Première Chambre** (also known as Chambre Dorée, or Gilded Chamber), where the Revolutionary Tribunal sat on 6 April 1793 and sentenced **Queen Marie Antoinette** to death.

In the "cathedral of chicanery," as **Balzac** called the **Law Courts,** a thicket of police, public *écrivains* (letter writers), and prisoners used to gather while hawkers sold newspapers and rented black judicial robes. Today, the lobby is still a chaos of black-robed barristers, plaintiffs, and judges dashing about. If you'd like to see a French Perry Mason putting *liberté, egalité,* and *fraternité* into action during the week, you may visit the courtroom proceedings (except the juvenile court). ◆ M-F 8AM-7:30PM. 2 Blvd du Palais. Métro: Cité. 43.29.12.55

Strolling on the Seine

Rhapsodically portrayed by such painters as Turner, Monet, and Sisley, the seven-mile stretch of the Seine that passes through Paris is the most famous and beautiful length of urban riverfront in the world. Within the city, the river is spanned by 33 bridges, and from the oldest (Pont-Neuf) to the dandiest (Pont Alexandre III) to the most humble and delicate (Pont des Arts), there is nary an ugly one among them. The Pont de Grenelle is of special interest to Americans; beside it is a replica of the Statue of Liberty. And along the banks of the gentle, green river is a panoply of famous monuments: the Eiffel Tower, the Grand Palais, the Musée d'Orsay, the Louvre, the Institute of France, the Conciergerie, Notre-Dame, and the famous penthouse restaurant Tour D'Argent, plus the former homes of Baudelaire, Voltaire, Rilke, Daumier, Balzac, and Corot, and the stately islands Ile de la Cité and Ile St.-Louis. Strolling along the tree-lined quays, one encounters lovers hand-in-hand, anglers casting their lines, clochards making their digs under the bridges, flower and bird markets, and, of course, *bouquinistes* peddling postcards, 19th-century pornography, and an occasional rare first-edition book from their zinc-topped boxes.

Restaurants/Nightlife: Red		**Hotels:** Blue
Shops/ ◆Outdoors: Green		**Sights/Culture:** Black

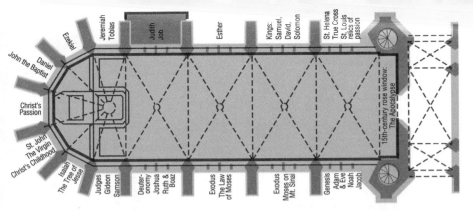

Ezekiel · Jeremiah Tobias · Judith Job · Esther · Kings: Samuel, David, Solomon · St. Helena True Cross St. Louis relics of passion

John the Baptist · Daniel · Christ's Passion · St. John The Virgin Christ's Childhood

Isaiah The Tree of Jesse · Judges Gideon Samson · Deuteronomy Joshua Ruth & Boaz · Exodus The Law of Moses · Exodus Moses on Mt. Sinai · Genesis Adam & Eve Noah Jacob

15th-century rose window: The Apocalypse

13 Ste.-Chapelle After Notre-Dame, this is the city's most significant medieval monument. **Saint Louis** (Louis IX, 1214-1270), France's only canonized king, erected this Gothic jewel of a chapel in 1248 to enshrine the relics he bought from Venetian merchants during his first crusade. His purchases included Christ's Crown of Thorns, two pieces of the True Cross, a nail from the Cross, the Roman soldier's lance that pierced Christ's side, and several drops of Christ's blood. For the relics, he paid 35,000 livres in gold, a sum far in excess of what it cost to construct Ste.-Chapelle.

Ste.-Chapelle was built in less than five years and is thought to have been designed by **Pierre de Montreuil.** It soars 67 feet without the aid of flying buttresses, a daring architectural accomplishment. In medieval times it was connected to the palace of St.-Louis, but today is hidden away in a side courtyard of the 19th-century **Palais de Justice.** Ste.-Chapelle is a two-tiered chapel; sequestered from view, the royal family worshiped upstairs in the light and airy **Chapelle Haute,** while members of the court prayed on the somber ground floor.

The chapel suffered considerable damage during the Revolution, when the gold reliquary was melted down and the structure was put to

use as a flour warehouse. In the 19th century the chapel was thoroughly made over by **Eugène-Emmanuel Viollet-le-Duc** (1814-1879), one of the **Baron Haussmann** architects who also restored Notre-Dame and cathedrals at Amiens and St.-Denis. **Steinheil,** a compatriot of Balzac and Baudelaire, restored the windows. Of the 12 apostle statues, only one (the bearded apostle fifth down on the left side) is original. Portions of the damaged originals are on exhibit in the Cluny Museum.

The chapel's spectacular windows are older than Notre-Dame's and comprise the largest expanse of stained glass in the world— 1,500 square yards, enough to cover three basketball courts. Created in an age of mass illiteracy, this illustrated Bible consists of 1,134 scenes. The windows read chronologically beginning on the left near the entrance and progressing clockwise around the chapel. Start with the lower left panel and read from left to right, row by row from bottom to top. The narrative begins with Genesis and the Old Testament, continues through the Crucifixion

Ste.-Chapelle

15

(illustrated in the choir apse), the acquisition of the relics, the construction of the chapel Ste.-Chapelle, and, finally, the Apocalypse. Notice that a liberated Saint Louis devoted entire windows to two women of the Old Testament, **Judith** and **Esther**. The thick, predominantly red-and-blue dyed glass of the 15 main windows contrasts sharply with the green-and-yellow hues of the flamboyant rose window (restored by **Charles VIII** in 1485) illustrating the Apocalypse. Because the windows are backlit by the sun, you must read along with the sun's rising and setting. Thus, you have to get up early to catch the Battle of Jericho and must come after lunch for David and Goliath. And, if the flies on Pharoah's face interest you, bring your opera glasses, because many of the panels, particularly the highest ones, are nearly impossible

The Islands

to decipher. Anyone who identifies even a few Bible characters in a short visit is doing well. Not long ago a Belgian Benedictine monk arrived at Ste.-Chapelle with his Bible and a pair of binoculars; it took him two full weeks, gazing every day from dawn to dusk, to complete the cycle.

For an initial visit, the best approach is to set aside your guidebook, gaze upward, and imagine yourself among the royal family in the 13th century watching as Saint Louis mounted the stairs to the gold reliquary to display the sacred Crown of Thorns. The crown (but not the more dubious relics Saint Louis purchased, such as a feather from the wing of the Angel of the Annunciation) now resides in Notre-Dame and is exhibited only on Good Friday. In addition to its visual splendors, the acoustics of Ste.-Chapelle are renowned; **Couperin** played the organ here in the 17th century. Nowadays, rather expensive evening concerts of classical music are held here several times a week between March and November. ♦ Admission. Daily 9:30AM-6:30PM, Apr-Sep; daily 10AM-5PM, Oct-Mar. 2 Blvd du Palais. Métro: Cité. 43.54.30.09

14 Les Deux Palais $ This corner café with Roaring Twenties mirrored columns serves omelets, good coffee, and hot lunch specials. ♦ M-Sa 6:30AM-8PM. 3 Blvd du Palais. No credit cards. Métro: Cité. 43.54.20.86

15 Cité Métro One of the original 141 Art Nouveau "dragonfly" métro station entrances designed by **Hector Guimard** in 1900.

The French spend about 28 billion francs on tobacco each year.

In the planned mixed community of architect Louis Le Vau on Ile St.-Louis, sumptuous mansions bordering the river were built for aristocrats, and modest town houses were built inland for carpenters and ironmongers. In the elegant houses on the *quais*, the largest, grandest salons faced the riverside for the view. This broke with 17th-century tradition, which placed the great rooms away from the street, behind a courtyard that acted as a barrier to noise and smells.

15 Place Louis-Lépine Named after a short Belle Epoque police chief remembered mainly for having armed Parisian *gendarmes* with whistles and truncheons, this square is a charming urban Eden surrounded by the grim walls of **Hôtel-Dieu Hospital**, the **Préfecture de Police**, and the **Commercial Tribunal**. One of the largest flower markets in Paris blooms here year-round with everything from chrysanthemums to lemon trees. On Sunday, the flower market is transformed into a bird market selling fresh seed and berries, bells and cages, and a veritable palette of colorful canaries, finches, and parrots. ♦ Métro: Cité

16 Préfecture de Police This bunker of a building is the headquarters of the fictional Inspector Clouseau of *Pink Panther* fame and the very real Paris police. On 19 August 1944, during the liberation of Paris, about a thousand Paris police officers revolted against the German occupation, barricaded themselves in the préfecture, hoisted the tricolor to a rousing chorus of the *Marseillaise*, and held off Nazi tanks and artillery for four days until the Allies arrived. In the ensuing battle, 280 died, and buildings around Notre-Dame's parvis are still pockmarked with bullet holes. ♦ Place Louis-Lépine. Métro: Cité

17 Rue St.-Jacques The city's oldest street, which begins at the Petit Pont, originated as a Roman road. A thousand years later, it was named after the crusading **Saint Jacques**, whose body miraculously washed up on the Spanish coast in the ninth century. Paris was the principal starting point of a one-thousand-mile pilgrimage to the Shrine of St. Jacques in Santiago de Compostela in Spain. In medieval times, pilgrims wearing scallop shells (the symbol of Saint Jacques) would set off down this street. The delicious contents of such shells are served throughout Paris as *Coquilles St.-Jacques*. ♦ Métros: Cité, St.-Michel

18 Petit Pont The *Little Bridge* on this site was first built in 1185 by **Bishop Maurice de Sully**, who also oversaw the construction of Notre-Dame. A 19th-century version now stands where, in the Middle Ages, minstrels used to cross toll-free. ♦ Métros: Cité, St.-Michel

19 Archaeological Crypt In 1965, while excavating for an underground parking lot, the city of Paris unearthed Gallo-Roman and medieval ruins, now preserved in this slightly eerie but intelligent archaeological site/museum beneath the parvis of Notre-Dame.

Designed by **André Hermant,** the crypt is worth a quick visit, if only to see the scale models of Paris, which show its evolution from a Celtic settlement during the Second Iron Age to a Roman city in 500 BC. Notice that the Romans, in anticipation of another barbarian invasion, reinforced the original ramparts with a second wall. This is one of the city's most accessible museums (commentary is in English and French). And if you're lucky, you may see a few trowel-and-toothbrush archaeologists still digging. ♦ Admission. Daily 9:30AM-7PM. Enter at the west end of the parvis. Métros: Cité, St.-Michel

20 Hôtel-Dieu Hospital Behind the double row of chestnut trees is **God's Hostel,** founded in AD 651 by **Saint Landry,** Bishop of Paris. The hospital was an important training facility for American doctors in the 19th century. The oldest known cabaret in Paris, **La Pomme de Pin,** stood on this site in 1400. It was frequented by **Rabelais, Villon, Molière,** and **Racine.** ♦ Parvis Notre-Dame. Métros: Cité, St.-Michel

21 Parvis of Notre-Dame In the Middle Ages, when miracle plays were performed, the square in front of Notre-Dame represented *paradise,* a name contracted over the centuries to *parvis.* Critics of **Baron Haussmann,** who enlarged the parvis sixfold in the 19th century, called it the "paved prairie." ♦ Métros: Cité, St.-Michel

21 Rue de Venise Paris in the Middle Ages was a snarl of narrow horse paths. Marked in the pavement of the parvis in front of the cathedral is the former position of this one-yard-wide medieval alley, no doubt once the narrowest street in Paris. ♦ Métros: Cité, St.-Michel

22 Charlemagne and His Vassals On the south side of the parvis rests a bronze statue created in 1882 of **Charlemagne,** the Frank who was crowned the first Holy Roman Emperor in AD 800. Under Charlemagne and his successors, Paris was merely a provincial town. The center of Charlemagne's empire was at Aix-la-Chapelle. (If you happen to be looking for public toilets, follow the tail of Charlemagne's prancing horse; it points west to nearby stairs leading underground.) ♦ Parvis of Notre-Dame. Métros: Cité, St.-Michel

23 Point Zéro All distances in France are measured from this brass compass star *(Point Zéro des Routes de France)* fixed in the pavement in front of the cathedral. Throughout France, highway signs tell you how far away you are (in kilometers) from *Paris Notre-Dame.* ♦ Métros: Cité, St.-Michel

24 Notre-Dame The cathedral of Notre-Dame, wrote **e.e. cummings,** does not budge an inch for all the idiocies of this world. For six centuries, this world-famous masterpiece of the Middle Ages has endured as a sonnet in stone, harmonizing mass and elegance, asymmetry, and perfection. Among its architectural triumphs are the Gothic ribbed vaulting and the flying buttresses, which opened up the church by permitting the erection of higher, more slender walls pierced by glories of stained glass.

Notre-Dame

In 1163 no less a personage than **Pope Alexander III** laid Notre-Dame's foundation stone, and the final masterful touches were not completed until 1345–more than two centuries later. (Ste.-Chapelle, by comparison, was erected in five years.) The design followed the sketches executed in 1159 by **Bishop Maurice de Sully** and was implemented by architects **Pierre de Montereau,** who was responsible for Notre-Dame's south transept, and **Jean de Chelles,** and by generations of anonymous workers.

To tour Notre-Dame is to stroll through French history. On this site the Romans built a temple in antiquity to **Jupiter** and the **Emperor Tiberius.** In the cathedral, during the Middle Ages, the homeless slept and were fed; trade unions met; passion plays were performed; and merchants from the Orient sold everything from ostrich eggs to elephant tusks. During the 12th century Notre-Dame's adjoining cathedral school became an intellectual center known throughout Europe and eventually gave birth to the Sorbonne. During the Revolution the cathedral was rechristened the *Temple of Reason,* with the dancer **Mademoiselle Maillard** chosen as Goddess of Reason; shortly thereafter, the cathedral was actually auctioned off to a demolition contractor for scrap building material. Though never actually demolished, Notre-Dame was in shambles in 1804 when **Napoléon Bonaparte** called **Pope Pius VII** from Rome to officiate at his coronation, which was held before the cathedral's high altar. After the anointing, Napoléon defiantly snatched the crown from the pontiff and crowned himself emperor, a dramatic scene captured by **Jacques-Louis David** in his famous painting that hangs in the Louvre.

West Facade At the base of the west facade, which is topped by two 69-meter (226-foot) towers, are three famous portals devoted to (from left to right) the Virgin Mary, the Last Judgement, and Sainte Anne, the Virgin's mother. Royalty couldn't stay out of the act; in the tympanum of the portal to Sainte Anne, a kneeling **King Louis VII** (far right) dedicates the cathedral with Bishop Sully (on the left with a crook in his hand), as the bishop's faithful secretary takes notes straddling a Gothic stool. The presence of **Barbedor,** the scribe, represents one of the first times an intellectual was honored in a cathedral facade.

Above the three portals is the **Gallery of Kings, Viollet-le-Duc's** 19th-century replicas of medieval masterpieces, which were once painted in vibrant yellow, cobalt, and scarlet. The 28 kings represent the kings of Judea and

The Islands

Gargoyles

Israel, thought in the Catholic Church to be the ancestors of Christ. In 1793 Revolutionaries mistook them for the kings of France and toppled and decapitated them. Fortunately, at the time, an educator spirited away the sculpted heads and buried them in his yard at 20 Chaussée d'Antin, near the present site of the Paris Opéra. They languished there until 1977, when they were unearthed in the course of excavations for a bank vault and put on exhibit at the Cluny Museum.

North and South Towers At the top of a spiraling 255-step climb up the north tower you will find not Victor Hugo's *Quasimodo,* the tormented hunchback of Notre-Dame's belfry, but an equally unsettling sight: **Viollet-le-Duc's** stone bestiary of gargoyles, gremlins, and demons. It was believed that the gargoyles kept evil spirits from the cathedral (a number of them serve as downspouts, squirting rain from their mouths—sheer entertainment in spring showers). The 90-meter spire was added during the heavy-handed Gothic Revival restoration of 1860. In addition, architect Viollet-le-Duc placed a statue of himself alongside the copper apostles and evangelists. The apostles stand on the cathedral roof looking outward, blessing the city, but the architect looks upward, admiring his work. (For a bird's-eye view of Viollet-le-Duc, the celebrated flying buttresses, and a splendid chain of bridges over the Atlantic-bound Seine, climb the last 125 steps to the top of the south tower. You won't regret it.)

Interior As you enter Notre-Dame, the nave appears more somber than the transept and altar. This is due, in part, to your eyes adjusting to the darkness, but the difference in hue is mostly a matter of dirt. At night, after the tourists and parishioners go home, the interior of the cathedral is washed section by section. But this delicate cleanup process, which requires using only warm water (no soap, solvent, or sandblasting is allowed), won't be completed until the mid-1990s.

Mays Paintings Every year in May during the Middle Ages, paintings called *Mays* were given by the Orfèvrerie, the gold workers' union. The paintings (among them a **Le Brun** and a **Le Sueur**) were originally hung between the church pillars; today, they are displayed in the side chapels.

Notre-Dame, West Facade

The massive organ, with more than 7,000 pipes, is France's largest, a masterwork installed in 1730 by **Aristide Cavaillé-Col**. A century later, the organ was restored. And now, following in the tradition of **Couperin, Franck,** and **Messiaen,** all of whom performed here, some of Europe's greatest organists offer free recitals here every Sunday in the late afternoon. These, as well as the candlelit Easter vigil and Christmas Eve Mass, draw ample crowds. The cathedral's seating capacity for Mass and organ concerts is nearly 10,000.

Each 11 November, in a deeply moving cathedral service, the Royal British Legion honors British and Commonwealth soldiers who died on French soil during WWI.

Windows New windows were installed in Notre-Dame's clerestory after WWII, but not because of damage caused by the Germans. In the 18th century **Louis XV** declared stained glass *déclassé,* destroyed the Gothic glass in the upper-level nave windows, and replaced it with clear glass, to give the cathedral interior a bright Protestant appearance. It was not until after the war that contemporary glass replicas of the original Gothic windows were installed. Of Notre-Dame's three famous rose windows (north, south, and west), only the north has the original 13th-century glass. The south and west rose windows glow most brilliantly at twilight, while the north window is best viewed

in morning light. The stained glass windows of the 13th and 14th century are thick, with small images predominantly portrayed in deep reds, blues, and purples (they're actually dyed into the glass). Over the centuries, it became possible to make thinner glass. Images became larger and were handpainted on the surface, and ways of making brighter greens and yellows were discovered. These developments are evident in the differences between the original windows and the modern replicas.

Wood Sculpture One of the cathedral's most charming decorations is the 14th-century Gothic relief on the north side of the chancel that depicts the life of Christ from the Nativity to the Last Supper. In the Nativity, Mary lies coyly posed in a proper bed, while the baby Jesus and animals from the manger are crammed together in a basket. In the next

scene, a slim, erect king with a pageboy haircut stands among the Magi offering gifts (supposedly, this is Saint Louis).

The new altar (in front of the old altar) betokens the liturgical changes in the 1960s that allowed the priest to say Mass facing the congregation instead of turning his back. In addition, Mass is now said in French, instead of the original Latin, but even so, given the cathedral's echoing acoustics, sometimes it sounds as if it could be Greek to most listeners. ◆ Daily 8AM-7PM. Rue d'Arcole (Rue du Cloître-Notre-Dame). Métros: Cité, Maubert-Mutualité

25 La Colombe ★★$$ Originally a 13th-century tavern and later a famous cabaret in the 1950s, The Dove restaurant is classified as a French historic landmark and, according to *Le Figaro* magazine, is the most photographed house in Paris. The sagging beamed ceilings, cages of cooing doves, and the profusion of fresh flowers complement the home-style menu of duck with seasonal fruit, *stroganoff au ris sauvage,* an excellent *soupe à l'oignon,* and a rich chocolate cake. The concierges at the Crillon and Plaza Athénée hotels have this on their list of American favorites. Dining on the arbored terrace is available in the summer. ◆ M 7:30PM-midnight; Tu-Sa noon-2PM, 7PM-midnight. 4 Rue de la Colombe. Métro: Cité. 46.33.37.08

When the Romans arrived in Paris in 52 BC, they overran the Parisii, a Gallic tribe of fishermen and river traders who had been living on the Ile de la Cité, the largest island on the Seine, since the third century BC. The Romans built a *cité* (fortified palace) called *Lutetia* (surrounded by water) and adopted as their symbol a sailing vessel, the logo of Paris to this day. The Romans stayed for about 500 years, and judging from the size of the remaining baths and amphitheater, Paris was a far less important Roman outpost than Arles. Although they first settled on the Ile de la Cité, the Romans constructed their town primarily on the left bank of the Seine—Rue St.-Jacques was the principal north-south street—where faint traces of their era remain: the amphitheater (off the Rue Monge), the baths (adjoining the Cluny Museum), a Roman forum (buried under the Rue Soufflot), and a theater (near Rue Racine).

The Seine river in Paris is only half as wide as the Thames at London Bridge, but it has 33 bridges, more than twice as many as the Thames in downtown London.

Restaurants/Nightlife: Red   **Hotels:** Blue
Shops/ 🌳 Outdoors: Green   **Sights/Culture:** Black

25 Rue de la Colombe This medieval street is cut where the old Roman wall once ran to protect Paris against barbarian invasions.
♦ Métro: Cité

26 La Lieutenance ★★$$$ Housed in a 16th-century building that once belonged to the canons of Notre-Dame, **Pierre Devigne's** fashionable restaurant caters at night to the show-biz crowd but is less frantic during lunch. Chef **Daniel Lemounier** serves his *St.-Pierre au beurre blanc* and *feuillete de 3 poissons.* ♦ Tu-F, Su noon-2PM, 8-11:30PM; Sa 8-11:30PM. 24 Rue Chanoinesse. Métro: Cité. 43.54.91.36

27 9-11 Quai aux Fleurs The sculpted heads on the face of this 19th-century building on the Quai aux Fleurs (which, by the way, sells no flowers) commemorates two of history's

most famous lovers, **Héloïse** and **Abélard,** who today cast plaintive glances at couples strolling arm-in-arm along the Seine. In 1118 Pierre Abélard (1079-1142), an iconoclastic theologian who helped found the University of Paris, fell in love with one of his students. She was Héloïse (circa 1101-1164), the brilliant niece of **Fulbert,** the foul-tempered canon of Notre-Dame. "Under the guise of study, we gave ourselves to love," wrote Abélard..."We exchanged more kisses than sentences." Their passionate affair was brought to an abrupt, brutal, and tragic end by her uncle, whose thugs emasculated Abélard. Héloïse and Abélard lived on, cloistered separately for many years, but were buried side-by-side in Père-Lachaise Cemetery. ♦ Métro: Cité

28 Le Vieux Bistro ★★$$/$$$ Far removed from the traffic and crush of tourists is this quiet, charming restaurant featuring the cuisine of Lyon. The roast quail in gin and cream sauce is delicious. ♦ Daily noon-2PM, 7:30-10:45PM. 14 Rue du Cloître-Notre-Dame. Reservations required. Métro: Cité. 43.54.18.95

29 Square Jean XXIII Cherry trees blossom here in the spring, lime trees shade in the summer, and the chestnut leaves are heaped ankle-deep in autumn. Notre-Dame's west face tower is above but it looks flat compared to its south and east sides shored by dramatic flying buttresses. Here is a place to pause and feed the birds or to perch on a wooden bench during an occasional outdoor concert given by a local police officers' orchestra. ♦ Métros: Cité, Maubert-Mutualité

30 Mémorial de la Déportation The Deportation Museum, designed by **G.H. Pingusson** in 1962, commemorates the 200,000 French who died during the Holocaust. Some 30,000 people from Paris alone were deported to Nazi death camps during WWII. Reflecting the Jewish tradition of paying homage to the dead by placing a stone on the grave, the memorial is constructed around a tunnel of 200,000 quartz pebbles. It also contains small tombs with earth from each of the concentration camps. The visitor here feels trapped visually and psychologically by the low ceiling and iron bars. Stark and simple, the memorial in the Square de l'Ile-de-France is one of city's most moving monuments. ♦ Daily 10AM-noon, 2-7PM, Apr-Sep; daily 10AM-noon, 2-5PM, Oct-Mar. Quai l'Archevêché. Métro: Cité

31 Pont St.-Louis Step lightly; this pedestrian bridge is the ninth on a site that has had a shaky, if not disastrous, history. The first bridge linking the two islands was erected in 1634 by developer **Jean-Christophe Marie;** it crumbled on opening day, drowning 20 people. And this wasn't the worst of Marie's bridge disasters; his **Pont Marie,** built the following year, later collapsed during a flood, killing 121 people. ♦ Métros: Cité, Pont-Marie

Ile St.-Louis

A world apart from the rest of Paris, this once-bucolic cow pasture and site of sword duels is jammed today with grand 17th-century town houses (which with few exceptions are closed to the public) and fashionable shops. Somehow it remains a peaceful oasis in the heart of a bustling city. Ile St.-Louis is named after **Louis IX,** the saintly French king who recited his breviary here among the cows. **Voltaire** considered this island the "second best" location in the world (his first choice was the straits of the Bosporus separating Europe from Asia).

Communities have only lived here for 300 years, yet the island is the oldest preserved section of the French capital, bisected by a single commercial street. When **Henri IV** decided to "urbanize" the pastoral Ile St.-Louis for his courtiers as an extension of Place des Vosges, he hired **Jean-Christophe Marie.** Between 1614 and 1630, Marie laid out one of the city's first real estate developments with straight streets on a grid, an avant-garde idea in an age when streets followed meandering medieval cow paths.

Only six blocks long and two blocks wide, Ile St.-Louis is an isolated village with no subway stop, four small hotels, and a baker whose ovens are fueled with wood. The 6,000 *Louisiens* (as island residents are called) are a proud, independent breed who don't always take kindly to interlopers (Ile St.-Louis was the first quarter in Paris to chase out the Nazis during the Liberation). When Louisiens leave the island, they say they are going "to Paris" or "to the continent" or "to the mainland,"a voyage that's less than the length of a football field. Many of the elder residents have not been off the island in years, and less than 20 years ago there was so little traffic on Sunday, the islanders played *boules* in the streets.

Soon after **Berthillon** opened its doors for business, ice cream became the rage of Paris, the island was rediscovered, and along with the notoriety came the inevitable chic tea salons and hordes of tourists. Among the island's better known residents: **Apollinaire, Balzac, Voltaire, Zola, Baudelaire, Cézanne, Courbet, Daumier, Delacroix, Colette, George Sand,** and **Georges Pompidou.**

32 Brasserie de Isle St.-Louis ★★$$ This Alsatian brasserie/tavern comes complete with the regional mascot—a stork perched on the old wooden bar. The bird, of course, is stuffed, and soon so are the neighborhood habitués who sit elbow-to-elbow dining on sausage, sauerkraut, ham knuckles, damson plum tarts, and *chopes* (steins) of Mutzig beer served by gruff waiters. The 1913 silver-plated espresso machine is a museum piece, as is the bartender, **Yvon Cottet.** This feisty Breton, who has worked for **Brigitte Bardot, Charles de Gaulle,** and **François Mitterrand,** has served in this noisy brasserie for the last 35 years. He is even immortalized by a statue in New York's Museum of Modern Art. Ask him for that story and you'll be his friend for life. ♦ M-Tu, F-Su noon-1:30AM; closed Aug. 55 Quai de Bourbon. No credit cards. Métro: Pont-Marie. 43.54.02.59

33 Le Flore en l'Ile ★★$ The sunniest tea-room in Paris boasts a three-star view of the Panthéon on the Left Bank and the flying buttresses of Notre-Dame. The good news is that it still offers music by Mozart and a good pot-au-feu, hearty breakfasts, Rocquefort salad, and chocolate cake. The bad news is that it has lost much of its cheerful charm. Lukewarm coffee and four-star toilets. ♦ Daily 10AM-2AM. 42 Quai d'Orléans. Métros: Maubert-Mutualité, Pont-Marie. 43.29.88.27

The famous Turgot Map of Paris was completed in 1739 after four years of labor by a team of artists led by Louis Bretez. Commissioned by Michel Etienne Turgot, who was in effect the mayor of Paris at the time, the extraordinary document is architecturally accurate right down to the window bays in the Louvre and the bushes in the Tuileries. The streets, however, are widened to keep them from disappearing behind the buildings. The maps featured at the beginning of each tour outlined in this book (for example, see pages 50 and 82) were inspired by the Turgot Map.

On the Right and Left banks, addresses on streets perpendicular to the Seine begin at the river with the number 1 and increase as they move away from the river.

33 La Chaumière en l'Ile ★★$$/$$$ Pink tablecloths, fresh-cut flowers, and the traditional French cuisine of **Gilles Ferron.** ♦ Tu 7-10:30PM; W-F, Su noon-2:30PM, 7-10:30PM; Sa noon-2:30PM, 7-11PM. 4 Rue Jean-du-Bellay. Métros: Maubert-Mutualité, Pont-Marie. 43.54.27.34

34 18-20 Quai d'Orléans Columnist **Walter Lippmann** lived here in 1938. ♦ Métro: Pont-Marie

34 10 Quai d'Orléans The author of *From Here to Eternity,* **James Jones,** resided here with his family from 1958 to 1975 and entertained the likes of **Henry Miller, Alexander Calder, William Styron, Sylvia Beach,** and **James Baldwin.** ♦ Métro: Pont-Marie

34 Adam Mickiewicz Museum The life and times of exiled Mickiewicz, the "Byron of Poland," as well as the poet's relationships

with the great Romantic French authors and musicians are brought to life on the second floor of this library and museum. The private library, established in 1852, contains some 200,000 volumes, as well as copies of nearly every Polish newspaper published in the 19th century. In the Chopin Room on the first floor are the composer's frayed armchair, his hand-penned mazurka scores, a death mask, and the world's only daguerreotype of the young **Chopin.** ♦ Guided tours: Th 3-6PM. Call for summer hours. 6 Quai d'Orléans. Métro: Pont-Marie. 46.34.05.44

35 St. Louis $ A British tea salon and tourist favorite serving true English scones, quiche Lorraine, tabbouleh, and 60 kinds of tea. ♦ M, W-Su noon-11PM; Tu noon-3:30PM. 81 Rue St.-Louis-en-l'Ile. Métro: Pont-Marie. 43.29.81.52

35 Alain Carion A rock collector's paradise. Minerals and malachites, geodes, and minuscule fossilized black nautiluses fashioned into earrings. ♦ Tu-Sa 10:30AM-1PM, 2PM-7:30PM. 92 Rue St.-Louis-en-l'Ile. Métro: Pont-Marie. 43.26.01.16

35 La Crêpe St.-Louis ★$ A Breton crêperie, genuine in every respect, from the gregarious patron **Jean-Pierre Ervé** to the 40 varieties of paper-thin pancakes filled with Rocquefort, *andouillette* sausage, curry, and spinach. For dessert try the flambé Irish mousse or the Almondine (vanilla ice cream, almonds, and chocolate). ♦ Daily noon-midnight. 86 Rue St.-Louis-en-l'Ile. Reservations recommended on the weekend. No credit cards. Métro: Pont-Marie. 43.26.34.21

Paris' version of Oprah Winfrey or Phil Donahue is Bernard Pivot, who leads a panel of authors who discuss literature on a TV show called "Apostrophes," which is watched by six million people every week. (The show can be seen on a Manhattan cable TV channel, too.) A former literary critic for the newspaper *Le Figaro,* Pivot got the first TV interview with Alexander Solzhenitsyn after the writer left Russia, and taped a secret interview with Lech Walesa in Poland.

36 Pylones The place where whimsical rubber jewelry and accessories sell as briskly as hot chestnuts on a winter afternoon. In lieu of that Boucheron diamond bracelet, wouldn't you rather be wearing a fanciful cactus, ice cream cone, monkey, or maybe an automobile accident on your wrist? Other novelties include children's bibs and rubber padded overalls, plus whimsical alligator knives, mallard forks, and New Wave egg cups. ♦ Daily 11AM-7PM. 57 Rue St.-Louis-en-l'Ile. Métro: Pont-Marie. 46.34.05.02

36 Hôtel St.-Louis $$$ The two-star cousin of the Lutéce and the Deux Iles, this modest hotel has exposed wooden beams, Louis XIII furniture, thick carpeting, and modern

The Islands

bathrooms, but *petit* bedrooms. Fifth-floor rooms have a view. ♦ 75 Rue St.-Louis-en-l'Ile. Métro: Pont-Marie. 46.34.04.80

36 Le Monde des Chimères ★★$$ This stone-and-beam bistro may lack the luster of its earliest days under **Jacques Manière,** one of the star chefs of nouvelle cuisine, but it remains a strong favorite of Ile St.-Louis natives. Among the specialties of chef **Cécille Ibane** are her 40-garlic chicken, *la brandade de morue,* and *magret* of duck with figs. ♦ Tu-Sa 12:15-2:30PM, 7:30-10:30PM; closed two weeks in Feb. 69 Rue St.-Louis-en-l'Ile. Métro: Pont-Marie. 43.54.45.27

36 Lutèce $$$ Named after the first Roman settlement in Paris, this restored 17th-century town house is now a three-star hotel. Ask for one of the brighter rooms on the top floor; they offer exquisite views of the island's rooftops and the dome of the Panthéon across the river. ♦ 65 Rue St.-Louis-en-l'Ile. Métro: Pont-Marie. 43.26.23.52

37 Rue de la Femme Sans Teste (Street of the Headless Woman) Shortly after the Revolution, the Rue Le Regrattier (named in the 17th century for an entrepreneur in the island development consortium) was dubbed the "Street of the Headless Woman" (in old French, *tête* was spelled with an *s*) after a decapitated statue at the corner of Rue Le Regrattier and Quai de Bourbon. "Headless woman," however, is a misnomer; the robed stone figure, severed at the torso, is believed to be Saint Nicholas, the patron saint of boatmen. His statue stands at the top of the stairs that once led down to the ferry. ♦ Métro: Pont-Marie

37 Wally le Sahrien ★★$$$ One of the most unusual and expensive couscous restaurants in Paris is run by a former Saharan camel driver named **Wally Chouaqui.** This shadowy restaurant is opulent with red velvet and inlaid ivory and serves plentiful couscous and spit-roasted lamb meals. ♦ M-Sa noon-2:30PM, 8-11PM. 16 Rue Le Regrattier. Reservations required. Métro: Pont-Marie. 43.25.01.39

37 Galerie Robert Burawoy Specializing in ancient Japanese armor, this gallery feels like the battlefield locker room for filmmaker Akira Kurosawa's next samurai epic. You will find a $15,000 coat of 19th-century mail (complete with a mustachioed mask), ceremonial stirrups, lacquered wooden saddles, and sabers sharp enough to carve sushi. Burawoy exhibits and sells museum-quality Japanese weaponry to collectors and Walter Mitty shoguns. ♦ W-Sa 2-7PM. 12 Rue Le Regrattier. Métro: Pont-Marie. 43.54.67.36

37 6 Rue Le Regrattier The voluptuous West Indian mistress of **Baudelaire, Jeanne Duval,** who was known as the "Black Venus," lived here. ♦ Métro: Pont-Marie

38 Aux Anysetiers du Roy ★$$ Originally called *Au Petit Bacchus* (the scorched remains of a 300-year-old effigy of the God of drink and revelry slouch above the entrance), this tavern used to serve the gamblers and jocks who frequented the ancient *jeu de paume* (tennis) court across the street at No. 54. The chef recommends the *moules marinières* and the *profiteroles au chocolat.* Don't leave without washing your hands in the 17th-century pewter bathroom sink upstairs. ♦ M-Tu, Th-Su 7PM-midnight. 61 Rue St.-Louis-en-l'Ile. Reservations required. Métro: Pont-Marie. 43.54.02.70

38 Deux Iles $$$ A 17th-century mansion-turned-hotel with an abundance of fresh flowers. The hotel bar with a fireplace in the cellar and the Renaissance-style ceramic tiles in the bathrooms are adequate compensation for the smallish pastel rooms. ♦ Bar: M-Sa 6:30PM-midnight. 59 Rue St.-Louis-en-l'Ile. Métro: Pont-Marie. 43.26.13.35

38 Hôtel Chenizot This former residence of the city's archbishops was also the home of **Theresia Cabarrus,** a noblewoman of insatiable sexual appetite. She offered herself to drawing-room Revolutionaries in 1789 and as a result of this gesture was dubbed *Notre-Dame de Thermidor.* While the plaster cornucopia and ferns in the first courtyard date from an 18th-century restoration, the mythological sea god over the front door and the sundial in the clammy rear courtyard are original 17th-century decorations. During the 17th century, wooden staircases were reserved for ordinary aristocrats, iron staircases were reserved for middle management, and stone or marble for those intimate with the royal family. Thus the wrought-iron balustrade near the entrance betrays the status of the original owner. ♦ 51 Rue St.-Louis-en-l'Ile. Métro: Pont-Marie

38 Librairie Ulysse I In 1971 the free-spirited **Catherine Domain** opened this vest-pocket shop specializing in travel books. She has crammed in, higgledy-piggledy, 20,000 French and English titles on everything from trekking in the Himalayas to canoeing in South America. Domain recently opened a second bookshop, **Ulysse II** (26 Rue St.-Louis-en-l'Ile, 43.29.52.10), specializing in books on

France, maps, and travel magazines. It's worth a special trip. ♦ Tu-Sa 2-8PM. 35 Rue St.-Louis-en-l'Ile. Métro: Pont-Marie. 43.25.17.35

38 Nos Ancêtres les Gaulois ★$$ A cavernous 240-person all-you-can-eat establishment tackily decorated with sheepskins, battered shields, and wild boars' heads (in sunglasses) to loosely evoke the Middle Ages. Earthy do-it-yourself salads, greasy sausage platters, grilled meat, chocolate mousse, and barely drinkable red wine are perennial hits with starving students and rowdy German tour groups. Always crowded. Arrive early and avoid Saturday nights, when the ambience is raucous, bordering on neanderthal. ♦ M-Sa 7PM-midnight; Su noon-2PM. 39 Rue St.-Louis-en-l'Ile. Reservations required. Métro: Pont-Marie. 46.33.66.07, 46.33.66.12

39 Post Office Cabins are available for making international phone calls. ♦ M-F 8AM-7PM; Sa 8AM-noon. 16 Rue des Deux-Ponts. Métro: Pont-Marie

39 Les Fous de l'Ile ★★★$/$$ Fresh-cut flowers and brass candlesticks on old wooden bistro tables, coupled with comfortable sofas, books to read, a wood-burning stove, wacky monthly art exhibitions, surrealist postcards, and music from Telemann to Talking Heads make this converted *épicerie* the island's most relaxing and hip restaurant/café. At lunch, famished drama students arrive for the *Chavignol aux fruits* (goat cheese and fruit salad), *magret de canard* with a red wine sauce, pot-au-feu, fish with crayfish sauce, and all-American brownies and carrot cake. ♦ M-Sa noon-midnight; Su noon-8PM. 33 Rue des Deux-Ponts. Métro: Pont-Marie. 43.25.76.67

39 Marcel Haupois The home of old-fashioned bakery bread cooked in wood-burning ovens (*four chauffé au bois*). ♦ M-W, Sa-Su 6:45AM-1:30PM, 3-8:30PM. 35 Rue des Deux-Ponts. Métro: Pont-Marie. 43.54.57.5

Berthillon

GLACES	SORBETS	Pamplemousse rose
Agenaise	Abricot	Péche
Cacahuète	Airelles	Poire
Caramel	Ananas	Quetsche
Chocolat	Cacao	Reine Claude
Chocolat au nougat	Cassis	Rhubarbe
Créole	Cerise	Thé
Dauphinois	Citron vert	**FRUITS**
Feuille de Menthe	Fraise	**EXOTIQUES**
Gianduja	Framboise	Banane
Grand-Marnier	Figue	Corossol
Marron glacé	Fraise de bois	Fruit de la Passion
Moka	Groseille	Goyave
Noisette	Mandarine	Kiwi
Noix	Melon	Kumquat
Nougat au miel	Menthe	Litchees
Pistache	Mirabelle	Mangue
Plombières	Mure	Noix de coco
Praliné aux pignons	Myrtille	Papaye
Vanille		

40 Berthillon ★★★$ The best ice cream and sorbet in Paris. This Ile St.-Louis landmark is so popular that around Christmastime the police show up to direct the flow of Parisians queuing around the block. Berthillon enjoys the luxury (or chutzpa) of closing two days a week and going on vacation at the height of the ice cream-eating season. Surly women in pink aprons scoop up more than 50 flavors made without an ounce of artificial ingredients. Sample the exotic fruit flavors in season: rhubarb, black currant, fig, kumquat, and fresh melon. ♦ W-Su 10AM-8PM; closed the last half of July, Aug, and during all school holidays. 31 Rue St.-Louis-en-l'Ile. Métro: Pont-Marie. 43.54.31.61

40 Au Gourmet de l'Isle ★★$$ A bustling bargain bistro famous for its breaded tripe—a nice dish if you can stomach it. Other less challenging specialties: artichoke hearts, and *ouillettes* and red beans, strawberry tarts, and Auvergne wines. ♦ M-Tu, F-Su noon-2PM, 7-10:15PM. 42 Rue St.-Louis-en-l'Ile. Dinner reservations required. Métro: Pont-Marie. 43.26.79.27

40 Hôtel du Jeu de Paume $$$ Deftly fashioned around a royal tennis court dating from 1624 (*jeu de paume* is the medieval precursor of the game now played at Wimbledon and Flushing Meadow), this refined 32-room hotel is the first new hostelry on the islands in two decades. Room No. 4 overlooks the garden, and No. 7 features a terrace. ♦ 54 Rue St.-Louis-en-l'Ile. Métro: Pont-Marie. 43.26.14.18

40 Madame Pierre Fain A toy-and-school supplies store so loved by Ile St.-Louis grade-schoolers that over the decades its walls have been papered with their crayon drawings of cheery Madame Fain and her stray cats. Among the Barbie dolls, racing cars, and purring Persians, you'll find a slick postcard series made from photographs she snapped on the island. ♦ M-Sa 10AM-3PM, 4-8PM; closed Aug. 34 Rue St.-Louis-en-l'Ile. Métro: Pont-Marie. 43.26.44.72

41 St.-Louis-en-l'Ile Church Popular for weddings and candlelit concerts, this Jesuit Baroque edifice was built in 1726 after the plans of island resident **Louis Le Vau,** the great French architect who designed portions of the Louvre and Versailles. Inside is a statue of Saint Louis in chain mail and crusader's sword, and next to the tomb of a Polish freedom fighter with a daunting name (**Damaiowicestrzembosz**) is a 1926 plaque that bears the inscription: "In grateful memory of St. Louis in whose honor the City of Saint Louis, Missouri, USA, is named." The church was heavily vandalized during the

Revolution, as you can see by the carved cherubs over the massive wooden west portal who look strangely empty-handed; they once held the king's *fleur-de-lis*. The only reason the church statues of Sainte Geneviève and the Virgin Mary survived the Revolution is because they were disguised as the goddesses of Reason and Freedom. Among the church's other curiosities is the iron spire, a 1765 replacement for the original Le Vau campanile destroyed by lightning. Evening concerts are held here frequently. ♦ Daily 9AM-noon, 3-7PM. 3 Rue Poulletier (19bis Rue St.-Louis-en-l'Ile). Métro: Pont-Marie

41 L'Orangerie ★$$$ A mini Maxim's with 18th-century decor and background harpsichord music that specializes in elegant late suppers. The ribs of beef and leg of lamb

The Islands

(cooked over a wood fire) and rich Bordeaux reds cause Rolls-Royce traffic jams out front. ♦ Daily 8:30PM-midnight; closed Aug. 28 Rue St.-Louis-en-l'Ile. Reservations required. Métro: Pont-Marie. 46.33.93.98

41 La Charlotte de l'Isle ★★$ A chocolate haunted house. Try the *gâteau du diable,* the half-moon cookies, or a wickedly delicious witch's broom (chocolate-dipped orange rinds) at this little-known tea salon. Sound diabolical? Charlotte, the hospitable kimono-clad owner, appears strangely obsessed with Halloween but swears she has yet to turn a customer into a toad. In the back room near the kitchen ("my laboratory" she calls it), you may sip a freshly brewed Chinese tea at one of three tiny tables nestled among the clutter of puppets, dried-flower bouquets, and an old stereo playing Poulenc, while under the spell of her changing entertainment. ♦ Th-Su 2-8PM; poetry readings Tu 8:30PM; puppet shows W at 2:30PM and 4PM; piano concert and tea F 6-8PM. 24 Rue St.-Louis-en-l'Ile. Métro: Pont-Marie. 43.54.25.83

42 24 Quai de Bethune In 1935 **Helena Rubinstein** demolished one of the island's finest town houses (constructed in1642) and built an Art Deco structure in its place, over which she reigned from the rooftop apartment. ♦ Métro: Pont-Marie

Before 1640 Parisian town houses had no indoor plumbing. Chamber pots were emptied into the street or courtyard from upper-story windows (hence the expression *gardez l'eau*), and men relieved themselves wherever they pleased (which is why royalty always had a nosegay within reach to cover the stench). The raw sewage made its way back into the Seine, thus explaining Parisians' preference for wine over river water. Today, tap water, referred to in restaurants as *Château de Chirac* (after Mayor Jacques Chirac), is filtered from the Seine and is certainly drinkable.

Many of the streets in Paris have gutters running down the middle, a holdover from the Middle Ages, when water was channeled through to wash them.

43 Square Barye At the eastern tip of the island, this pocket park is all that remains of the terraced gardens of **Duc de Bretonvillier**. You might glimpse sunbathers or witness a schoolboys' fishing competition here on the cobblestone *quai*. Across the river is an open-air sculpture park and, alas, one of the Left Bank's architectural eyesores, the Faculty of Science tower at Jussieu. ♦ Métros: Pont-Marie, Sully-Morland

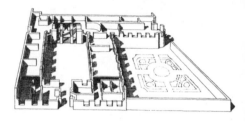

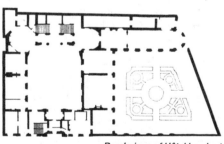

Renderings of Hôtel Lambert

44 Hôtel Lambert Probably the most opulent of 17th-century private residences in Paris, this frescoed and pilastered *hôtel particulier* was designed by **Louis Le Vau** in 1640 for **Lambert the Rich**. Its lavish gilded ceilings by **Charles Le Brun** predate and rival his Great Hall of Mirrors at Versailles. After the 1830-31 insurrection, Polish **Prince Adam Czartoryski** fled to France, married **King Louis-Phillipe's** granddaughter, and bought the Hôtel Lambert for his digs. Over the years, Czartoryski's residence served as a salon for expatriate Polish royalty and intelligentsia and as a rehearsal hall for **Frédéric Chopin**. Later it functioned as a girls finishing school and a safe house for Allied fighter pilots shot down in France. **Voltaire** briefly nested here with his lover, the **Marquise de Châtelet,** while writing the **Henriade.** Since 1972 the house has belonged to the **Rothschilds.** Behind the locked gate is a horseshoe-shaped courtyard large enough to stable 20 thoroughbreds and the famous **Galerie d'Hercule** with the **Le Sueur** frescoes and **Jacques Rousseau** trompe l'oeil landscape paintings. Open to the public on rare occasions. ♦ 2 Rue St.-Louis-en-l'Ile. Métros: Pont-Marie, Sully-Morland

44 Librairie Libella This dissident Polish bookstore and small press smuggled out the sermons of priest **Jerzy Popieluszko** in 1984 and published them shortly before his murder. Libella stocks everything from Polish fairy tales to Solidarity literature in French and English. The Lambert Gallery next door exhibits the works of contemporary Polish and Eastern European painters such as **Jozef Czapski** and **Jan Lebenstein;** the owner boasts that Lebenstein nosed out **Mark Rothko** for top honors at the first Biennale in Paris. ♦ Bookstore and gallery: Tu-Sa 9AM-noon, 2:30-7PM. 12 Rue St.-Louis-en-l'Ile. Métros: Pont-Marie, Sully-Morland.

44 5 Rue St.-Louis-en-l'Ile The expatriate literary agent **William Aspenwall Bradley,** who represented **Thornton Wilder, Edith Wharton, Katherine Anne Porter,** and **John Dos Passos,** lived here. Bradley was the one who closed the deal for publication of the *Autobiography of Alice B. Toklas* by **Gertrude Stein.** ♦ Métro: Pont-Marie

45 9 Quai d'Anjou The 19th-century illustrator and satirist, **Honoré Daumier,** lived here off and on for 17 years in the company of distinguished islanders such as poet **Baudelaire** and fellow artist **Delacroix.** It was on the Ile St.-Louis that Daumier sketched his mordant portrayals of life and politics and painted masterpieces such as *La Blanchisseuse* (The Washer Woman), which hangs in the Louvre. ♦ Métros: Pont-Marie, Sully-Morland

46 Hôtel Lauzun Louis Le Vau built a mansion in 1656 for a corrupt French army caterer, **Charles Gruyn des Bordes,** who was arrested soon afterward. That is why the building is named for its second tenant, **Saint Simon's** brother-in-law, the dandy **Duke of Lauzun.** The roll call of residents and visitors to the Hôtel Lauzun includes **Rilke, Wagner, Daumier, Delacroix,** and **Steinheil** (who restored the Ste.-Chapelle windows). In 1834 **Baudelaire** gathered his bohemian "hashish club" in an upstairs room and conducted the hallucinatory research for his book *Les Paradis Artificiels.* Some of the gaudiest suites in all of Paris are the *chambres de parade* (parade rooms), which are cluttered with golden nymphs, cut-velvet walls, trompe l'oeil murals, and allegorical figures. The gilded rainspouts and pouting stone lion in the courtyard (supporting a 20th-century afterthought, the bathroom) are alone worth the trip. In 1928 the city bought and restored it as a residence

for visiting heads of state. ♦ Currently under renovation; call ahead for visits arranged by the Centre d'Accueil de la Ville de Paris. 17 Quai d'Anjou. Métros: Pont-Marie, Sully-Morland. 42.76.54.04

47 29 Quai d'Anjou In 1922, with a hand-printing press, American **William Bird** established his **Three Mountains Press** here. Under the editorial aegis of **Ezra Pound,** it published **Ernest Hemingway** and **Ford Madox Ford.** ♦ Métros: Pont-Marie, Sully-Morland

47 37 Quai d'Anjou When he arrived in France in 1921 after the acceptance of his first major novel, *Three Soldiers,* **John Dos Passos** rented a room in this building. ♦ Métros: Pont-Marie, Sully-Morland

48 Au Franc Pinot ★★$$/$$$ One of the last of the island's original 92 taverns, this 300-

year-old watering hole originally catered to sailors who anchored cargo ships next to the Pont-Marie. The metal grape cluster over the door dates from 1656. Not as old but agelessly satisfying are the Loire Valley reds served with homemade minced duck *rillettes* in the upstairs wine bar. For dinner, venture downstairs into the 17th-century vaulted wine cellar/restaurant where you may enjoy, among other specialties, the roast pigeon in cereal. ♦ Tu-Sa noon-2PM, 7-11PM. 1 Quai de Bourbon. Métro: Pont-Marie. 43.29.46.98

48 Pont Marie King Louis XIII laid the first stone of this bridge, which was completed in 1635 and partially destroyed by the 1658 spring thaw. The thaw caused a flood that dumped 22 of the bridge's four-story houses into the Seine, drowning 121 residents and shopkeepers. The bridge is not named after **Marie de Médici, Henri IV's** widow, who commissioned the work, but after **Jean-Christophe Marie,** the contractor hired to develop Ile St.-Louis and the *quais.* ♦ Métro: Pont-Marie

48 3 Quai de Bourbon Explaining the plainness of the facade of this real-estate agency is a story in itself. The sumptuous Empire-style windows and storefront you don't see at **No. 3** were purchased by **J. Pierpont Morgan** and moved in 1926 to the Metropolitan Museum of Art in New York. They now serve as the entrance to the museum's Wrightsman Galleries, which house a superb collection of Louis XVI furniture and porcelain. ♦ Métro: Pont-Marie

The term *hôtel* in Paris often refers not to that overnight institution with room service, but rather to a *hôtel particulier,* meaning a town house or mansion.

Restaurants/Nightlife: Red   **Hotels:** Blue
Shops/ 🎋 Outdoors: Green   **Sights/Culture:** Black

Alain Senderens
Chef, Lucas-Carton

Passage Véro-Dodat in Bernard Gauguin's shop, browsing for some old cookbooks; lunch at **Lipp** on a Saturday; and scrambled eggs for lunch in the summer at **Aux Deux Magots** while watching people pass by.

Jogging through the **Luxembourg Gardens** in the evening; joining friends for a drink at the **Hôtel Bristol bar;** then dining either at **Benoît's** on the Rue St.-Martin, **La Fermette du Sud-Ouest** on the Rue Coquillière, or on Moroccan food like pastillas at **El Aouina** on the Rue Magdebourg.

Seeing a good film, then dining downstairs at **Castel's.**

The **Eiffel Tower** at night.

The Islands

Andrée Putman
Paris-based Interior Designer

Dining at **Chez la Vieille.** This tiny bistro opens only at lunchtime, Monday through Friday. They offer exceptional French home-cooking—the pot-au-feu, stuffed tomatoes, and crayfish are out of this world.

Visiting **Mémorial de la Déportation,** located at the tip of Ile de la Cité, on the Pont St.-Louis side, behind Notre-Dame. A narrow staircase leads to a very impressive bit of architecture, built in 1957 by G.H. Pingusson, commemorating the thousands of French who died during the Holocaust.

Touring the **Musée d'Histoire Naturelle.** It has a winter garden containing a large variety of tropical plants; a botanical section with 10,000 species of plants; a menagerie and snake area; and paleontology, minerology, and paleobotany sections.

Hammam St.-Paul (Turkish baths), which has a good restaurant where you can have a light dinner in your terry-cloth robe.

Maria di Mase
Publisher

I love the mystery of the **Rue Broca,** a curved, narrow, tortuous, and sunken street that's unlike any other. It's inhabited by people who, much like me (I am an editor of tales), love their stories.

Régine
Owner of Régine's restaurant and nightclub

Lunch at the **Relais Plaza, Stresa, Le Pré Carré,** or the **Bar des Théâtres.**

The **Louvre** and **Georges Pompidou** museums.

Clothes from **Alaïa, Ungaro,** and **Jean Claude.**

The power of the monarchy and the revolutionaries' struggle are evoked clearly at the Museum of the Police. Royal orders for arrests (called *lettres de cachet*) were carried out without due process of law, and many of these historic documents are on display, including warrants for Danton, Lavoisier, Beaumarchais, and Madame Roland.

Comtesse Anna de Bagneux
Château du Marais

The **Jardin du Luxembourg** and its elegant palace and fountains were created in the seventh century by the Italian queen mother Marie de Médici. They have been altered little since then, and are still beautiful. Artists and students cross these gardens to reach Boulevard St.-Michel, where the old university **La Sorbonne** stands.

On the Quai de Conti, you can see beautiful 17th-century architecture at the **Palais de l'Institut** and 18th-century buildings at the **Hôtel de la Monnaie.** On Quai Voltaire, don't miss **La Frégate,** a little restaurant with old wainscoting.

On the other side of the Seine, you find the **Louvre** and **Tuileries Gardens** (very famous, but I like them all the same!), as well as **Rue de Rivoli,** with its arcades and two English bookstores. For the best hot chocolate in Paris, go to the ancient tearoom, **Angélina.**

I don't care much for the Champs-Elysées, but it is large and lively. If you're in the area and want high-quality food and a very agreeable welcome, turn right on Rue de Berri to find **Le Val d'Isére** restaurant.

Les Invalides, founded in the 17th century by Louis XIV for his wounded soldiers, is a harmonious place with gardens and a large esplanade leading down to the Seine. It contains a museum of French-army history.

Don't miss the **Musée Rodin,** located in a beautiful ancient *hôtel particulier* on the Boulevard des Invalides at the corner of Rue de Varenne.

Versailles!

Gonzague Saint Bris
Author

Paris is the world's best city for a love affair. It is like the compartmentalized shell of a snail, or the plan of a brothel that Leonardo da Vinci once drew, where the clients never run into each other. You move to another quarter and you're unrecognized. Thus, some people can carry on several love affairs at the same time, as long as they don't have two mistresses in one neighborhood.

The most cinematic place to take a girl is the **Château Raray,** where **Jean Cocteau** made the film *Beauty and the Beast.*

The best secret place in Paris is the varnished wooden cabin in the sky that **Gustave Eiffel** built at the top of the tower that bears his name; it was for seducing adventurous visitors.

Best place to break up: **Françoise Sagan** says there is no better spot than the table near the door of the **Brasserie Lipp**—you know so many people coming in that you have to greet them endlessly, never allowing time to try to explain your questionable conduct to your companion. Thus, one does avoid long, sad justifications.

Best hotels: For a night of love, the room at the **Hôtel Bristol.** For writing, **Oscar Wilde's** room at **L'Hôtel** on the Rue des Beaux-Arts. For dreaming, the roof of the **Crillon Hôtel** in the golden dawn, from which you can contemplate the **Place de la Concorde** (Curzio Malaparte said, "The Place de la Concorde isn't a place, it's an idea").

My favorite place: the **Palais Royal,** where I can sing under the window of **Inès de la Fressange,** the most beautiful woman in Paris and a former top model for Chanel.

My favorite museum: **Le Musée Carnavalet.**

My favorite restaurant: **Le Grand Véfour.**

My favorite garden: the one on the **Champs-Elysées,** where the infant **Proust** played with my great-grand-mother in the sandpile. I also like the public gardens, where, in summer, without asking permission, I give rustic dinner parties (particularly in the **Place du Canada,** which is hidden from view with its woods and romantic rocks).

My favorite rendezvous spot: on **Rue de Rivoli,** across from the **Louvre** under the statue of my ancestor, **General Desaix,** a rival and friend of **Bonaparte.** He was killed in civilian costume because he arrived late to the Battle of Marengo. He had superb long hair.

My simplest pleasure: walking my dog, Byron, through any street in Paris.

Gérard Titus-Carnel
French Painter and Poet

Aux Fins Gourmets on the Boulevard St.-Germain for its cassoulet.

The greenhouse in the **Jardin des Plantes** for dreaming.

Museum of African and Oceanic Art (especially for the crocodile pit).

The **Albert Kahn Gardens.**

A few streets with strange names from my childhood: **Rue de la Dhuis, Rue de la Py,** and **Rue Le Bua.**

The **Gustave Moreau Museum.**

Ste.-Chapelle for the light.

Passage Panorama, Passage Joffroy for the **Hôtel Chopin,** and **Passage Verdeau** for the old bookstores.

Peter Dawson
Author

My favorite places for a rendezvous:

The summer house in the **Parc de Bagatelle** that dominates the prettiest rose garden in Paris. Enchanting in any season.

At the counter of **Ma Bourgogne,** in the **Place des Vosges,** sipping a simple wine and nibbling a *croque monsieur.*

In the main salon at **Angélina,** eating a ruinous **Mont Blanc** and drinking the richest hot chocolate in the world, protected by the last vestiges of old Europe.

The **Espadon** bar of the **Ritz** for a cocktail at 6PM and maybe an impromptu performance by Gainsbourg on the piano.

The top-floor bar of the **Concorde Lafayette** at the Porte Maillot at sundown, with a glass of champagne.

The **Ste.-Chapelle** on the night of a candlelit concert.

Le Vivarois for whatever brilliant entrée **Claude Peyrot** may recommend that day.

The **Bistro 121** for their *poireaux vinaigrette,* which you must order when you make your reservations (it raises the humble leek to an art form), and the *poule-au-pot.*

The **Cochon d'Or** for the best grilled *pied de cochon* in the world and the finest piece of grilled French beef.

Chez Allard for the *pâté de foie de volaille* and the *canard aux olives.*

Chez Georges at Porte Maillot for the perfectly cooked *train de côtes de boeuf.*

Chez La Vieille at lunchtime for the best home-cooking in Paris.

The **Train Bleu** for a *saucisson chaud de Lyon* and the illusion of travel in the most stunning fin-de-siècle decor.

Baroness Gabrielle Van Zuylen

The lake in the **Bois de Boulogne** in the winter when it's frozen, and the **Parc de Montsouris,** anytime.

Sunday morning at the market on the **Rue de Buci,**

then lunch at **Lipp,** followed by a walk in the **Père-Lachaise Cemetery.**

Walking over the **Pont des Arts;** the movie theater **La Pagode** on the Rue de Babylone, inside and out; **Madame Loo's** Chinese extravaganza on the Rue de Courcelles (now an antique gallery); the greenhouses of **La Ville de Paris** at the Porte d'Auteuil; **Musée des Monuments Français** on the Place du Trocadéro; the **Colonial Museum** at the Port Dorée; the **Eiffel Tower** at night; and **Place du Furstemberg** in the spring.

Joel Katz
Partner, Katz Wheeler Design, Philadelphia

Musée des Arts et Metiers—an incredible collection waiting for a real museum to display it well. Amazing globes, timepieces, and instruments of weight, measure, and astronomy.

The violinist in the courtyard of the **Hôtel de Sully** at dusk, who's posed like the gypsy violinist in the Kertesz photograph.

A walk through **Ile de la Cité,** ending with **Notre-Dame** and the monument to the 200,000 deported—the contrast between the most elegant and the most brutal monuments to faith.

The overpriced but superbly crafted paintboxes in art-supply stores on Rue Jacob.

The **Musée d'Orsay.**

Ever wonder what happened to the guillotined bodies during the Reign of Terror? In some cases, their skin was used to bind books. One poor soul's flesh ended up as the cover of a two-by-three-inch Christian prayer book that's part of the rare book collection at the University of California at Berkeley. Inside the book's cover is the following inscription: "During the French Revolution, there were tanneries devoted to curing the skins of the victims of the guillotine. The fine grain made these skins particularly suitable for binding books. Although the centuries have removed the macabre or even horrible implications, it remains a curious evidence of gross insensitivity that human skin should have been employed on a religious book. Or was it, perhaps, a grim jest of the overwhelming anticlerical movement of the period?"

M **St.-Michel**

La Bûcherie—*in winter get a table by the fireplace*

Musée de Cluny—*a former monk's quarters located atop Roman baths that now holds French Medieval art*

M **Maubert-Mutualité**

Le Balzar—*Camus and Sartre had their last argument in this literary brasserie*

La Sorbonne—*sign up for a crash course in French at Paris' most famous university, or go to Richelieu's tomb on 21 October or 4 December and wait for his red hat to drop from the ceiling*

Parisians find the sounds of Louis Armstrong, Miles Davis, and other American jazz greats at **Crocojazz**

Voltaire, Rousseau, and Victor Hugo lie in the rather depressing crypt of the **Panthéon**

Le Bistrot de la Nouvelle Mairie—*enjoy a glass of Beaujolais or Gamay outdoors at one of the city's finest wine bars*

On 26 December 1898, Pierre and Marie Curie discovered radium in a ramshackle lab at the Sorbonne School of Physics and Chemistry

The Latin Quarter

This section of the city is Roman Paris, the university, and the Bohemian quarter. The **Henri Burger** novel *La Vie Bohème*, which became the **Puccini** opera *La Bohème*, was set here. The Latin Quarter was once the home of **Verlaine** and **Descartes**, and is still the home of the **Sorbonne**, old book-shops, student cafés, publishing houses, jazz clubs, and, more recently, expensive boutiques. For seven centuries, this was a city within a city, where scholars had a tongue of their own (Latin), were exempt from the civil law, and recognized no authority except for the Pope. Latin, which hasn't been spoken here since the Revolution, was replaced on the streets of the Left Bank by the Moroccan, Greek, and Vietnamese of immigrant families selling the couscous, souvlaki, and Imperial rolls that supplement the basic Bohemian diet of bad coffee and cheap cigarettes.

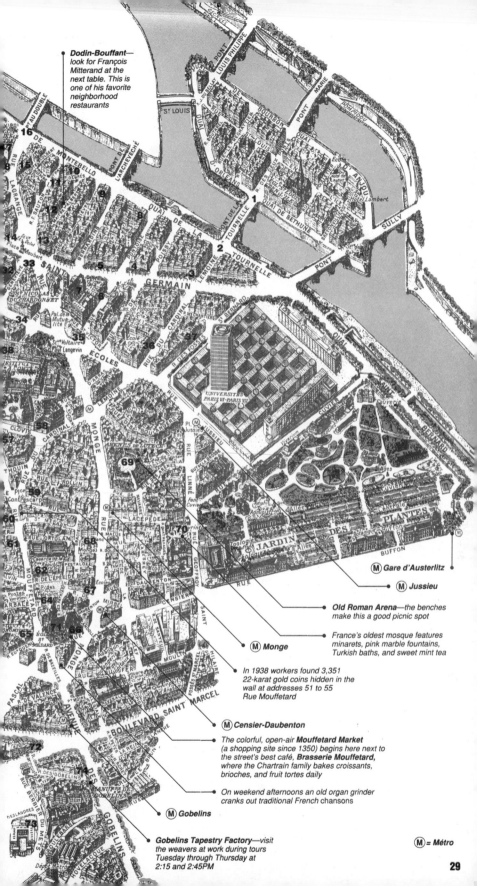

Dodin-Bouffant—look for François Mitterand at the next table. This is one of his favorite neighborhood restaurants

(M) *Gare d'Austerlitz*

(M) *Jussieu*

Old Roman Arena—the benches make this a good picnic spot

France's oldest mosque features minarets, pink marble fountains, Turkish baths, and sweet mint tea

(M) *Monge*

In 1938 workers found 3,351 22-karat gold coins hidden in the wall at addresses 51 to 55 Rue Mouffetard

(M) *Censier-Daubenton*

The colorful, open-air **Mouffetard Market** (a shopping site since 1350) begins here next to the street's best café, **Brasserie Mouffetard**, where the Chartrain family bakes croissants, brioches, and fruit tortes daily

On weekend afternoons an old organ grinder cranks out traditional French chansons

(M) *Gobelins*

Gobelins Tapestry Factory—visit the weavers at work during tours Tuesday through Thursday at 2:15 and 2:45PM

(M) = *Métro*

Pont de la Tournelle

This walk begins at the **Pont de la Tournelle,** in front of the famed penthouse restaurant, **La Tour d'Argent,** and passes by the booksellers along the Seine and a splendid view of **Notre-Dame's** flying buttresses. Next comes **François Mitterrand's** house, two funny, offbeat museums—the **Musée des Hôpitaux de Paris-Assistance Publique** (Museum of Public Health and Welfare) and

The Latin Quarter

the **Musée des Collections Historiques de la Préfecture de Police** (Police Museum)—and then the **Rue des Ecoles** to the Sorbonne and the **Collège de France,** which for centuries have been the most celebrated seats of learning in Europe. At the end of the street are the Roman baths adjoining the extraordinary medieval **Cluny Museum.** Climbing **Montagne Ste.-Geneviève,** named after the patron saint of Paris, you pass **King Philippe Auguste's** 13th-century city wall, the **Panthéon,** and a landmark for oenologists, the **Bistrot de la Nouvelle Mairie,** one of the best wine bars in Paris. It's all literally downhill from there. At the **Place de la Contrescarpe,** the more adventuresome may peel off for a detour past a Roman arena and a Turkish mosque complete with minarets, arriving at the zoo and botanical gardens—a nice spot for a picnic lunch purchased in the **Place-Monge** or **Mouffetard Market.** On the **Rue Mouffetard,** a medieval market street frequented this century by the likes of **Ernest Hemingway** and **Josephine Baker,** you might meander past stalls selling everything from tropical mangoes to African monkey bread and end up at **Gobelins,** the old royal weaving mills, for a possible afternoon tour. If you hunger for a meal, you will find inexpensive Vietnamese and Greek shish-kebab restaurants abounding along Mouffetard around Gobelins. For the more pricey establishments, including **Dodin-Bouffant, Brasserie Balzar,** or La Tour d'Argent, and the night spots in this vicinity, such as the **Paradis Latin** or **Les Trois Maillets,** head back to the beginning of this walk toward the Rue des Ecoles and the Seine.

Paris street names often honor individuals or their professions or tell the street's destination.

1 Sainte Geneviève On the **Pont de la Tournelle,** one of the Seine's newest bridges (1928) and the fifth in a long line that dates back to 1369, is a missilelike statue of the city's patron. Apparently ready for a heavenly liftoff, the angular obelisk effigy of Sainte Geneviève by **Landowski** turns her back on Notre-Dame and faces upriver, guarding the city as her spirit has done since 450. In that year, the prayers of the then 27-year-old nun were credited with halting **Attila the Hun's** advance on Paris, after his army of barbarians had just sacked Cologne and brutalized 10,000 of its maidens.

In 473, while the city was under siege by the Franks, Geneviève courageously smuggled 11 boatloads of food to starving Parisians through enemy lines. She lived on this Left Bank mountain until the ripe age of 89, and like France's other virgin sainte, **Jeanne d'Arc,** was consigned to flames, but not until 1,281 years after her death. The fanatic anticlerics of the Revolution burned her remains and cast the ashes into the river. ◆ Métros: Cardinal-Lemoine, Pont-Marie

2 La Tour d'Argent ★★★★$$$$ This may no longer be the best restaurant in Paris, but its penthouse panorama of Notre-Dame's flying buttresses and the barges passing on the Seine has helped make it the city's most famous, expensive, and spectacular eating establishment. Tour d'Argent is successor to an earlier *auberge* that occupied the same site, the **Café Anglais,** which was founded in 1582. The Café Anglais was mentioned by **Madame de Sévigné** in her famous letters and provided the setting for a **Dumas** novel. It is said that this is also where the fork was first used in Paris. On the ground floor of the restaurant is a table set with the original silver, crystal, and china that were used on 7 June 1867 to serve a dinner at the Café Anglais attended by **Czar Alexander II,** the **Czarevitch, Wilhelm I,** and **Bismarck.**

The touch of class is evident throughout the Tour d'Argent, from the Grand Siècle-style elevator to the traditional blue cornflower in the jacket lapel of restaurant owner and dandy **Claude Terrail,** master of the dinner-with-a-view formula. The Tour d'Argent's pièce de résistance is its pressed duck flambé, first served in 1890 to **Edward VII,** then Prince of Wales. More than 600,000 ducklings later, the dish is still a hit. The kitchen keeps a running tally of the number of ducklings pressed (which must be where McDonald's got the idea), and each order arrives at the table with a numbered card. Other recommended dishes include cold Lagardère lobster, flambéed peaches, and bittersweet chocolate cake. The wine list draws from the 300,000 bottles in the vaulted cellars underground. You can tour the cellars after dessert and watch Terrail's little sound-and-light show while sipping a vintage liqueur. In the rooftop restaurant you must reserve your table far in advance; ask for one by the picture window. Bear in mind, however, that lunch is just half the price of dinner and midday is when Parisians eat out. The Tour d'Argent is popular with Americans and Japanese, and the only French speakers in the place at dinner may be the waiters. ♦ Tu-Su noon-4PM, 8PM-1AM. 15 Quai de la Tournelle. Reservations required. Métro: Maubert-Mutualité. 43.54.23.31

2 Les Comptoirs de la Tour d'Argent If you want to take one of the Tour d'Argent's trademark blue-and-white Limoges plates home as a souvenir but lack the gall to pinch one (or an overcoat large enough to conceal it), step across the street into the gourmet boutique of **Claude Terrail,** the enterprising restaurateur who has become the Pierre Cardin of French cuisine. Here, instead of dinner for $180, you can buy a menu for $18, fresh *foie gras de canard* to go, or an entire Tour d'Argent place setting, including fluted champagne glass, coffee spoon, and ashtray. Prices start at $4 for 140 grams of Dijon mustard and escalate to more than $2,000 for a bottle of Fine Clos du Griffier 1788. Service can be as snooty as the setting is opulent. ♦ Tu-Sa 10AM-midnight; Su noon-midnight. 2 Rue du Cardinal-Lemoine. Métros: Cardinal-Lemoine, Maubert-Mutualité. 46.33.45.58

3 Chez René ★★$$/$$$ An authentic bistro with amusing waiters and very tasty daily specials that range from Monday's pot-au-feu to Friday's *blanquette de veau* (veal in white sauce). Also on the menu are cucumbers and cream, country sausages, mutton with white

beans, *entrecote Bercy,* and in the autumn, *pleurotes provençales* (fresh wild mushrooms baked with garlic). ♦ M-F 12:15-2:15PM, 7:45-10:15PM; closed Aug and holidays. 14 Blvd St.-Germain. Reservations recommended. No credit cards. Métros: Cardinal-Lemoine, Maubert-Mutualité. 43.54.30.23

4 Chez Toutoune ★★$$$ Colette Toutoune Dejean offers traditional home-style meals at old-fashioned prices. The five-course menu chalked on the blackboard changes daily, but you can always count on the pot-au-feu, braised guinea hen with cabbage, mussels with endive, grilled leg of lamb, currant tarts, and creamy Brie. ♦ M 8-10:45PM; Tu-Sa noon-2PM, 8-10:45PM. 5 Rue de Pontoise. Dinner reservations recommended. Métro: Maubert-Mutualité. 43.26.56.81

4 La Marée Verte ★★$$ A bargain seafood restaurant known for its hearty fisherman's plate, turbot souffle (which rivals the one served around the corner in the chic Dodin-

Bouffant), and delicious meringue tarts. ♦ Tu-Th noon-2PM, 7:30-10:30PM; F-Sa noon-2PM, 7:30-11PM. 9 Rue de Pontoise. Reservations recommended. Métro: Maubert-Mutualité. 43.25.89.41

4 Le Bistro d'Hannah ★$ At this unassuming bistro, restaurateurs **Eric** and **Sonia Marcyz** serve four flavorful cuts of Aberdeen Angus beef from the sole supplier in France, accompanied by refreshing Beaujolais *crus.* ♦ M noon-2:30PM; W-Su noon-2:30PM, 7:30-10:30PM. 9 Rue de Pontoise. Métro: Maubert-Mutualité. 43.54.68.23

5 Diptyque Run by English and French artists who met while studying at the Ecole des Beaux-Arts after WWII, this tiny corner shop specializes in elegant antique bead necklaces, rose-petal sachets, Welsh bedspreads, Shetland plaids, and candles scented with the fragrance of the forest floor on a damp May morning. ♦ Tu-Sa 10AM-7PM. 34 Blvd St.-Germain. Métros: Cardinal-Lemoine, Maubert-Mutualité. 43.26.45.27

5 HG Thomas The boutique of **Hervé Gerald Thomas** offers the *chicest* in gifts: Italian luggage, *double* umbrellas, hunting knives, Braun clocks, and whiskey flasks. The inventory ranges from designer ballpoints to Weber barbecues. Most everything at HG Thomas comes in black. ♦ Tu-Sa 10:30AM-8PM. 36 Blvd St.-Germain. Métro: Maubert-Mutualité. 46.33.57.50

5 Au Pactole ★★$$$ Another one of **François Mitterrand's** preferred seafood restaurants. The delicacies of chef **Roland Magne** encompass *marbre de poissons aux algues*, lobster sautéed in ginger, and Argentine steak with a red wine sauce. The decor has been totally redone: could the color of the walls be called orange-lemon? ◆ M-F noon-2:30PM, 7-10:45PM; Sa 7-10:45PM; closed Christmas Day. 44 Blvd St.-Germain. Reservations recommended. Métro: Maubert-Mutualité. 43.26.92.28, 46.33.31.31

6 Pontoise Swimming Pool and Club Quartier Latin Squash Club Surrounded by rows of old lockers and changing rooms, this pretty indoor pool is one of the few in Paris where lap swimming is the norm and lane markers are actually respected. Downstairs is an athletic club with four squash courts, Jacuzzi, sauna, dance classes, lounge, and a snack bar where salads, steaks, and fruit juices are served. Passes to the pool

The Latin Quarter

and squash club are available by the day. ◆ Gym and squash club: M-F 10AM-10PM; Sa-Su 9:30AM-7PM. Pool: M-F 11AM-1:45PM, 5-9PM; Sa-Su 11AM-9PM. 19 Rue de Pontoise. Métros: Cardinal-Lemoine, Maubert-Mutualité. 43.54.82.45

7 St.-Nicolas-du-Chardonnet Built in 1709, this sanctuary was originally a 13th-century chapel standing in a field of *chardons* (thistles). Later redesigned by **Charles Le Brun,** it now houses the Le Brun family chapel, along with Charles Le Brun's *The Martyrdom of Saint John*. The beautiful wood carving over the side door on the Rue des Bernadins is also by Le Brun. St.-Nicolas-du-Chardonnet happens to be one of the most liturgically conservative in Paris: Mass is performed entirely in Latin. ◆ 239 Blvd St.-Germain. Métros: Cardinal-Lemoine, Maubert-Mutualité

8 Jean-Pierre Stella Legions of lead soldiers stand at attention and ready to serve. Stella's petite shop on the *quai* also deals in military medals, samurai armor, Napoleonic helmets, and vintage weaponry. ◆ M-Sa 10:30AM-noon, 2-7PM; closed Aug. 67 Quai de la Tournelle. Métro: Maubert-Mutualité. 46.33.40.50

8 Musée des Hôpitaux de Paris—Assistance Publique (Museum of Public Health and Welfare) Tucked away in this 17th-century mansion, which after the Revolution was converted into the central pharmacy for the city's hospitals, is one of Paris' most offbeat yet pleasurable museums. Unknown to most Parisians, this museum of French medicine contains an extraordinary collection of old ceramic apothecary jars, Roman medicine vials, hospital rosters, old glass baby bottles, pewter syringes, copper basins, blocks of marble that were pulverized to powder baby bottoms, and a mechanical model of a quasi-night deposit box that 19th-century nuns

invented for abandoned babies. ◆ Admission. W-Su 10AM-5PM; closed Aug and holidays. 47 Quai de la Tournelle. Métro: Maubert-Mutualité. 46.33.01.43

8 45 Quai de la Tournelle After being discharged from the American Ambulance Corps in the spring of 1919, **John Dos Passos** sublet a playwright's apartment here and began what would become his first successful novel, *Three Soldiers*. ◆ Métro: Maubert-Mutualité

9 Rue de Bièvre This unpretentious street of abandoned shops and couscous restaurants is barricaded at both ends and guarded round the clock. That's because French **President François Mitterrand** lives at **No. 22.** Though the Elysée Palace is the official presidential residence, Mitterrand, a socialist, has departed from tradition and returns here each night to sleep. A blue police van parked on the *quai* is the tip-off that the president is at home. *Bièvre,* which comes from the Latin word for beaver, was named after a tributary of the Seine. At **No. 12,** a statue of Saint Michel slaying the dragon marks the former site of **Collège St.-Michel.** ◆ Métro: Maubert-Mutualité

10 Chez Maître Albert ★$$ Named after the 13th-century alchemist who worked here, the restaurant features the obligatory Left Bank exposed beams, a grand fireplace, a small menu (including marinated salmon, fish sausage in sorrel, Meaux Brie cheese, and frozen strawberry soufflé), and unbeatable prices. It attracts bargain-seekers by the horde. ◆ M-Sa 7:30PM-midnight. 1-3-5 Rue Maître-Albert (at the angle of 73 Quai de la Tournelle). Reservations recommended. Métro: Maubert-Mutualité. 46.33.13.78, 46.33.06.44

10 Jean-Louis Barbéry Barbéry and his wife run this smart shop specializing in French books, etchings, and illustrations from the 16th century to 1930. A modest collection of sculpture is displayed in their back room. ◆ Tu-Sa 1-7PM. 2 Rue des Grands-Degres. Métro: Maubert-Mutualité. 43.25.33.76

11 Galerie Urubamba Traditional Indian art from the Americas is the speciality of this gallery/folk-art shop: Guatemalan weaving, handpainted Mexican masks, feathered Brazilian headdresses, and Panamanian shirt panels. You could spend hours perusing the ethnographic books and curios here. ◆ Tu-Sa 2-7:30PM. 4 Rue de la Bûcherie. Métro: Maubert-Mutualité. 43.54.08.24

11 Sylvain Eden This lush indoor rain forest of palms, bamboo, and ferns is cultivated by a team of landscape architects who will foliate your next gallery opening or terrace barbecue with all manner of jungle flora for rent. All this verdure recalls **Greenpeace,** the worldwide environmental organization that formerly occupied this building and was the target of clumsy French terrorist cloak-and-dagger diplomacy (see page 181). ◆ M-F 9AM-6PM. 1-3 Rue de la Bûcherie. Métros: Maubert-Mutualité, St.-Michel. 46.34.61.18

12 Patchworks du Rouvray Like the Galerie Urubamba across the square, this quilt emporium is run by an American woman. **Diane de Obaldia's** shop is named after a 14th-century farmhouse near Chartres, where she started her business. Today, she sells traditional American Midwest patchwork quilts from the 1930s: log cabins, grandmother's flower gardens, and double wedding rings. She offers about 40 different quilting classes (in French and English) and 700 varieties of cotton fabric for inspired quilters. ♦ M 2-6:30PM; Tu-Sa 10:30AM-6:30PM; closed the week surrounding 15 Aug. 1 Rue Frédéric-Sauton. Métro: Maubert-Mutualité. 43.25.00.45

12 Chieng-Mai ★★$$ An excellent Thai restaurant serving beef *satay,* squid and mint salad, spicy pork brochette, and, for dessert, grilled flan with coconut milk. The pineapple salad is divine. ♦ M-Sa noon-2:30PM, 7-11:30PM. 12 Rue Frédéric-Sauton. Reservations required. Métro: Maubert-Mutualité. 43.25.45.45

12 Dodin-Bouffant ★★$$ One of the best seafood restaurants in Paris, Dodin-Bouffant (named after a fictional extravagant gourmet in a **Marcel Rouff** novel) orders 500 pounds of fish daily, smokes its own herring and salmon, and has oysters delivered every day from Brittany and Ireland. Order the steamed scallops with fresh pasta or the curried sole with squash fondue and discover why this warm, casual bistro is one of François Mitterrand's favorite neighborhood restaurants. ♦ M-Sa 12:30-2PM, 7:45PM-11PM; closed Aug and two weeks at Christmas. 25 Rue Frédéric-Sauton. Reservations required. Métro: Maubert-Mutualité. 43.25.25.14

13 Than Binh This little Vietnamese grocery store supplies the many Southeast Asian restaurants and families clustered around Place Maubert. The exotic spices and bewildering assortment of food (rice steamed in banana leaves, tapioca in grape leaves, and shrimp muffins) will transport your imagination to the Mekong Delta. ♦ Tu-Su 9AM-7:30PM; 29 Place Maubert. Métro: Maubert-Mutualité. 43.54.03.34

14 Place Maubert The name *Maubert* is probably a contraction of **Maître Albert,** a Dominican teacher at the University of Paris in the Middle Ages. For centuries, this wide spot in the road was a crime-ridden skid row, a resort for tramps drinking *gros rouge* (cheap red wine), and the site of public executions. Here, in 1546, during the reign of **François I,** the printer and humanist philosopher, **Etienne Dolet,** was burned at the stake as a heretic; his own books were used to kindle the fire. In addition to serving as an execution ground, from the Middle Ages hence this crossroads has been a bustling open-air market. ♦ Métro: Maubert-Mutualité

15 Colbert $$ From many of the 16 rooms in this former 18th-century residence (parts of the building date back to 1500), you can contemplate Notre-Dame while having breakfast in bed. The decor is a bit grim, but the rooms are quiet and simply furnished, and the beds have luxuriously smooth sheets (**No. 41** is a

studio with an especially fine view). The **Duke of Windsor** once sponsored an animal hospital on the site of the present courtyard garden. ♦ 7 Rue de l'Hôtel-Colbert. Métro: Maubert-Mutualité. 43.25.85.65

16 Quai de Montebello Booksellers The *bouquinistes* who work in the shadow of Notre-Dame practice one of the city's oldest trades, selling old Daumier prints, volumes on everything from Balzac to bebop, and the occasional nasty postcard out of their green boxes on the quai. These famous, free-spirited cowboys of the book business open and close their sidewalk stalls when they please and sell only what interests them. If you are in the market for old French cookbooks, seek out **Monsieur Bardon** at Box 11, Quai de Montebello (42.60.27.50). At stall No. 102, across the Ile de la Cité on the corner of the Pont de Notre-Dame, is **Monsieur Leleu,** who restores old manuscripts and has a private collection consisting primarily of leatherbound books from the 18th century. ♦ Daily 11AM-7PM, depending on the weather. Located on the Quai de Montebello from the Petit Pont to the Pont de l'Archevêché. Métro: St.-Michel

Quai de Montebello

16 Pont au Double The only bridge in Paris whose toll was double—two *sous* instead of one. ♦ Métro: St.-Michel

17 St.-Julien-le-Pauvre This odd, ungraceful amalgam of Romanesque and Gothic church architecture is devoid of bell tower, transepts, or organ, and squats on a small square lined with acacia trees. With its iron-caged well in front, it looks more like a humble country church than a Parisian monument. Started in 1165 (and restored in 1250 and 1651), St.-Julian-the-Poor (named after a martyred third-century bishop who gave all his money to the penniless) claims to be the oldest church in Paris. (Construction began two years after the Notre-Dame's started, but St.-Julien-le-Pauvre was completed first. The bell tower and part of the nave in the church of St.-Germain-des-Prés antedate St.-Julien-le-Pauvre, but purists point out that when St.-Germain-des-Prés was built, it stood outside the city walls and therefore was not, strictly speaking, a Parisian sanctuary.)

The Latin Quarter

In the 12th century, when renegade theologian **Pierre Abélard,** the most famous scholar in the Christian world, quit Notre-Dame, he took more than 3,000 students along with him and established a new university at St.-Julien. The church thus became the seat and meeting place for the new University of Paris. In 1524 students critical of a new rector ransacked and nearly destroyed the church. After the Revolution, St.-Julien-le-Pauvre was used variously as a salt storehouse, a wool market, and a flour granary. Since 1889 it has belonged to the Greek Orthodox church. The enormous stone slab beside the well came from the fourth-century Roman highway that became the Rue St.-Jacques. ♦ Daily 9AM-1PM, 2:30-6:30PM. 1 Rue St.-Julien-le-Pauvre. Métro: St.-Michel

17 Square René-Viviani In this lovely little park stands what is reputed to be the oldest tree in Paris. This false acacia *(Robinia pseudoacacia)* leans on stone crutches, infirm but erect, and blooms every spring. Not bad for a sprout that crossed the ocean from Guyana to be planted in 1680 by **Jean Robin.** As you sit for a moment on one of the park benches, notice the pieces of worn and broken statuary surrounding you; they were once part of Notre-Dame.
♦ Métros: Maubert-Mutualité, St.-Michel

17 Les Trois Maillets The Three Mallets, started in the 13th century as a tavern to serve the stonemasons constructing Notre-Dame, was transformed into a post-war jazz club at first frequented by American GIs. It has one of the best piano bars in Paris. ♦ Admission. W-Su 7PM-3AM. Dim sum and music: 10:30PM-2:30AM. 56 Rue Galande. Métros: Maubert-Mutualité, St.-Michel. 43.54.00.79

18 Rue du Fouarre Seated on *fouarres* (forage or bundles of straw), undergraduates in the Middle Ages attended open-air lectures along this alley of rowdy intellectuals, notorious throughout Europe. In an attempt to ease ten-

sions in 1358, **Charles V** chained the street at both ends and closed it at night. During his visit to Paris in 1304, even **Dante** harkened to the scholars here and later made reference in his writing to this *vico degli strami* (the road of straws). ♦ Métro: Maubert-Mutualité

18 La Fourmi Ailée ★★$/$$ This women's bookstore has a tearoom in the rear, where on a chilly day you can order a hot goat cheese salad, sit back in a caned bentwood chair by the marble-mantel fireplace, and peruse your purchase of some work by Simone de Beauvoir or Colette. ♦ M, W-Su noon-7PM. 8 Rue du Fouarre. Métro: Maubert-Mutualité. 43.29.40.99

18 Rue Galande The beginning of the old Roman road to Lyon, this meandering street was named in 1202 after a family who lived nearby. It was one of the fancier neighborhoods in 17th-century Paris. ♦ Métro: Maubert-Mutualité

18 Studio Galande A cinema famous for its nightly showings of *The Rocky Horror Picture Show.* Being surrounded by funkily costumed French college students enjoying their umpteenth viewing of this crazy cult film, singing and miming the lines, is 90 minutes of guaranteed bellylaughs. Whether or not you go to the film, glance up at the 14th-century stone relief of **Saint Julien** crossing the Seine, which originally stood over the portal of nearby **St.-Julien-le-Pauvre** church. ♦ 42 Rue Galande. Métro: Maubert-Mutualité. 43.54.72.71

19 Rue des Anglais In medieval times this street was a favorite haunt of English students attending the Sorbonne. ♦ Métro: Maubert-Mutualité

20 Librairie Gourmande The celebrated *bouquiniste,* **Madame Baudon,** has graduated from her stall on the *quai* to a shop where she sells books on food and wine from the 17th century to the present. ♦ Daily 10AM-7PM. 4 Rue Dante. Métros: Maubert-Mutualité, St.-Michel. 43.54.37.27

20 Album From *Action* comics to *Zot,* and Donald Duck to Dick Tracy, this *bande dessinée* shop specializes in new and vintage American comic books. For the seriocomic art collector, there are oil paintings of Batman and portraits and statues of Mr. Spock. ♦ Tu-F 10AM-8PM. 6 Rue Dante. Métros: Maubert-Mutualité, St.-Michel. 43.54.67.09

20 A l'Imagerie The largest old print and poster shop in Paris, specializing in Art Deco, Art Nouveau, and late 19th-century Japanese prints and stamps. ♦ Tu-Sa 10:30AM-1PM, 2-7PM, July-Aug; M 2-7PM, Tu-Sa 10:30AM-

1PM, 2-7PM, Sep-June. 9 Rue Dante. Métros: Cluny-La Sorbonne, Maubert-Mutualité. 43.25.18.66

21 Auberge des Deux Signes ★$$$ **Monsieur Dhulster,** the Auvergnat restaurant owner, shops every day before dawn at the Rungis market for the raw materials that his chef, **Christophe Fraichard,** transforms into a sublime array of dishes, such as filet of sole with shrimp raviolis and foie gras *d'oie en brioche.* The inn's setting, which includes a stone spiral staircase, a vista of Notre-Dame (splendid at night), and St.-Julien-le-Pauvre's gardens, could not be more medieval. ♦ Daily noon-2:30PM, 7-10:30PM. 46 Rue Galande. Reservations recommended. Métro: Maubert-Mutualité. 43.25.46.56, 43.25.00.46

22 Rue St.-Julien-le-Pauvre The magnificent gate at **No. 14** marks the 17th-century home of the governor of the old Petit-Châtelet prison. Also, don't miss the house of the dwindling windows at **No. 10;** they start with the largest ones on the ground floor and shrink all the way up to the maids' rooms in the attic. ♦ Métros: Maubert-Mutualité, St.-Michel

22 The Tea Caddy ★$ Looking like your prim and proper English great-aunt's library, with dark wood paneling and thick-paned windows, this is the place for afternoon tea and crumpets. Light lunches and suppers of quiche, salads, and omelets are also served. ♦ M, W-Su noon-7PM. 14 Rue St.-Julien-le-Pauvre. No credit cards. Métros: Maubert-Mutualité, St.-Michel. 43.54.15.56

22 Caveau des Oubliettes A nightclub that looks like what it used to be: the dungeons of the old **Petit-Châtelet** prison. Be ready for such quaint medievalties as waiters in minstrel garb, bawdy songs, a guillotine, ancient torture instruments, and chastity belts on the walls. Inquire about the late-night tour of the *oubliettes* (dungeons) below the stairs. ♦ M-W 9PM-1AM; Th-Sa 9PM-2AM. 1bis Rue St.-Julien-le-Pauvre. Métros: Maubert-Mutualité, St.-Michel. 43.54.94.97

22 Esmeralda $$ This popular small hotel is a favorite of traveling actors and artists. Rooms with views of Notre-Dame are subjected to the midnight noise of *The Rocky Horror Picture Show* crowd exiting the Studio Galande cinema. ♦ 4 Rue St.-Julien-le-Pauvre. Reservations required. Métros: Maubert-Mutualité, St.-Michel. 43.54.19.20

23 Rue de la Bûcherie A *bûcherie* is a woodshed, and this part of the *quai* is where firewood-laden barges dropped their cargo. ♦ Métros: Maubert-Mutualité, St.-Michel

23 Shakespeare and Company Septuagenarian **George Bates Whitman**—who was raised in China, speaks five languages (including Russian), and claims the poet **Walt** as a distant forebear—has for the last 40 years run this charitable bookstore/inn for authors, vagabond intellectuals, and literature professors. Spiritual heir to **Sylvia Beach** (whose famous Paris bookstore of the same name on

the Rue de l'Odéon supplied **Hemingway** with free reading material and was the only house that would publish **Joyce's** *Ulysses*), Whitman bought part of her collection and borrowed the name Shakespeare and Company. In his late sixties he fathered a daughter whom he named **Sylvia Beach Whitman**. Throughout the years, Whitman's chaotic stacks, which defy the Dewey decimal or any other system of categorization, have been frequented by the likes of **Lawrence Durrell, Henry Miller, J.P. Donleavy,** and beat poet **Lawrence Ferlinghetti.** Although Whitman is rarely in the bookstore, if he appears while you're browsing he may well offer you a cup of tea and, if you happen to be penniless and show promise as a writer, may invite you to spend the night (or week) in the **Writer's Room** or bed down on the floor of his upstairs library. To the left of the bookshop, which has one of the world's most eclectic bulletin boards, Whitman keeps his own private collection and

his motor scooter. Per Whitman's wishes, the bookstore no longer has a phone; Whitman has a private line but he doesn't answer that either. Any book purchased in the shop is stamped with an inscription that reads: *Shakespeare and Co. Kilometer Zero Paris.* ♦ Daily noon-midnight. 37 Rue de la Bûcherie. No phone. Métro: Maubert-Mutualité.

23 La Bûcherie ★★$$/$$$ **Bernard Bosque's** menu, featuring stuffed cabbage with crayfish, ocean salmon with chives, and wild duck and oysters in champagne, hasn't changed in years and may be one of the Left Bank's best values. Expect a crowd at this restaurant (illustrated above), and try getting a table near the crackling fireplace. At all costs avoid sitting behind the chimney, where famished customers can go unnoticed for days. ♦ Daily noon-12:30AM. 41 Rue de la Bûcherie. Reservations recommended. Métros: Maubert-Mutualité, St.-Michel. 43.54.78.06

24 Petit Pont **Bishop Maurice de Sully** was responsible for the construction of both the majestic Notre-Dame and this little bridge, which was in earlier days animated by jugglers, sharpers, and dog trainers. At the end of the bridge was once the **Petit Châtelet,** a fortress and prison that was a more diminutive version of the **Grand Châtelet** on the Right Bank. ♦ Métro: St.-Michel

Restaurants/Nightlife: Red   Hotels: Blue
Shops/ 🌳Outdoors: Green   Sights/Culture: Black

35

25 Café de Cluny ★$ Set at one of the Latin Quarter's busiest corners, this sprawling café commands a front-row seat on the boulevards St.-Michel and St.-Germain. Upstairs in the quiet plush booths, Sorbonne professors take their morning coffee or have a dish of ice cream with their graduate students in the afternoon. ♦ M-Th, Su 6AM-midnight; F-Sa 24 hrs. 102 Blvd St.-Germain. Métro: St.-Michel. 43.26.68.24

26 Le Select Latin $ Popular with Sorbonne students, this large corner café/restaurant serves French-American breakfasts of ham, eggs, and fresh croissants. ♦ M-Th 7AM-2:30AM; F-Sa 24 hrs. 25 Blvd St.-Michel. Métro: St.-Michel. 43.26.98.90

27 Hôtel de Cluny, Museum, and Palais des Thermes This magnificent mansion, built by the abbots of Cluny in 1330 and rebuilt in 1510, is one of the oldest private residences in Paris. It straddles the ruins of second-century Roman baths and houses one of the world's

finest collections of French medieval art, including the mysterious and beautiful *Lady and the Unicorn* tapestries.

The baths date from **Marcus Aurelius** (161-180); **Julian the Apostate,** proclaimed Roman Emperor in 360, lived in the adjoining palace. The baths and palace were sacked during numerous barbarian invasions, and in 1340, **Pierre de Châlus,** abbot of Cluny, the wealthy Benedictine abbey in Burgundy, bought the ruins and erected the Hôtel de Cluny as a pied-à-terre to lodge the abbots when they visited Paris. Shortly after the Revolution, the Cluny was occupied by a cooper, a laundress, French Navy astronomers, and a surgeon who used the chapel for his dissections. Among the mansion's tenants in 1833 was **Alexandre du Sommerard,** an art collector who had specialized in Gothic and Renaissance art for decades. When he died in 1842, the state bought the building as well as du Sommerard's collection and appointed his son **Edmond** as the museum's first curator.

As you enter the museum courtyard by the Rue du Sommerard, notice the polygonal stair tower sprinkled with carved shells *(coquilles St.-Jacques),* the symbol of the patron saint of **Jacques d'Amboise,** the abbot of Jumiéges, who between 1485 and 1510 rebuilt the hotel in its present flamboyant Gothic style. The first rooms of the museum are replete with delicate ivory carvings, embroidered Egyptian silks, and Flemish tapestries of gentlemen setting off for the hunt.

Notre-Dame Gallery In this stark white room are the stone sculptures (1210-1230) of the heads of 21 noseless but nevertheless majestic kings. They represent the kings of Judea and Israel, who, according to Saint Matthew's genealogy, were ancestors of Christ. Like most men too closely associated with religion and royalty at the time of the Revolution, they lost their heads. But theirs is a case of mistaken identity. Originally enshrined in the **Gallery of Kings** on **Notre-Dame's** west facade, they were toppled in 1793 by an angry mob who assumed they were the kings of France. In 1977, during excavations for a new bank in the Hôtel Moreau near the Opéra, these 21 sculpted heads were unearthed; the discovery is considered one of the 20th century's major archaeological finds.

Roman Baths The towering roof of the *frigidarium* (cold bath) is the largest Roman vault in all of France. The ceiling has survived 18 centuries of wear and tear, not the least of which was the eight feet of topsoil heaped on it by an abbot who rooted his apple orchard and kitchen garden on the roof. The ship prows decorating the base of the groined vaulting are the building signatures of the powerful Boatmen's Guild of Paris. Nearby is the *Boatmen's Pillar,* one of the oldest pieces of sculpture in Paris. It was supposed to be a column from Jupiter's Temple, which stood, during the reign of Roman emperor **Tiberius** (AD 14-37), where Notre-Dame is today.

Treasury Upstairs is a dazzling display of Gallic, Barbarian, and Merovingian jewelry, including six gold Visigoth crowns, two 13th-century gold double crosses, and the

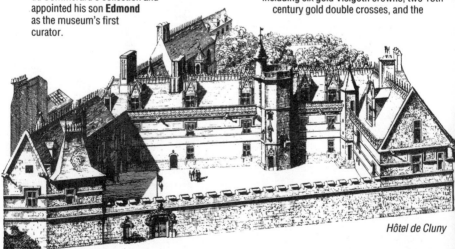

Hôtel de Cluny

sublimely delicate 14th-century *Golden Rose*, probably fashioned by an Italian goldsmith in Avignon, that was presented to the Bishop of Basel by **Pope Clement V**. The designs are so modern, so elegant, you get the impression that you're not admiring jewelry from the Middle Ages, but rather window-shopping around the Place Vendôme.

Stained Glass Among the medieval stained-glass windows in the upstairs corridor are religious scenes from the Ste.-Chapelle and the St.-Denis cathedrals. Take a close look; in the actual churches—even with a strong pair of opera glasses and a stiffly craned neck—you won't get a view this good. Three large windows and the surrounding stonework come from the church of St.-Jean-de-Latran, demolished in 1859 to make way for the Rue des Ecoles built between the Cluny and the Sorbonne.

Abbots' Chapel One of the few surviving interior details of the original mansion, this chapel was used as the ancient oratory of the abbots and is an architectural masterpiece. The flamboyant vaulting sprouts palmlike from a single slender pillar. In a room near the chapel is a 1383 eagle lectern and a 12th-century gilt copper altar table.

Tapestries Saving the best for last, enter the rotunda-shaped room on the top floor, dimly lit to protect the world-famous *Lady and the Unicorn* tapestry series. In 1844, quite by accident, writer **George Sand** discovered the tapestries hanging at the **Château de Boussac**; supposedly they were a wedding present in the 15th century from magistrate **Jean Le Viste** to his bride (the Le Viste coat of arms appears in each panel). The artist, who remains unknown, is thought to have designed the similar set of six tapestries that is now hanging in the Cloisters museum in New York City. The delicate tapestries allegorically depict the five senses. In *Sight*, we find the noble unicorn gazing into the mirror of a bejeweled blond woman. *Sound* is identified by the miniature organ, and *Touch* by the blond woman grasping a banner in one hand and the unicorn's horn in the other. In *Taste*, she takes a sweet from a bowl, and in *Smell* she holds a rose to her nose (as does the monkey below her). In the mysterious sixth tapestry, the woman's tent is emblazoned with the words *A Mon Seul Desir* (To My Only Desire), thought to represent mastery of all five senses. Notice that the woman on the red *millefleur* (literally *one thousand flowers*) background, changes from one sumptuous gown to another in a veritable fashion show as you progress around the room. ♦ M, W-Su 9:30AM-5:15PM. 6 Place Paul-Painlevé. Métros: Cluny-La Sorbonne, Maubert-Mutualité, St.-Michel. 43.25.62.00

28 Au Vieux Campeur France's best mountain-climbing outfitters this side of Chamonix. Pitons, ice axes, alpine sleeping bags, and giant spools of brightly colored climbing rope for your next ascent up Everest or the Eiffel Tower. If a bivouac at a wine bar atop the Montagne Ste.-Geneviève's slopes is more your aim, pause on the sidewalk and watch France's next generation of rock climbers sampling new equipment, rappelling down an indoor version of what looks like the Eiger's North Face. This is one of the Vieux Campeur's nine stores on the Left Bank. ♦ M 2-7PM, Tu-Sa 10AM-8PM, Oct-July; Tu-Sa 10AM-7PM, Aug-Sep. 48 Rue des Ecoles. Métros: Maubert-Mutualité, St.-Michel. 43.29.12.32

29 Collège de France $$ A quiet bed-and-breakfast hotel offering a glimpse of the Notre-Dame towers from some of the sixth-floor rooms. ♦ 7 Rue Thénard. Métros: Maubert-Mutualité, St.-Michel. 43.26.78.36

30 Prosciences This store stocks supplies for high school biology classes and all the Collège de France research laboratories. Amid the test tubes and life-size plastic skeletons (shrouded in tinsel at Christmas) are

glass beakers and white porcelain pitchers that French householders love to buy, not for their children's chemistry experiments, but as measuring cups for the kitchen. Also, the 125-centiliter pitchers make dandy creamers. ♦ M-Th 8:30AM-5:30PM; F 8:30AM-4:30PM. 44 Rue des Ecoles. Métro: Maubert-Mutualité. 46.33.33.00

31 Beauvais College Chapel One of the Sorbonne's first college chapels, which was built in 1380 and is now restored. This tiny sanctuary has been used since 1882 by the Romanian Orthodox church. ♦ Services: M-Th 11AM-noon; F 11AM-noon, 6-7PM; Su 10AM-1PM. 9bis Rue Jean-de-Beauvais. Métro: Maubert-Mutualité. 43.54.67.47

32 Musée des Collections Historiques de la Préfecture de Police (Police Museum) This fascinating, often grisly, little collection surveys the city's most notorious crimes, from the 16th century to the present. Exhibits include a graphic representation of the 1563 punishment of the **Duc de Guise's** murderer (quartering by four horses); orders for the arrest of **Dr. Guillotin** in 1795; an account of **Charlotte Corday's** murder of **Marat** in his bath; a book stained with blood from the 1932 assassination of French **President Paul Doumer;** and **Verlaine's** statement of his attempted murder of fellow poet **Rimbaud**. Among the more ingenious weapons on display are a strangling cord made of twisted paper, metal knuckle-dusters, a knife concealed in a lady's fan, and a guillotine blade used during the Revolution. Children and whodunit fans alike are intrigued by this petit Guignol, which requires Holmesian perspicacity to find. Enter the lobby of the fifth arrondissement police headquarters, gumshoe your way up the stairs, and knock on the door marked Musée. ♦ Free. M-F 9AM-5PM. 1bis Rue des Carmes. Métro: Maubert-Mutualité. 43.29.21.57

33 Montagne Ste.-Geneviève This French Parnassus, the central point of the old University of Paris, is named after the city's sanctified patroness (Saint Denis is the male patron saint). It is admittedly steep, but to call any of the city's seven hills a mountain must certainly have been Roman grandiosity. The summit of Ste.-Geneviève is gracefully crowned with the **Panthéon,** whose columned dome dominates the Left Bank. Here was the convent where **Saint Thomas Aquinas** wrote his *Summa Theologica,* upon which the orthodox philosophy of Catholicism is based. It is a vicinity rich in intellectual history: **Ignatius Loyola** and **Calvin** studied here; **Marat** drew up his pamphlets; and **Pascal** died a stone's throw from the place where **Verlaine** was to pass away many generations later. The hill counts among its educational institutions the world-famous **Sorbonne,** the **Collège de France,** prestigious medical and law schools, and three large *lycées* (secondary schools), and was at one

time the site of the **Ecole Polytechnique,** France's equivalent to MIT. In 1804 the Rue de la Montagne-Ste.-Geneviève was the scene of a plot to murder **Napoléon Bonaparte.** ♦ Métro: Maubert-Mutualité

34 Rue des Ecoles This street name celebrates the presence of all the academic institutions and university establishments hereabouts. ♦ Métro: Maubert-Mutualité

35 Librairie Presence Africaine Need a few *Wolof* lessons before visiting Gambia? Looking for a Senegalese cookbook? A black gospel concert on the Left Bank? This African bookstore includes a Third World periodical section and a bulletin board for Afrophiles. ♦ M-Sa 10AM-7PM. 25bis Rue des Ecoles. Métro: Cardinal-Lemoine. 43.54.15.88

35 Da Capo Claude Fihman runs this postage stamp-sized shop dealing in 78-rpm records, old sheet music, and opera programs. ♦ M-Sa 1-7PM. 14 Rue des Ecoles. Métro: Cardinal-Lemoine. 43.54.75.47

36 Le Paradis Latin This glittering offspring of **Jean-Marie Riviére's** other nightclub, the Alcazar, has one of the top ten dinner-floor shows. ♦ Dinner: M, W-Su starting at 8PM. Shows start at 10PM, but you must be there 30 minutes in advance. 28 Rue du Cardinal-Lemoine. Métro: Cardinal-Lemoine. 43.25.28.28

37 Moissonnier ★★★$$/$$$ The earthenware bowls spilling over with Lyonnais salads, the friendly waiters, generous charcuterie, and homey setting have earned this Left Bank establishment a loyal clientele. Specialties

include roast kidneys, duck with turnips, tripe baked with onions and white wine, creamy au gratin potatoes, and delicious Brouilly and Bordeaux. ♦ Tu-Sa noon-2:30PM, 7-10:30PM; Su noon-2:30PM; closed Aug. 28 Rue des Fossés-St.-Bernard. Métro: Jussieu. 43.29.87.65

38 Ecole Polytechnique These massive buildings once housed France's equivalent of MIT. Founded as an Army-run engineering school by **Gaspard Monge,** the mathematician who accompanied **Napoléon** to Egypt, the Ecole Polytechnique's best known graduates are car designer **André Citroën** and former French President **Valéry Giscard d'Estaing.** Its annual grand ball at the opéra is pretty famous, too. Several years ago the prestigious university moved to the suburbs. ♦ Rue de l'Ecole Polytechnique. Métros: Cardinal-Lemoine, Maubert-Mutualité

39 Jean-Baptiste Besse How affable **Papa Besse** (since 1932 one of the most respected wine merchants in Paris) manages to find what he's looking for in his helter-skelter corner store is anybody's guess. A little man who sports a beret and a peasant's guileless smile, Besse has a story and a vintage for every occasion. If a customer is unpleasant, Besse will let him or her leave with run-of-the-mill wine, but he'll invite those he likes into his cobweb-covered cellars for some serious choosing. ♦ Tu-Sa 10:30AM-2:30PM, 4:30-8:30PM; Su 11AM-1PM; closed Aug. 48 Rue de la Montagne-Ste.-Geneviève. Métro: Maubert-Mutualité. 43.25.35.80

39 Shobudo International A building on this tranquil 17th-century courtyard houses Europe's oldest judo school. If you don't have time for a self-defense class and would like to fake it in hopes of intimidating those muggers back home, you can buy a black belt and the latest kung fu paraphernalia in the **Budo Store** on the second floor. Or walk to the end of the courtyard, turn left, and squeeze into the spectators' gallery for a few bouts of *ken-jitsu,* a Japanese martial art predating the shoguns. The judo school is in a building that was once part of the **Hostel of the 33** (named after the number of years Christ lived), established by monk **Claude Bernard** as a dormitory for theology students. The door buzzer will admit you into quite another world. ♦ M-Sa 9AM-7:30PM. 34 Rue de la Montagne-Ste.-Geneviève. Métro: Maubert-Mutualité. 43.29.00.41

39 Crocojazz This cubbyhole of a record shop resounds with the music of Art Blakey, Miles Davis, Louis Armstrong, and Coleman Hawkins. Jack Daniels whiskey bottles on the wall, the occasional country twang of Hank Thompson and Ricky Skaggs, and the worn Levis and ersatz cowboy boots of the French clientele round out the ambience of this American LP import mecca. ♦ Tu-Sa 11AM-1PM, 2-7PM. 64 Rue de la Montagne-Ste.-Geneviève. Métro: Maubert-Mutualité. 46.34.78.38

40 La Nef Parisienne On this small square, as on city schools and other public structures throughout Paris, is affixed a sailing vessel (*la nef* is the nave of a ship), which has been the city's coat of arms since 1260, when Saint Louis appointed the Boatmen's Guild to administer the affairs of the city. *Fluctuat nec mergitur* (float never sink) is the city motto. In addition to adorning public buildings and faculties, *La Nef Parisienne* is embossed on everything from the mayor's stationery to police officer's badges. ♦ Métros: Cardinal-Lemoine, Maubert-Mutualité

41 Le Coupe-Chou ★$$ This seductive inn occupies the site of a famous Parisian barbershop whose proprietor slit the throats of his customers, whom his neighbor the butcher then made into pâté. If you can manage to cast that grisly chapter out of your mind, you will probably enjoy this attractive restaurant serving salmon raviolis, lamb with mint, magret of duck with peaches, and hot homemade puff pastries, although you may opt to stay away from the pâté. ♦ M-Sa noon-2PM, 7PM-9AM; Su 7PM-midnight. 11 Rue de Lanneau. Métro: Maubert-Mutualité. 46.33.68.69, 43.54.36.54

42 Collège de France First called the Three-Language College because Hebrew and Greek were taught here as well as Latin, this college, founded by **François I** in 1529, counts among its famous faculty **Frédéric Joliot-Curie**, who split a uranium particle; the physicist **André-Marie Ampère**, after whom a unit measuring electric current is named; poet **Paul Valéry**; and the more contemporary scholars **Roland Barthes, Michel Foucault,** and **Claude Lévi-Strauss**. ♦ 11 Place Marcelin-Berthelot. Métro: Maubert-Mutualité. 44.27.12.11

It is not true that the French dislike Americans. In fact, America has been quite fashionable in France of late. There is, however, always just a soupçon of superiority in the French manner. America, they like to say, is the only country that went from the barbarian stage to the decadent stage without passing through a civilized stage.

BRASSERIE BALZAR

43 Balzar ★★$$ **Camus** and **Sartre** had their last argument at the Balzar, and **James Thurber, Elliot Paul, William Shirer,** and the old *Chicago Tribune* crowd gathered here for the beer and *choucroute* (sauerkraut) *garni*. The Balzar's literary clientele, its old wood paneling and mirrors, and its waiters in long white aprons creates an ambience that makes it one of the best brasseries in Paris. Getting a table for lunch is not difficult; dinner, however, is a different story. At night, especially after the theater, the vinyl banquettes are jammed with university professors, actors, editors, journalists, and aspiring poets dining on hearty fare such as the pig's feet Sainte-Memehould, *cervelas* rémoulad, cassoulet, and calf's liver niçoise washed down with a bottle of Bordeaux. This restaurant is worth a

The Latin Quarter

visit, even if you only stop for a Kir or coffee on the terrace. Conveniently, when the Balzar is closed, the **Lipp,** another literary shrine (on the Boulevard St.-Germain) stays open, an arrangement dating from the days when they were under the same management. Another attractive quality of the Balzar is its refusal to admit customers accompanied by poodles or Doberman pinschers. ♦ Daily 8AM-11:30PM; closed Aug and Christmas through New Year's Day. 49 Rue des Ecoles. Reservations recommended. Métro: Maubert-Mutualité. 43.54.13.67

44 Place de la Sorbonne This square, lined with cafés and lime trees, was a focal point for the student-worker protest of 1968. That year, on 10 and 11 May, police and students clashed violently, resulting in the injury of 400 participants and the arrests of hundreds of others. Today you will find a graffiti-marred statue of **Auguste Comte** (1798-1857), who was fired from his job as examiner in mathematics at the prestigious Ecole Polytechnique for his revolutionary ideas. Comte is best remembered as the founder of Positivism, a philosophy that strongly influenced John Stuart Mill. ♦ Métros: Cluny-La Sorbonne, Luxembourg (RER)

44 Hôtel Select $$ Located on the Place de la Sorbonne, this 70-room hotel is a quiet, ideal location for exploring the Latin Quarter. In 1937, 25-year-old **Eric Sevareid** checked into a 50-cents-a-night room here on the square and headed off to work for the *Paris Herald,* soon accomplishing feats such as an interview with **Gertrude Stein**. ♦ 1 Place de la Sorbonne. Métros: Luxembourg (RER), St.-Michel. 46.34.14.80

Restaurants/Nightlife: Red	**Hotels:** Blue
Shops/ ♥ Outdoors: Green	**Sights/Culture:** Black

45 Sorbonne France's most famous university began in 1253 as humble lodgings for 16 theology students. In medieval times, the university was not a mass of edifices, pedants, and bureaucrats, it was a loose assembly of soapbox academics giving street-corner lectures to students who boarded at inns throughout Paris. However, by the end of the 13th century, when the Sorbonne became the administrative headquarters for the University of Paris, there were 15,000 undergraduates studying in the city. **Saint Thomas Aquinas** and **Roger Bacon** were among the Sorbonne's great teachers; **Saint Ignatius Loyola, Dante, Erasmus,** and **John Calvin** were students there. The Sorbonne grew in size and power and frequently contradicted the authority of the French throne. During the Hundred Years' War (1337-1453), the Sorbonne had the audacity to side with England against France. It recognized **Henri V** as king of France and cravenly sent one of its best prosecutors to Rouen to try **Jeanne d'Arc.**

The Latin Quarter

In 1642 **Cardinal Richelieu** (pictured at right) was elected grand master of the Sorbonne; he commissioned architect **Jacques Lemercier** to restore the dilapidated college buildings and erect a Jesuit-style church.

Years passed and the Sorbonne closed down in 1792 during the Revolution, and remained empty until 1806, when **Napoléon** headquartered his **Académie de Paris** there. Following the May 1968 student-worker demonstration, the state unceremoniously rechristened the Sorbonne as "Paris University IV," nominally tossing it into the archipelago of institutions of higher learning scattered about the city.

Don't be shy about wandering down the long stone corridors of the Sorbonne and visiting the university's lecture halls, such as the **Amphithéâtre Descartes** or **Salle Doctorat.** (Unfortunately, the ornate **Grand Amphithéatre** with its famous *Puvis de Chavannes* fresco is strictly reserved for ceremonies of state.) In the event that you enroll (as hundreds of Americans do every year) for a four-month crash course in French, you may come to know the dusty domed ceiling and stiff wooden benches of the shabbier **Richelieu Amphithéâtre** intimately. ◆ M-Sa 8AM-10PM. For an admission application, contact the Cours de Civilisation Française de la Sorbonne. Galerie Richelieu. 45-47 Rue des Ecoles. Métro: Cluny-La Sorbonne. 40.46.26.64, 40.46.26.75

November is France's official *Mois de la Photo,* with photography shows in dozens of museums and galleries throughout Paris.

45 Ste.-Ursule-de-la-Sorbonne Nothing of **Richelieu's** Sorbonne remains save **Jacques Lemercier's** chapel (1642), which was the first completely Roman-style building in 17th-century Paris. Richelieu is buried here. Above **François Girardon's** beautiful white marble tomb (1694), which depicts a half-recumbent Richelieu, his red cardinal's hat still hangs by a few slender threads from the ceiling. According to tradition, the hat will remain there until Richelieu's soul is freed from Purgatory, at which time the threads will rot and the hat will drop. The chapel is closed to the public except during its special exhibitions of stained glass, tapestry, and old manuscripts. ◆ Church services are held in the chapel on 21 October (the feast day of Sainte Ursule) and 4 December (the anniversary of Richelieu's death). Place de la Sorbonne. Métros: Cluny-La Sorbonne, Luxembourg (RER)

46 Lycée Louis le Grand Founded in 1550, this 1,500-student state-run high school numbers among its former pupils **Molière, Voltaire, Robespierre, Hugo, Baudelaire, Pompidou, Giscard d'Estaing, Chirac,** and **Senghor** (the former president of Senegal). For information on touring the building, contact the lycée's secretary on the second floor. ◆ M-F 9AM-noon, 2-5PM. 123 Rue St.-Jacques. Métros: 1 Luxembourg (RER), St.-Michel. 43.29.12.06

46 Perraudin ★★★$/$$ Popular among Sorbonne students and their profs, this bargain canteen with archetypal bistro decor (lace curtains, red-and-white checked tablecloths, and tiled Deco floors) offers a panoply of *cuisine bourgeoise*: lamb and kidney beans, beef stew, au gratin potatoes, and rough red wines. ◆ M, Sa 7:30-10:15PM; Tu-F noon-2:15PM, 7:30-10:15PM; Su noon-2:15PM; closed evenings in Aug. 157 Rue St.-Jacques. No credit cards. Métro: Luxembourg (RER). 46.33.15.75

47 Bibliothèque Ste.-Geneviève This library, constructed in 1850 on the Place du Panthéon, occupies the site of the old **Collège Montaigu**

where **Erasmus, Calvin,** and **Loyola** studied. Architect **Henri Labrousté's** revolutionary use of steel frame and masonry construction (further elaborated in his other library, the Biblio-thèque Nationale, which was finished in 1868) makes this building one of the most important 19th-century forerunners of modern architecture. While you may peek inside, the library itself is restricted to visitors with a valid reader's card. ♦ Place du Panthéon. Métro: Cardinal-Lemoine

48 Rue Soufflot Looking down the Rue Soufflot (named for the architect of the Panthéon), you will see two matching buildings, the **City Hall** of the fifth arrondissement and the **University of Paris Faculty of Law** building with the **Luxembourg Gardens** and **Eiffel Tower** in the distance. Eighteen feet below the Rue Soufflot lie the remains of a Roman forum, discovered by 19th-century archaeologists; however, the ruins are not open to the public. ♦ Métros: St.-Michel, Odéon

49 Les Fontaines ★★$$ This bistro may look like it lost its soul somewhere in all the cigarette smoke, but it serves surprisingly good hearty fare for quite reasonable prices. Co-owner **Roger Lacipière**, once a butcher, still roams through the markets at Rungis during the pre-dawn hours two or three times a week to purchase rib steaks for the menu that are as thick as the Gideon Bible, and he offers a superlative *gigot* and *fricassée de volaille de Bresse aux girolles*. ♦ M-Sa 8PM-midnight, closed Aug. 9 Rue Soufflot. Métros: Maubert-Mutualite, Odeon. 43.26.42.80

50 Terrenoire ★★$$ In this classy Italian restaurant with fresh flowers and pink linen on every table, **Albano Casanova** offers delicious carpaccio, lasagna, *piccata al limone,* and filet Casanova (steak with mushrooms and prosciutto in a cream sauce), as well as *tiramisu* and *zabaglione* ice cream for dessert. ♦ Daily noon-2:45PM, 7:30-11:30PM. 18 Rue des Fossés-St.-Jacques. Reservations recommended. Métro: Luxembourg (RER). 43.54.83.09

50 Ferme Sainte-Suzanne ★★$ A neighborhood restaurant off the **Place de l'Estrapade** with a fine selection of Brie, Camembert, and Chabichou (goat) cheeses. ♦ M-F 11:30AM-2:30PM, 7:30-10PM. 4 Rue des Fossés-St.-Jacques. Métro: Luxembourg (RER). 43.54.90.02

51 Le Bistrot de la Nouvelle Mairie ★★★ $/$$ One of the city's finest wine bars, which is located on the pretty **Place de l'Estrapade.** The clientele varies from lawyers with watch fobs to butchers in aprons. On a warm summer afternoon, order a plate of Camembert, charcuterie, or *pâté de foie de porc*, and enjoy a cellar-cool Beaujolais or Gamay at one of the outdoor tables. ♦ M-F 9AM-11PM; Sa 11AM-3PM. 19 Rue des Fossés-St.-Jacques. Métro: Luxembourg (RER). 43.26.80.18

51 Hôtel des Grands Hommes $$$ Comfortable and right in the heart of the Latin Quarter, this is a fine place to stay if you can hack the lobby with its plastic plants and disco music.

52 Panthéon When **Louis XV** recovered from gout at Metz in 1744, he vowed, in gratitude, to build a great temple honoring **Sainte Geneviève.** The architect, **Jacques-Germain Soufflot,** chose to construct a classical edifice based on the form of a Greek cross (339 feet long and 253 feet wide). Soufflot, who had been inspired by his trips to Italy, intended his building to resemble the Panthéon of Agrippa in Rome (the Paris Panthéon's lofty 52-pillar dome and handsome Corinthian colonnade, however, wound up being much more suggestive of St. Paul's in London). Finished by **Guillaume Rondelet,** one of Soufflot's students, in 1850, the Panthéon was secularized into the Temple of Fame, a necropolis for the distinguished atheists of France. In its rather depressing crypt lie the likes of **Voltaire, Rousseau, Victor Hugo** (whose coffin passed a ceremonial night under the Arc de Triomphe and was carried to the Panthéon in the hearse of the poor), **Gambetta, Emile Zola, Louis**

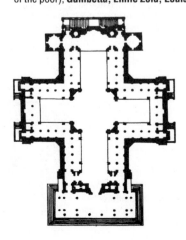

Braille (the 19th-century Frenchman who, blinded at age three, went on to invent the system of embossed dots that enables the sightless to read), **Jean Jaurès** (the celebrated leftist politician and orator who was assassinated in 1914), and **Jean Moulin** (the Resistance leader in WWII who was tortured to death in the Occupation). After the Revolution, the Panthéon's 42 tall windows were walled up, and today the monument looms over the square like a prison, grandiose and austere. ♦ Daily 10AM-12:30PM, 4-5:30PM. Place du Panthéon. Métros: Cardinal-Lemoine, Luxembourg (RER). 43.54.34.51

53 Lycée Henri IV Dating from Napoleonic times, the Lycée Henri IV is one of the city's most prestigious high schools; **Jean-Paul Sartre,** the French novelist and playwright who refused the Nobel Prize for Literature in 1964, taught here. The school's most notable architectural feature is the **Tour de Clovis,** a Gothic belfry. The tower is all that remains of

The Latin Quarter

the **Abbaye Ste.-Geneviève,** built by **King Clovis** after he was converted to Christianity by his wife, **Clotilde of Burgundy,** and Sainte Geneviève. **Saint Thomas Aquinas** (1225-1274) taught at the abbey. ♦ Closed to the public. 23 Rue Clovis. Métro: Luxembourg (RER)

53 St.-Etienne-du-Mont (St.-Stephen-of-the-Mount) Its mélange of triple classical pediments, Gothic rose window, medieval-style belfry, and Renaissance dome defy the laws of architectural purity. Its low-hanging chandeliers are a menace to anyone over six feet tall; it must be the only church in Paris that closes for lunch, but, *mon Dieu!,* it's beautiful. Constructed in 1626, St.-Etienne-du-Mont is home to two graceful 16th-century spiral staircases, an extraordinary wooden pulpit (1650) shouldered by a grimacing Samson, and the only rood screen left in Paris, as well as the tombs of **Pascal, Racine,** and **Marat.** The church surrounds a shrine to Sainte Geneviève, which Paris fathers have visited the first Sunday of each year for hundreds of years. During the annual pilgrimage on 3 January 1857, while bowing to bless a child, **Monseigneur Sibour,** Archbishop of Paris, was stabbed to death by an unfrocked priest named **Verger,** who apparently objected to the ban on marriage that compelled priestly celibacy. A marker at the rear of the center aisle indicates the spot where the murder was committed. ♦ M-Sa 7:30AM-noon, 2:30-7:15PM; Su 7:30AM-12:30PM, 4-7:30PM. Place Ste.-Geneviève. Métro: Cardinal-Lemoine. 43.54.11.79

54 Au Vieux Paris ★$/$$ In the shadow of the St.-Etienne-du-Mont church, **Jean Vergez's** restaurant of wooden beams and stone pillars serves rich food from France's southwest: foie gras, *confit de canard,* blood sausage, eggs piperade, and its special tournedos Rossini. Dessert might be *charlotte aux poires,* following entrées washed down with the house Burgundy or Beaujolais. ♦ M-Sa noon-2PM, 7-10:45PM. 2 Place du Panthéon. Reservations recommended. Métros: Cardinal-Lemoine, Luxembourg (RER). 43.54.79.22

54 51 Rue de la Montagne-Ste.-Geneviève **James Joyce** shared a flat here with French writer **Valéry Larbaud.** ♦ Métro: Cardinal-Lemoine

55 Le Raccard ★★$$ The Swiss chalet decor may be heavy-handed, but the all-you-can-eat raclette is as authentic and delicious as it comes. In winter, fondues made with Gruyère or Vacharin are served. ♦ Tu-Su 7:30PM-1AM; closed Aug. 19 Rue Laplace. Reservations recommended. Métro: Cardinal-Lemoine. 43.25.27.27, 43.54.83.75

56 La Truffière ★$$/$$$ A rich antithesis of nouvelle cuisine. This restaurant serves specialties from Périgord: black truffles, foie gras, and generous portions of goose and duck prepared in every conceivable fashion. Have an apéritif near the fireplace in the sitting room before proceeding to dinner. ♦ Tu-F, Su noon-2PM, 7-10:30PM; Sa 7-10:30PM; closed first two weeks of Aug. 4 Rue Blainville. Reservations required. Métros: Cardinal-Lemoine, Place-Monge. 46.33.29.82

St.-Etienne-du-Mont

56 9 Rue Blainville The site of the first public library in Paris. ♦ Métros: Cardinal-Lemoine, Place-Monge

56 Randy & Jay's ★★$$ Randy is from Seattle, and Jay is from Angola; together they brew up the best barbecue sauce in town. Decorated with checked tablecloths and homey Americana, this hole-in-the-wall restaurant also serves corn on the cob, red beans and rice, potato salad, coleslaw, homemade pies (pecan, apple, blueberry, and sweet potato), and special house cocktails such as *Lemon Boogie, Blue Troubles,* and *Monkey Business.* No charge for Randy's extemporaneous stand-up comedy. ♦ Tu-Su 7:30PM-2AM. 14 Rue Thouin. Métro: Cardinal-Lemoine. 43.26.37.09

57 Rue Descartes This street carries the name of French mathematician and philosopher **René "I-think-therefore-I-am" Descartes** (1596-1650). He lived on Montagne Ste.-Geneviève from 1613 to 1619 and again in 1625, but it is doubtful he ever lived on this street, which was then known as la **Rue des Bordels** (the street of brothels). Descartes emigrated to Sweden, where he died in the arms of **Queen Christina.** ♦ Métro: Cardinal-Lemoine

57 39 Rue Descartes A plaque above the awning conspicuously marks the house where poet **Paul Verlaine** (1844-1896) died. Later there was a hotel at the same address, where in 1922 **Ernest Hemingway** once rented a room, which he later described in *A Moveable Feast.* ♦ Métro: Cardinal-Lemoine

57 47 Rue Descartes At the end of the passageway in this historic 17th-century, half-timbered Norman-style house is another section of **King Philippe Auguste's** medieval city wall. ♦ Métro: Cardinal-Lemoine

58 Rue Clovis This short street is named after **Clovis** (AD 466-511), king of the Franks, who defeated the Romans at Soissons, consequently ending the Roman Empire in Gaul and founding France. The narrow sidewalk on the south side of the street (near No. 5) is practically blocked by the ivy-draped ruins of **King Philippe Auguste's** fortified wall. It was originally 33 feet high, with a pathway on top, and was patrolled by the city sentries (during the 19th century, a bronze regiment of these sentries was enshrined on the roof of the City Hall in the Place de l'Hôtel de Ville). Construction of the wall started in 1190, and it marked the city limits of Paris until the 17th century. The wall was pulled down when **Louis XIV** left Paris for Versailles. At the bottom of the hill at **No. 67 Rue du Cardinal-Lemoine** is the house where **Pascal** died in 1662. ♦ Métro: Cardinal-Lemoine

59 Place de la Contrescarpe In the Middle Ages, this dark, dangerous neighborhood lay outside **King Philippe Auguste's** city wall, beyond the moat, on the counter-escarpment. Since the days of Hemingway's *A Moveable Feast,* the public urinals and bus stop have

disappeared, but a certain seediness remains. In winter, the local *clochards* (street people) still huddle over the heating duct and live off spoils from the markets and spare change from tourists. On summer weekends, harmless bikers in black leather congregate here. ♦ Métros: Cardinal-Lemoine, Place-Monge

59 1 Place de la Contrescarpe The name **Maison de la Pomme de Pin** (Pine Cone Cabaret) is carved into the wall above the *boucherie* and Italian restaurant at this address. It marks the site of an old café frequented by satirist **François Rabelais** (1494-1553), author of *Pantagruel* (1532) and *Gargantua* (1534). ♦ Métros: Cardinal-Lemoine, Place-Monge

59 La Chope ★$ Once a **Hemingway** haunt, this café is crowded with stout butchers drinking Calvados and students from the Lycée Henri IV playing pinball. You will also find chef's salads and, believe it or not, banana splits. ♦ Daily 7AM-2AM. 2 Place de la

Contrescarpe. Métros: Cardinal-Lemoine, Place-Monge. 43.26.51.26

60 Rue Mouffetard Leading out of the **Place de la Contrescarpe** is the 13th-century Rue Mouffetard. As you descend the narrow street, let your imagination take you back to the time when it was the main Roman road to the southeast, Lyon, and Italy. During the 12th century the area near the **Bièvre River** was filled with the country homes of rich Parisians. Within four centuries the Bièvre became a foul-smelling stream polluted by the animal wastes and dyes flushed by tanners, skinners, and the Flemish tapestry weavers from the Gobelins factory. In 1910 the river was covered over and incorporated into the sewer system.

Some guess the name Mouffetard comes from *mouffette,* French for skunk; more likely it is a corruption of the Roman name of the hill it traverses, **Mont Cétar.** Prior to the Revolution the poor of Paris lived here in utter wretchedness. The unadorned mansard-roofed 17th-century houses that still line the Rue Mouffetard were built for ordinary folk. In the 1600s one French writer said more money could be found in one single house of the Faubourg St.-Honoré than in all of those combined on the Rue Mouffetard. ♦ Métros: Censier-Daubenton, Place-Monge

"Though one Frenchman meeting another will never ask directly what the other did during the war, that will be the first thing he will try to find out."
                                                Clyde H. Farnsworth,
                                The New York Times (20 February 1973)

Window-shopping is an honorable pastime everywhere; in France it's known as *léche-vitrine* (which translates literally as "lick the window").

Restaurants/Nightlife: Red   Hotels: Blue
Shops/ 🌳Outdoors: Green   **Sights/Culture:** Black

60 12 Rue Mouffetard Façade Above a diminutive American-style supermarket is an astounding painting that looks more suited to early Little Rock than Paris. *Le Nègre Joyeux* (The Happy Negro) portrays a stereotyped grinning black servant in striped pants serving tea to his mistress. ♦ Métro: Place-Monge

60 51 to 55 Rue Mouffetard In 1938 workers discovered 3,351 coins of 22-karat gold weighing 16.3 grams each and bearing the image of **Louis XV.** Hidden inside the wall, the buried treasure, according to an accompanying note, belonged to **Louis Nivelle,** the royal counselor who mysteriously disappeared in 1757. ♦ Métros: Censier-Daubenton, Place-Monge

61 Pot-de-Fer Fountain What appears to be an Italianate roadside dungeon is actually a restored historic monument. Behind this wall is one of the 14 fountains constructed in 1624 at the behest of **Marie de Médici.** The fountain was designed to handle the overflow from the

The Latin Quarter

Gallo-Roman aqueduct that she had refurbished to supply water for her new palace in the Luxembourg Gardens. What a sprinkler system it must have been! ♦ 60 Rue Mouffetard. Métro: Place-Monge

62 Chaussures Georges This dinky one hundred-year-old shoe store run by a garrulous Armenian named **Georges** supplies the neighborhood butchers, fishmongers, and masons with their rubber boots and wool-lined French *sabots* (wooden shoes). These are shoes for function, not fantasy, proclaims Georges, who keeps all his footwear in 19th-century boxes with pewter handles. He also sells plain espadrilles—the *real* ones from Spain, not Chinese imitations. ♦ Tu-Sa 9:30AM-12:30PM, 2:15-7:30PM; Su 9:30AM-12:30PM. 64 Rue Mouffetard. Métro: Place-Monge. 47.07.16.66

62 61 Rue Mouffetard Look for the back door of the old **Garde Républicaine** barracks. ♦ Métro: Place-Monge

62 Le Vieux Chêne ★★$/$$ This modest little restaurant, known for its earthy homemade pâté, is adorned with a miniature oak tree (the restaurant's namesake), which is believed to have been carved from a ship's masthead. ♦ Tu-Sa noon-2PM, 8-11PM. 69 Rue Mouffetard. Reservations recommended. Métro: Place-Monge. 43.37.71.51

63 10 Rue Vauquelin On 26 December 1898, working out of a ramshackle ground-floor laboratory here at the **Sorbonne School of Physics and Chemistry** (which is now housed in a shiny new redbrick-and-glass building), **Marie Curie** and her husband, **Pierre,** discovered radium. The discovery of radioactivity not only earned them a Nobel prize in 1903 (the first of two for Marie), but triggered a fundamental rethinking of theoretical physics. A few months after their discovery, the quantum theory was published. ♦ Métro: Censier-Daubenton

63 Jardin des Plantes It was begun in 1626 by **Louis XIII** as a royal medicinal herb garden planted on an old rubbish heap. Today, the 74-acre botanical garden hosts a floral orgy of peonies, irises, roses, geraniums, and dahlias from April through October. The garden, bounded by streets named after great French naturalists and botanists (**Jussieu, Geoffroy St.-Hilaire, Daubenton, Buffon,** and **Lacépède**), contains a pedestal inscribed to the French scientist **Lamarck,** the founder of the doctrine of evolution (tough luck, Charles Darwin) and another honoring **Chevreul,** the director of the Gobelins dye factory who lived to a ripe 103 and whose color-spectrum research informed the Impressionist painters.

Within the park is France's oldest public zoo, a menagerie with a rather pathetic history. Established shortly after the Revolution to display survivors from the Royal Menagerie at Versailles (one hartebeest, one zebra, one rhinoceros, and a sheepdog), it was originally called the **People's Democratic Zoo.** In 1795 the first elephants arrived, in 1805 the bear-pit opened, and in 1827 an Egyptian prince gave the Jardin des Plantes its first giraffe. The zoo grew in size and popularity until the Siege of Paris in 1870 and1871, when the poor beasts were eaten. For several weeks, it is said, the privileged of Paris dined on elephant steaks the size of manhole covers. The zoo has never recovered from the slaughter, and conditions remain on the shabby side (animals are still jailed in Second-Empire pavilions and rumors of stray cats being fed to snakes and reptiles run rampant). However, children still seem to love visiting the zoo despite its faults.

Legend holds that the park's famous *Cedar of Lebanon,* now 40 feet in circumference, is now 40 feet in circumference, traveled in 1735 as a seedling in the hat of naturalist **Bernard de Jussieu,** who had carefully preserved it during confinement as a prisoner of war. But in truth, it was given to him after his release.

The park's **Museum of Natural History** has four departments, Paleontology, Paleobotany, Mineralogy, and Entomology, and it possesses one of the world's richest mineral collections and some of the oldest fossilized insects on earth. ♦ Garden: daily 8AM-8PM. Zoo: daily 9AM-6PM. Greenhouses: M, W-Su 1-5PM. Museum: daily 10AM-5PM. Enter at Rue Buffon, Rue Cuvier, or Place Valhubert. Métros: Gare d'Austerlitz, Jussieu, Place-Monge. 40.79.30.00

64 Musée de Sculpture en Plein Air This outdoor sculpture museum, built in 1980, was once **Henri IV's** bathing beach. The king would pour water here from a royal hat over the young Dauphin as the preamble to a swimming lesson. Today this spot on the banks of the Seine holds permanent and temporary sculpture exhibitions. But avoid this place after dark; a less desirable brand of exhibitionist prowls then. ♦ Quai St.-Bernard. Métros: Gare d'Austerlitz, Jussieu

64 L'Institut du Monde Arabe ★★$$ Opened in December 1987, this sociocultural institution was established to promote relations between France and the Arab world. It contains a library, an exhibition space, and a top-floor tearoom/restaurant that serves shish kebab, smoked salmon, baklava, and a better river view than the Tour D'Argent at half the price. Even if you don't have an appetite, the building itself is worth a visit. The architect, **Jean Nouvel,** has given Islamic references a stunning space-age interpretation. Take note of the south facade: the wall is made up of thousands of cameralike shutters that can be opened and closed to regulate the amount of light inside. ♦ Institute: Tu-Su 1-8PM. Restaurant: Tu-Su 1-7PM. 23 Quai St.-Bernard. Métro: Jussieu. 46.33.47.70 (restaurant); 40.51.38.38 (general information)

64 Le Village Afro-Brésilien Known to every African and Brazilian in Paris, this exotic spice and produce stall sells bouquets of dried fish from Réunion, monkey bread from Senegal, vegetable sponges and spices from Togo, crushed shrimp from Benin, pulverized nutmeg from Madagascar, Yucca grain, and Brazilian manioc flour. The store seems to have been lifted off a back street in Bamako or Dakar. The adventuresome Frenchman **Jacques Joulin,** who opened the shop 20 years ago after hitchhiking through Africa, also sells carved masks and colorful Senegalese fabric. ♦ Tu-F 9AM-2:30PM, 4-7PM; Sa 9AM-7PM; Su 9AM-12:30PM. 2bis Rue de l'Arbalète. Métro: Censier-Daubenton. 43.31.67.81, 47.07.14.74

The University of Paris was founded in 1215 after dissident theologian Pierre Abelard and his students were banished from Notre-Dame; they packed up and moved to the Left Bank in quest of intellectual freedom and established their new campus near the ruins of the Roman baths. In 1253 Robert de Sorbon, the king's confessor, created a college for indigent theological students in a house the king had given him, and he left his name on what would become one of the world's most distinguished universities. In 1469 Louis XI further enhanced the Latin Quarter as a world center of learning when he invited three printers (Ulric Gering, Martin Crantz, and Michel Friburger) from Mainz, Germany, to the Sorbonne to crank up France's first printing press. The final coup in the intellectual occupation of the Left Bank came in 1530, when François I founded the Collège de France to challenge the powerful and scholastically dogmatic Sorbonne.

65 A la Bonne Source (At the Good Spring) The bas-relief of two boys drawing water dates from the time of **Henri IV** (1589-1610) and is the oldest house sign on the street. ♦ 122 Rue Mouffetard. Métro: Censier-Daubenton

65 Facchetti & Co. Charcuterie Fine A first-rate gourmet Italian delicatessen. The main reason for stopping here is not to buy pasta and Parmesan but to admire, outside the shop, the bucolic mural of peasants at work below a pair of stags and wild boars. ♦ Tu-Th 8:15AM-1PM, 4-7:30PM; F-Sa 8:15AM-3:30PM; Su 8:15AM-1:30PM. 134 Rue Mouffetard. Métro: Censier-Daubenton. 43.31.40.00

66 Mouffetard Market A bustling pedestrian street market has convened at the bottom of the hill ever since 1350. It begins at the Rue de l'Epée-de-Bois. Among the gastronomical items purveyed here are mangoes, blood oranges, horse meat, wild boar, sea urchins, Colombian coffee, and hundreds of marvel-

ously smelly cheeses. Take a self-guided tour: just follow your nose. Be sure to peruse the African bazaar on the Rue de l'Arbalète, and go down the Rue Daubenton and Passage Passé Simple to visit the flower shops and the stalls specializing in Auvergnat sausage. As you wander, remember the two cardinal rules of marketing in Paris: first, *don't touch the produce;* and second, *the vendor, not the customer, is always right.* ♦ Tu-Sa 9AM-1PM, 4-7PM; Su 9AM-1PM. Métro: Place-Monge

67 La Tuile à Loup Run by the affable **Marie-France** and **Michel Joblin,** this crowded shop specializes in French regional arts and crafts. You will find earthenware pottery dishes, hand-carved wooden bowls, toys by well-known French artist **Roland Roure,** and a vast selection of books on French folklore, rural architecture, and ecology. ♦ Tu-Sa 10:30AM-1PM, 3-7:30PM; Su 11AM-1PM (call ahead to confirm Sunday hours). 35 Rue Daubenton. Métro: Censier-Daubenton. 47.07.28.90

68 Place Monge This square is named after the mathematician **Gaspard Monge** (1746-1818), who in 1794 founded the prestigious Ecole Polytechnique. Near the bustling small farmers' market is the old barracks of the **Garde Républicaine,** whose famous Horse Guards parade up the **Champs-Elysées** on Bastille Day, 14 July. ♦ Market: W, F, Su 7AM-1PM. Métro: Place-Monge

69 Arènes de Lutèce (Roman Arena) After the Roman Baths, this enormous first century amphitheater is the city's most important Roman ruin. Its 325- by 425-foot oval shape once seated 15,000 spectators, and it was accidentally discovered (and partially destroyed) in 1869. With its surrounding gardens and benches, the arena provides an island of tranquility for young parents pushing strollers and old men playing *boules*, and, in summer, campy medieval jousts in the arena. A nice spot for a picnic lunch of sourdough rye bread and charcuterie from the Place-Monge Market. ◆ Enter at Rue de Navarre and Rue des Arènes. Métros: Cardinal-Lemoine, Jussieu, Place-Monge

Keeping Fit in France

Although it may seem as if Parisians do most of their huffing and puffing on cigarettes, there are a variety of athletic centers in Paris, and it is possible

to maintain your exercise regime while you're away from home. Municipal tennis courts abound, and some of the larger hotels have health clubs that are amenable (in varying degrees) to offering one-day or monthly passes to nonguests for reasonable fees.

Health Clubs and Gyms:

Club Jean-de-Beauvais 15 Rue Jean-de-Beauvais, 46.33.16.80

Hôtel Méridien 81 Boulevard Gouvion-St.-Cyr, 40.68.34.34

Hôtel Nikko 61 Quai de Grenelle, 45.75.62.62; 45.75.25.25

Samourai 26 Rue de Berri, 43.59.04.58

SIEM 6 Rue de Lapparent, 43.20.35.10

Horseback Riding:

Manège de Neuilly 19bis Rue d'Orléans, 45.01.20.06

Poney-Club de la Cartoucherie Bois de Vincennes, 43.74.61.25

Swimming Pools:

Deligny 25 Quai Anatole-France, 45.51.72.15

Henry-de-Montherlant 32 Boulevard Lannes, 45.03.03.28

Jean-Taris 16 Rue Thouin, 43.25.54.03

Piscine de la Porte de la Plaine 13 Rue du Général-Guillaumat, 45.32.34.00

Tennis Courts:

Centre de Tennis du Jardin du Luxembourg Luxembourg Gardens, 43.20.67.64

Centre Sportif d'Orléans 14 Avenue Paul-Appell, 45.40.55.88

Cours du Polygone de Vincennes Avenue du Tremblay, 43.74.78.70

Mondial Tennis Country Club 58 Avenue du Président Wilson, 46.07.62.69

70 La Mosquée de Paris This Moorish ensemble of soaring minarets, pink marble fountains and crescent moons is the oldest mosque in France. It was constructed in 1926 by Arab artisans and three French architects. In gratitude for North African support during WWI, France gave the French Arab community the funds to build the mosque. Arabs from the poor Belleville and Barbès quarters gather at this enclave of Islam to read the Koran at the **Muslim Institut.** During Ramadan, hundreds of North Africans kneel facing Mecca and pray to Allah on a sea of Persian carpets spread beneath the mosque's delicately carved dome. Nearby, behind a dark curtain, the women intone their prayers. A guided tour (unfortunately brief and in French) of the building, central courtyard, and Moorish garden offers a worthwhile introduction to Islam. You may leave feeling as though you've passed the afternoon in Riyadh or Istanbul. ◆ M-Th, Sa-Su 9AM-noon, 2-6PM. Place du Puits-de-l'Ermite. Métro: Place-Monge. 45.35.97.33/34/35

70 Café de la Mosquée ★$ Flaky Moroccan pastries, sweet mint tea, and Turkish coffee are served during the summer on a white patio shaded by leafy fig trees. In winter tea is served in a quiet lounge adjoining the *hammam* (Turkish steam bath). No alcohol is served. ◆ Café: daily 10AM-10PM; closed Aug. Restaurant: daily noon-2:30PM, 7:30-9:30PM. Baths: (for women) M, W 11AM-8PM, Th 11AM-9PM, Sa 10AM-9PM; (for men) F 11AM-8PM, Su 10AM-8PM. 2 Rue Daubenton (39 Rue Geoffroy-St.-Hilaire). No credit cards. Métro: Censier-Daubenton. 43.31.18.14

70 Brasserie Mouffetard ★★$ The best café on the street. The croissants, brioches, and fruit tarts are made fresh daily by the friendly **Chartrain** family, the café owners. It's noisy, always crowded with vendors and students, and in winter the windows steam up with animated conversation. Light lunches and snacks are available, too. ◆ Tu-Sa 7AM-9PM; Su 7AM-4PM; closed July. 116 Rue Mouffetard. Métro: Place-Monge. 43.31.42.50

71 St.-Médard This rustic village church, built in 1773, is an architectural conglomeration of flamboyant Gothic and Renaissance styles and has a story for every predilection. French literature majors may remember this as the church in which Jean Valjean accidentally encounters Javert in **Victor Hugo's** *Les Misérables.* Trade unionists point out correctly that St.-Médard was turned into the *Temple of Labor* during the Revolution. Art historians will recall the notorious painting of **Sainte Geneviève,** which for centuries was erroneously ascribed to Watteau. And finally, the occultists in the crowd will appreciate a most famous corpse buried here, that of Saint Médard's deacon, a young Jansenist named **François Paris,** who died in 1727. Within two years, crowds of more than 800 hysterical convulsionists flocked to his grave where they groaned and trembled in hopes of miraculous cures. (The frenzied gatherings were finally outlawed by **Louis XV** in 1732, but Paris' tomb remains beneath the unmarked stones of what is now the Chapel of the Virgin.) The majority of the church's construction was financed by fines imposed on Protestants; the money ran out while the vaulted ceiling was being installed, so it was completed in wood. At least that's how the story goes. ◆ 141 Rue Mouffetard. Métro: Censier-Daubenton

72 Le Petit Marguery ★★$/$$ A lively 1900s-style neighborhood bistro with an inventive menu of leeks with truffles and venison with celery root. ◆ Tu-Sa noon-2PM, 7:30-10PM; closed Aug. 9 Blvd de Port-Royal. Reservations recommended. Métro: Gobelins. 43.31.58.59

73 Mobilier National (National Storehouse) What is as supersecret as the French CIA, answers directly to the president, and is littered with Napoléon-era love seats and andirons? Answer: the Mobilier National, the nation's attic. This singular institution was created in 1667 by **Colbert** as a royal storehouse at the same time he transformed the Gobelins factory. It is the state's interior decorator, responsible for furnishing government ministries and embassies with everything from inkwells to curtains. The institution, which at one time also kept the crown jewels, is quartered within the Gobelins complex in an unremarkable redbrick structure designed by **Auguste Perret.** In 1964 **André Malraux,** then Minister of Culture, offered studio space in the Mobilier National to contemporary French furniture designers who would be willing to create and sell their prototypes to French manufacturers. Thus, the Mobilier National takes credit for the boldly modern furniture used in former president **Georges Pompidou's** office at the **Elysée Palace.** You can pass by the Mobilier National on the Gobelins tour, but the warehouse itself is off-limits to the public. ◆ Rue Berbier-du-Mets. Métro: Gobelins

LES MOVLINS DES GOBELLIN

74 Gobelins Tapestry Factories The factory, the avenue, and the neighborhood all take their name from the brothers **Jean** and **Philibert Gobelin,** who in the 15th century established their famous dyeworks along the stinking **Bièvre River.** Although the name *Gobelins* has become synonymous with tapestry, the two brothers never wove a thread. Their claim to fame in the tapestry world was making a special scarlet dye. In 1662 **Jean-Baptiste Colbert, Louis XIV's** famous minister, persuaded the king to take over the Gobelins property. There, under the management of court painter **Charles Le Brun,** Colbert assembled a craft colony of about 250 Flemish weavers. Colbert's goal was twofold: to compete with Flanders' tapestry industry and to cover the vast expanse of walls in the *Sun King's* sumptuous palace at Versailles. (Within Gobelins' first courtyard stands a marble statue of Le Brun [1907] by **Cardier,** followed in the next courtyard by a statue of his boss, Colbert [1894], by **Aube.**) In time, Gobelins became so celebrated that **Marie Antoinette** and **Louis XVI** (in 1790) and the **Pope** (in 1895) paid personal visits to the humble workshops.

Today scores of weavers at the Gobelins factory manufacture tapestries with the ancient

techniques, working on century-old wooden looms. Using wools from a palette of 14,920 colors, weavers may spend two to four years completing woven panels, the designs of which are based on modern paintings by artists such as **Matisse, Picasso,** and **Miró.** Three days a week, the state-owned Gobelins mills offer 75-minute guided tours of the tapestry factory and the allied **Savonnerie** (carpet) and **Beauvais** (horizontal loom weaving) workshops, a treat for anyone interested in weaving and crafts. You can visit the studios where weavers, trained from the age of 16, work quietly, occasionally glancing up at mirrors before them to view the reverse side of the tapestry. If you can't get to the factory, you can see Gobelins tapestries hanging at Versailles as well as other places reserved for the privileged: the Paris Opéra, the National Library, the Elysée Palace, and the Luxembourg Palace. ◆ Tours: Tu-Th 2-3PM. To arrange group tours, call Caisse Nationale des Monuments Historiques at 44.61.20.00. 42 Ave des Gobelins. Métro: Gobelins. 43.37.12.60

In 1980 French men measured an average height of 5 feet, 7 inches.

The Rue St.-Jacques was once the Via Superior, an ancient Roman road stretching south towards Orléans. Christian pilgrims began their journey to the shrine of Santiago de Compostela in Spain, one of France's most popular pilgrimages, on this road during the Middle Ages. Thus, the street was named Rue St.-Jacques (French for Santiago). Compostela, a city near the Atlantic coast of Spain, was rich in scallop shells (*coquilles St.-Jacques*), which the pilgrims brought back as proof of their voyage and devotion.

Restaurants/Nightlife: Red   Hotels: Blue
Shops/ ◆ Outdoors: Green   **Sights/Culture:** Black

Baron Eric de Rothschild
Co-owner/Manager, Château Lafitte Rothschild
Bordeaux Wines

Strolling in the **Albert Kahn Gardens** in Boulogne.

Having tea and chocolate cake in one of the little bistros in the **Buttes-Chaumont.**

Sunday lunch in the **Parc de Montsouris.**

Seafood at **Le Duc** on the Boulevard Raspail with Rieussec (dry white wine) for dinner.

Feasting on pot-au-feu for lunch on Saturday at **Balzar.**

Perusing the wine list at **Benoît** on Rue St.-Martin.

Pierre Rosenberg
Head Curator, Department of Paintings, Louvre

The **Henner** and **Hébert** museums, exhibiting 19th-century paintings, are two excellent yet seldom visited

places. Other interesting but less well known museums are the **Nissim de Camondo Museum,** for 18th-century furniture; and the charming and centrally located **Cognac-Jay Museum,** featuring 18th-century French paintings. In the **Bourdelle Museum,** at Montparnasse, or in the **Musée des Monuments Français,** you need not fear intrusive museum guards.

César
French Sculptor

Coffee in the morning, either at the **La Rotonde café** or the **Select** on Montparnasse, and dinner at **Lipp, La Coupole, Chez Benoît, Tong Yen,** or downstairs at **Castel's.**

I love going to the flea market and visiting the antique dealers on Rue Jacob, Rue de l'Université, Rue du Bac, and Rue de Seine.

I live near the Rue Daguerre where there is a wonderful open-air market and a nice little Greek restaurant.

Rudolph Chelminski
American Author

The view at night of the islands and the Left Bank, from the point where the Pont des Arts jumps over the Seine from the Institut de France to the Right Bank. Anyone who sees this and doesn't instantly agree that Paris is the most beautiful city in the world is a churl or a New Yorker, which is usually the same thing, anyway.

A four-corner, right-of-way blockage at an intersection where everyone has *priorité* over everyone else and refuses to budge. In one beautiful flash, you entirely understand French civilization.

A walk through the **Marais** ending at the **Place des Vosges** and wondering why in hell you didn't have the brains to buy an apartment there 25 years ago.

A Christmas dinner of oysters, *dinde aux marrons,* and champagne in **La Coupole** (the brasserie side, of course).

The third girl from the left in the **Crazy Horse Saloon's** chorus line. For sheer beauty it's a toss-up between her and the **Ste.-Chapelle,** but she's more kinetic.

The **Pont Alexandre III** at twilight, when the Belle Epoque lanterns have been turned on but there is enough sky left to give a Magritte effect.

The **Luxembourg Gardens,** not jogging (what an idea), but watching the murderous old men playing a game of *boules.*

All the open-air markets, especially the **Buci** and the **Mouffetard.**

Père-Lachaise, the cemetery that makes death seem like fun.

Dinner at **Taillevent, Vivarois,** or **Lucas-Carton,** if some rich publisher is buying. If not, any of the following will do just fine: **L'Ambassadeur d'Auvergne, L'Aquitaine, Chez les Anges, Chez Georges, Le Cochon d'Or, Aux Charpentiers, L'Entrecôte, Léon, Les Saints-Pères, La Providence, Le Récamier, Le Val d'Or,** or **Chez la Vieille.** And that's just a star

Susy Davidson
New York-based Food Consultant

My favorite Paris bistros are **Louis XIV, L'Ami Louis, Benoît,** and **Chez Georges.**

If I'm not dining at my favorite bistros, I can be found at one of these brasseries: **Le Vaudeville, Chez Francis,** and **La Coupole.**

My favorite restaurants are **Robuchon** (Restaurant Jamin) and **Apicius** on the Avenue de Villiers.

For a little chocolate indulgence, stop by **La Maison du Chocolat** on the Rue François I.

My favorite bars and wine bars are **Closerie des Lilas, Le Bourbon** in the Hôtel Sofitel, **Willi's Wine Bar, Le Rubis** on the Rue du Marché-St.-Honoré, **La Cloche des Halles,** and **Le Sauvignon.**

Count Jean d'Harcourt
Gentleman Farmer

Hot chocolate, croissants, and the papers at **Café Flore** Sunday mornings; walking along **Rue Jacob** browsing for rare editions; lunch at **Willi's Wine Bar;** the **St.-Séverin** and **St.-Julien-le-Pauvre** churches; tea at the **Tea Caddy** next to St.-Julien-le-Pauvre; dinner at **Morot Gaudry** on Rue de la Cavalerie; a special evening at **Douchka,** where you can hear the best Russian singers in Paris; buying books at **Galignani** on Rue de Rivoli; and taking a stroll in the **Tuileries Gardens.**

Andrew Harvey
Poet and Novelist

The allegorical figures on the **Pont Alexandre III.**

The **Place Georges-Cain** outhouse of the **Musée Carnavalet.**

Sitting on the benches by the **Seine.**

Glimpses of the secret courtyards from the street in the **Marais** and the **sixth arrondissement.**

The **Bossuet** figure on the fountain at **Place**

St.-Sulpice, and the two Baroque fonts in the church of St.-Sulpice.

An evening of medieval concerts in Ste.-Chapelle.

All the Chardin paintings in the Louvre.

Jacques Grange
Interior Designer

Walking all around Paris.

Crossing from the Left Bank to the Right Bank on the Pont des Arts.

Bargaining with many of the antique dealers on Rue de Beaune, Quai Voltaire, and Rue Jacob (especially Comoglio).

The Fontaine des Médicis in Luxembourg Gardens.

Lunch at La Coupole.

The Palais Royal. The garden and shops under the arcade such as Didier Ludot, where you can find old luggage and handbags and Madame Orsoni, who sells antique porcelain and china in the Galerie de Valois.

Sunday mornings at the Clignancourt flea market, particularly the Marché Paul Bert, followed by lunch in spring or summer in the Chez Marie garden (next to Paul Bert).

All kinds of sweets at Madame Acabo on Rue La Fontaine.

The Delacroix towers in the church of St.-Sulpice, and dining in the café on the square.

Another antique dealer in a charming passage— Eric Philippe at Vero Dodat.

Lunch at Pauline on Rue Villedo.

Tea or a before-dinner drink on the terrace of the Samaritaine department store in the spring or summer months.

Summer dining on the terrace at Le Vert Galant.

Drinks in the bar of the Hôtel Pont-Royal.

The two cafés across from the Hôtel Drouot (auction house) for beer on draft and hard-boiled eggs.

Riding the No. 63 bus.

Jennifer Bartlett
Painter

Luxembourg Gardens, La Coupole, Le Chaméléon, Place de la Concorde, V.O. movies on the Boulevard Montparnasse, St.-Sulpice, Poilane, Fauchon, La Tour d'Argent, Louvre, Marmottan Museum, La Cafetière, Orangerie, Jeu de Paume, lemon tarts, Rue de Buci Market, Boulevard St.-Germain, Bois de Boulogne, Left Bank shops, and Nos Ancétres Les Gauloises.

Françoise Gilot
Artist

Walking along Le Canal St.-Martin (built by Gustave Eiffel, who built the Eiffel Tower) with its small bridges and waterlocks.

The charming Place des Vosges for its early 17th-century architecture, the Victor Hugo Museum (which is a curiosity rather than a full-fledged museum) and all the small shops and restaurants around the square. The Coconnas has always been popular, although recently it hasn't quite lived up to its reputation.

Some of architect François Ledoux's gates to the city of Paris built in the 17th century, particularly the one at the Jaurès métro station, or those at Denfert-Rochereau or Monceau.

One of the enclosed galleries at the Passage des Panoramas and the nearby Musée Grevin, which is the Parisian equivalent of Madame Tussaud's. The Passage Choiseul is also interesting.

The old section of the Père-Lachaise cemetery. It's romantic in the springtime, with trees growing everywhere and statues tilting in one direction or another.

Gustave Moreau Museum, located in the artist's home and studio on Rue de la Rochefoucauld.

Rue Réaumur, where you can see the many Art Nouveau, Art Deco, and purely outrageous buildings along the street. Newspapers are published here, and, at the turn of the century, this was the headquarters for the textile magnates.

The Latin Quarter

Madame Kaki Borgeaud
Director of J.L. Scherrer

Climbing to the top of the Eiffel Tower.

A ride on the Seine on a *bateau mouche,* anytime of the year.

The smell of Paris' streets in the morning.

Stopping in any small bistro to have a cup of coffee.

Dining in Chinese restaurants at night.

Roaming through the Hôtel Drouot (the auction house) in search of a bargain.

The boutiques on Rue de Tournon.

The buffet at the Gare de Lyon—marvelous food and a classic monument.

Dinner in a cozy atmosphere at La Maison d'Automne on Rue des Plantes.

Marion Pike
Painter

Walking along the Seine in the sun on the Right Bank, from the Pont Neuf to the Pont Alexandre III; then, on the Left Bank, in the shade, from Pont St.-Michel to Pont des Arts. On this latter side, you pass a number of strange boats.

Sunset on the Pont des Arts.

A ham-and-eggs breakfast and a dinner at Lipp.

The Rue de Nevers, straight out of the Middle Ages (it starts just where Rue Dauphine ends and intersects Rue de Nesle). Also the Passage Dauphine, which runs between Rue Dauphine and Rue Mazarine, and the beautiful Cour de Rohan, with entrances on three sides: Boulevard St.-Germain, Rue Dauphine, and Rue St.-André-des-Arts.

The pastels upstairs in the Pavillon de Flore at the Louvre, and the lion by Barye downstairs.

The Sunday morning bird market (*marché des oiseaux*) on Ile de la Cité, where a flower market is located during the rest of the week.

In the fifties Jean-Paul Sartre and Simone de Beauvoir held Existential court at **Café Flore**— a great place to savor a real bacon-and-eggs breakfast

Ⓜ *Solférino*

Make advance reservations to tour the extraordinary **Glass House** (see page 59)

Ⓜ *Rue du Bac*

Ⓜ *St.-Sulpice*

Ⓜ *Sèvres-Babylone*

← 15

A destitute Hemingway used to capture and strangle pigeons for lunch here at the **Luxembourg Gardens**

A small bronze replica of the Statue of Liberty graces the gardens here

The site of a beekeeping school run by an Esperanto-speaking Dominican friar

St.-Germain

The tree-lined **Boulevard St.-Germain** originates near the tip of Ile St.-Louis, then traverses the heart of literary Paris, and finally arrives back at the Seine at the **Pont de la Concorde** in that *Noble Faubourg* quartier fashionable during the reign of Louis XV. This is the home of the **Académie Française**, the world's oldest café (**Le Procope**), prestigious publishing houses, bookbinders, and that conclave of intellectual watering holes where **Fitzgerald**, **Hemingway**, and other American scriveners wrote or drank away rejection-slip depression. And in the 1950s, this is where Sartre gave birth to existentialism.

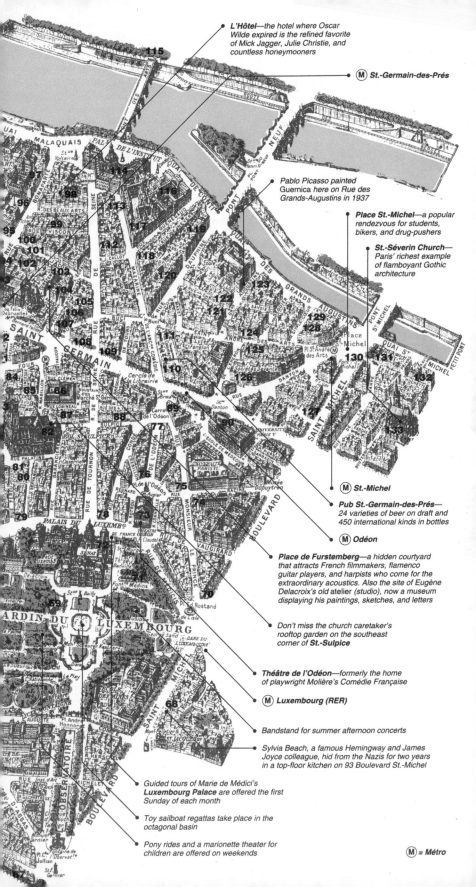

L'Hôtel—the hotel where Oscar Wilde expired is the refined favorite of Mick Jagger, Julie Christie, and countless honeymooners

(M) St.-Germain-des-Prés

Pablo Picasso painted Guernica here on *Rue des Grands-Augustins* in 1937

Place St.-Michel—a popular rendezvous for students, bikers, and drug-pushers

St.-Séverin Church—Paris' richest example of flamboyant Gothic architecture

(M) St.-Michel

Pub St.-Germain-des-Prés—24 varieties of beer on draft and 450 international kinds in bottles

(M) Odéon

Place de Furstemberg—a hidden courtyard that attracts French filmmakers, flamenco guitar players, and harpists who come for the extraordinary acoustics. Also the site of Eugène Delacroix's old atelier (studio), now a museum displaying his paintings, sketches, and letters

Don't miss the church caretaker's rooftop garden on the southeast corner of **St.-Sulpice**

Théâtre de l'Odéon—formerly the home of playwright Molière's Comédie Française

(M) Luxembourg (RER)

Bandstand for summer afternoon concerts

Sylvia Beach, a famous Hemingway and James Joyce colleague, hid from the Nazis for two years in a top-floor kitchen on 93 Boulevard St.-Michel

Guided tours of Marie de Médici's **Luxembourg Palace** are offered the first Sunday of each month

Toy sailboat regattas take place in the octagonal basin

Pony rides and a marionette theater for children are offered on weekends

(M) = Métro

The St.-Germain quartier is also the home of the inviting **Luxembourg Gardens,** the **Ecole des Beaux-Arts,** and a plethora of art galleries. In this neighborhood, the painter **Corot** walked the quais; **Manet** lived on **Rue Bonaparte;** and **Delacroix** resided in the **Place de Furstemberg. Ingres, Baudelaire,** and **Wagner** stayed on **Quai Voltaire,** and **Picasso** painted *Guernica* on **Rue des Grands-Augustins.**

The St.-Germain walk covers half of the boulevard—the most interesting portion is in the vicinity of the church of **St.-Germain-des-Prés,** where the remains of the city's oldest abbey stand. The promenade takes you down alleys where bookshops, poster stores, antique dealers, and picture restorers do business side-by-side with chic dress shops and cafés frequented by aging students.

This is a stroll you can make in blue jeans and a sweater. Start at the **Musée d'Orsay,** a former Belle Epoque train station that is now devoted to art and culture—spanning the era from 1848 to World War I. En route to the Boulevard St.-Germain, take Rue du Bac and stop at **Deyrolle,** an amusing taxidermy shop. On the boulevard, you'll encounter **Madeleine Gély's** handmade-umbrella shop, an essential for those frequent April downpours. You might consider having an early lunch and watching the world go by at one of those literary shrines: **Lipp, Flore,** or **Deux Magots.** When you can't eat another bit of Lipp's *choucroute* (sauerkraut), visit the shaded Place de Furstemberg to look for the old studio of **Delacroix,** browse for antiques along **Rue Jacob,** or tour the African art galleries along **Rue de Seine.**

The narrow **Cour du Commerce St.-André** is where the guillotine was invented and where the firebrand **Marat** had his printing press. You'll pass the **Buci Market,** where Picasso bought his sausages, and **Le Bonaparte** café, where Sartre philosophized with **Simone de Beauvoir.** At **Rue de Tournon,** nature lovers will want to detour through the Luxembourg Gardens, one of the **Queen Marie de Médici** legacies to the city.

At the day's end, consider dining at a classic, old-world bistro such as **Allard.** Or you could catch an early Cary Grant film at the **Action Christine,** then dine in the splendor of **Jacques Cagna** around the corner of Rue des Grands-Augustins. After dinner, wander toward the river via **La Palette,** where you can have a beer at the bar, or venture into the hole-in-the-wall **Caveau de la Boulée** to sit in on a midnight game of chess.

St.-Germain

1 Hôtel Solférino $$ This hotel has Oriental rugs, pastel walls, floral-patterned wallpaper, small rooms, and a veranda where you can enjoy breakfast. ♦ 91 Rue de Lille. Métro: Solférino. 47.05.85.54

2 Palais de la Légion d'Honneur Built by Pierre Rousseau for German **Prince Frédéric III de Salm-Kyrbourg** in 1786, this palace (pictured above) is architecturally the most significant **Louis XVI** building in Paris. In 1804 **Napoléon** acquired it for the *Légion d'Honneur.* (The city of San Francisco built a copy of the palace and turned it into an art museum.) The *légion* was a society started by Napoléon to honor men, and later women, who greatly served France. Members may emblazon themselves with a woven bud of red wool stitched to their left lapel. ♦ Légion museum: Tu-Su 2-5PM. 2 Rue de Bellechasse. Métro: Solférino

The Musée d'Orsay is constructed of almost twice as much metal as the Eiffel Tower. Standing 453 feet long, 131 feet wide, and 105 feet high, it has roughly the same exterior dimensions as the Georges Pompidou Center. The 56,416 square feet of exhibition space is half of what the Louvre has.

3 Musée d'Orsay In December 1986 a long train of effort chugged into the Gare d'Orsay, and when the steam cleared, there stood a magnificent museum, a Paris showcase for 19th-century art and culture. The Musée d'Orsay houses the art that chronologically links the Louvre collections with those at the Pompidou Center, bridging the end of Romanticism and the origins of Modern Art. The museum transports us back to a time of grace and with the works of such geniuses as **Henry James, Edouard Manet, Sarah Bernhardt,** and **James McNeill Whistler.**

The Musée d'Orsay collection includes all the glorious Impressionist paintings formerly in the **Jeu de Paume;** the post-Impressionist and Nabi works from the **Palais de Tokyo** (among them are 400 paintings by **Odilon Redon**); and selected works that were formerly in the Louvre, including paintings and sculptures by artists such as **Courbet** and **Millet,** who were born after 1820, and various late paintings by **Delacroix, Corot, Ingres,** and the **Barbizon landscape painters.**

History The Quai d'Orsay site was once occupied by the **Palais d'Orsay,** a government building that was devastated (as were the Hôtel de Ville and the Tuileries Palace) by the May 1871 fires set by the Commune at the end of France's tragic civil war period. The Orléans Rail Company bought the property and hired **Victor Laloux** (1850-1937), the architect who had rebuilt the Hôtel de Ville, to design a railway station and hotel. Construction lasted from Sepember 1898 to July 1900 and was accomplished by a crew of 380 men working in round-the-clock shifts.

At one time, 200 trains a day used the Gare d'Orsay, but the growing electrification and lengthening of trains made Orsay's short plat-

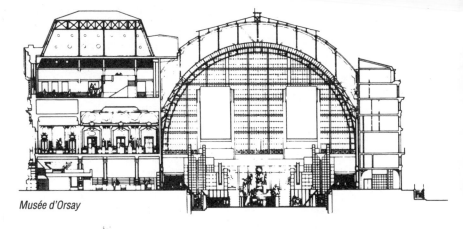

Musée d'Orsay

forms obsolete in the late 1930s. Over the years, the station took on other functions. Prisoners of war were garrisoned here after the Liberation; **General de Gaulle** announced his return to power at the Gare d'Orsay hotel on 19 May 1958; **Orson Welles** made a film version of the **Franz Kafka** book *The Trial* here in 1962; and in 1970, **Bernardo Bertolucci** used it as a setting for part of his film, *The Conformist.*

As early as 1961, plans to raze the station and build a modern 870-room hotel complex were nearly realized; **Le Corbusier** even competed for the design job. In 1971 the station was

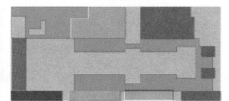

Upper Level

Middle Level

declared a historic landmark. In 1979 **ACT Architecture** (a group of three associated architects: **Pierre Colboc, Renaud Bardon,** and **Jean-Paul Philippo**) was selected to renovate the building for use as a museum. The famed Italian designer **Gae Aulenti** was the interior designer.

St.-Germain

Ground Level This floor features painting, sculpture, photography, and decorative arts dating from 1848 to 1870. The front of the gallery contains sculptures by **Rude, Préault,** and **Pradier,** and a great animal bronze by **Barye.** At the rear of the gallery stands *The Dance* by **Carpeaux.** Rooms at the end of the courtyard are dedicated to the **Paris Opéra** and its architect, **Charles Garnier.**

To the right of the courtyard are paintings by Romantics such as **Delacroix** and **Ingres,** as well as works by the eclectics and symbolists such as **Puvis de Chavannes** and **Gustave Moreau,** along with the pre-1870 work of **Edward Degas.** To the left of the courtyard are works by Realists, including **Daumier, Corot, Millet,** and the **Barbizon painters.** They are neighbors to the masterpieces of **Edouard Manet,** such as *Olympia* and *Déjeuner sur L'Herbe,* in addition to the pre-1870 work of **Monet, Bazille,** and **Renoir.**

Upper Level The tour jumps to the upper level (to follow the chronological order of the artwork), where the light streaming through the museum's glass roof shows off the post-1870 flowering of Impressionism. Here **Manet, Degas, Monet,** and **Renoir** are joined by **Sisley, Pissarro, vanGogh,** and **Cézanne.** Nearby, post-Impressionists such as **Seurat, Signac, Cross,** and **Gauguin** are shown with the Pont Aven and Nabi schools, including **Denis, Bonnard, Vallotton,** and **Vuillard.** There's also a special room devoted to graphic arts and photography from 1880-1914, including the works of early photographers **Atget, Emerson, Steichen,** and **Stieglitz,** as well as **Bonnard** and **Degas,** who are best known for their painting. After you have feasted your eyes on this floor's treasures,

Ground Level

■Painting   ■Bookstore
■Sculpture   ■Rooftop Café
■Decorative Arts   ■Art Nouveau
■Architecture   ■Birth of the Filmmaker
■Temporary Exhibitions ■Restaurant

Main Entrance

Information Area

go downstairs for **Nadar, Legray, Baldus, Carroll,** and **Cameron.**

Middle Level The terraces above the courtyard display the sculpture of **Rodin, Maillol,** and **Bourdelle.** The rooms along the Seine have figures created during the Third Republic, including works by symbolists **Burne-Jones** and **Delville.** Eight rooms are devoted to the sinuous era of Art Nouveau, with works by the Belgians **Horta** and **van de Velde,** by **Gallé** and **Majorelle** of the Nancy School, and pieces by **Guimard** and **Thonet,** the dean of bentwood furniture. On the Rue de Lille side, you will find the 20th-century paintings of **Klimt** and **Matisse,** heralding the advent of Modern Art. Also on this level is an exhibition showing the evolution of the film industry.

Impressionists The famous French Impressionist collection is displayed on the ground and upper levels. The term "Impressionism" was coined by a derisive critic after seeing Monet's painting *Impression: Sunrise.* The name stuck, and the movement effected as dramatic a change in the course of art history as the Renaissance had. Instead of choosing

St.-Germain

heroes, mythic deities, or saints for their subject matter, the Impressionists painted ordinary people in cafés as well as trains chuffing into Gare St.-Lazare with vivid color and undisguised brush strokes.

Americans in Paris The Orsay collection also includes paintings by more than 36 American artists, including **John Singer Sargent, William Merritt Chase, Robert Henri, George Inness,** and **Winslow Homer,** many of whom worked and studied in Paris. And this is where you can visit that emblem of American art, *The Artist's Mother,* by Whistler. A rooftop café, a bookstore, and a 380-seat auditorium round out the museum. ♦ Admission. Tu-W, F-Sa 10AM-5:30PM; Th 10AM-9:15PM (opens at 9AM, 20 June-20 Sep); Su 9AM-5:30PM; closed Christmas day and 1 May. 1 Rue de Bellechasse. Métro: Solférino. 45.49.48.14, 45.49.11.11 (recorded information)

Within Musée d'Orsay:

Museum Restaurant ★$$ Housed in the dining room of the old hotel, the restaurant is an ornately gilded period piece that has a ceiling covered with painted deities by **Gabriel Ferrier,** winner of the 1872 *Prix de Rome.* The decor is the real attraction here, not the food. Don't bother asking the waiter for absinthe, but try the next best thing: Pernod on ice. ♦ Tu-W, F-Su 11:30AM-2:30PM, 4-5:50PM (tea), 7-9:30PM; Th 11:30AM-2:30PM, 7-9:30PM. 45.49.48.14

4 **Bonpoint** This pricey chain store offers a touch of the couture for the little darlings in your life. Sister stores are nearby. ♦ M-Sa 10AM-7PM. 67 Rue de l'Université. Métro: Rue du Bac. 45.55.63.70

4 **Galerie Berggruen** Alas, Berggruen, an éminence grise in the art world, sold his gallery, but the new owner, **Mendiharat,** has not sacrificed quality: Galerie Berggruen still shows select new artists and some of the best available engravings by **Klee, Kandinsky, Ernst, Chagall,** and others of their ilk. ♦ Tu-Sa 10AM-1PM, 2:30-7PM. 70 Rue de l'Université. Métro: Rue de Bac. 42.22.02.12

5 **Rue du Bac** The barracks that housed the swashbuckling heroes of *The Three Musketeers* by **Alexandre Dumas** were located on this street, which was built in 1564 and named after the *bac* (ferry) that used to transport Vaugirard quarry stone across the Seine to the construction site of the Tuileries Palace. ♦ Métro: Rue du Bac

6 **Le Maconnais** ★$$ An attractive bistro serving *poulet fricassé à la crème,* Maconnais salad *(foie de volaille vinaigrette),* and a sweet *marquise au chocolat* and *gratin à l'orange* for dessert. ♦ M-F 11:45AM-2:30PM, 6:45-10:30PM; Sa 6:45-10:30PM; closed between Christmas and New Year's Day, one week at Easter, three weeks in Aug. 10 Rue du Bac. Reservations recommended. Métro: Rue du Bac. 42.61.21.89

6 **Lefèbvres Fils** Among the former shoppers at this century-old firm selling earthenware china and fanciful trompe l'oeil dishes were **Victor Hugo, Marcel Proust,** and **Georges Feydeau.** ♦ M-Sa 10:30AM-noon, 2:30-6PM; closed in Aug. 24 Rue du Bac. Métro: Rue du Bac. 42.61.18.40

JEAN SAFFRAY

6 **Jean Saffray** Buy an ice cream bust of your favorite French politician, whether it's François Mitterrand, Georges Marchais, Jacques Chirac, or Valèry Giscard d'Estaing. ♦ Tu-Sa 7AM-8PM; Su 7:30AM-7PM; closed in Aug. 18 Rue du Bac. Métro: Rue du Bac. 42.61.27.63

6 **Design 95** An unassuming shop filled with reasonably priced objects such as hand-blown wine and water glasses and champagne flutes ♦ M-Sa 3-7PM. 23 Rue du Bac. Métro: Rue du Bac. 42.61.17.43

6 **Christian Constant** ★$ This tearoom-cum-chocolate-and-pastry shop serves 36 kinds of tea accompanied by five varieties of sugar, acacia honey, and fresh brioches, as well as great hot chocolate and kiwi tarts, but the pièce de résistance is its one hundred percent pure bittersweet chocolate bars. ♦ Daily 8AM-8PM. 26 Rue du Bac. Métro: Rue du Bac. 47.03.30.00

7 **Maxoff Restaurant** ★$$/$$$ The menu's highlights include tarama, herring *à la Russe,* a Baltic salad, salmon *à tartare,* Russian caviar, *caviar d'aubergines,* Ukrainian borscht, strudels, tortes, and blinis. ♦ Tu-Sa 12:30-2PM, 7:30-10:30PM; closed in Aug. 44 Rue de Verneuil. Reservations recommended. Métro: Rue du Bac. 42.60.60.43

7 Ravi ★★$$$ Spicy and pricey, along with its sister restaurant (214 Rue de la Croix-Nivert, 45.31.58.09), this aptly named Indian restaurant (*Ravi* means *sun* in Hindi) outshines its competitors with Madras curries, kabobs, and outstanding Tandoori prawns. ♦ Daily 12:10-2PM, 8:15-11PM. 50 Rue de Verneuil. Reservations recommended. Métro: Rue du Bac. 42.61.17.28

7 Tan Dinh ★★★$$$ The most elegant—and expensive—Vietnamese restaurant in Paris is located conveniently around the corner from the Musée d'Orsay. Delicate smoked-goose ravioli, light noodles with piquant shrimp, and lobster beignet of *coquilles St.-Jacques* with ginkgo, prepared by the affable **Vifian** brothers, who alternate nights in the kitchen. Exotic sorbets and remarkable Bordeaux. ♦ M-Sa noon-2PM, 7:30-11PM; closed first half of Aug. 60 Rue de Verneuil. Dinner reservations recommended. Métro: Rue du Bac. 45.44.04.84

7 50 Rue de l'Université The former site of the **Hôtel de l'Intendance,** where **Edna St. Vincent Millay** wrote her Pulitzer prize-winning poem, *The Ballad of the Harp-Weaver,* in 1921. ♦ Métro: Rue du Bac

8 Le Rideau de Paris After 35 years in business, this crowded little linen shop has cornered the neighborhood market in one hundred-percent French cotton dishtowels and lace bistro curtains. ♦ M 2-6:30PM; Tu-F 10AM-6:30PM; Sa 2:30-6:30PM. 32 Rue du Bac. Métro: Rue du Bac. 42.61.18.56

8 Nina Borowski-Archéologie One of the world's most renowned dealers in rare Greek and Near Eastern antiquities, Borowski also deals in New York by appointment (212/439.9722). She numbers among her clients the great museums of Europe and America. Don't miss her collection of ancient Greek and Roman rings and other jewelry. ♦ M 2-7PM; Tu-Sa 10:30AM-12:30PM, 2-7PM; closed in Aug. 40 Rue du Bac. Métro: Rue du Bac. 45.48.61.60

9 Galerie Adrien Maeght The owner of this bookstore/gallery comes from a famous family of art dealers and sells drawings and prints by modern artists from **Matisse** to **Cucchi,** as well as **Calder** posters, **Miró** T-shirts, and deluxe art books. ♦ Tu-Sa 9:30AM-1PM, 2-7PM. 42 and 46 Rue du Bac. Métro: Rue du Bac. 45.48.45.15

9 Lenôtre The owner, **Gaston Lenôtre,** wrote the book on pastry, and this is only one of his five outlets in Paris. You can almost gain weight by just looking in the delectable shop window, so why not slip inside and sample the *palet d'or* or go for broke with the Concorde chocolate meringue cake? ♦ M-Sa 9AM-8PM; Su 9AM-1PM; closed the end of July through the end of Aug. 44 Rue du Bac. Métro: Rue du Bac. 42.22.39.39

9 Deyrolle A 150-year-old taxidermy shop with everything from mounted polar bears, tigers, and bewildered baby elephants to cobras and many other citizens of Noah's Ark staring out of their glass eyes. Deyrolle also acquires rare butterflies, tastefully stuffed cocker spaniels, and just about every crystal, geode, and mineral on earth except kryptonite. Kids could be left here for hours. The question is, when you retrieve them, will they have glass eyes, too? ♦ M-F 9AM-12:30PM, 2-6PM; Sa 9AM-12:30PM, 2-5:30PM. 46 Rue du Bac. Métro: Rue du Bac. 42.22.30.07

10 L'Oeillade ★★$$ An ever-changing, moderately priced three-course menu is offered by chef **Jean-Louis Huclin,** who makes all the sausages, terrines, and pasta himself. He also serves perfectly stewed pot-au-feu salad, cassoulet in a gleaming copper saucepan, succulent roast chicken, and mousse au

chocolat. Small but affordable wine list. ♦ M-F noon-2:30PM, 7:30-10:30PM; Sa 7:30-10:30PM. 10 Rue St. Simon. Métro: Rue du Bac. 42.22.01.60

10 Hôtel Duc de St.-Simon $$$ A cozy antique-furnished 34-room hotel (illustrated above) run by a Swedish couple on a hideaway street just off the Boulevard St.-Germain. Popular among transatlantic diplomats and intellectuals (**Edward Albee,** author of *Who's Afraid of Virginia Woolf?,* stays here). Reservations for newcomers may be difficult, but keep trying. And garden lovers should ask for room No. 25, which has a flower-bedecked terrace. ♦ 14 Rue St.-Simon. Métro: Rue du Bac. 45.48.35.66

The number of newspapers in France is declining—and so is readership. Only one person in five reads a newspaper in France, compared to one in three in the United States and one in two in Britain. French newspapers also cost two to three times as much as their American and British counterparts. On the other hand, the number of magazines is skyrocketing, making the French the world's most avid magazine readers, with 1,345 copies printed for every 1,000 citizens. This is twice the rate in Britain and 25 percent more than in the United States.

11 The General Store For homesick Americans whose taste buds languish without delicacies such as Paul Newman's spaghetti sauce, Hellman's mayonnaise, taco shells, Cheerios, maple syrup, peanut butter, and pecans. The General Store also sells stuffed turkeys and homemade pumpkin pies during Thanksgiving week and cookbooks such as *La Cuisine Americaine* for French gourmands researching recipes for meatloaf or succotash. ♦ M-Sa 10AM-7:15PM. 82 Rue de Grenelle. Métro: Rue du Bac. 45.48.63.16

11 Chez Tourrette ★$ Across the street from the Four Seasons Fountain, **Madeleine Delaistre** serves a rib-sticking pot-au-feu and beef Bourguignonne for lunch in a quaint hole-in-the-wall restaurant/bar (one of the smallest in Paris) that's favored by lawyers and blue-collar workers. Delaistre's little dog, **Salers,** is all bark, and the fare is all bite. ♦ M-F 9AM-9PM. 70 Rue de Grenelle. No credit cards. Métro: Rue du Bac. 45.48.49.68

12 Superlatif Not as elegant as its former incarnation, **Papier +,** this stationery shop sells colored paper, designer pens, and assorted

LA COUR DE VARENNE

St.-Germain

doodads. ♦ M 1-7PM; Tu-Sa 10AM-7PM. 86 Rue du Bac. Métro: Rue du Bac. 45.48.84.25

12 Olivier de Sercey This tiny printing and engraving shop makes those dignified business cards dealt out by the ambassadors and government ministers whose offices are nearby. Wedding and party invitations are made here as well. ♦ M-F 9AM-7PM; closed in Aug, holidays. 96 Rue du Bac. Métro: Rue du Bac. 45.48.21.47, 45.49.20.80

12 La Boîte à Musique This antique shop specializes in 19th-century music boxes from France, England, and Switzerland. ♦ M 2-7:30PM; Tu-Sa 11AM-7:30PM; closed in Aug. 96 Rue du Bac. Métro: Rue du Bac. 42.22.01.30

Parlez Vous Anglais?

If English is your first—or only—language, and you need a book fix in Paris, here are the English-language bookstores of choice:

Albion 13 Rue Charles V	....	42.72.50.71
Attica 34 Rue des Ecoles	....	43.26.09.53
Brentano's 37 Avenue de l'Opéra	....	42.61.52.50
Galignani 224 Rue de Rivoli	....	42.60.76.07
Shakespeare and Company 37 Rue de la Bûcherie	....	No phone
Trilby's 18 Rue Franklin	....	45.20.40.49
Village Voice 6 Rue Princesse	....	46.33.36.47
W.H. Smith and Son 248 Rue de Rivoli	....	42.60.37.97

13 La Cour de Varenne The back door of this snobbish antique store opens onto a lovely courtyard where the servants' quarters of **Madame de Staël** still stand. There are two floors of carved wooden columns, clocks, 17th- and 18th-century furniture, Japanese lacquer, mother-of-pearl-framed mirrors, and early 19th-century paintings of hot-air balloons. ♦ Tu-F 10AM-1PM, 2-7PM; Sa 10AM-1PM, 2-6PM; closed in Aug. 42 Rue de Varenne. Métros: Rue du Bac, Sèvres-Babylone. 45.44.65.50

14 110 Rue du Bac After the sale of *The Artist's Mother* to the French government in 1893, **James McNeill Whistler** moved into a ground-floor apartment here and consorted with his artist-intelligentsia friends such as **Henry James, Edgar Degas, Edouard Manet,** and **Henri Toulouse-Lautrec.** ♦ Métro: Rue du Bac

15 La Pagode Those **Truffaut** and **Renoir** classics you've always sighed over may demand a new orientation in this authentic Chinese pagoda, the most unusual cinema in Paris. ♦ 57bis Rue de Babylone. Métro: St.-François-Xavier. 47.05.12.15

16 Au Bon Marché The oldest department store in Paris is especially famous for its *épicerie* (food market), which is the largest of its kind in the city (2,750 square meters) and sells everything from fresh oysters to foie gras. ♦ M-Sa 9:30AM-6:30PM. Epicerie: 8:30AM-9PM. 22 Rue de Sèvres. Métro: Sèvres-Babylone. 45.49.21.22. Epicerie: 45.48.47.94

17 La Vie Naturelle This beauty salon-cum-health food store run by the talented coiffeur and ex-Le Mans racecar driver **Jean-Pierre Régnier** proffers everything from honey shampoo and carrot cake to a smart haircut. ♦ M 1-7PM; Tu 10AM-7PM; W-Th 9:30AM-7PM; F 10AM-7:30PM; Sa 9AM-noon. 101 Rue du Bac. Métro: Rue du Bac. 45.48.90.58

18 Diners en Ville Tablecloths, candlesticks, china, earthenware, flatware—everything for the well-dressed table. ♦ 27 Rue de Varenne. Métro: Rue du Bac. 42.22.78.33

Restaurants/Nightlife: Red
Shops/ 🌳 Outdoors: Green
Hotels: Blue
Sights/Culture: Black

18 Kenzo Everyone's favorite Japanese designer splashes gorgeous colors to create amusing, informal clothes and accessories. ♦ M 11AM-7PM; Tu-Sa 10AM-7PM. 17 Blvd Raspail. Métro: Rue du Bac. 45.49.33.75

19 Fontaine des Quartre-Saisons The Four Seasons Fountain was designed in 1730 by **Bouchardon** to supply water to aristocrats in the wealthy Faubourg St.-Germain. This sculpture's magnificence is, as **Voltaire** once complained, squandered on a narrow street. ♦ 57-59 Rue de Grenelle. Métro: Rue du Bac

19 Roland Barthélemy Fromager The Elysée Palace buys its cheese at Barthélemy, which offers more than 50 kinds of chèvre (fresh goat cheese), the finest Vacherin (from October to February), and its special *boulamour,* a ball of enriched cow's cheese covered with kirsch-soaked raisins. ♦ Tu-F 8:30AM-1PM, 4-7:30PM; Sa 8:30AM-1:30PM, 3:30-7:15PM. 51 Rue de Grenelle. Métro: Rue du Bac. 45.48.56.75

20 Issey Miyake Artist **Shiro Kuramata's** white-plaster drapes make a stunning backdrop for Miyake's sculptural clothes. A fashion purist, this Tokyo-based designer creates all

his own fabrics, and dresses his followers for maximum comfort and ease of motion. Nearby are two other Miyake boutiques: **Hommes** (the men's store at 33 Blvd Raspail) and **Plantation** (the moderately priced unisex line at No. 17). ♦ M-Sa 10AM-12:30PM, 1:30-7PM; closed three weeks in Aug. 201 Blvd St.-Germain. Métro: Rue du Bac. 45.48.10.44, 45.44.60.48

21 Un Moment en Plus ★$ This bookshop/tea salon offers the latest in political journals and comic books, plus scrumptious tabouleh, onion tarts, and *fondant au chocolat* (chocolate mousse cake). The popular hangout is always crowded with students of the prestigious Ecole Science Politique, or Science Po, as the *intimes* dub it. ♦ M-F 10:30AM-8PM; Sa 12:30-7:30PM; closed in Aug. 1 Rue de Varenne. Métro: Rue du Bac. 42.22.23.45

22 Hotel Lutetia $$$ Fashion designer **Sonia Rykiel** spruced up the interiors of this turn-of-the-century luxury hotel with elegant gray and violet fabrics as well as Art Deco frescoes. ♦ 45 Blvd Raspail. Métro: Sèvres-Babylone. 45.44.38.10

Tourists often hum "April in Paris" with great hopes of clear weather, but Parisians know sunshine and spring don't hit town until May, when three long weekend holidays (Labor Day, Ascension, and Pentacost) give a foretaste of the summer vacations ahead. May is also the month for polo matches at the Club de Paris (otherwise closed to the public), and the glamorous French Tennis Open at Roland-Garros (but tickets are as rare as counterfeits are rife because the seats at center court are sold out by January to corporate clients from IBM and Christian Dior).

23 Atelier Guillaume Martel Have a special 17th-century portrait or modern print you need framed? Martel, a graduate of the prestigious **Ecole du Louvre,** specializes in *dorure froide* for both antique and contemporary prints. ♦ Tu-Sa 9-11AM, 3-7PM; closed in Aug. 2 Rue du Regard. Métro: Sèvres-Babylone. 45.49.02.07

24 Café Parisien ★★★$/$$ This modest café has garnered a large reputation. Its weekend brunches, pot-au-feu, hearty *plats du jour,* and *tarte tatin* draw a lively, often literary, throng. ♦ Daily noon-3PM, 8-11:30PM. 15 Rue d'Assas. Reservations recommended. No credit cards. Métro: Rennes. 45.44.41.44

25 Le Petit Bacchus ★★$$ The Left Bank wine bar owned by **Steven Spurrier** offers a respectable selection of Bordeaux, Côtes-du-Rhône, and Loire Valley wines. Delicious quiches, vegetable tarts, Auvergne charcuterie, country cheeses, and wines by the glass are further temptations. ♦ Tu-Sa 10:30AM-8:30PM. 13 Rue du Cherche-Midi. Métro: Sèvres-Babylone. 45.44.01.07

St.-Germain

25 Jule des Pres Ravishing dried-flower sculptures are designed by the much-imitated shop that opened nearly a decade ago in the Marais. Each piece is signed with a red-wax seal. ♦ M-Sa 11AM-7PM. 19 Rue du Cherche Midi. Métros: St.-Suplice, Sèvres-Babylone. 45.48.26.84

26 Soleil de Provence This friendly shop imports virgin olive oil, tapenade, almond soap, and herbs from Provence. Quite simply, it has much of the best that the sunbathed southern French province has to offer. ♦ Tu-Sa 10AM-7PM; closed in Aug. 6 Rue du Cherche-Midi. Métro: Sèvres-Babylone. 45.48.15.02

26 Poilâne The most famous baker in France, if not the world, **Lionel Poilâne** continues a family tradition started by his Norman father, **Pierre,** in 1933. The round sourdough country loaf baked in wood-fired ovens is served in some 400 Parisian restaurants and flown daily to expensive gourmet shops in New York and Tokyo. **Catherine Deneuve** and **Pierre Cardin** order specially decorated loaves for their parties, and **King Hussein** has it jetted to his palace.

If he's not too busy and you ask politely, Lionel may even take you down into the bakery's 12th-century cellars, where a bare-chested baker in shorts and a cap, like a Daumier cartoon, feeds lumps of dough into a wood-burning brick oven. ♦ M-Sa 7:15AM-8:15PM. 8 Rue du Cherche-Midi. Métro: Sèvres-Babylone. 45.48.42.59

27 **Le Recamier** ★★$$$ Situated in a serene cul-de-sac in the well-trodden St.-Germain shopping district, this elegant restaurant caters to the Paris publishing crowd and has one of the city's most peaceful outdoor terraces. Owner **Martin Cantegrit** features dishes from his native Burgundy: fricassee of snails and wild mushrooms, beef Bourguignonne *sans pareil,* as well as salmon tartare, an excellent summer starter. Cantegrit's wine list, which he calls "my little Bible," merits the appellation. ♦ M-Sa 12:30-2:30PM, 8-10:30PM. 4 Rue Recamier. Métro: Sèvres-Babylone. 42.22.51.75

28 **Au Sauvignon** ★$/$$ A trendy old wine bar papered with the inevitable maps of French wine regions. Still, in summer, it's not such a bad thing to order a plate of country-cured ham, some Cantal cheese, and a Sancerre rosé and sit at one of the sidewalk tables watching

St.-Germain

the world stroll by. ♦ M-Sa 8:30AM-10PM; closed in Aug. 80 Rue des Sts.-Pères. No credit cards. Métro: Sèvres-Babylone. 45.48.49.02

28 **Maude Frizon** More than 1,500 styles of handcrafted footwear are carried here. Next door at **Maude Frizon Club,** the shoes are almost as pretty, but they're machine-made and one-third the price. ♦ 83 Rue des Sts.-Pères. Métro: Sèvres-Babylone. 45.49.20.59

28 **Cassegrain** There's nothing quite like a proper thank-you note, or an engraved-in-gold place card. This stationer has been setting the standard since 1919. ♦ 81 Rue des Sts.-Pères. Métro: Sèvres-Babylone. 42.22.04.76

29 **31 Rue du Dragon** The **Académie Julian,** which was once here, admitted hundreds of aspiring American painters who were hoping to study on the GI bill after WWII but were unable to meet the stricter entrance requirements of the **Ecole des Beaux-Arts.** ♦ Métro: St.-Germain-des-Prés

29 **Chez Claude Sainlouis** ★$ For more than 25 years, the unfailingly popular restaurant of ex-stuntman **Claude Piau** has played it safe, serving an unchanging menu: steak, lamb chops, salad, and chocolate mousse. ♦ M-Sa 12:15-2:45PM, 8-11PM; closed one week at Easter, one week at Christmas, and Saturday evenings in Aug. 27 Rue du Dragon. Reservations recommended. No credit cards. Métro: St.-Germain-des-Prés. 45.48.29.68

30 **Yakijapo Mitsuko** ★★$/$$ One of the best sushi bars in Paris also serves sashimi and *yakitori* (broiled skewered meats and vegetables) at reasonable prices. ♦ Daily noon-2:30PM, 7-11:30PM. 8 Rue Sabot. Métro: St.-Germain-des-Prés. 42.22.17.74

31 **Brasserie Lipp** ★★$$ This famous Alsatian brasserie counts among its clients **Yves Saint Laurent** and **François Mitterrand.** A literary landmark, where waiters still dress in black waistcoats and long white aprons, Lipp is always replete with editors (from *Grasset, Gallimard,* and *Hachette*) and politicians. **De Gaulle** and **Pompidou** used to lunch at these tables, and **Ben Barka,** a Moroccan militant, was arrested here.

The ceilings are covered with buxom nudes; the walls are festooned with Art Nouveau ceramics and conveniently hung with mirrors so large you never need to crane your neck to watch the celebrities pass by. Lipp used to be run by the formidable **Roger Cazes** (whose father bought the establishment in 1920 from an Alsatian named **Lippman**), who seemed not to care for Americans of less cultural stature than **William Styron.** The best ploy for getting seated was to arrive on a rainy day in February just before 2AM—or shortly after a morning bomb scare.

During the reign of Cazes, anyone who was anyone sat on the main floor; upstairs was more or less Siberia. After his death, the new management restored the second floor so diners there need no longer feel banished. It is, of course, always possible to enjoy a Bavarian dark beer or cup of hot chocolate on the terrace; just don't tell anyone that's where you sat. The food is solid, though often disappointing. Stick with oysters, smoked salmon, and potato salad: they're hard to ruin. ♦ Daily 8AM-2AM. 151 Blvd St.-Germain. Reservations required. Métro: St.-Germain-des-Prés. 45.48.53.91

31 **Le Drugstore** ★$/$$ Here you can enjoy such French delicacies as le hamburger, le ice cream, and le Coca-Cola. Downstairs you can buy le newspaper *(The International Herald Tribune),* which arrives at 1AM the morning of publication. ♦ Store: daily 10AM-2AM. Restaurant: daily 9AM-2AM. 149 Blvd St.-Germain. Métro: St.-Germain-des-Prés. 42.22.92.50

32 **Baxter** Old prints, etchings, and lithographs abound in this charming shop that specializes in European architectural and botanical illustrations from the 17th to 19th centuries. The friendly staff has both a knowledge of and affection for the wares. Framing services are available, too. ♦ M 1-7PM; Tu-Sa 10AM-7PM. 15 Rue du Dragon. Métro: St.-Germain-des-Prés. 45.49.01.34

32 **Korean Barbecue** ★$/$$ The cook-it-yourself fare includes marinated beef and vegetables that you grill over a gas stove at your table. ♦ Daily noon-3PM, 7-11PM. 1 Rue du Dragon. No credit cards. Métro: St.-Germain-des-Prés. 42.22.26.63

33 **Restaurant Sts.-Pères** ★$/$$ At this century-old bistro, the waitresses in black uniforms with white collars look like they've just been fired from the household staff of Marcel Proust. The specialties include *poireaux*

vinaigrettes, coq au vin, *petit salé,* wild boar stew (in winter), and blueberry tarts. ♦ M-Tu, F-Su noon-2:20PM, 7-9:45PM; closed 15 Aug-15 Sep. 175 Blvd St.-Germain. Reservations recommended. No credit cards. Métro: St.-Germain-des-Prés. 45.48.56.85

34 Sts.-Pères $$$ The tastefully renovated hotel was designed in 1658 by **Alphonse Daniel Gittard,** who founded the Academy of Architecture under **Louis XIV** and whose portrait hangs behind the reception desk. If dozing off while staring up at a 17th-century ceiling painting of the *Crowning of Jupiter* is your idea of luxury, ask for Room No. 100. ♦ 65 Rue des Sts.-Pères. Métro: Sèvres-Babylone. 45.44.50.00

35 The Twickenham ★★$$ A favorite haunt of contemporary French philosopher and bestselling author **Bernard Henry Levy,** this English-style pub/restaurant is dimly lit, with plush red-leather booths and an elegant varnished bar. ♦ M-F 9:30AM-2AM; Sa 9:30AM-7PM; closed in Aug. 70 Rue des Sts.-Pères. Métro: Sèvres-Babylone. 42.22.96.85

35 Sabbia Rosa Sexy teddies and other alluring lingerie can be purchased for or by the femme fatale. ♦ M-Sa 10AM-7PM; closed last half of Aug. 73 Rue des Sts.-Pères. Métro: St.-Sulpice. 45.48.88.37

36 La Maison de Verre (Glasshouse) The extraordinary glasshouse of **Pierre Charreau** and **Bernard Bijovet** is a must for any student of 20th-century design. You can get a glimpse of the exterior from the courtyard, but for a look at the inside of the early 1930s building—a tour de force in glass-block-and-steel construction—you must make a reservation in advance. ♦ Send requests to: A.P. Vellay-Dalsace, 31 Rue St.-Guillaume, 75007 Paris. Métro: Sèvres-Babylone. 42.22.01.04

37 Edouard and Gabriel Bresset The Bressets are the leading French specialists in haute Epoque: wood carvings, furniture, sculptures, and paintings. ♦ M-Sa 10:15AM-12:30PM, 2:30-7PM; closed in Aug, first week of Sep. 197 Blvd St.-Germain. Métro: Rue du Bac. 45.48.18.24

38 Madeleine Gély Since 1834 the finest umbrella shop in Paris has been selling and repairing handmade *parapluies.* A limp isn't the only reason to buy one of Madeleine Gély's 400 unusual canes, which include duck- and bulldog-

headed canes, watch canes, whiskey-flask canes, and even a cane to measure the withers of a horse. ♦ Tu-Sa 9:30AM-7PM; closed in Aug. 218 Blvd St.-Germain. Métro: Rue du Bac. 42.22.63.35

39 Bar du Pont Royal ★★$ The dark, oak-paneled basement bar where right- and left-wing political columnists once came to argue over the Algerian war is today the turf of nattily dressed publishers courting promising reporters/novelists. ♦ M-Sa 11:30AM-1AM. 5 Rue de Montalembert. Métro: Rue du Bac. 45.44.38.27

39 Pont Royal $$$ Named for the nearby bridge, this comfortable hotel run by the Best Western chain has small rooms, courteous service, and a loyal clientele of international editors and publishers. ♦ 7 Rue de Montalembert. Métro: Rue du Bac. 45.44.38.27

40 Bistrot de Paris ★★$$/$$$ **Michel Oliver,** whose father owns the Grand Véfour, created this chic bistro, which has an innovative one-two punch: ravishing 1880s' decor with Belle Epoque mosaics and a classic menu of crab soup, braised pig's trotters, stewed beef in

wine sauce, and reliable Bordeaux. ♦ M-F noon-2PM, 8-11PM; Sa 8-11PM. 33 Rue de Lille. Reservations recommended. Métro: Rue du Bac. 42.61.16.83

41 Quai Voltaire This quai honors Voltaire, whose triumphant return in 1778 from 30 years of exile was greeted by a torchlight parade that wound from the **Comédie Française** (where his tragedy *Irène* had just opened) across the river to **No. 27,** where he died months later on 30 May 1778. The quai's history includes many artists: **Jean-Dominique Ingres** died on 14 January 1867 at **No. 11; Delacroix** and **Corot,** at different times, rented the top-floor studio at **No. 13;** in the hotel at **No. 19, Baudelaire** penned *Les Fleurs du Mal* in 1857; and **Wagner** composed *Die Meistersinger* here between 1861 and 1862. Today, it is a bazaar of first-rate antique shops and galleries. Side-by-side are well-known dealers such as **H. Berès Bailly** (No. 25), **De Jonckheere** (No. 21), **Jean Max Tassel** (No. 15), and **Michel Segoura** (No. 11). ♦ Métro: St.-Sulpice

Even though 500,000 French men and women are bitten by dogs each year (3,500 of the victims are postal carriers), dogs remain Parisians' best friends. Canines are welcome in some of the poshest restaurants in France, and they may even be served rice or pasta prepared by the master chef.

Every decade a new face is chosen to represent Marianne, the symbol for the French republic. Catherine Deneuve was her incarnation in the eighties. For the nineties, Inez de la Fressange, Chanel's top model, was given the honor, but she was dumped by Chanel shortly thereafter, based on charges of divided loyalty.

41 Restaurant Voltaire ★$$/$$$ Frequented by antique dealers and upper-class English folks, this restaurant/café has a maître d'hôtel with a knack for recognizing everyone—even on their first visit. ♦ Café: Tu-Sa 7:30AM-7PM. Restaurant: Tu-Sa 12:30-2:30PM, 7:30-10PM. Closed three weeks in Aug, one week in Feb, one week in May. 27 Quai Voltaire. Reservations recommended. No credit cards. Métro: Rue du Bac. 42.61.17.49

41 Quai Voltaire $$ **Baudelaire, Oscar Wilde, Richard Wagner,** and **Jean Sibelius** each came to this hotel looking for a room with a view. Do the same: ask for a front room (if you don't mind the traffic noise) and wake up to a vista of the Seine and the Tuileries. ♦ 19 Quai Voltaire. Métro: Solférino. 42.61.50.91

41 Sennelier A celebrated art-supply store patronized by the Left Bank's finest ꓹpainters. Even if you couldn't draw an apple to save your life, step inside and rub shoulders with the Beaux-Arts students shopping for linseed oil,

St.-Germain

blocks of brilliantly colored pastel chalks, and wooden palettes. ♦ M 9AM-noon, 2-6:15PM; Tu-Sa 9AM-6:15PM; closed in Aug. 3 Quai Voltaire. Métro: Rue du Bac. 42.60.72.15

42 7 Rue de Beaune **Henry James,** whose classic novel *The Ambassadors* featured American expatriates in Paris, came to visit **James Lowell** here in 1872, and as an added bonus found **Ralph Waldo Emerson** and his daughter, **Ellen,** in the sitting room. ♦ Métro: Rue du Bac

42 9 Rue de Beaune While living here at the Hotel Elysée in July 1920, **Ezra Pound** convinced **James Joyce** to move from Trieste and bring his family to Paris, where they lived nearby in a small hotel at **9 Rue de l'Université.** ♦ Métro: Rue du Bac

42 Le Cabinet de Curiosité Lined with panels from a late 18th-century pharmacy, this amusing shop displays scientific instruments, ancient technical books, monkey skeletons from Madagascar, brass hourglasses, ladies' shoes from the Louis XVI epoch, and an exquisite collection of Gothic keys and locks. Owner **Jean-Claude Guerin** is an expert in fine wrought iron. ♦ M-Sa 11AM-7PM; closed in Aug. 23 Rue de Beaune. Métro: Rue du Bac. 42.61.09.57

43 Université $$$ This smugly stylish hotel in a 17th-century town house is decorated with tapestries, antiques, and a small courtyard. ♦ 22 Rue de l'Université. Métro: Rue du Bac. 42.61.09.39

43 2-4 Rue de l'Université In 1776 **Benjamin Franklin** lived here at the former **Hôtel d'Entragues** while he was drumming up support for the American Revolution. ♦ Métro: Rue du Bac

44 Lenox $$$ The then 22-year-old **T.S. Eliot** spent a romantic summer here in 1910 on the old man's money, just before he took a job in a London bank and wrote *The Love Song of J. Alfred Prufrock.* Restored with chic simplicity and a slightly New Wave bar, the Lenox is a favorite of visiting fashion models. The women come and go thinking of Valentino. ♦ Bar: daily 5PM-2AM. 9 Rue de l'Université. Métro: Rue du Bac. 42.96.10.95

45 Debauve and Gallais This wood-paneled chocolate shop with a semicircular counter began as a pharmacy nearly 200 years ago when medicated chocolate was a nostrum for flatulence, anemia, and other ills. Today, in addition to delicious nonmedicinal chocolate, Debauve and Gallais sell an assortment of exotic teas from old metal canisters and ornate Chinese tea bricks used as legal tender for paying imperial taxes under the Sung Dynasty. ♦ Tu-Sa 10AM-7PM; closed last week of July, and the month of Aug. 30 Rue des Sts.-Pères. Métros: Rue du Bac, St.-Germain-des-Prés. 45.48.54.67

46 Coffee Parisien ★★$$ An American brunch is served all day. Franco-New Yorker **Jonathan Goldstein** (who manages Le Coffee Shop across the street, as well as Café Parisien on Rue Assas) serves pancakes with maple syrup, hash browns, bagels and cream cheese, eggs Benedict, bacon cheeseburgers, and more. The food is jazzed up with live blues performances on Friday nights. Goldstein's personal collection of Americana, which includes a 1950s Lucky Strike ad and *The New York Times* front page from 22 November 1963— the day President John F. Kennedy was assassinated in Dallas—decorate the walls. ♦ M-Th, Sa-Su 10AM-7PM; F 10AM-midnight. 5 Rue Perronet. Reservations recommended. Métro: St.-Germain-des Prés. 40.49.08.08

The French Are Famous for More Than Just Fries

Where would the world be without the croissant, the omelet, and mayonnaise, not to mention these other culinary gifts from the French:

Bouquet Garni—First used in French recipes in the mid-17th century, the combination of thyme, bay leaf, and parsley is a staple for sauces and soup stocks.

Peach Melba—August Escoffier created this luscious dessert in 1899 for singer Nellie Melba: a ripe peach with vanilla ice cream and fresh raspberry sauce.

Chicken Fricassee—The French method of frying chicken in fat, then adding a little liquid to create a sauce, has been around since the 15th century.

Food Processor—Created in 1964 by Pierre Verdun, this machine and its descendents revolutionized food preparation.

Pressure Cooker—Invented in 1679, it was first called a "steam digester" by its creator Denis Papin.

Soufflé—This most French of recipes made its first appearance in a 1730 cookbook.

60

46 Than ★★$ Don't let the crowds in the aisle or the swordfish teeth on the wall scare you away. This tiny Asian canteen is a popular bargain in the pricey St.-Germain quarter. For 24 years the affable Mr. Than has been serving delicious and affordable Cantonese and Vietnamese specialties to neighborhood editors, publishers, and medical students. He brags about the lacquered duck and carmelized spare ribs. ♦ M 7-11PM; Tu-Sa noon-2PM, 7-11PM. 42 Rue des Sts.-Pères. Métro: St.-Germain-des Prés. 45.48.36.97

47 Jean-Michel Beurdeley and Cie Proprietor of one of the boulevard's most inviting Asian art galleries, Beurdeley displays 18th-century Japanese paintings and eighth-century Chinese porcelain figures, but his most treasured item is an enormous second-century BC bronze drum from Southwest Asia. ♦ M-Sa 10AM-noon, 2:30-7PM; closed in Aug. 200 Blvd St.-Germain. Métro: Rue du Bac. 45.48.97.86

47 Galerie André-François Petit This fanciful surrealist gallery has brass door handles, whimsically designed by an artist named **Jette,** that look like a typesetter's nightmare. ♦ Tu-Sa 10:30AM-noon, 2:30-6:30PM; closed 14 July-15 Sep. 196 Blvd St.-Germain. Métro: Rue du Bac. 45.44.64.83

47 Relais St.-Germain ★★$$ Dine on respectable cuisine at prices even struggling writers can afford. Profiterole addicts swear by this place. ♦ M-Th, Su 12:15-2:30PM, 7:30-11PM; F, Sa 12:15-2:30PM, 7:30-11:30PM. 190 Blvd St.-Germain. Reservations recommended. Métro: Rue du Bac. 42.22.21.35, 45.48.11.73

48 Rue des Sts.-Pères Known in the 13th century as the **Chemins aux Vaches** (Cow Path), this street became **Rue de St.-Pierre** in the 16th century in honor of the Holy Fathers. ♦ Métros: Rue du Bac, St.-Germain-des-Prés

48 St.-Vladimir le Grand To catch a glimpse of Mother Russia, come on a Sunday morning and watch the rosy grandmothers wearing babushkas enter this Ukrainian church. ♦ 49-51 Rue des Sts.-Pères. Métros: Rue du Bac, St.-Germain-des-Prés

49 Orient-Occident The scholarly proprietor **Jean-Loup Despras** is an expert in hieroglyphics and acquires some of the most exquisite Egyptian, Greek, Roman, and Etruscan artifacts in Paris for this shop. His partner, **Yvonne Moreau-Gobard,** handles bronze, stone, and wood sculpture from China, India, Thailand, and Cambodia. ♦ M-Sa 10AM-12:30PM, 2-7PM; closed in Aug. 5 Rue des Sts.-Pères. Métros: Rue du Bac, St.-Germain-des-Prés. 42.60.77.65 (Jean-Loup Despras), 42.60.88.25 (Yvonne Moreau-Gobard)

The city of Paris employs a person to clean out the streets' gutters on a regular basis, which is once a day on most roads. The street cleaner has a special wrench to unleash a flood of water. And the same unpurified river water that cleans the streets also supplies the fire hydrants and irrigates the public gardens.

50 Alain Brieux This eclectic curio shop specializes in prints, Arabic astrolabes, and rare medical books that date back to the 14th century. Everything in the store is for sale except the gruesome model incorporating a real baby's skeleton and the alligator hanging from the ceiling. This latter item was a traditional feature in old apothecaries and alchemists' labs. ♦ M-F 10AM-1PM, 2-6:30PM; closed in Aug. 48 Rue Jacob. Métro: St.-Germain-des-Prés. 42.60.21.98

50 Angleterre $$$ Formerly the English Embassy, **Benjamin Franklin** refused to enter

the building to sign the US Declaration of Independence because he considered it British soil. Angleterre is now a picturesque hotel with a garden patio (**Hemingway** once lived in a small second-floor room). Ask for the large front room, No. 7. The bar and piano lounge are open 24 hours for hotel clients only. ♦ 44 Rue Jacob. Reservations required. Métro: St.-Germain-des-Prés. 42.60.34.72

50 Il Casanova ★★$/$$ A smiling Irish waitress serves visiting graduate students delicious tomato and mozzarella salad, minestrone soup, lasagna, and tortellini with mushrooms at this small, inexpensive Italian restaurant. ♦ M, W-Su noon-3PM, 6-11:30PM. 42 Rue Jacob. Dinner reservations recommended. Métro: St.-Germain-des-Prés. 42.60.36.83

51 Démons et Merveilles You'll find folk costumes from Romania, Hungary, Poland, Afghanistan, Tibet, and India, and all the garb you need to run away with the Gypsies here. **Faty,** the Tunisian owner, ran away from his law practice to start this shop. ♦ M-Sa 10AM-8PM. 45 Rue Jacob. Métro: St.-Germain-des-Prés. 42.96.26.11

51 Rue Jacob This street named after the Old Testament patriarch is chock-full of book and antique shops selling everything from autographs and old manuscripts to theater props and scientific instruments. ♦ Métro: St.-Germain-des-Prés

52 Le Petit St.-Benoît ★★$/$$ Offering indigent Left Bank intellectuals the same menu for 125 years now (including a respectable roast veal with mashed potatoes), this popular coach-house bistro has prices difficult to beat. And, as a bonus, the WC features a celebrated blue-and-white checked washbowl. ♦ M-F noon-2:30PM, 7-10PM. 4 Rue St.-Benoît. No credit cards. Métro: St.-Germain-des-Prés. 42.60.27.92

53 St.-Germain-des-Prés $$ In the heart of bustling St.-Germain, this small hotel is convenient but hardly tranquil. Breakfast is served in the garden room. ♦ 36 Rue Bonaparte. Métro: St.-Germain-des-Prés. 43.26.00.19

54 Shu Umura If you like art supply and stationery stores you'll love this Japanese cosmetics shop, which has some of the fascination of both. Compacts, lipstick, nail polish, creams, and brushes in every hue and shape imaginable are on display. This is but one of an international 6,000-shop chain created 20 years ago by makeup artist Shu Umura, who embellished the faces of Japan's most famous movie stars. ♦ M 11AM-7PM; Tu-Sa 10AM-7PM. 176 Blvd St.-Germain. Métro: St.-Germain-des-Prés. 45.48.02.55

55 Café de Flore ★★$$ **Jean-Paul Sartre** wrote of hanging out in this great café during WWII: "Simone de Beauvoir and I more or

St.-Germain

less set up house in the Flore. We worked from 9AM till noon, when we went out to lunch. At 2PM we came back and talked with our friends till 4PM, when we got down to work again till 8PM. And after dinner, people came to see us by appointment. It may seem strange, all this, but the Flore was like home to us: even when the air-raid alarm went, we would merely feign leaving and then climb up to the first floor and go on working ...." You don't have to be Sartre, **Camus,** or any other genius of a Flore regular to divine that the drink to order here in winter is hot grog (rum, tea, and lemon slices). And ask for extra slices because they never bring enough. If you're an early bird, the Flore is an excellent place to passionately peruse *Le Monde* and have a *real* breakfast of *oeufs au plat* (fried eggs), bacon, and croissants. ♦ Daily 7AM-1:30AM. 172 Blvd St.-Germain. No credit cards. Métro: St.-Germain-des-Prés. 45.48.55.26

55 La Hune Wedged between Café de Flore and Aux Deux Magots is one of the liveliest bookstores in Paris. La Hune provides literary sustenance to the Parisian men and women of letters (and those trying to resemble them) who frequent shrines to caffeine-driven cogitation. ♦ M 2PM-midnight; Tu-F 10AM-11:45PM; Sa 10AM-7:30PM. 170 Blvd St.-Germain. Métro: St.-Germain-des-Prés. 45.48.35.85

55 Le Montana Piano-Bar ★★$ Champagne at dawn, *pourquoi pas?* The surly, therefore authentic, bartender serves a seductive *Montana Fantaisie* made of pears, grenadine, orange juice, and champagne enhanced by live jazz in the evenings. ♦ Daily noon-6AM. 28 Rue St.-Benoît. Métro: St.-Germain-des-Prés. 45.48.93.08

55 Hôtel Montana $$ The lady knitting at the front desk sits in visual counterpoint to some of the hipper rock 'n' roll types that frequent this 19-room hotel. ♦ 28 Rue St.-Benoît. Métro: St.-Germain-des-Prés. 45.48.62.15

55 Le Bilboquet ★$$ On the former site of **Club St.-Germain,** an old existentialist haunt, this upbeat dinner-jazz club serves grilled rack of lamb and sides of beef. ♦ Restaurant: daily 8PM-2 or 3AM. Jazz starts at 10:30PM. 13 Rue St.-Benoît. Métro: St.-Germain-des-Prés. 45.48.81.84

55 Aux Deux Magots ★★★$/$$ If you've read *The Sun Also Rises,* you never need to be alone at this café. This is where Jake Barnes meets up with Lady Brett, and it is peopled with fictitious memories. **Hemingway** and his cronies met here to drink away the sting of rejection slips, a pastime he later reminisced about in *A Moveable Feast.*

The name of the café has nothing to do with fly larvae, but comes from the two statues of paunchy Chinese commercial agents—*magots*—that hang high on one of the pillars. They sit on money boxes. So does the new manager of Aux Deux Magots, who paid some $1.4 million in 1985 to purchase this literary mecca. Boasting that the Deux Magots is "The Rendezvous of the Intellectual Elite," the menu offers 25 kinds of whiskey and little pots of strong espresso. From May through August, the sidewalk entertainment on the terrace opposite the St.-Germain-des-Prés bell tower is always amusing and occasionally brilliant. ♦ Daily 7:30AM-1:30AM. 6 Place St.-Germain-des-Prés. No credit cards. Métro: St.-Germain-des-Prés. 45.48.55.25

55 Arthus-Bertrand This 150-year-old establishment casts reproductions of some of the Louvre's treasures in sterling or in 18-karat gold. It also supplies 80 percent of the military medals and decorations for African nations. (Business is usually brisk owing to the high turnover in excellencies.) For $6,000 to $20,000, they custom design the ceremonial swords worn by the "immortals" accepted into the Académie Française. The firm has a seriousness and a price list that will curb any idle browser. ♦ Tu-F 10AM-6:15PM; Sa 10AM-12:30PM, 2-6:15PM. 6 Place St.-Germain-des-Prés. Métro: St.-Germain-des-Prés. 42.22.19.20

56 **Embâcle** This sculpture (whose name means blockage in French) is not a ruptured water main but a practical joke of a fountain by **Charles Daudelin**. It was created in 1985. ♦ Métro: Blvd St.-Germain (Rue de Rennes). St.-Germain-des-Prés

57 **Hôtel de l'Abbaye** $$$ This 18th-century convent-turned-hotel has stone arches, antique furniture, plenty of peacefulness, and fresh cut flowers. Ground-floor rooms Nos. 2 and 3 open onto the trellised garden. ♦ 10 Rue Cassette. Reservations required. Métro: St.-Sulpice. 45.44.38.11

58 **58 Rue Madame** The oldest brother of **Gertrude Stein, Michael Stein,** and his artist wife, **Sarah,** moved here in 1903 and began buying the canvases of their close friend **Henri Matisse.** Within two decades, the Steins had assembled in this apartment one of the finest collections of Matisses, **Renoirs, Gauguins,** and **Picassos** in the world. ♦ Métro: St.-Sulpice

59 **Perreyve** $$ A quiet, newly renovated hotel just a minute's stroll from the Luxembourg Gardens. ♦ 63 Rue Madame. Métro: St.-Sulpice. 45.48.35.01

60 **Hôtel de l'Avenir** $$ This small hotel near the Luxembourg is tremendously popular with students. ♦ 65 Rue Madame. Métro: St.-Placide. 45.48.84.54

61 **La Table de Fès** ★★$$ Excellent North African couscous, chicken and lemon *tajine* (stew), and peppery *merguez* (lamb sausage) keep this Moroccan restaurant crowded and hopping. The spicy change of pace from all those French buttery cream sauces is welcome. This spot is best late at night. ♦ M-Sa 7:45PM-12:15AM; closed 15-31 Aug. 5 Rue Ste.-Beuve. Reservations recommended (call after 5PM). Métro: Vavin. 45.48.07.22

61 **Hôtel Ste.-Beuve** $$ This handsome hotel, ideally situated equidistant from La Coupole and the Luxembourg Gardens, was decorated by the master designer, **Christian Badin.** Any advice (on restaurants, gallery openings, concerts) received from **Alain** at the front desk is golden. ♦ 9 Rue Ste.-Beuve. Métro: Vavin. 45.48.20.07

62 **26 Rue Vavin** This luxury terraced apartment building was designed in 1925 by French architect **Henri Sauvage.** The splendid blue-and-white tile complex, complete with ground-floor shops and indoor parking, was an early attempt at a self-contained building: what Le Corbusier would call *unité d'habitation.* ♦ Métro: Vavin

62 **Marie-Papier** Attracting customers from Los Angeles to Tokyo, this famous French stationery store promotes an elegant line of colored paper in single sheets or large albums. ♦ M-Sa 10:30AM-7PM. 26 Rue Vavin. Métro: Vavin. 43.26.46.44

62 **Rouge et Noir** Games galore! This handsome shop sells fine-crafted miniature billiard tables, roulette wheels, hand-carved dominoes, Chinese checkers, Monopoly, and, yes, even Trivial Pursuit. ♦ Tu-Sa 10:30AM-1PM, 2-7PM. 26 Rue Vavin. Métro: Vavin. 43.26.05.77

63 **La Coupole** ★★$$ Along with the Brasserie Lipp and Le Balzar, La Coupole is the most popular café with a history. **Jean-Paul Sartre** dined here, as did **Eugène Ionesco,** who liked his coffee *liégeois.* **Alberto Sordi** lost himself in the curry while **Roman Polanski** played coy behind his menu. **Josephine Baker** frequented La Coupole accompanied by her lion cub. Novelists **Hemingway, Fitzgerald,** and **Joyce** also consorted here. When American breakfasts were the specialty at La Coupole, **Henry Miller** would come for his morning porridge. **Man Ray, Matisse,** and the famous **Kiki** of Montparnasse were part of the local fauna, too.

La Coupole was conceived in 1926 by **René Lafond.** While working at the Dôme Café, he negotiated a 20-year lease on the wood and coal depot across the street. He transformed

the building with red-velvet booths, jazz-age chandeliers, and a dozen columns painted by Montparnasse's artistic community. The story goes that the painter **Auffray,** whose studio was in Montparnasse, first suggested that real artists paint the Coupole's 12 columns. Lafond paid for the supplies and gave each artist a few good meals as an honorarium. **Léger's** contribution is to the left of the bar; the black rat dancing on the head of a flutist is by **Vassilief.** Other columns were painted by **Gris, Ribiera, Soutine, Chagall, Delaunay, Brancusi,** and **Foujita.** Matching the artist with his pillar has been a favorite Parisian pastime over dessert at La Coupole ever since.

Purchased for more than $10 million and restored by brasserie czar **Jean-Paul Boucher,** the cavernous dining room is classified as a historic monument, and therefore its columns have been preserved. La Coupole today is a watering hole for politicos, neighborhood merchants, aspiring actors, wandering poets, Scandinavian models, editors, and, most recently, the suburban hordes that invade the Montparnasse movie theaters on Saturday nights. La Coupole, so it is said, has the densest population of beautiful women in Paris here on weeknights; it is most chic, however, to make an appearance Sunday night. But on any night the atmosphere will be smokily festive. Expect a good time, but don't expect haute cuisine. The fare is simple and serviceable. In the basement is an enormous ballroom where the dance is so inviting, revelers literally kick off their shoes. ♦ Café: daily 7:30AM-2AM. Ballroom: F-Sa 9:30PM-4AM (tea dancing: Su 3-7PM). 102 Blvd du Montparnasse. No reservations taken after 8:30PM. Métro: Vavin. 43.20.14.20

Restaurants/Nightlife: Red
Shops/ 🌱Outdoors: Green

Hotels: Blue
Sights/Culture: Black

64 Dominique ★★$$ This restaurant/deli is as Russian as balalaikas. Grab a stool at the counter and snack on smoked salmon, pressed caviar, hot borscht, and blinis with sour cream. ♦ Downstairs take-out counter: daily 9:30AM-2:30PM, 5:15-10:30PM. Upstairs restaurant: daily 12:15-2:15PM, 7:15-10:30PM; closed mid-July to mid-Aug, one week in Feb. 19 Rue Bréa. Reservations recommended. Métro: Vavin. 43.27.08.80

65 Académie de la Grande-Chaumière Any closet Cézannes, budding Bonnards, or rising Renoirs in your traveling party? At this modest art academy you can draw or paint your own masterpiece from live models and carry it home for less than the cost of those imitation Toulouse-Lautrec posters sold on Rue de Rivoli. ♦ Painting and drawing: M-Sa 9AM-noon. Sketching: M-Sa 3-6PM; closed in Aug. 14 Rue de la Grande-Chaumière. Métro: Vavin. 43.26.13.72

66 La Caméléon ★★$$ A bohemian bastion for famished painters in the 1960s, La Caméléon has changed (regrettably retaining its black wallpaper, however) into a thriving neighbor-

St.-Germain

hood bistro serving the classic veal stew, hot sausage, smoked haddock, and a wide selection of salads. Those with a sweet tooth swoon for the white chocolate mousse and iced tea (with fresh mint) soufflé, a recipe the owners borrowed from their children, who operate **Gerard et Nicole,** a first-rate Montparnasse restaurant. Splurge on a delicious old Bourgueil wine with your meal. ♦ Tu-Sa 12:15-2:15PM, 8:15-10:30PM; closed in Aug. 6 Rue de Chevreuse. Dinner reservations recommended. No credit cards. Métro: Vavin. 43.20.63.43

67 La Closerie des Lilas ★★$$ This legendary restaurant is where lilacs once bloomed, where **Hemingway** and **Henry James** hung out, where the defenders of Dreyfus plotted, and where **Gide, Verlaine, Châteaubriand, Ingres,** and **Trotsky** expounded. (Trotsky, **Lenin,** and the Russian crowd actually preferred La Rotonde, which opened down the street around 1911, 103 years after La Closerie des Lilas. Serious drinkers convened at Le Dôme Café, and the American crowd hung out at La Coupole—both are located down the block.) Today La Closerie des Lilas is frequented by young French film stars and other constellations of the pretty and superchic. It's expensive and a little pretentious, but not bad for an after-dinner drink or a weekend lunch in the mottled light of its outdoor terrace, especially during August when the rest of Paris shuts down. Try the steak tartare, *pigeon de Bresse rôti, rumsteack Hemingway flambé au Bourbon,* or the best-selling *turbotin grillé.* The piano kindles a certain warmth as well. ♦ Daily 10:30AM-1:30AM. 171 Blvd du Montparnasse. Reservations required. Métro: Port Royal. 43.26.70.50, 43.54.21.68

68 93 Boulevard St.-Michel During WWII, the Nazi's searched for two years for **Sylvia Beach,** founder of the famous Paris **Shakespeare and Company** bookstore (see page 35), who hid here in a top-floor kitchen. ♦ Métro: Luxembourg (RER)

69 Luxembourg Gardens As a part of his draconian remodeling of Paris, **Baron Haussmann** had a plan to change this precious green expanse but was thwarted when 12,000 Parisians signed a petition to save the park. In the heart of the Left Bank, the 60-acre playground is graced with fountains, sculptures, ponds, flowerbeds, tennis courts, pony rides, a marionette theater, and outdoor band concerts. The open-air café is dappled with a light filtering through the leaves of the surrounding trees that recalls the most pleasant moods of Impressionism. The park is under heavy surveillance by officious *gardiens* (guards) enforcing regulations stating that "the park is out of bounds to the drunk, beggars, and the indecently dressed; the playing of cards is restricted to the northwest corner of the gardens; the kicking of balls and sitting on the grass is prohibited entirely; and the park must be vacated precisely 30 minutes before sunset." Doing their duty, uniformed guards trill their whistles to chase lingerers from the gardens.

As for those ever-amusing Americans in Paris: in 1900 **Isadora Duncan** was wont to dance here at 5AM, when the gardens opened, and **Hemingway** at his most destitute used to capture and strangle pigeons from the garden in order to come up with something for lunch. Do not miss the Luxembourg's many hidden delights: the small bronze replica of the Statue of Liberty; a series of statues of French queens and famous 19th-century women standing among the crocuses, daffodils, and azaleas; a beekeeping school run by Esperanto-speaking Dominican friar **René-Jean Marmou,** curator of the apiary, who gives practical classes on Tuesday and Saturday from April to September through the Centrale d'Apiculture (41 Rue Pernety, 45.42.29.08); and the *pétanque* bowlers and chess players sequestered in their respective corners of the gardens. On weekends, a swarm of smartly dressed Latin Quarter grade-schoolers romp here (attended by their white-collar parents) and compete in the park's tricycle races and toy sailboat regatta held in the octagonal basin at the center of the park. ♦ Métros: Luxembourg (RER), N.D. des Champs, St.-Sulpice

70 Dalloyau ★★$$ To sip a civilized cup of Chinese tea or indulge in a stately scoop of homemade ice cream or a delicate pastry while gazing over the Luxembourg Gardens from Dalloyau's terrace is to taste the luxury and leisure of an earlier, more gracious era. ♦ M-Sa 9:30AM-7:30PM; Su 9AM-7:00PM. 2 Place Edmond-Rostand. Métro: Luxembourg (RER). 43.29.31.10

70 Rue Monsieur le Prince Monsieur le Prince is what every French king's brother was traditionally called. During the last century, this street was a veritable American alley, as evidenced by the events that took place at the following addresses. **No. 14:** in March 1959 **Martin Luther King Jr** visited black novelist **Richard Wright** in his third-floor apartment. **No. 22:** in 1892 **James McNeill Whistler** had a studio on the courtyard, where he completed a portrait of **Count Robert de Montesquieu** (years later, the count sold the painting for an exorbitant sum, thereby greatly offending Whistler. The portrait now hangs in the Frick Museum in New York). **No. 49:** the poet **Henry Wadsworth Longfellow** lived here in June 1826. He made his contribution of $36 a week to the Parisian economy, which gained him not only a room in the *pension de famille* of **Madame Potet,** but also French lessons with her daughters and free laundry service. **No. 55:Oliver Wendell Holmes** lived here (now the site of the **Lycée St.-Louis**) from 1833 to 1835 while he studied to be a doctor. To be on the safe side, the following year he obtained a second medical degree from Harvard. ♦ Métro: Odéon

70 Slice ★★$ If you crave mozzarella and an aroma of Manhattan, Slice serves the best New York pizza in town. You will also find highly respectable chocolate chip cookies and brownies and a moist banana-chocolate cake. ♦ Daily 11AM-11PM. Delivery: noon-2:30PM, 6:30-11PM anywhere in Paris. 62 Rue Monsieur-le-Prince. No credit cards. Métros: Luxembourg (RER), Odéon. 43.54.18.18

71 Médici Fountain At the end of a long, somewhat slimy pool filled with goldfish is one of the few Italianate stonework remnants of **Marie de Médici's** day. White marble nude lovers, *Acis* and *Galatea,* are eyed from above by the bronze Cyclops *Polyphemus,* who waits to do the Greek mythic version of kicking sand in the face of the 98-pound weakling before making off with the girl. Notice the trompe l'oeil effect of having the water appear to flow uphill into the grotto. On the back side of the fountain is a delightful bas-relief of *Leda and the Swan* by **Valois.** ♦ 15 Rue de Vaugirard. Métro: Luxembourg (RER)

72 Luxembourg Palace In 1610 the assassin **Ravaillac** could hardly have imagined that his murder of **Henri IV** would result in the creation of this splendid palace and gardens. (Indeed he didn't live long enough after committing his dastardly deed to imagine much of anything.) The widow of Henri IV, **Queen Mother Marie de Médici,** tired of the Louvre, decided to build a palace that would recall her native Italy. She bought this vast property at the southern edge of the city from **Duke François de Luxembourg** and dispatched an architect to Florence to study her family residence, the Pitti Palace, before making plans for the new palace. Obediently, **Salomon de Brosse** designed Luxembourg Palace for her. Work began in 1615, but, ironically, by the time the residence reached completion in 1631, Marie had been banished by her own son, **Louis XIII,** for turning against **Cardinal Richelieu.** She died penniless in Cologne 11 years later. During the Revolution, the palace served a short stint as a prison; it was here that "Citizen Paine," the American **Thomas Paine,** languished as an enemy Englishman for more than 10 months during the 1793 Reign of Terror and narrowly escaped execution.

St.-Germain

Subsequently, Luxembourg Palace was remodeled to house the newly created French Senate, which met for the first time in 1804 and still resides here. Few of the trappings of Marie de Médici's time remain; the 19th-century architect **Chalgrin** (who also designed the Arc de Triomphe) made sure of that in his democratic remodeling. The 24 images of the queen's life story created by **Rubens** were moved to the Louvre and the Uffizi Gallery in Florence. Chalgrin festooned the library with the paintings of **Delacroix** in homage to Virgil, Homer, and Dante. On the one day each month that the palace is open, visitors queue around the block, looking disturbingly like a bread line. For guided tours, call the **Caisse Nationale des Monuments Historiques** at 44.61.20.00. ♦ Closed to the public except the first Sunday of each month at 10:30AM. 15 Rue de Vaugirard. Métro: Luxembourg (RER)

Le Beaujolais nouveau est arrivé! Every third Thursday in November the arrival of the new Beaujolais makes headlines around the world. Once considered too young to be of enological interest, today this fruity wine from southern Burgundy enjoys the French wine industry's finest hour of marketing. Two-thirds of the Beaujolais Nouveau are sold abroad, mostly in the United States, Japan, and Canada. On Beaujolais Nouveau Thursday, wine bars throughout Paris are giddy with bacchanalian enjoyment. The rowdy crowd at the tiny but popular Le Rubis (10 Rue du Marche-St.-Honoré) overflows onto two city blocks. Other popular Beaujolais *dégustation* points include Taverne Henri IV (13 Place du Pont-Neuf) and Au Sauvignon (80 Rue des Saints-Peres). Vilfeu Glacier (3 Rue de la Cossonnerie) celebrates the occasion with a refreshing Beaujolais Nouveau sorbet.

73 Théâtre de l'Odéon City architects **Marie-Josephe Peyre** and **Charles de Wailly** designed this rather clumsy building in 1782, intending it to look like an antique temple. With 1,913 seats, it was the largest theater in Paris. The **Beaumarchais'** *Marriage of Figaro* premiered here on 27 April 1784 in an atmosphere of success and scandal; the author was jailed. After WWII, **Jean-Louis Barrault** and **Madeleine Renaud** revived interest in the theater with their productions of works by

St.-Germain

Beckett, Ionesco, Albee, and Claudel, which became the talk of the town and, for a short period, made the theater the most popular in Paris. ♦ Ticket office: daily 11AM-6:30PM. 1 Place Paul-Claudel. Métro: Luxembourg (RER). 43.25.70.32

74 Polidor ★★$/$$ For more than a century, Polidor's home-cooking has lured writers such as **Hemingway, Joyce, Valéry,** and **Verlaine** out of their garrets for the earthy consolations of the pumpkin soup, roast chicken, bacon and lentils, and rabbit in mustard sauce. Since its founding in 1945, little has changed; Polidor still has the classic bistro decor, homey lace curtains, and tiny wooden drawers where the regulars store their linen napkins. One customer has dined here every evening for 40 years. Even the prices have stayed within a garret-dweller's means. ♦ Daily noon-2:30PM, 7PM-12:30AM. 41 Rue Monsieur-le-Prince. No credit cards. Métros: Luxembourg (RER), Odéon. 43.26.95.34

75 Chez Maître Paul ★★$$/$$$ Like a country cottage hidden deep in the Franche-Comté region of eastern France, this restaurant comes with white tablecloths and a warm welcome from the **Gaugain** family. The kitchen is famous for its variety of wine sauces and a winning way with chicken and veal. ♦ Tu-Sa noon-2:30PM, 7-10:30PM; closed in Aug, Christmas, and New Year's Day. 12 Rue Monsieur-le-Prince. Reservations recommended. Métros: Luxembourg (RER), Odéon. 43.54.74.59

Although Paris is home to only about 20 percent of the regional population, the central city employs approximately 40 percent of its workers.

76 La Mediterranée ★$$ This old haunt of **Marlene Dietrich** and **Jean Cocteau** serves seafood specialties such as marinated mussels, bouillabaisse, and *barre grillé.* ♦ Daily noon-3PM, 7PM-2AM. 2 Place de l'Odéon. Métro: Odéon. 43.26.46.75

77 12 Rue de l'Odéon From 1921 to 1940 this was the famous bookstore **Shakespeare and Company,** run by **Sylvia Beach,** daughter of a Presbyterian minister from Princeton, New Jersey. Her shop was a Parisian hearth and home for American and British writers such as **Ezra Pound, Archibald MacLeish, Thornton Wilder,** and **F. Scott Fitzgerald,** to whom she served as guardian angel. She was constantly lending books and money to **Ernest Hemingway,** who came to Paris in 1921 and, after the publication of *The Sun Also Rises,* became the city's most famous expatriate writer, influencing many generations of American fiction writers as well.

Beach was devoted to literature in general and to one writer in particular: **James Joyce.** If it hadn't been for this amazing woman, perhaps the most important literary event of the day might never have happened: the publication, in full, of *Ulysses.* Beach accomplished that feat by becoming Joyce's secretary, editor, agent, and banker. She nearly went blind typing his illegible manuscript, and the publishing costs practically bankrupted Shakespeare and Company. ♦ Métro: Odéon

78 19 Rue de Tournon In May 1790 the American Revolutionary naval officer **John Paul Jones,** having served a year in the Russian navy, moved to Paris, where he was welcomed as a national hero for his epic 1779 capture of the *Serapis,* a British warship. Jones died destitute in this second-floor flat on 18 July 1792. The fact that he received a full-scale state funeral paid for by the French government was no consolation and no small irony. ♦ Métro: Luxembourg (RER)

79 Grand Hôtel des Principautés Unies $$ In a top-floor flat, **William Faulkner** set to work on his first novel, *The Mosquitoes,* in the summer of 1925. Perhaps you will be so inspired here. ♦ 42-44 Rue de Vaugirard. Métro: St.-Sulpice. 46.34.11.80

80 Au Bon St.-Pourçain ★★$$ One of the few remaining authentic Lyonnais bistros in Paris. Chef **Daniel Pesle** fuels his regulars from the neighborhood with aioli, cassoulet, and his quick wit. ♦ M-F noon-3PM, 8-11:15PM. 10bis Rue Servandoni. Métro: Mabillon. 43.54.93.63

81 Le Petit Journal Jazz of every stripe, from Dixieland to fusion and back again to bebop, can be heard in **Claude Bolling's** favorite club. Other performers here include **Sacha Distel, Bill Coleman, Sugar Blue, Doctor Feelgood,** and the **Metropolitan Jazz Band.** ♦ Daily 10PM-2AM; closed in Aug. 71 Blvd St.-Michel. Métro: Luxembourg (RER). 43.26.28.59

81 Rue Férou Stroll down the street of the following artistic addresses. **No. 2:** painter/photographer **Man Ray** occupied an *atelier* (studio) with a high ceiling here in 1951; **No. 6: Hemingway** lived in this sphinx-protected *hôtel particulier* in 1926 while writing *A Farewell to Arms,* having left his wife, **Hadley,** for French *Vogue* staffer **Pauline Pfeiffer;** and **No. 13:** painter **Henri Fantin-Latour** had an apartment here in 1858, where he was sketched by his friend **James McNeill Whistler** (whose drawing was later purchased by the Louvre). ♦ Métro: St.-Sulpice

82 Place St.-Sulpice One of the most serene squares in Paris has a café, pink-flowering chestnut trees, and the marvelous stone *Fountain of the Cardinal Points* by **Visconti,** (pictured above) featuring four famous French clergymen oriented north, south, east, and west, with four regal lions snarling at their feet. Once flanked by shops peddling ivory crucifixes, rosary beads, and clerical garments, the square today is graced by two **Yves Saint Laurent** boutiques and hosts antique and book fairs in summer, and, for many, the finest of the Bastille Day balls. ♦ Métro: St.-Sulpice

<hr>

Roll over Descartes. Although the French educational system is firmly rooted in the Cartesian tradition of accepting no idea without rigorous critical analysis, an enormous proportion of France pays homage to astrology, fortune-telling, and other forms of divination. Major Parisian corporations are known to consult handwriting analysts and astrologers before hiring job candidates. More than 40,000 professional astrologists (which is more than the number of Catholic clergy in Paris) declare their income to tax authorities, and a full 15 percent of the revenues earned by the Minitel, the state-owned videotex system, is generated by astrology services.

<hr>

Restaurants/Nightlife: Red **Hotels:** Blue **Shops/ 🌳 Outdoors:** Green **Sights/Culture:** Black

82 Church of St.-Sulpice Interrupted by insurrection, insolvency, and even bolts of lightning, the construction of this church required

the services of architects, including the notable **Louis Le Vau,** over a span of 134 years. Its dramatic classical style was the inspiration of **Giovanni Servandoni,** a Florentine known for his theater and stage-set designs. The disparity of the two towers, an odd couple indeed, was the result of shifting architectural sands and patronly indecision. Named after **Saint Sulpicius,** the sixth-century archbishop of Bourges, and dubbed the Temple of Victory during the Revolution, the church hosted a lavish banquet for 1,200 after Napoléon returned from his victories in Egypt. Inside the front door are two holy water stoups made from enormous shells given to **François I** by the Venetian Republic. The first chapel on the right was frescoed by an aging **Eugène Delacroix.** In a chapel at the rear of the church is the extraordinary *Virgin and Child* by **Jean-Baptiste Pigalle.** The organ, designed in 1776 by **Chalgrin,** with 6,588 pipes, numbers among the largest in the world.

In the floor, running along the north-south transept, is a bronze meridian line, a testament to France's 19th-century passion for science. Three times a year, on the equinoxes and the winter solstice, sunlight strikes the line so precisely that light runs along the metal strip, glances off an obelisk and globe at its top, and finally illuminates a cross. The inscription on the obelisk translates, more or less, as "Two Scientists with God's Help." Outside on the sunny southeast corner of the church you can glimpse the caretaker's rooftop garden; during particularly hot summers, he sells his bumper crop of strawberries and tomatoes to tourists. ♦ Daily 8AM-7PM. Place St.-Sulpice. Métro: St.-Sulpice. 46.33.21.78

83 Djuri ★★$$ In his intimate basement club, venerable guitarist and singer **Djuri Cortez** performs Russian, Yiddish, Romanian, and Gypsy folk music into the wee hours. Nice things happen here: the ravishing Yugoslav at the next table may entice you to dance, for example. Djuri's upstairs restaurant serves Hungarian goulash, chopped liver, stuffed peppers, and Transylvanian cabbage. ♦ Restaurant: Tu-Su 7PM-2AM; closed in Aug. Club: Tu-Su 10:30PM-1:45AM; closed in Aug. 6 Rue des Canettes. Métro: Mabillon. 43.26.60.15

84 Grand Hôtel des Balcons $$ A comfortable, reasonably priced hotel down the street from the Théâtre de l'Odéon. ♦ 3 Rue Casimir-Delavigne. Métros: Luxembourg (RER), Odéon. 46.34.78.50

84 Bartolo ★★$$ The service is sauntering and the prices inflated at this Italian restaurant, but *Madonna*, the pizzas and pasta al dente are delicious. ♦ Tu-Sa 7-10:30PM. 7 Rue des Canettes. Métro: Mabillon. 43.26.27.08

84 Chez Georges ★★$ Locating an alley called Duckling Street, faced with superabundant

St.-Germain

Italian restaurants, the footloose walker stumbles onto this classic old French bar wallpapered with mug shots of the singers who perform in the cabaret downstairs. It's a nice place for a glass of Côtes-du-Rhône or Beaujolais before dining on canelloni and pizza down the street. ♦ Tu-Sa noon-2AM. 11 Rue des Canettes. No credit cards. Métro: Mabillon. 43.26.79.15

84 The Village Voice In the intelligent tradition of those famous interwar Left Bank bookstore/salons run by women such as Sylvia Beach and Adrienne Monnier, the English bookshop of **Odile Hellier** is a busy crossroads for Anglophone writers, artists, and literati in Paris. Hellier has something for everyone: a fine selection of classical, contemporary, and small-press fiction, exceptional author readings, and the latest issues of *The New York Review of Books, The New Yorker,* and (naturally) *The Village Voice.* ♦ M 2-8PM; Tu-Sa 11AM-8PM; closed two weeks in Aug. 6 Rue Princesse. Métro: Mabillon. 46.33.36.47

84 Bistro Henri ★★$ The first-rate neighborhood bistro is known for its delicious *magret de canard*, green bean vinaigrette, *foie de veau*, baked goat-cheese salad, au gratin potatoes, and homemade tarts. ♦ M 7:30PM-midnight; Tu-Sa noon-2PM, 7:30PM-midnight. 16 Rue Princesse. Reservations required. No credit cards. Métro: Mabillon. 46.33.51.12

In France, the ground floor of a building is called the *rez-de-chaussée* (which is what Americans would call the first floor) and the *premier étage* (first floor) is considered the second floor of the building, and so forth.

84 Castel's ★$$$ The most private of the city's private clubs, Castel's caters to dandies, back-biting gossips, the most clean-cut "BCBGs" (the French term for yuppies), and former cabinet ministers with socialite dream girls on their arms.

Technically, no one crosses **Jean Castel's** threshold unaccompanied by a card-carrying member (some privileged 2,500 people), but if you're dressed acceptably (coat and tie) and speak some French to **Corinne** at the box office window...*peut-être*. The decor is tacky, the food unremarkable, and the disco floor crowded—so what's all the fuss about? ♦ Restaurant: M-Sa 9PM-1AM. Disco: M-Sa 11:30PM-dawn. Ground-floor canteen: M-Sa 9PM-5AM. 15 Rue Princesse. Métro: Mabillon. 43.26.90.22

84 Birdland ★★$ The jazzy bar serves chili con carne and plays classic **John Coltrane** and **Charlie Parker.** ♦ M-F 7PM-dawn; Sa 10PM-dawn. 18 Rue Princesse. Métro: Mabillon. 43.26.97.59

Artists' Ateliers

If you'd rather see where art begins instead of where it ends up, the following artists' *ateliers* (studios) are open to the public:

Constantin Brancusi The sculptor willed his Montparnasse atelier and its contents of more than 110 works to France on the condition that they be maintained in the place that had been his home for 30 years. His wishes were met, in spirit. The former four-room Montparnasse atelier has been reconstructed in the Beaubourg and has been dubbed the Pompidou Center's potting shed. ♦ Admission. M, W-F noon-10PM; Sa-Su 10AM-10PM. Georges Pompidou Center. Métros: Hôtel-de-Ville, Rambuteau. 42.77.11.12, 42.77.12.33

Emile-Antoine Bourdelle This conglomeration of workshops, galleries, and gardens pays homage to the work of the sculptor who spent 15 years with Rodin as pupil, assistant, collaborator, and friend. The museum, which is run by his daughter, Madame Rhodia Dufet-Bourdelle, contains 21 studies of Beethoven, with whom he was fascinated, as well as casts of his sculptures and busts of Ingres, Rodin, and Rembrandt. ♦ Admission. Tu-Su 10AM-5:40PM. 16 Rue Antoine-Bourdelle. Métros: Falguière, Montparnasse-Bienvenue. 45.48.67.27

Eugène Delacroix In 1857 Delacroix took these rooms for their proximity to St.-Sulpice and for their privacy. He had given up the profligate ways of youth for painting. "I go to work as other men run to their mistresses," he said. ♦ Admission. M, W-Su 9:45AM-12:30PM, 2-5:15PM. 6 Rue de Furstemberg. Métro: St.-Germain-des-Prés. 43.54.04.87

Gustave Moreau No starving artist here. Moreau moved into this elegant town house with his parents in 1854 and stayed here until he died in 1898. The four-story mansion contains more than 1,100 paintings, drawings, and illustrations. ♦ Admission. W-Su 10AM-1PM, 2-5PM. 14 Rue de la Rochefoucauld. Métro: Trinité. 48.74.38.50

85 Aux Charpentiers ★★$$ Formerly the lunch hall of an 18th-century carpenters guild, this reasonably priced bistro serves chef **Pierre Bardeche's** simple but well-prepared bacon and lentils, beef stew, sautéed veal, and other daily specials. ♦ M-Sa noon-3PM, 7-11:30PM. 10 Rue Mabillon. Reservations recommended. Métro: Mabillon. 43.26.30.05

85 Guy ★★$$ Brazilian music, spicy shrimp with pepper, and the delicious (but unpronounceable) *empajadas de camarao* and *feijoada churrascos* lure expatriates from Rio. A live Brazilian band plays during Saturday lunches. ♦ M-F 7:45PM-1AM; Sa noon-3:30PM, 7:45PM-1AM; closed in Aug. 6 Rue Mabillon. Reservations required. No credit cards. Métro: Mabillon. 43.54.87.61

86 Marché St.-Germain The old covered market bustles with cobblers, fishmongers, dairymaids, and tripe peddlers. Next to the market are an underground basketball court and a 25-meter public swimming pool, the Piscine St.-Germain. ♦ Market: Tu-Sa 9AM-1PM, 4-7:30PM; Su 9AM-1PM. Pool: Tu 7-8:30AM, 11:30AM-1:30PM, 5-8PM; W 7-8:30AM, 11:30AM-6PM; Th-F 7-8:30AM, 11:30AM-1:30PM; Sa 7AM-6PM; Su 8AM-6PM. (Hours vary during summer holidays and school vacations.) Rue Mabillon (Rue Lobineau). Métro: Mabillon

Jazz Joints

In the forties and fifties, when the Latin Quarter's underground dives resonated to the sounds of saxophones, Paris was the undisputed jazz capital of the world. In the sixties, seventies, and eighties, cities in the United States and Japan laid claim to that fame, but now Paris is staging a comeback. Here are some of the city's best spots for all that jazz:

Au Duc des Lombards
42 Rue des Lombards 42.36.51.13

Baiser Sale 4 Rue des Lombards 23.33.37.71

Le Bilboquet 13 Rue St.-Benoît 45.48.81.84

L'Eustache 37 Rue Berger 40.26.23.20

Jazz Club Lionel Hampton Hôtel Meridien, 71 Boulevard Gouvion-St.-Cyr 47.58.12.30

Magnetic Terrace
26 Rue de la Cossonnerie 42.36.26.44

Le Mecene 4 Rue des Lombards 42.77.40.25

Le Montana 28 Rue St.-Benoît 45.48.93.08

Montgolfier Hôtel Sofitel,
8 Rue Louis Armand 40.60.30.30

New Morning 7-9 Rue des
Petites-Ecuries 45.23.51.41; 47.45.82.58

Le Petit Journal/Montparnasse 13 Rue du Commandant Rene Mouchotte 43.21.56.70

Le Petit Opportun 15 Rue des Lavandieres Ste.-Opportune 43.21.56.70

Le Sunset 60 Rue des Lombards 40.26.46.60

Le Village 7 Rue Gozlin 43.26.80.19

87 Le Petit Vatel ★★$ One of Paris' smallest and cheapest restaurants is filled with famished students and artists huddling around three tables by a lavender stove. Tasty daily specials include Brazilian red beans, ratatouille, moussaka, roast pork, poached fish, and chocolate cake. ♦ M-Sa noon-3PM, 7PM-midnight; Su 7PM-midnight; closed one week at Christmas. 5 Rue Lobineau. Métro: Mabillon. 43.54.28.49

88 Au Savoyard ★★$$$ For 32 years this colorful restaurant has been serving authentic French Alpine cuisine in the midst of Paris. The wooden chairs, wild-game trophies, paintings of mountain scenes, and peacock feathers provide an appropriately rustic setting for the fine Alpine fare of chef **Leao**. House specialties are raclette (melted raclette cheese, potatoes, and ham), Savoyard fondue, and smoked Savoie sausages. Au Savoyard is a regional gem. ♦ Daily noon-2:30PM, 7-11:30PM; closed in Aug. 16 Rue des Quatre-Vents. Reservations recommended. Métro: Odéon. 43.26.20.30

St.-Germain

89 Carrefour de l'Odéon A crossroads of sorts ruled over by a great pigeon-limed bronze of **Danton,** that Revolutionary leader whose statements such as "We need audacity, more audacity, audacity forever..." cost him his head when he was sent to the guillotine by **Robespierre** in 1794. ♦ Métro: Odéon

89 Christian Tortu One of the hottest new florists in town. Tortu creates opulent and original designs with flowers and vegetables. Garden furniture is also sold. ♦ M-F 9AM-7PM; Sa 9AM-6PM. 6 Carrefour de l'Odéon. Métro: Odéon. 43.26.02.56

90 Rue de l'Ecole de Médecine During the Revolution, **Jean-Paul Marat** founded the biting journal *L'Ami du Peuple* and was forced to hide in the Paris sewers. The radical democrat was elected to the National Convention three years later with the support of **Danton** and **Robespierre** but soon learned that you can't please all of *le peuple* all of the time. On 13 July 1793 Marat was stabbed while taking a bath in his house along this street. His killer was Girondist **Charlotte Corday,** who had hidden a cheap knife in her bodice. For the surprisingly ungory details of this assassination, see **David's** painting in the Louvre's Salle des Etats. ♦ Métro: Odéon

91 Rue des Ciseaux Named after a scissors craftsman who once resided here, this short street is home to three Japanese restaurants and an Italian pizzeria. ♦ Métro: St.-Germain-des-Prés

The length of the average French business lunch is 124 minutes, compared to the average American business lunch of 67 minutes.

92 Le Village ★$/$$ For 34 years this was the site of a dark and dingy post-war bar run by the **Carydes** brothers, whose stools were filled with old-timers waxing nostalgic for the intellectual glory days of St.-Germain-des-Prés. In 1987 **Christian Samoyault** and his wife, **Lydia,** transformed the landmark watering hole into a jazz club and restaurant. The house specialties include homemade foie gras and grilled salmon with mustard sauce. ♦ Daily noon-2AM. 7 Rue Gozlin. Métro: St.-Germain-des-Prés. 43.26.80.19

93 St.-Germain-des-Prés For more than 15 centuries a church has stood on this corner, which in Roman times was *prés* (open pasture). The first church, built in AD 452 by Merovingian **King Childebert,** was repeatedly destroyed by invading Normans and finally rebuilt, to last, in 1163. The Romanesque western gate tower is faintly reminiscent of the great abbeys on the outskirts of Paris. During the Middle Ages, the St.-Germain-des-Prés, named after Saint Germanus (AD 496-576), bishop of Paris, became a focal point for Easter fairs, with hundreds of

St.-Germain

stalls, performing theater troupes, and dancing bears. (None of this has changed today save the dancing bears, which have been replaced, more or less humanely, by street musicians of the imitation-Dylan school.)

Inside the church of St.-Germain is an altar dedicated to the victims of the Sepember 1793 massacre, a shameful chapter of French history, when Paris was ruled by a bloodthirsty mob called the *sans culottes* (because they wore linen trousers instead of aristocratic knee breeches). In 1793, after a mock trial on the weekend of 2-3 Sepember, almost 200 prisoners sequestered in the church were led into the courtyard (at the corner of what is now **Rue Bonaparte** and **Blvd St.-Germain**), where they were stabbed and hacked to death by hired killers. Ministers of **Louis XVI,** his father confessor, and the Swiss Guards were slaughtered. The carnage was followed by an auction of the victims' personal effects. The skull of **René Descartes,** the 17th-century mathematician and philosopher, along with the body of **John Casimir,** a 17th-century king of Poland who was abbot of St.-Germain, are buried inside the church.

Today, however, the edifice is best known for its evening concerts of classical music. It provides a cool place to meditate on muggy summer days. ♦ Daily 8AM-8PM. Guided tours Tu, Th 1-5PM. Place St.-Germain-des-Prés. Métro: St.-Germain-des-Prés. 43.25.41.71

93 Picasso Sculpture In the small park to the left of the church's main portal is a bronze bust of a woman by **Pablo Picasso,** given to the city in 1958 in memory of his friend, the poet **Guillaume Apollinaire** (1880-1918), who lived and died nearby at 202-204 Boule-

vard St.-Germain. (A short street nearby also honors Apollinaire.)

Of Polish origin (his last name was **Kostrowitzki**), Apollinaire wrote the famous *Alcools* in 1913 and was an early leader of the Paris avant-garde. Eventually renowned for his poetry, Apollinaire was best known in his time as the man who stole the *Mona Lisa.* The scandal began when Apollinaire's former personal secretary lifted two inconsequential Phoenician statues from the Louvre and sold them to Picasso. Coincidentally, the *Mona Lisa* disappeared shortly afterwards. Apollinaire, trying to protect his secretary and Picasso from suspicion and incarceration, turned in the statues and was jailed for four days. The *Mona Lisa* eventually resumed her place in the Louvre, and Apollinaire was exonerated. He never, however, recovered his self-esteem. ♦ Métro: St.-Germain-des-Prés

94 Librairie Le Divan The bookstore of the Gallimard publishing house has works by all its latest authors, plus other literature and a large collection of *bandes dessinés* (comic books), such as *Tin Tin Chez le Psychanalyste.* Also notable are the black-and-white author photos tacked to the walls. ♦ M-Sa 10AM-7:30PM. 37 Rue Bonaparte. Métro: St.-Germain-des-Prés. 43.26.84.73

94 Réunion des Musées Nationaux It's Tuesday. You forgot to buy a poster or catalog at the Louvre to take home, and now the museum is closed. Don't fret. This bookstore stocks all the catalogs and posters published by the national museums in France since 1966. ♦ M-F 9AM-12:30PM, 2-5PM. 10 Rue de l'Abbaye. Métro: St.-Germain-des-Prés. 43.29.21.45

95 24 Rue Bonaparte In the spring of 1928 **Henry Miller** stayed here with his wife, **June.** ♦ Métro: St.-Germain-des-Prés

96 Ecole des Beaux-Arts The city's **School of Fine Arts** was established by **Louis XIV** and trained many of the architects and artists who have designed and decorated Paris over the centuries. The school is worth a quick detour to view the lovely Renaissance archway, fountain, and sculpture, and the changing exhibitions of student work. Two well-known architects, **Richard Morris Hunt** and **Bernard Ralph Maybeck,** were among the first Americans to be educated here, and each employed his own version of the Beaux-Arts style in the US in the late 19th century. ♦ M 2:15-4:30PM; Tu-F 9AM-noon, 2:25-4:30PM. 14 Rue Bonaparte. Métros: Rue du Bac, St.-Germain-des-Prés. 42.60.34.57

96 Buci Market One of the prettiest street markets is named after **Monsieur Buci,** president of the French Parliament during the Renaissance. The intersection of Rue de Buci and Rue de Seine is thronged with operatic hawkers hustling endives, homemade fettuccine, fresh ground Colombian coffee, wild strawberries, fresh cherries, hot baguettes, and pink tulips. From here, Rue de Seine shoots off toward the river, becoming a thoroughfare of art galleries. Bear that in mind when passing by in the early evening: a crowded gallery is most likely hosting a *vernissage* (literally a "varnishing"), or exhibition opening. Manifest your best French accent, join the party, and talk art while sipping a glass of champagne. ♦ Tu-Sa 9AM-1PM, 4-7PM; Su 9AM-1PM. Métro: Odéon

96 Le Fournil de Pierre In the vanguard of the new artisanal bakeries, Le Fournil de Pierre prides itself on its whole-grain breads. Its *pain de 6 céréales* possesses more fiber than a Presto log and might even inspire you to buy a toaster for your hotel room. ♦ M 11AM-8PM; Tu-Sa 8AM-8PM; Su 8:30AM-1PM. 64 Rue de Seine. Métro: Odéon. 46.34.17.59

96 La Louisiane $$ If you want to stay right in the heart of Paris, there's no better choice than this hotel. Located around the corner from the Rue de Buci street market, the Louisiane has hosted some very famous French literati, including **Jacques Prévert** and **Jean-Paul Sartre.** The noise level is likely to be high at all times, so light sleepers should give it a pass. ♦ 60 Rue de Seine. Métros: Mabillon, Odéon. 43.29.59.30, 43.29.79.30

97 8 Rue Bonaparte The young Corsican conqueror once lived here, but this street wasn't named for him until 1852, when his nephew, **Napoléon III,** became emperor. ♦ Métro: St.-Germain-des-Prés

98 Restaurant des Beaux-Arts ★★$/$$ A bargain canteen usually filled with art students. Go early to miss the lines but not the coq au vin, beef Bourguignonne, *confit de canard,* and cassoulet. ♦ Daily noon-2:30PM, 7-11PM. 11 Rue Bonaparte. No credit cards. Métro: St.-Germain-des-Prés. 43.26.92.64

98 Robert Duperrier Here you'll find a lively combination of Indonesian, North American, and African art, from Gabonese amulets to Ibo statues. ♦ M-Sa 10AM-12:30PM, 3-7PM; closed in Aug. 14 Rue des Beaux-Arts. Métro: St.-Germain-des-Prés. 43.54.38.64

98 Franco Maria Ricci Editore This is the Paris headquarters of the celebrated Milan publisher whose eclectic and elegant series of fine arts books and literature ranges in subject from decorative ceramics and iconography to deluxe Italian re-editions of **Saki, Kafka, Borges,** and **Poe.** ♦ Tu-Sa 10AM-1PM, 2:30-7PM. 12 Rue des Beaux-Arts. Métro: St.-Germain-des-Prés. 46.33.96.31

98 L'Hôtel $$$$ This pretentiously generic name is befitting for a hostelry with true snob appeal—the snug and refined favorite lodgings of **Mick Jagger, Julie Christie,** and

countless honeymooners. Formerly the **Hôtel d'Alsace,** this is where **Oscar Wilde** stayed in 1899 after his release from Reading Gaol (the prison). He expired here the following year sighing, "I am dying beyond my means." *Dorian Gray* fans can actually occupy the room where Wilde lived out his last days. Or, if you prefer, book the Art Deco bedroom of dance-hall belle **Mistinguett.** The hotel's five-story well is a triumph of Directoire architecture. All in all, it's a unique hotel with a special romantic ambience. ♦ 13 Rue des Beaux-Arts. Reservations required. Métro: St.-Germain-des-Prés. 43.25.27.22

Within L'Hôtel:

Le Belier ★★$$$/$$$$ This romantic, expensive restaurant maintains a reputation for excellent, if somewhat stilted, service. The specialties include veal tournedos with mozzarella, sole and salmon in saffron, and meringue with mangoes and chocolate. ♦ Daily 12:30-2PM, 7:30PM-12:30AM. Reservations required. 43.25.27.22

Bar de l'Hôtel ★★$$ Popular with young art and antique dealers treating fancy San

Francisco friends to the Parisian scene. Piano bar. ♦ Daily 6AM-2AM. 43.25.27.22

98 Galerie Claude Bernard One of the city's best, this internationally known gallery shows such modern heavyweights as **Balthus, Giacometti, David Hockney, Louise Nevelson,** and **Jim Dine.** ♦ Tu-Sa 9:30AM-12:30PM, 2:30-6:30PM; closed in Aug. 7-9 Rue des Beaux-Arts. Métro: St.-Germain-des-Prés. 43.26.97.07

98 5 Rue des Beaux-Arts **Edouard Manet** was born here in 1835. A wall plaque commemorates that truly blessed event. ♦ Métro: St.-Germain-des-Prés

99 24 Rue Visconti This was once the home of **Racine.** According to a historian's account, the brilliant 17th-century dramatist died here on 21 April 1699 of a combination of dysentery, erysipelas, rheumatism, a liver ailment, and, possibly, "the chagrin of no longer being in favor with the king." ♦ Métro: St.-Germain-des-Prés

99 17 Rue Visconti Young **Balzac** set up his print shop at this cultural address. A few years later, in 1836, **Delacroix** moved in. It was here that he painted his portraits of **George Sand** and her lover **Frédéric Chopin.** ♦ Métro: St.-Germain-des-Prés

100 Atelier Depretz In a courtyard off Rue Jacob, **Jean-Claude Depretz,** a master-painting restorer, repairs damaged canvases with rabbit-skin glue while his assistant camouflages the scars. At this same address is a bookbinder in the **Atelier Pinault** employing tools that haven't changed in five centuries. ♦ M 10:30AM-12:30PM, 2-7PM; Tu-F 9AM-12:30PM, 2-7PM; Sa 9AM-12:30PM; closed in Aug. 30 Rue Jacob. Métro: St.-Germain-des-Prés. 43.26.60.14

100 Claude Boullé Some of the cut and polished stones (ranging from $30 to $150) at this gallery are the mineral counterparts of **Frederick Turner's** seascapes on canvas. ♦ M 2-7PM; Tu-Sa 10:30AM-12:30PM, 2-7PM. 28 Rue Jacob. Métro: St.-Germain-des-Prés. 46.33.01.38

100 La Maison Rustique Green thumbs will enjoy browsing in this agricultural and horticultural bookstore. ♦ M-Sa 10AM-7PM. 26 Rue Jacob. Métro: St.-Germain-des-Prés. 43.25.67.00

100 La Maison Comoglio This outrageous but poetic antique shop used to rent **Jean Cocteau** the zany props he employed in his plays and films. This tradition of specializing in the strange and bizarre may be threatened by the new owner's intention to peddle furniture and decorator fabrics. ♦ M 2:30-7PM; Tu-Sa 10:30-7PM; closed in Aug. 22 Rue Jacob. Métro: St.-Germain-des-Prés. 43.54.65.86, 42.60.77.33

101 14 Rue Jacob German opera composer **Richard Wagner** lived here from 1841-1842. ♦ Métro: St.-Germain-des-Prés

St.-Germain

102 La Villa à St.-Germain-des-Prés $$$ This hotel has a slick new interior design but the same small and charming rooms as its former incarnation, the Isly hotel. ♦ 29 Rue Jacob. Métro: St.-Germain-des-Prés. 43.26.60.00

102 27 Rue Jacob The prestigious French publishing house, **Editions du Seuil,** has its offices in the building where **Ingres,** the master of French classical painting, lived more than 150 years ago. ♦ Métro: St.-Germain-des-Prés

102 Les Marronniers $$ Named after the two chestnut trees in its garden, this charming hotel, classified as a national monument, is set back on a peaceful courtyard. It is justly popular. ♦ 21 Rue Jacob. Reservations required. Métro: St.-Germain-des-Prés. 43.25.30.60

102 Des Deux Continents $$ This cozy hotel occupies two adjacent houses along a quiet street. ♦ 25 Rue Jacob. Métro: St.-Germain-des-Prés. 43.26.72.46

Baron Georges-Eugène Haussmann (1809-1891), the ogre-genius of urban planners, changed the face of Paris more than anyone else in history. When he took office in 1853 as prefect of the Seine under Napoléon III, Paris was a dense welter of streets and alleys. Haussmann created two dozen squares and parks and cut wide boulevards through old neighborhoods (Boulevard St.-Germain among them), opening up what had been a claustrophobic density, but also destroying the Paris of Diderot, Voltaire, and Balzac. The grim reality, however, is that although the avenues were created partly to improve the city's circulation, the greater strategic purpose was to allow Napoléon's soldiers to more easily suppress uprisings and worker riots.

103 Yveline Tucked away in the **Furstemberg Square** (pictured above) is a charming antique shop. ♦ M-Sa 11AM-6:30PM; closed in Aug. 4 Rue de Furstemberg. Métro: St.-Germain-des-Prés. 43.26.56.91

103 Delacroix Museum The old *atelier* (studio) of **Eugène Delacroix,** where he lived, worked, and in 1863, died, is now a museum displaying his paintings, sketches, and letters. A quick tour will give you some idea of why **Baudelaire** described Delacroix as a "volcanic crater artistically concealed beneath bouquets of flowers." ♦ Admission. M, W-Su 9:45AM-12:30PM, 2-5:15PM. 6 Rue de Furstemberg. Métro: St.-Germain-des-Prés. 43.54.04.87

103 7 Rue Jacob In 1656, at the age of 17, **Racine** lived here with his uncle. ♦ Métro: St.-Germain-des-Prés

103 Librairie Maritime et d'Outre-Mer This bookstore specializes in maritime books. ♦ M-Sa 10AM-7PM. 17 Rue Jacob. Métro: St.-Germain-des-Prés. 46.33.47.48

103 Studio V.O./ V.F. Want to star in the next Polanski thriller set in Paris? Need to gesticulate more effectively at surly waiters and postal clerks? Adult acting classes in French or English are taught here by highly professional American and French drama instructors. ♦ 11 Rue Jacob. Métro: St.-Germain-des-Prés. 40.46.01.92

104 Manuel Canovas A wallpaper and fabric designer whose sumptuous work is often featured in *Vogue* and *Architectural Digest,* Manuel Canovas sells to professional and amateur decorators alike. ♦ M-Sa 9:30AM-6:30PM. 7 Rue de Furstemberg. Métros: Mabillon, St.-Germain-des-Prés. 43.25.75.98

104 La Boutique Shoes, handbags, placemats, linens, and scarves fashioned from the cheery fabrics of Manuel Canovas, the next-door neighbor, are featured here. ♦ M-Sa 10AM-7PM. 5 Rue de Furstemberg. Métros: Mabillon, St.-Germain-des-Prés. 43.26.89.31

104 2 Rue Cardinale The Black Sun Press operated at this address under the aegis of **Harry** and **Caresse Crosby,** a couple of wild surrealists of the 1920s. They were the first to publish the **D.H. Lawrence** book *Sun.* Harry, who was a nephew of **J.P. Morgan,** died in a double suicide with his mistress at the **Hôtel des Artistes** in New York. ♦ Métro: Mabillon

104 Place de Furstemberg Named after **Egon de Furstemberg,** a 17th-century abbot of St.-Germain-des-Prés, this hidden treasure attracts French filmmakers, flamenco guitar players, and harpists who like to play in the courtyard with its extraordinary acoustics. At the center of the square is a white-globed lamppost and four paulownia trees that **Henry Miller** described in *Tropic of Cancer* as having "the poetry of T.S. Eliot" (see illustration at left). In spring the trees burst into fragrant lavender bloom; Paris never smells as sweet anywhere else. ♦ Métro: St.-Germain-des-Prés

105 Hôtel de Seine $$ This hotel has an English-style lounge with armchairs downstairs. Beat poet **Lawrence Ferlinghetti,** owner of City Lights Bookstore in San Francisco, stays here. ♦ 52 Rue de Seine. Métro: Odéon. 46.34.22.80

105 Mimi La Sardine A rainbow variety of velours has been stitched into everything from headbands to skirts. ♦ M 2-7:30PM; Tu-Sa 10AM-7:30PM. 54 Rue de Seine. Métro: Odéon. 46.34.11.66

105 La Table d'Italie At the best Italian delicatessen in Paris, **Silvio Beluti** imports Roman porchette, Milanese panettone, and regional wines. Everything but the fresh-daily pasta comes from his homeland. Lurking beneath the Parma hams dangling from the ceiling is a small counter serving inexpensive but generous pasta snacks. ♦ Tu-Sa noon-3PM, 7-11PM. 69 Rue de Seine. Métro: Mabillon. 43.54.34.69, 46.33.15.29

105 Galerie Documents Since 1954 **Michel Romand** has owned the city's most distinguished antique poster shop, specializing in *affiches* from 1875 to 1930, particularly the works of **Toulouse-Lautrec, Grasset, Mucha,** and **Steinlen.** ♦ Tu-Sa 10:30AM-12:30PM, 2:30-7PM. 53 Rue de Seine. Métro: Odéon. 43.54.50.68

105 Galerie Arts des Amériques If pre-Columbian art from Central and South America is your passion, this gallery has treasures in store for you. ♦ M 2-5PM; Tu-Sa 10:30AM-12:30PM, 2-5PM. 42 Rue de Seine. Métros: Mabillon, St.-Germain-des-Prés. 46.33.18.31

105 La Palette ★★$ A bohemian café right out of a Jean Rhys novel. In fact, **James Ivory** filmed part of that down-and-out tale *Quartet* (with **Alan Bates, Maggie Smith,** and **Isabelle Adjani**) here in 1981. The artists' palettes that hang on the wall are more interesting than the paintings themselves, but don't miss the humorous 1920s tiled murals in the back room. House specialties include Gruyère omelet, chef's salad, country ham served on Poilâne country bread, and a delicious *tarte tatin*. Bearded waiter **Jean-François** is grouchy but kindhearted and plays the part of a little Bonaparte. You must order quickly and without indecision or he'll ignore you until you've learned your lesson. The WC is an "authentic porcelain kangaroo trap," as one

Aussie regular calls the crouch-style toilet. ♦ M-Sa 8AM-1:30AM; closed in Aug. 43 Rue de Seine. No credit cards. Métro: Odéon. 43.26.68.15

105 Cosi ★★$ This gourmet Italian sandwich and salad counter serves everything from salmon carpaccio to roasted red peppers—all on bread baked in wood-fired pizza ovens. Tuscan wines, opera by Verdi, and daily editions of *La Repùbblica*, lend to Cosi's Latin charm. Take-out or, if you prefer, eat here in the upstairs seating area. ♦ Daily 11AM-midnight. 54 Rue de Seine. Métro: Odéon, St.-Germain-des-Prés. 46.33.35.36

106 L'Echaudé ★$$ Yet another romantic lace-curtain restaurant run by the three famous **Layrac** brothers—this one off the Rue de Buci. Chef **Jean-Paul Chossat** makes a *filet de rascasse* with puree of prawns and a duck with raspberries and escargots in puff pastry that will provide more than sufficient memories to fill your next postcard home. ♦ Daily noon-2:15PM, 7PM-2AM (last orders taken at 12:30AM). 21 Rue de l'Echaudé. Reservations required. Métro: Mabillon. 43.54.79.02

St.-Germain

106 Le Chai de l'Abbaye ★★$ One of the few good wine bars in Paris not crawling with yuppies. ♦ Open daily 24 hours. 26 Rue de Buci. Métros: Mabillon, Odéon. 43.26.68.26

106 2 Rue du Bourbon le Château Buzz yourself in and have a look at the circular-well courtyard in this 1824 structure. (L'Hôtel on Rue des Beaux-Arts is another example of this architectural device.) Try to imagine how items such as grand pianos are hoisted up to the fifth floor through the windows. ♦ Métro: Mabillon

107 Rhumerie Martiniquaise ★$ Upper-crust rum imbibers, along with the rabble out for a good time, keep this place packed. However, the stiff punches made with 130 kinds of the sugarcane elixir make it worth fighting for a table. In addition to the usual daiquiris and planter's punch, try the *Père Serge,* named after a priest at St.-Germain-des-Prés, which is made with rum, lemon, and sugarcane syrup. ♦ Daily 9AM-3AM. 166 Blvd St.-Germain. No credit cards. Métro: St.-Germain-des-Prés. 43.54.28.94

The French have more dogs per person than any other nation in Western Europe. In Paris alone there are 161,000 pooches, twice the number of children. However, Paris, unlike New York, has no pooper-scooper law. According to city surveys, pedestrians are likely to encounter canine droppings every 262 feet. Eighty-one *caninettes*—bright green motorbikes equipped with rotating brushes and suction hoses—scour 1,500 miles of sidewalk each day, collecting some 20 tons of dog waste by quitting time.

Restaurants/Nightlife: Red
Shops/ ♀Outdoors: Green
Hotels: Blue
Sights/Culture: Black

108 Le Fürstemberg ★$ Gay Paree decor reigns in this small cellar room that offers both exotic cocktails and the attractions of the venerable **André Persiany's** sing-along piano music. Food can be ordered for a short time in the evening, and a jazz quartet plays into the wee hours. ◆ Daily 6PM-3AM. Restaurant: daily 7:30-8:30PM. Jazz quartet: daily 10:45PM-3AM. 27 Rue de Buci. No credit cards. Métro: Mabillon. 43.54.79.51

108 Le Muniche ★$$ Delicious fish soup, grilled sardines, fresh briny oysters, four kinds of choucroute, and an honest plate of liver and onions are some of the fare at this crowded

St.-Germain

Alsatian bistro. In summer, reserve a table on the sidewalk. ◆ Daily noon-3AM. 27 Rue de Buci. Métros: Mabillon, Odéon. 46.33.62.09

108 La Boutique Layrac Traiteur The windows at this expensive late-night delicatessen/caterer are capable of bringing any passing gourmand to a dead stop. Duck *à l'orange,* curried chicken, ornamented whole poached salmons, and impeccable pastries join a fine selection of wines, liqueurs, breads, and regional French specialties. ◆ Daily 9:30AM-3AM. 29 Rue de Buci. Métros: Mabillon, Odéon, St.-Germain-des-Prés. 43.25.17.72

109 Vagenende ★★$/$$ With a full effulgence of 1885 Belle Epoque and Tiffany glass decor, this poor man's Maxim's has starred in films such as *Travels with My Aunt* and *Murder on the Orient Express.* Homemade foie gras, fresh shellfish, and pot-au-feu are several good dishes to try. ◆ Daily noon-3PM, 7PM-1AM. 142 Blvd St.-Germain. Métro: St.-Germain-des-Prés. 43.26.68.18

110 Le Procope ★★$$ Founded in 1686 by Sicilian **Francesco Procopio dei Coltelli,** and assured success by the 1689 opening of the **Comédie Française** in a tennis court-turned-theater across the street, the Procope advertises itself as the world's oldest café (the second star rating is for its history). Customers

have included Olympian talents **La Fontaine, Rousseau,** and **Voltaire;** 18th-century revolutionaries including **Benjamin Franklin, Thomas Jefferson, Robespierre, Danton, Bonaparte,** and **Marat;** ageless literati like **Victor Hugo, Honoré de Balzac, Paul Verlaine, George Sand,** and **Mallarmé;** and in the 1950s, when the tavern/café became a restaurant, **Simone de Beauvoir** and **Jean-Paul Sartre.** These days, the best part of dining at Le Procope is adding your name to the distinguished guest list. Its 18th-century decor, red walls, and crystal chandeliers never seem to compensate for the slow service and disappointing cuisine. Safest bets are the classics: pot-au-feu and grilled lamb. ◆ M-F 8AM-11PM; Sa-Su 8AM-1AM. Jazz: M-Sa 11PM-2AM; closed in July. 13 Rue de l'Ancienne-Comédie. Métro: Odéon. 43.26.99.20

111 Pub St.-Germain-des-Prés ★★$$ Along with 24 brands of draft beer and 450 international varieties of bottled brew, this 600-seat pub offers such basic grub as mussels and beef cooked with—guess what?—beer. By the end of the evening, you may feel that you have been similarly stewed yourself. It's a favorite of American students abroad. ◆ Open daily 24 hours. 17 Rue de l'Ancienne-Comédie. Métro: Odéon. 43.29.38.70

111 Rue St.-André-des-Arts Running from Rue Mazarine to Place St.-Michel, this eclectic little street seems more like a pedestrian mall and is always host to a few guitar duos passably imitating Simon and Garfunkel. ◆ Métro: Odéon

111 St.-André-des-Arts $$ A comfortable, modest pension run by a friendly staff. ◆ 66 Rue St.-André-des-Arts. Métro: Odéon. 43.26.96.16

111 Le Mazet Street musicians, lowlifes, and professional pinball players frequent this down-and-out bar. You know the kind: beer-foamed mustaches, numerous dogs underfoot, and a pall of cigarette smoke in the air. If you choose to slum here, watch your billfold. ◆ M-Th 10AM-2AM; F-Sa 10AM-3AM. 61 Rue St.-André-des-Arts. No credit cards. Métro: Odéon. 43.54.68.81

111 Cour du Commerce St.-André Built in 1776, the city's first covered shopping mall was a hive of activity during the Revolution and inspired 17 other *passages* that sprang up on the Right Bank in the 19th century. Through the windows at **No. 4,** you can glimpse the remains of one of the towers in the city wall. At **No. 8** in 1789, **Marat** printed revolutionary exhortations in his inflammatory journal *L'Ami du Peuple.* Nearby, a German carpenter named **Schmidt** patiently perfected the hideous guillotine (named after **Dr. Guillotin,** who recommended this philanthropic apparatus for decapitation). Schmidt practiced on sheep, and the street ran red with the blood of the unfortunate beasts. It was also here that the artist **Balthus** had a studio and painted his famous picture *The Passage du Commerce St.-André* in 1954 (don't look for the shop he painted with the golden key; it has long since been abandoned). ◆ 59-61 Rue St.-André-des-Arts. Métro: Odéon.

Within the Cour du Commerce St.-André:
Monsieur Baudrillart If you decide to have your Paris journal recovered in leather, the bookbinding shop of Monsieur Baudrillart is the place to go. ◆ M-F 9AM-noon, 2-7PM. 46.33.19.88

A La Cour de Rohan ★★$ This British teashop is decorated in garden-fresh whites and greens and offers lobster bisque, broiled goat cheese on toast, savory tarts, toothsome cakes, scones, crumbles, exotic teas, and a 17th-century heirloom recipe for spicy marmalade. No smoking allowed. ◆ Tu-F, Su noon-7:30PM; Sa 12:30-11:30PM; closed 15-30 Aug. No credit cards. 43.25.79.67

111 La Datcha des Arts ★$/$$ The proprietor of this Central European restaurant keeps a guitar on the wall for those who prefer their own singing to the piped-in mazurkas. Start with borscht and a lemon vodka, a dollop of beluga caviar, then move on to the *Assiette Datcha* (Danish salmon, sprats, tarama, eggplant caviar, and three kinds of Baltic herring with fresh blinis). He also sells 15 kinds of vodka, Matroszka dolls, and blinis-to-go. ◆ Daily noon-midnight. 56 Rue St.-André-des-Arts. Métro: Odéon. 46.33.29.25

112 Librairie Fischbacher A bookshop with a stunning collection of fine arts editions and books on history, primitive arts, and autobiographies in French, English, and German. ◆ M-F 9AM-7PM; Sa 10AM-7PM. 33 Rue de Seine. Métro: Odéon. 43.26.84.87

113 12 Rue Mazarine Here the young **Molière** made his acting debut and later, with an inherited nest egg, opened a theater in an abandoned tennis court; this was the genesis of the **Comédie Française.** In 1673 after he died on stage, the company was orphaned and evicted. But the troupe started anew in another old tennis court at 14 Rue de l'Ancienne Comédie in 1689 after a decade of inactivity. ◆ Métro: Odéon

114 Institut de France Situated across the **Pont des Arts** from the **Louvre,** this 17th-century masterpiece, designed by **Louis Le Vau** at the same time he was working on the Louvre, houses the prestigious **Académie Française.** The academy began in 1635 as a salon of intellectuals who gathered informally to discuss French rhetoric and usage. Shortly thereafter, **Cardinal Richelieu** charged them with the protection and proliferation of the French language, hoping that Parisian French would eventually obliterate the less refined regional dialects. Academy membership is limited to 40 "immortals," making each member literally one in a million among the French population. The academy doesn't stint on panoply: at their induction ceremonies, the members wear silver-embroidered green robes and cocked admirals' bonnets and carry jeweled swords. The immortals don their robes for secret meetings, which are held every Thursday afternoon. Their responsibilities are to safeguard the mother tongue and to prepare new editions of the academy's dictionary, which first appeared in 1694.

Election to the academy is reserved for great writers, and even the list of runners-up comprises a pantheon of French literature: **Descartes, Diderot, de Maupassant, Balzac, Flaubert, Verlaine, Stendhal,** and **Proust** among them. **Molière,** the playwright/director/actor, was invited to join the academy on the condition that he give up acting. He refused the honor. No actor has ever been admitted to date. **Emile Zola** campaigned for election 13 times unsuccessfully; Nobel prize winners **André Gide** and **Albert Camus** never

Institut de France

even tried. In 1981 women's history was made when **Marguerite Yourcenar** was inducted into the sacred ranks of the academy and became the first female immortal (her cloak was personally designed by **Yves Saint Laurent**). The left wing of the institute (toward the mint building) is the site of the notorious **Tour Nesle,** from whence, according to **Dumas, Queen Margot** (the first wife of **Henri IV**) would catapult that night's lover into the Seine. Among the exemplary statuary in the institute rotunda is a totally nude **Voltaire.** ♦ Métro: Odéon

115 Pont des Arts Providing a pedestrian crossing between the **Institut de France** and the **Louvre,** this wooden-planked structure with its latticed arches was the first iron bridge in Paris. Designed by an engineer named **Dillon** in 1804, this footbridge was originally landscaped with potted orange trees, rosebushes, and hothouses full of tropical plants. Hordes of easel-toting artists from the nearby **Ecole des Beaux-Arts** come here to sketch and daub that familiar compendious view spanning the **Ile de la Cité,** the rose-gray facade of **Place**

St.-Germain

Dauphine, the dignified form of the **Pont-Neuf,** and the spires of **Notre-Dame** and **Ste.-Chapelle** in the distance. ♦ Métro: Odéon

116 Hôtel des Monnaies The austere classical-style French mint (pictured above) is where the nation's centime and franc coins are designed and struck. In 1775, shortly after the original mint by **Jules Hardouin-Mansart** was demolished, the present edifice was built by **Jacques-Denis Antoine.** The **Musée des Monnaies** traces the history of French coins back to **Charlemagne's** day and houses a collection of medals, currency, and commemorative coins. Hundreds of gold and silver medals are also for sale in the nearby museum shop (M-F 10AM-5:45PM; Sa 10-11:45AM, 2-5:30PM. 2 Rue Guénégaud. 40.46.56.66). ♦ Museum tours: Tu-Su 1-6PM. Free tours of production area: M, W 2PM. 11 Quai de Conti. Métro: Odéon. 40.46.58.92

116 Impasse de Conti Here on the street in 1792, a young Corsican named **Napoléon Bonaparte** rented an attic room in the **Hôtel de Guénégaud,** built by **François Mansart** in 1659. Twelve years later, he conquered Europe and crowned himself emperor of France. ♦ Métro: Odéon

117 Le Balto ★$ An animated bar/tabac livened up by local architecture students who pass their afternoons playing table soccer. Best for Gruyère on Poilâne bread or a nightcap standing up. Every Wednesday at 9:30PM the **Fanfare des Beaux-Arts,** a rowdy horn ensemble, performs. ♦ M-F 7AM-11PM. 15 Rue Mazarine. Métro: Odéon. 43.26.02.29

117 Michel Cachoux Dig through the fossils, lapis, amethysts, and star-shaped calcites—there's something for everyone's hard-rock fantasy here. ♦ Tu-Sa 11AM-12:30PM, 2:30-7:30PM, or by appointment; closed in Aug. 16 Rue Guénégaud. Métro: Odéon. 43.54.52.15, 43.25.46.20

117 Galerie Couvrat Desvergnes The last time you saw such an elegant Art Deco setting was probably in an Ernst Lubitsch film. If you can afford it, this is the place to start your own collection of French Art Deco furniture and accessories designed by period luminaries such as **Rhulmann, Charreau,** and **Cheuret.** Imagine a bronze torchiere by **Brandt** with light filtering through an alabaster shade in your living room. ♦ Tu-Sa 11AM-1PM, 2-7PM; closed in Aug. 12 Rue Guénégaud. Métro: Odéon. 43.29.72.70

118 La Cafetière ★★$$ Co-owner **Jean Romestant** greets you with a voice that should have been in a Truffaut movie. The specialties of his warmly lit restaurant are the *canard sauvage* (wild duck) and hot apple crêpes. *Cafetière* means coffeepot, hence the collection that's scattered about. ♦ Daily 12:30-2:30PM, 7:30-10:30PM. 21 Rue Mazarine. Reservations required. Métro: Odéon. 46.33.76.90

118 Galerie Isy Brachot From the vastness of the repertoire of jokes deriding Belgians, you might conclude that the French are lacking in respect for the people of that country. This quite respectable gallery reflects the Belgian view of surrealism (representing the artists **Magritte** and **Delvaux**) and is more than worth a look. ♦ Tu-Sa 11AM-1PM, 2-6:30PM; closed 10 July-10 Sep. 35 Rue Guénégaud. Métro: Odéon. 43.54.22.40

119 Rue de Nevers This 13th-century alley ends near a remnant of the **King Philippe Auguste** city wall (circa 1200) and passes beneath an arch chiseled with an excerpt of the 17th-century poem *Le Paris Ridicule,* by **Claude Le Petit,** which forecasted the collapse of **Henri IV's** noble Pont-Neuf. The paper edition of this caustic verse was publicly burned in the **Place de Grève,** along with its author. ♦ Métro: Odéon

120 Le Monde en Marche Step into a magical world of wooden toys, puppets, and puzzles that are gaily colored and made by hand. ♦ Tu-Sa 10:30AM-7:30PM; closed part of Aug. 34 Rue Dauphine. Métro: Odéon. 43.26.66.53

20 Hôtel le Régent $$ This recently renovated 25-room hotel is nicely located midway between the Seine and the Rue de Buci, which proffers the prettiest outdoor market in Paris. ◆ 61 Rue Dauphine. Métro: Mabillon. 46.34.59.80

21 Jacques Cagna ★★$$$/$$$$ In his elegant old inn, Jacques Cagna features traditional French cuisine with a nouvelle flourish. The prices are heavy, but the sauces are light and the vegetables are treated with the gentility they deserve. Specialties include asparagus, lobster, and wild mushrooms in puff pastry; braised veal sweetbreads with truffles and oysters; delicately fried sole and mullet with Béarnaise sauce; duck with red Burgundy and orange; oysters cassolette with lobster; and sliced hot apples with cinnamon ice cream. The wine cellar stocks 60,000 bottles in 550 varieties. ◆ M-F noon-2PM, 7:30-10:30PM; open two Saturday nights per month from Sep-Nov; closed holidays, 23 Dec-2 Jan and in Aug. 14 Rue des Grands-Augustins. Reservations required. Métro: Odéon. 43.26.49.39

21 Relais Christine $$$ A 16th-century monastery was converted into this plush, well-run, fashionable hotel in 1980. Choose from among modern or antique rooms and singles or split-level apartments, some of which offer luxurious marble bathrooms and access onto a secluded courtyard. The basement breakfast room alone is worth the visit. Highly recommended. ◆ 3 Rue Christine. Reservations required. Métro: Odéon. 43.26.71.80

21 5 Rue Christine After being ignominiously kicked out of their apartment on Rue de Fleurus, **Gertrude Stein** and **Alice B. Toklas** moved here in 1938. During the war, they fled to the countryside; in their absence, 5 Rue Christine was visited by the Gestapo, who attached a note to one of Stein's **Picasso** paintings reading "Jewish trash, good for burning." Stein died on 19 July 1946, and Toklas lived on here for another 18 years. The two women are buried side-by-side in the **Père-Lachaise** cemetery. ◆ Métro: Odéon

21 Boulevard St.-Michel This was one of the great boulevards of **Baron Haussmann,** scythed through the Left Bank from the edge of the Seine in a broad, tree-lined swath. The boulevard was named in 1867 in memory of the ancient chapel of **St.-Michel** that stood here once upon a time. ◆ Métro: St.-Michel

22 Action Christine Two adjacent revival houses keep aficionados of **Hitchcock** and **Lubitsch,** as well as fans of **Bogie** and **Bacall** classics, happy. ◆ Daily 2-10:30PM. 4 Rue Christine and 10 Rue des Grands-Augustins. Métro: Odéon. 43.29.11.30

123 7 Rue des Grands-Augustins From 1936 to 1955, **Pablo Picasso** lived in this imposing house, where he painted *Guernica* in 1937. His friends **Gerald** and **Sara Murphy,** the quintessential American expatriates in the 1920s, had an apartment in the pink building around the block on the Quai des Grands-Augustins. It was Picasso who got them work painting sets for **Diaghilev** and the **Ballet Russe.** They were also the models **Fitzgerald** used for Dick and Nicole Diver in *Tender Is the Night.* ◆ Métro: Odéon

123 Quai des Grands-Augustins In 1313 one of the first *quais* (embankments) in Paris was constructed next to the monastery of **St.-Augustin.** Hundreds of years later, **Thomas Jefferson** idled away many an afternoon here, browsing along this stretch of riverside, which is still known for its book- and print-sellers. ◆ Métro: St.-Michel

123 Lapérouse ★★$$$/$$$$ Chef **Patrick Gillot** is attracting multitudes of gourmands to this Old World *quai*-side restaurant with culinary sonnets such as lobster lasagna, lobster soup with julienne of vegetables, and warm apple

tarts. ◆ Tu-Th 12:30-2:30PM, 7:30-10:30PM; F-Sa 12:30-2:30PM, 7:30-11PM; Su 12:30-2:30PM. 51 Quai des Grands-Augustins. Reservations required. Métro: St.-Michel. 43.26.68.04

124 46 Rue St.-André-des-Arts Sixty years ago, in a building housing two bookshops, **e.e. cummings** rented a single room. ◆ Métros: Odéon, St.-Michel

124 Maison Woerli As you stroll down Rue St.-André-des-Arts, you can't miss this neighborhood *épicerie* with large candy jars as sentinels out front. ◆ Tu-Sa 8AM-8PM; Su 8AM-1PM; closed on Aug. 36 Rue St.-André-des-Arts. Métros: Odéon, St.-Michel. 43.26.89.49

125 28 Rue St.-André-des-Arts In *Satori in Paris,* Jack Kerouac described pleasant evenings spent here at what was then a bar called **La Gentilhommière** (circa 1962) and is now a pizzeria. ◆ Métros: Odéon, St.-Michel

125 Allard ★★$$ One of the old-time, honest bistros, with two zinc bars, sawdust-strewn floors, and a rotating selection of *plats du jour* as perennial as the clientele. The **Allard** family, who played host here to the **Aga Khan, Brigitte Bardot,** and **Georges Pompidou,** sold the restaurant, but it retains much of the old feeling. ◆ M-F noon-2PM, 7:30-10PM; closed in Aug, holidays. 41 Rue St.-André-des-Arts. Reservations required. Métros: Odéon, St.-Michel. 43.26.48.23

A recent survey revealed that more than half of the residents of Paris, given the opportunity, would live elsewhere. Reasons cited: property prices, cost of living, pollution, noise, and traffic jams. And when asked to describe the principal personality traits of Parisians, 91 percent said stressed and nervous.

126 Katyoushka ★$ Formerly **La Tchaika,** this Russian tea salon has a drawing-room atmosphere in which Chekhov, Tolstoy, or any princeling for that matter, would have been comfortable. Slavic hors d'oeuvres such as borscht, tarama, caviar, blinis, and smoked salmon, are still served, along with cheesecake. Perfect for an afternoon tea or a quick meal. ♦ M-F noon-2:30PM, 7:30-11PM; Sa 7:30-11PM. 9 Rue de l'Eperon. Métros: Odéon, St.-Michel. 43.54.47.02

127 La Lozère ★★$/$$ This crowded canteen with its bare wooden tables is a trip straight to the Lozère region in France's heartland. Try one of the robust regional specialties such as *confit de porc,* mutton tripe vinaigrette, or *aligot d'Aubrac* (a heavenly concoction of mashed potatoes, garlic, and Cantal cheese, served only on Thursday), or snack on slices of country ham, herb sausage, and *Bleu d'Auvergne.* ♦ Tu-Sa noon-2PM, 7:30-10:30PM; closed in Aug and last week of Dec. 4 Rue Hautefeuille. Reservations recommended. Métro: St.-Michel. 43.54.26.64

128 Rue Gît-le-Coeur The name means "Where the Heart Lies," a French phrase that's a good

St.-Germain

deal more romantic than the street's preceeding moniker: **Gilles-le-Cook.** Nos. 1-9 were originally one mansion, built in the 16th century by **François I** for his love at the time, the **Duchess d'Etampes.** ♦ Métro: St.-Michel

128 Hôtel de Vieux Paris $ In the 1950s this was a pay-as-you-go crash pad for the American Beat generation. **John Dos Passos, e.e. cummings,** and **William S. Burroughs** all hung out here at various times and discussed what existentialist effronteries might be perpetrated next. ♦ 40 Rue St. André-des-Arts. Métro: St.-Michel. 43.54.41.66

128 Caveau de la Bolée ★$ A wooden door leads into a 13th-century dungeonlike cavern filled with late-night chess and checkers aficionados. Dinner is served upstairs starting at 9PM. Downstairs a cabaret act plays nightly starting at 10:30PM. ♦ Daily 6:30PM-4AM. 25 Rue de l'Hirondelle. Métro: St.-Michel. 43.54.62.20

129 L'Ecluse ★★$/$$ This wine bar overlooking the Seine offers a spectrum of 70 reds (18 of which can be ordered by the glass). Bordeaux are the specialties, and they go wonderfully well with the plates of smoked goose, carpaccio, and Chavignol crottin cheese served here. ♦ Daily noon-2AM. 15 Quai des Grands-Augustins. Reservations recommended. Métro: St.-Michel. 46.33.58.74

130 Place St.-Michel A gathering spot on hot Saturday nights for a relatively nonviolent crowd of students, bikers, and drugpushers. The passable restaurants around the square cater to pizza- and souvlaki-eaters. ♦ Métro: St.-Michel

130 St.-Michel Fountain In 1860 **Gabriel Davioud** designed this 75-foot-high and 15-foot-wide sprouting monster (pictured above). The bronze of Saint Michel fighting the dragon is by **Duret.** ♦ Métro: St.-Michel

130 St.-Michel Métro One of the Art Nouveau métro entrances designed by **Hector Guimard** in 1900.

Le St. Séverin

130 Le St. Séverin The best people-watching perch in Place St.-Michel, with ice cream from the famous Berthillon. The hot chocolate is not bad either. ♦ Daily 7AM-2AM. 3 Place St.-Michel. Métro: St.-Michel. 43.54.19.36

131 Rue de la Harpe Named after **Reginald the Harper,** this medieval street, along with **Rue de la Huchette,** is one of the city's oldest. A downright moyen-âge air emanates from the cheap restaurants and taverns jammed with a host of impoverished students along this narrow, bustling street. ♦ Métro: St.-Michel

131 Rue de la Huchette In medieval times this ancient thoroughfare was called Street of Roasters, because it had a plethora of barbecue pits. Couscous and shish kebab joints continue the carnivorous tradition by roasting whole lambs and pigs in their front windows. You can always find cheap, if sometimes risky, street food here. ♦ Métro: St.-Michel

---

The first street-name signs didn't appear in Paris until 1729. For permanence, they were chiseled in stone and set into the walls of corner buildings. During the anticlerical fervor of the Revolution, the words "Saint" and "Sainte" were effaced from many of these signs, and the erasures still stand. In 1923 the stone markers were superseded by the black-and-white enamel nameplates you see virtually everywhere today.

Restaurants/Nightlife: Red **Hotels:** Blue
Shops/ 🌳Outdoors: Green **Sights/Culture:** Black

31 28 Rue de la Huchette Outside the Hôtel Mt.-Blanc is a plaque commemorating a WWII resistance fighter in the Rainbow unit that reads "Here fell Jean-Albert Bouillard, dead in the course of duty, killed by the Gestapo 17 May 1944 at 20 hours." ♦ Métro: St.-Michel

31 Théâtre de la Huchette Ever since Eugène Ionesco finished them in the mid-1950s, two of his plays, *The Bald Soprano* and *The Lesson,* have been running nonstop at this 85-seat theater. ♦ 23 Rue de la Huchette. Métro: St.-Michel. 43.26.38.99

31 Caveau de la Huchette Another crowded, dingy jazz cellar on a street that once rang with bebop. ♦ Cover. M-Th, Su 9:30PM-2:30AM; F 9:30PM-3AM; Sa 9:30PM-4AM. 5 Rue de la Huchette. Student discount available. Métro: St.-Michel. 43.26.65.05

31 10 Rue de la Huchette For several months here in 1795, a young brigadier-general languished in a sparsely decorated back room. Unemployed, unloved, and (he thought) dying of hunger, he saw no hope for the future. Soon thereafter, he dispersed a mob by firing grapeshot into its midst, and from then on **Napoléon Bonaparte** was never ignored. ♦ Métro: St.-Michel

32 Rue du Chat-qui-Pêche The Street of the Fishing Cat, most likely named after a medieval fishmonger, is one of the narrowest and, arguably, grungiest alleys in Paris. ♦ Métro: St.-Michel

St.-Séverin

133 Rue de la Parcheminerie This narrow street was crammed with scribes, copyists, and parchment peddlers in the Middle Ages. ♦ Métro: St.-Michel

133 St.-Séverin This lesser-known edifice, which was constructed around 1220 on the burial site of a sixth-century hermit named **Séverin,** is the official church of the **University of Paris.** Recognized as the city's richest example of flamboyant Gothic architecture, it was expanded between 1414 and 1520 with a bullet-shaped nave, a gaggle of gargoyles, and a five-aisled symphony of ribbed vaulting and stained glass. In 1673 the distinguished **Jules Hardouin-Mansart** tried his hand at enhancing the church, adding a small communion hall.

Don't miss the double ambulatory's slender medieval columns that shoot into vaulted arches, creating an effect that **Joris-Karl Huysmans** compared to being in a palm grove. The modern windows are by **Jean Bazaine,** the French abstract painter who created the mosaics for the UNESCO building and the Cluny-Sorbonne métro station. **Saint-Saëns** and **Fauré** performed on the 18th-

St.-Germain

century rococo organ in front of the west window; today the organ is frequently used for recitals. ♦ M-F 11AM-1PM, 3:30-7:30PM; Sa 11AM-11PM; Su 9AM-8PM. Rue des Prêtres-St.-Séverin. Métro: St.-Michel

Gregory Usher
Head Chef, Hôtel Ritz
Former Director, Cordon Bleu School of Cooking and Pastry

My ten favorite Parisian restaurants:

Au Franc Pinot One can easily spend half a day exploring the villagelike streets of the historic Ile St.-Louis. Au Franc Pinot, located in the middle of the island, is a quiet place for a quick bite to eat: cheeses, cold meat platters with green salad, and wines by the glass.

Benoît Owner Michel Petit is not *petit* at all; he is a giant man who delights in good food and wine. Benoît has to be one of the prettiest bistros in Paris, with its sparkling brass and etched-glass room dividers and fun turn-of-the-century posters and paintings. The food is prepared with care, and many traditional French dishes have been updated and lightened. Good and reasonably priced wine list.

Brasserie Balzar I would swim across the Seine any day to have the reward of a slice of sautéed calf's liver at this small brasserie next to the Sorbonne. Clients

St.-Germain

delight in people-watching in the mirrored interior. Start with the steamed mussels. Meringues with thick ribbons of Chantilly cream are a favorite dessert. Excellent beer on tap.

Chartier This place must be seen to be believed. It's one of the last great 19th-century workers' restaurants where even today it's difficult to spend more than 40 francs per person. Braised dishes are often the best here. Don't expect anything fancy and be prepared to share a table with others.

Chez Michel One of the first restaurants I went to when I arrived in Paris in 1970. I was smitten, badly, by the made-in-heaven lobster omelet. I make a yearly pilgrimage to sample it as well as some of their aged delicious Normandy specialties. The dessert soufflés and fruit tarts are smashing finales. It would be difficult to find a more spotless restaurant; the glasses literally sparkle.

Chez René A true family-run Paris bistro, and the food is simple and hearty. The daily specials are delicious (lamb and white-bean stew is sometimes Tuesday's specialty); the pan-fried crayfish is a tempting starter; spritzy Beaujolais wines come from owner Cinquin's property; and for dessert, the caramelized rice pudding is a substantial treat.

Chiberta Probably my favorite Paris restaurant. I love the salmon. And I love the gray-and-black-hued contemporary dining room, where each table is flatteringly lit. The owner, Richard, is a true professional who runs the front of the house with a firm hand, and the service is excellent. Chef Jean-Michel Bédier resides in the kitchen, and his cooking is superb, thoroughly modern, but neither pretentious nor precious. They serve one of the best cheese platters in Paris, and the desserts are stunning, elaborate creations that taste just as good as they look.

Le Vaudeville This bustling, Art Deco brasserie on the Rue Vivienne is part of a small chain that includes

Flo, Julien, and Terminus-Nord and was founded by the enterprising Alsatian chef Jean-Claude Boucher in 1968. The oyster bar is one of the city's best. This is the place to try a grilled pig's foot, if you have never had one. Good daily specialties.

Pile ou Face Chef Claude Udron and director Alain Dumerque run a small, well-appointed restaurant. Take a look at the painted ceiling in one of the rooms that was once a dairy. The dishes are influenced by southwestern French cooking and are a good value. Save room for dessert; the chef is trained as a pastry chef, too, and his fanciful sweets should not be missed.

Taillevent No restaurant is perfect, but Taillevent always seems to come the closest. The second-generation owner, Jean-Claude Vrinat, oversees every aspect of this Paris gastronomic institution. The kitchen, however, is entrusted to its highly capable chef, Claude Deligne, whose carefully balanced cuisine walks a tightrope between classic and nouvelle; he is a perfectionist when it comes to seasoning. We all deserve to be spoiled once in a while, and Taillevent does the best job in Paris.

Martine Guerrand-Hermès
Associate of Hermès

Crossing the **Place des Vosges,** the **Carrousel,** or **Tuileries** early in the morning or late at night; the two little bistros in the **Palais Royal;** the **Place St.-Georges;** the quai in front of **L'Institut de France;** the hardware floor (*bricolage*) in the BHV department store (they have everything); Delacroix's house on the **Place de Furstemberg;** lunch at **Gildo's** on Rue de Grenelle; dinner at **Le Pavillon de l'Elysée** for a great wine list, marvelous view, and good truffles; and the **Place du Palais Bourbon** and its two little restaurants.

Louis Cane
Artist

The 18th-century French paintings in the **Louvre,** the **Picasso Museum, National Museum of Modern Art (Georges Pompidou Center), Jardin des Tuileries, La Cour Palatiale du Palais-Royal, Rodin Museum** and the open-mouthed serpent inside **Notre-Dame** at the foot of a stoop on the northern end.

The art galleries **Daniel Templon, Beaubourg, Maeght-Lelong,** and **de France.**

The **Foundry SUSSE** for casting sculpture in Arcueil, outside of Paris.

Jean Gillet
General Manager, Hôtel Meurice

Favorite deluxe hotel: **Hôtel Ritz** on the Place Vendôme.

Favorite small hotel: **L'Hôtel** on the Rue des Beaux-Arts.

Favorite hotel restaurant: **Hôtel Bristol's** restaurant.

Favorite place for drinks: **Fouquet's** on the Champs-Elysées.

Marie "Bootsie" Galbraith

Wife of a former ambassador to France and a long-time resident of Paris

Backstage at the **Comédie Française,** where old costumes, hats, and wigs are made. There are two ladies there who use 18th-century irons to press ruffles onto the shirts.

Etienne Vatelot—the workshop of Monsieur Vatelot (on Rue Portalis), an expert maker and repairer of violins, violas, and cellos. He represents the fourth generation in his family to do so.

Musée de Sèvres—call ahead to get permission to see the workers making French china.

Walking through the **Cour du Commerce St.-André**— a passage *(galerie)* within a city block that remains unknown to most Parisians. Enter from Boulevard St.-Germain, Rue St.-André-des-Arts, or Rue de l'Ancienne-Comédie. It's like walking into a small village of the past.

Church of **St.-Julien-le-Pauvre**—one of the oldest churches in Paris. And it has Paris' oldest tree in its yard. Go during the service so you can hear the men's choir.

Les Petits Chanteurs du Croix du Bois—a famous boys choir that sings at **St.-Sulpice** church. On the Rue St.-Sulpice, you can buy tall church candles.

Montmartre—see the vineyards where they make their own wine.

La Villette and its **Science Museum**—the best part of it is **La Géode,** the huge golden sphere that houses an enormous movie screen and theater.

The **Musée des Automates in Neuilly** is full of 18th-century mechanical dolls, figures, and animals.

The **Garde Républicaine** has honor-guard dressage demonstrations in their own special buildings.

Walk anywhere in the old parts of the **Marais,** punch door buttons, and enter the wonderful courtyards.

Musée de Carnavalet in the Marais—a gorgeous building and collection.

Patrick Guerrand-Hermès

Executive Vice President, Hermès, and grandson of the company's founder

Rowing in the **Bois de Boulogne.**

Strolling in the rose gardens at **Bagatelle** in the spring.

Visiting the hothouses in **Boulogne-sur-Seine.**

The Japanese Gardens **(Albert Kahn Gardens)** on the Rue des Abondances.

Walking through the **Parc de Montsouris** and eating at one of its two restaurants.

Going to lesser-known museums, such as **Boudelle, Marmottan, Gustave Moreau,** and the **Army Museum** at Les Invalides (great for children, too).

Seeing old movies at small art cinemas.

Lunch at **Lipp.**

Saturday or Sunday mornings at the flea market **(Marché aux Puces),** followed by either a fantastic lunch at **La Barrière de Clichy** or a steak and french fries at one of the little bistros in the flea market.

Caserne de la Garde Républicaine.

Jim Dine

American Artist

Every time I visit Paris, I immediately go to the **Bon Marché** department store and make a complete tour of it because it's the kind of dopey store you used to be able to find in Cincinnati in the 1940s. There's a sales clerk in the luggage department who must think I'm some kind of pervert because she sees me looking at luggage all the time. She sells those aluminum suitcases that were once used by soldiers and blue metal trunks. I buy espadrilles, art supplies, and great stationery there. I go to their bicycle and sports department, and I go to the hardware department, which is where I found a very good etching tool (it's a rotary sanding disk on Velcro that enables you to erase without creating circular marks).

I also always visit the **Rodin Museum** because it's on the way from my hotel to Crommelynck's (my printer). I like to admire the roses in the garden.

I used to go to the **Bois de Boulogne** every day to ride my bike, but my back is so bad now that I don't. It's great because you can see the prostitutes flashing in the woods.

St.-Germain

I shop along the **Avenue de la Grand-Armée,** which is the continuation of the **Champs-Elysées,** because that's where some very good bike shops are located.

St.-Sulpice's Delacroix murals are always worth a visit!

I always go to the **Café Flore** for breakfast and order toast. My wife, Nancy, and I like their soft-boiled eggs, too. We also dine at **Brasserie Balzar,** and we have tea at **Christian Constant,** where they've got the finest cocoa I've ever tasted.

I go to the **Louvre** to look at antiquities and tour the Pavillon de Flore, which houses Spanish paintings and French bronzes by Barais.

The **Picasso Museum** is tastefully designed and is a great homage to the artist. I love the Giacometti furniture and the lighting fixtures—although everything about the museum is beautiful.

Daniel Templon

Paris Art Dealer

L'Ami Louis for the best foie gras in Paris.

Clara-Clara, a sculpture by Richard Serra in the **Parc de Choisy** in the 13th arrondissement.

Les Nymphéas by Monet in the **Orangerie.**

Paris Opéra House, Pont des Arts, Ste.-Chapelle, the bar in **L'Hôtel, Bar de l'Hôtel Pont-Royal,** and **Lucas-Carton.**

Claire Stoullig

Curator of Modern Art, Georges Pompidou Center Editor-in-Chief, *Art Studio Magazine*

Le Train Bleu at the Gare de Lyon, **Chapelle de la Salpêtrière, Villa Boulard** in the 14th arrondissement, **Atelier Gustave Moreau,** the *ateliers* along the Quai de Loire, **Passage Vivienne,** the trees in the **Parc de Montsouris, La Fontaine des Innocents,** and **La Bibliothèque Fornet.**

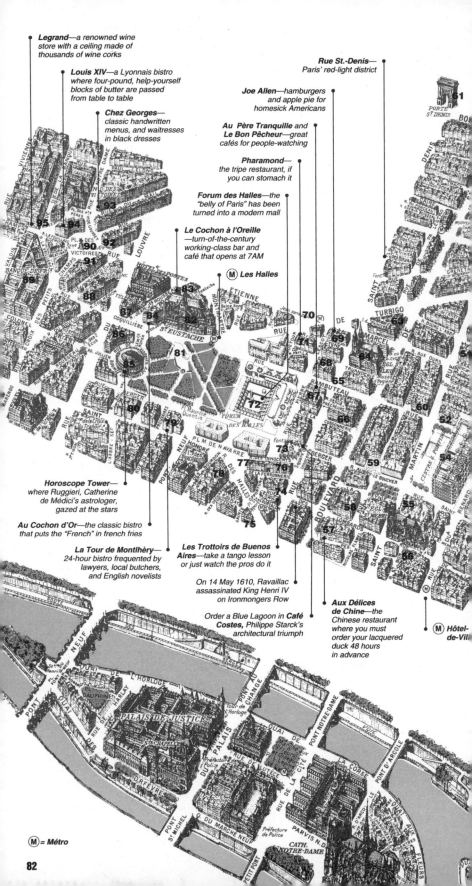

Legrand—a renowned wine store with a ceiling made of thousands of wine corks

Louis XIV—a Lyonnais bistro where four-pound, help-yourself blocks of butter are passed from table to table

Chez Georges—classic handwritten menus, and waitresses in black dresses

Rue St.-Denis—Paris' red-light district

Joe Allen—hamburgers and apple pie for homesick Americans

Au Père Tranquille and **Le Bon Pêcheur**—great cafés for people-watching

Pharamond—the tripe restaurant, if you can stomach it

Forum des Halles—the "belly of Paris" has been turned into a modern mall

Le Cochon à l'Oreille—turn-of-the-century working-class bar and café that opens at 7AM

Ⓜ **Les Halles**

Horoscope Tower—where Ruggieri, Catherine de Médici's astrologer, gazed at the stars

Au Cochon d'Or—the classic bistro that puts the "French" in french fries

La Tour de Montlhèry—24-hour bistro frequented by lawyers, local butchers, and English novelists

Les Trottoirs de Buenos Aires—take a tango lesson or just watch the pros do it

On 14 May 1610, Ravaillac assassinated King Henri IV on Ironmongers Row

Order a Blue Lagoon in **Café Costes,** Philippe Starck's architectural triumph

Aux Délices de Chine—the Chinese restaurant where you must order your lacquered duck 48 hours in advance

Ⓜ Hôtel-de-Vill

Ⓜ = *Métro*

82

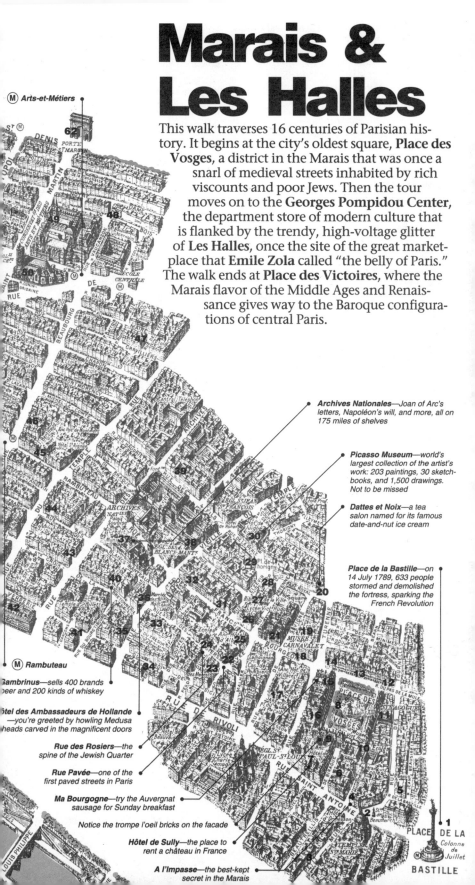

Marais & Les Halles

This walk traverses 16 centuries of Parisian history. It begins at the city's oldest square, **Place des Vosges**, a district in the Marais that was once a snarl of medieval streets inhabited by rich viscounts and poor Jews. Then the tour moves on to the **Georges Pompidou Center**, the department store of modern culture that is flanked by the trendy, high-voltage glitter of **Les Halles**, once the site of the great marketplace that **Emile Zola** called "the belly of Paris." The walk ends at **Place des Victoires**, where the Marais flavor of the Middle Ages and Renaissance gives way to the Baroque configurations of central Paris.

Ⓜ Arts-et-Métiers

Archives Nationales—Joan of Arc's letters, Napoléon's will, and more, all on 175 miles of shelves

Picasso Museum—world's largest collection of the artist's work: 203 paintings, 30 sketchbooks, and 1,500 drawings. Not to be missed

Dattes et Noix—a tea salon named for its famous date-and-nut ice cream

Place de la Bastille—on 14 July 1789, 633 people stormed and demolished the fortress, sparking the French Revolution

Ⓜ Rambuteau

Gambrinus—sells 400 brands beer and 200 kinds of whiskey

Hôtel des Ambassadeurs de Hollande—you're greeted by howling Medusa heads carved in the magnificent doors

Rue des Rosiers—the spine of the Jewish Quarter

Rue Pavée—one of the first paved streets in Paris

Ma Bourgogne—try the Auvergnat sausage for Sunday breakfast

Notice the trompe l'oeil bricks on the facade

Hôtel de Sully—the place to rent a château in France

A l'Impasse—the best-kept secret in the Marais

PLACE DE LA
Colonne de Juillet

BASTILLE

Kick off this tour with a breakfast of eggs and Auvergnat sausages at **Ma Bourgogne,** then browse the boutiques in Place des Vosges, or visit the **Musée Carnavalet** (the Historical Museum of the City of Paris) to peruse its collection of Revolution memorabilia and 18th-century shop signs, both of which are a big hit with children. Lunch could be at one of the fashionable new tea salons (**Le Loir dans la Théière,** for example) or a quick falafel or pastrami sandwich purchased somewhere on **Rue des Rosiers,** the main artery of the old Jewish quarter, which is lined with storefront synagogues and kosher bakeries (remember that much of the street closes on Saturday, the Jewish Sabbath). Your dessert will be the **Picasso Museum** in the **Hôtel-Salé** on Rue de Thorigny. (If

visiting the Marais in the summer, inquire about the **Festival du Marais,** a series of opera, chamber music, and drama performances in the district's exquisite 17th-century mansions.)

Upon reaching the Pompidou Center, you'll find that late-night restaurants, cafés, and clubs abound around Les Halles. **Au Cochon d'Or, L'Ami Louis,** and **L'Escargot Montorgueil** are three classic French restaurants to choose from. Great dancing may be found at the funky **Les Bains Douches** or the more Latin **Le Tango.** Complete your Les Halles rite of passage by sipping a Blue Lagoon at midnight on the terrace at **Café Costes** or indulging in a steak at 3AM with local butchers at **La Tour de Montlhéry.** Plan on sleeping late the next morning.

Marais

Since Roman times, this district in eastern Paris has been known as the *Marais* (marsh). It was once a vast, oozy swampland on the northern branch of the Seine. In the 12th century the marsh was drained, making it habitable for humans but inhospitable to all the creatures who wanted it wet. Like New York's fashionable SoHo district, the Marais is now a mélange of ruin and restoration, past and present. The historically rich neighborhood possesses at least one Roman road (along the François-Miron and St.-Antoine streets), what may be the city's oldest house

Marais & Les Halles

(a 14th-century, half-timbered house at 3 Rue Volta), the site of the (long-since destroyed) Bastille prison, and numerous twisting, huddled medieval streets.

Among those streets are three (Rue des Rosiers, Rue des Ecouffes, and Rue Ferdinand-Duval) that are the backbone of the celebrated Jewish quarter, formed in the 13th century when **King Philippe Auguste** "invited" the Jewish merchants living in front of Notre-Dame to move outside of his new city wall.

Seven French kings made the Marais their royal residence, starting with **Charles V** (1337-1380). **Henri II** (1519-1559) was the last; he died during a freak jousting accident when the shattered lance of **Montgomery,** the captain of his Scots Guards, pierced the visor of his helmet. Henri's wife, **Catherine de Médici,** tried to ease her grief by having their royal **Maison des Tournelles** in the Marais demolished.

A half-century after the accident, **Henri IV** chose to construct the **Place Royale** on the leveled crown land in the Marais. Its name was changed in 1800 to **Place des Vosges** to honor the Vosges in eastern France, which was the first provincial department to pay its taxes after the Revolution. "It's the blow of Montgomery's lance," **Victor Hugo** later wrote, "that created the Place des Vosges."

The Marais and Place Royale (Vosges) figured prominently in Henri IV's building boom in the 17th century, which also included **Pont-Neuf, Place Dauphine,** and **Ile St.-Louis.** In the Marais, the king employed the leading architects of the day: **Louis Le Vau, François Mansart,** and **Jules Hardouin-Mansart.**

During this era, **Molière, Racine, Voltaire,** and **Madame de Sévigné** were exchanging witty, learned party conversation in the great salons of the Marais that Molière parodied in his play *Précieuses Ridicules.* Within a century the former swamp had become the heart of intellectual Paris. In 1630 **Cardinal Richelieu,** a Marais resident, founded the **Académie Française** here, and years later a seven-year-old Mozart played his first Paris concert in Marais. This area became an island of urban civility and sophistication, far removed from the wild boars and party boors of Versailles.

After the Revolution the elegant town houses were abandoned or carved into small factories and rooming houses. Squatters took over, and the Marais fell into a shocking state of ruin. Over the centuries, 29 of the grand *hôtels particulières* were destroyed; nearly one hundred remained, dilapidated and on the verge of collapse. In 1964 **André Malraux,** Minister of Culture under **Charles de Gaulle,** came to the rescue and designated the Marais the first historic preservation district in Paris. With 1,500 architecturally important structures, it is the largest historic district in France.

Many of the old buildings have been given new life, as you'll see when you visit the **Archives Nationales, Musée Carnavalet** (the city's historical library), the famous Place des Vosges, and the **Picasso Museum.** The Marais quarter, a juxtaposition of splendor and squalor, is on a fashionable rebound.

The *International Herald Tribune,* the century-old English-language daily newspaper based in Paris, has a paid circulation of 178,000 and is distributed in about 164 countries. Today less than half of the readership is American. The paper was founded by James Gordon Bennett Jr., who ran the *New York Herald* until a scandal sent him fleeing to Paris in 1877 (legend holds that he urinated in his fiancée's fireplace in front of shocked guests at a New Year's Eve party). He controlled the New York paper from France and, in 1887, decided to start a European edition.

Most Paris métro stations are equipped with television screens broadcasting everything from music videos and aerobic dance classes to news shows.

Restaurants/Nightlife: Red   Hotels: Blue
Shops/ 🌳 Outdoors: Green   Sights/Culture: Black

1 Place de la Bastille On 14 July 1789, 633 people stormed the **Bastille** (the French counterpart to the Tower of London), captured its ammunition depot, released its prisoners (only seven, and none political), lynched its governor, and demolished the fortress, thus sparking the French Revolution. Every year the 14th of July is celebrated in Paris with parades and dancing in the streets.

The eight-towered Bastille was built in 1370 by Provost **Hugues Aubriot** as a fortified palace for **Charles V,** and was later transformed by **Cardinal Richelieu** into a holding tank where political prisoners were detained without trial. During its baleful history, the Bastille held **Voltaire,** who was imprisoned for penning his biting verse, as well as the **Marquis de Sade** and the notorious, enigmatic "Man in the Iron Mask." The paving stones, laid where Rue du Faubourg-St.-Antoine intersects the square, mark the site of the original towers. The figure perched on top of the 170-foot **July Column** in the middle of the square is not an allegory of Liberty as many suppose, but a winged Mercury. ◆ Métro: Bastille

1 Bastille Opéra Not long ago, the French government appointed **Carlos Ott,** a Canadian-Uruguayan architect, to design what was to be the largest opera house in the world on the Place de la Bastille. The facility, billed as the "people's opera house," entertains an estimated 960,000 ticket-holders a year and includes an amphitheater and a studio stage for smaller performances. Its opening was planned in conjunction with the July 1989 bicentennial of the storming of the Bastille and the French Revolution, but dissensions of an administrative nature, such as the axing

(figuratively at least) of the director, delayed the opening of the amphitheater until 1991. The opera house finally opened in 1992. ◆ Métro: Bastille

2 Statue of Beaumarchais The 18th-century comedies of **Caron de Beaumarchais** (1732-1799), *The Barber of Seville* (1775) and *The Marriage of Figaro* (1784), were respectively transformed by **Rossini** and **Mozart** into operas whose factotum hero was regarded as dangerously, even revolutionarily, independent. The radical sympathies of Beaumarchais were played out in real life, too: his office was secretly running guns to American revolutionaries. In keeping with the dramatist's satiric tradition, residents of the Bastille neighborhood are constantly dressing up his statue in outrageous costumes. ◆ Métro: Bastille

3 Le Maraîcher ★★$$ Authentic in every detail, from the wooden beams and old photos of the Marché St. Antoine to the patron himself. **Valentin Corral** studied cooking with Alain Senderens, decoration and presentation at Ledoyen, and fine wines in Bordeaux. Hence the exotic flowers, well-chosen wine list, and, above all, the seasonally inspired menu with gems such as *pot au feu de canette au coriandre, magret de canard* with honey and spices, and scallop raviolis with zucchini and

Marais & Les Halles

thyme. Just as impressive are the prices, with an incredibly inexpensive lunch-time menu. ◆ M 8-11PM; Tu-Sa noon-2PM, 8-11PM. 5 Rue Beautreillis. Reservations recommended. Métro: Sully-Morland. 42.71.42.49

4 A l'Impasse ★★$/$$ One of the best-kept secrets in the Marais can be found tucked away in a narrow alley. This old neighborhood bistro serves delightful meals in a pleasantly renovated dining room. Baked goat cheese salads, terrines of rabbit and girolle mushrooms, filet of duck in blueberry sauce, and rich chocolate profiteroles are among the delights offered here at bargain prices. The service is warm and attentive. ◆ Tu-F noon-2PM, 7-11PM; Sa 7-11PM; closed in Aug. 4 Impasse Guéménée. Reservations recommended. Métros: Bastille, St.-Paul. 42.72.08.45

5 Bofinger ★$$/$$$ One of the oldest and most overrated brasseries, Bofinger dates from 1864; house legend holds it was the first in the city to pour draft beer. Specialties include nostalgia, *fruits de mer*, Alsatian *choucroute*, wine from the Côtes-du-Rhône, and more nostalgia. Popular with Americans, whom the restaurant, as a matter of course, segregates from its French regulars. ◆ Daily noon-3PM, 7:30PM-1AM. 5-7 Rue de la Bastille. Reservations recommended. Métro: Bastille. 42.72.87.82

6 Hôtel de la Place des Vosges $$ Just down the street from the King's Pavilion entrance to the famous square sits this cozy, rather than regal, hotel. ◆ 12 Rue de Birague. Métro: St.-Paul. 42.72.60.46

7 Hôtel de Sully The most richly decorated private mansion in Paris dates from the time of **Louis XIII** and was designed in 1630 by architect **Androuet du Cerceau** for the notorious gambler **Petit Thouars,** who is said to have lost his entire fortune in one night. Ten years later, the mansion was bought by the **Duc de Sully,** a minister to **Henri IV.** Inside at the information office of the Caisse Nationale des Monuments Historiques et des Sites (Bureau of Historic Monuments and Sites), you may rent any of 40 châteaux or historic mansions throughout France for private receptions, weddings, or conventions. ♦ M-F 9AM-noon, 2-6PM; Sa 10:30AM-noon, 2-6PM. 62 Rue St.-Antoine. Métro: St.-Paul. 44.61.20.00

8 Place des Vosges The oldest and perhaps most beautiful square in Paris. This symmetrical ensemble of 36 matching pavilions with red and gold brick and stone facades, steep slate roofs, and dormer windows was designed in 1612 by **Clément Metezeau.** For the first time in Paris an arcade was used to link houses, and balconies were employed for more than decorative purposes.

Commissioned by **Henri IV,** the square's original function was to house a silk factory and its workers. The goal was to provide **Marie de**

Marais & Les Halles

Médici, his estranged queen, with lingerie cheaper than what could be imported from Genoa. Despite Henri's good intentions, his silkworkers' housing project was gentrified before the last brick was laid. Into the apartments with 16-foot-high ceilings, red marble fireplaces, and parquet floors moved **Richelieu, Corneille, Molière,** and a covey of courtiers, cavaliers, ministers, and marquises.

It remained a high-class neighborhood until the summer of 1686, when **Louis XIV** moved to Versailles and the French aristocracy followed. In the early 18th century the Marais continued to decline and eventually became the city's industrial East End. Heavy machinery was bolted to the elegant floors of the great spaces, and magnificent salons were subdivided into minuscule apartments. The neighborhood was not pulled out of its nosedive until the early 1960s, when Minister of Culture **André Malraux** had the Place des Vosges and the Marais declared a historic district. Nowadays in the Place des Vosges you will find, weather permitting, grandmothers knitting, toddlers digging in the dirt, or perhaps a group of North African immigrants enjoying an impromptu soccer game beside an equestrian statue of a smirking **Louis XIII.** ♦ Métros: Bastille, St.-Paul

9 Hôtel de Coulanges The **Marquise de Sévigné,** whose correspondence with her daughter in Provence became one of the most famous series of letters in French literature, was born here on 6 February 1626. Private residence. ♦ 1 Place des Vosges. Métro: St.-Paul

9 3 Place des Vosges You have to get pretty close to notice that the bricks are painted on. The newer buildings constructed on the square are masterpieces of trompe-l'oeil. The facades are made of plaster on wood framing, and they are painted to resemble brick. ♦ Métro: St.-Paul

10 Coconnas ★$$ Boasting a Louis XIII dining room and sidewalk terrace overlooking the mansions and garden of the Place des Vosges, this casual restaurant (run by **Claude Terrail** of La Tour d'Argent) has built its reputation on serving Good King Henri's *poule-au-pot* (commemorating Henri IV's famous political promise of a chicken in every pot) and *marquise au chocolat.* Crowded with American tourists and expatriates. ♦ W-Su noon-2PM, 7:30-10PM; closed 15 Dec-15 Jan. 2bis Place des Vosges. Reservations recommended. Métros: Bastille, St.-Paul. 42.78.58.16

11 La Chope des Vosges ★$/$$ Architects working on restorations in the historic district hang out in this simple café/restaurant. Not found on any gourmet's restaurant roster, it serves a *fait maison* foie gras and meals with a warm welcome. ♦ Daily 8:30AM-12:30AM, May-Sep; Tu-Sa 8:30AM-12:30AM, Su 8:30AM-2:30PM, Oct-Apr. 22 Place des Vosges. Reservations recommended. Métros: Bastille, St.-Paul. 42.72.64.04

11 Mythes et Légendes This museumlike shop sells antiques and archaeological artifacts, bronze Buddhas, Flemish tapestries, and magnificent Mayan and Aztec pieces. ♦ M-Sa 10AM-12:30PM, 2-7PM; closed two weeks in Aug. 18 Place des Vosges. Métros: Bastille, St.-Paul. 42.72.63.26

11 18 and 23 Place des Vosges These are two of the best portals on the square. Also, don't miss the door knockers at **No. 4** and **No. 17.**♦ Métros: Bastille, St.-Paul

11 Pavillon de la Reine $$$ One of the most elegant hotels in the Marais, this 17th-century mansion, discreetly distanced by its own garden courtyard, is quietly opulent, with antique tapestries, Persian carpets, grand fireplaces, marble floors, and soft leather couches. The Pavillon de la Reine is operated in conjunction with the chic **Relais Christine** across the Seine. ♦ 28 Place des Vosges. Métro: Chemin-Vert. 42.77.96.40

11 Musée Victor Hugo This museum was the French writer's home from 1833 until 1848, when **Napoléon III** came to power and Hugo's voluntary exile in the Channel Islands began. The museum's eclectic assortment of Hugo mementos includes the cap he wore during the 1871 Siege of Paris, his bust sculpted by **Rodin,** and a model of an elephant sculpture that he proposed for Place de la Bastille. Haunting but poetic postage stamp-sized pen-and-ink doodles of Rhine castles and ships at sea, and macabre sketches of witches, demons, and the hanging of John Brown show a nightmarish side to the author of *The Hunchback of Notre-Dame* (1831) and *Les Misérables* (1862).

The drawings are counterbalanced by the hodgepodge of Oriental furnishings Hugo designed for the Guernsey home of **Juliette Drouet,** his mistress for more than half a century. Don't leave the museum without viewing the Place des Vosges from one of Hugo's upstairs windows and glancing at the **Nadar** photo of an old but ageless Hugo on his deathbed, 22 May 1885. ♦ Admission. Tu-Su 10AM-5:40PM. 6 Place des Vosges. Métros: Bastille, Chemin-Vert, St.-Paul. 42.72.10.16

13 Jardin de Flore Founded by renowned French architect **Fernand Pouillon,** this remarkable small publishing house reissues deluxe limited editions of antique manuscripts, illustrations, and maps. Pouillon employs Renaissance bookmaking techniques and prints on handmade paper. The books are bound in tooled, gold-leaf leather, and illustrations are colored by hand. Among the wares on display are the masterful *Apocalypse* engravings (1498) of **Albrecht Dürer,** the illustrated *Venise* (1610) by **Giacomo Franco,** and the famous three-foot-diameter globes that Venetian cartographer **Vincenzo Maria Coronelli** created for **Louis XIV** in 1693. In 1984 another French head of state, **President François Mitterrand,** ordered a pair of

Marais & Les Halles

12 André Bissonnet Some years ago, a butcher named André Bissonnet laid down his meat cleaver, redecorated his *boucherie,* and began buying and, in his cold-storage room, restoring antique musical instruments. On any given day you might find a 1747 viola da gamba, a 17th-century harp, a porcelain trumpet, ancient hurdy-gurdies, or a black serpent, a bizarre 18th-century horn used to accompany chanting priests. Bissonnet claims to be an accomplished player of the Breton bombardon and upon request will proudly bleat out a few bars. ♦ M-Sa 2-7PM; closed in Aug. 6 Rue du Pas-de-la-Mule. Métro: Bastille. 48.87.20.15

13 21 Place des Vosges Cardinal Richelieu (1585-1642), the French prime minister under **Louis XIII** and the man who founded the **Académie Française** in 1635, lived here. ♦ Métros: Bastille, St.-Paul

13 La Guirlande de Julie ★$$/$$$ At his newest restaurant on the square, **Claude Terrail,** owner of the celebrated Tour d'Argent, presents a small seasonally inspired menu. Start with something light, such as the *terrine de poisson,* followed by the excellent pot-au-feu or mullet fricassee, accompanied by wines from the Cave de la Tour d'Argent. Conclude with the popular *émincée de pommes chaudes Guirlande* (cinnamon ice cream over crunchy baked apple slices). In summer reserve a table outside beneath the brick arcade. ♦ W-Su noon-2PM, 7:15-10PM; closed in Jan. 25 Place des Vosges. Reservations recommended. Métros: Bastille, St.-Paul. 48.87.94.07

these globes (at $12,000 apiece) for his Elysée Palace office—personalized with his portrait floating in the South Atlantic. The Art Nouveau doorway of ersatz marble is by sculptor and jeweler **Jean Filhos.** ♦ Tu-Su 2-6PM. 24 Place des Vosges. Métro: St.-Paul. 42.77.61.90

14 Rue des Francs-Bourgeois Originally called *Rue des Poulies* (Street of Spools) after a local community of weavers, this thoroughfare became known as the *Street of the Free Citizens* in the 14th century, when the local parish built an almshouse (on the site of 34-36 Rue des Francs-Bourgeois) for citizens so poor they were *francs* (free) of any obligation to the state tax jackals. ♦ Métro: St.-Paul

14 Carnavalette Old newspapers, political cartoons, fin-de-siècle theater programs, 19th-century satirical newspapers, and fashion catalogs from the 1930s are for sale here. ♦ Daily 10:30AM-6:30PM. 2 Rue des Francs-Bourgeois. Métro: St.-Paul. 42.72.91.92

15 Ma Bourgogne ★★$/$$ Owned by **Aimé Cougoureux,** this arcade-sheltered café is where the locals go for Sunday breakfast. Specialties include sausages from Auvergne, foie gras *des Landes, andouillette,* veal tripe, and spicy steak tartare. Sample one of the sublime Burgundies from the 15,000-bottle wine cellar. The building's history is less tasteful. It once belonged to a **Robert Aubrey,** whose wife, it was said, hated him so much she sometimes urinated in his soup. ♦ Daily 8AM-1AM; closed in Feb and one week in Mar. 19 Place des Vosges. No credit cards. Métros: Bastille, St.-Paul. 42.78.44.64

16 Hôtel de Chaulnes The second floor belongs to the elite one hundred-member **Architecture Academy.** Monthly guided tours of this building and the **Hôtel de Sully** are given by the members of the Caisse Nationale des Monuments Historiques; architecture buffs will find the tour worthwhile (there is a fee) and it offers yet another chance to polish up those French skills. ♦ 9 Place des Vosges. Métro: St.-Paul

16 L'Ambrosie ★★★$$$/$$$$ One of the few Michelin three-star restaurants in Paris is L'Ambrosie. The small ever-changing menu of owner and chef **Bernard Pacaud,** who trained under Claude Peyrot at Le Vivarois, fulfills the restaurant's promise of ambrosia. The menu changes every two or three months; some past favorites that haven't been forgotten include artichokes with foie gras, red pepper mousse, skate with sliced cabbage, veal sweetbreads with shallots and fresh pasta, and the puff-pastry desserts. ♦ Tu-Sa noon-1:30PM, 8-9:30PM; closed two weeks in Feb, three weeks in Aug. 9 Place des Vosges. Reservations required. Métro: St.-Paul. 42.78.51.45

17 Auberge de Jarente ★$/$$ A simple restaurant serving such Basque specialties as

Marais & Les Halles

piperade and paella at modest prices. ♦ Tu-Sa noon-2:30PM, 7:30-10:30PM; closed in Aug. 7 Rue de Jarente. Reservations recommended. Métro: St.-Paul. 42.77.49.35

18 L'Arlequin Ancient and beautiful glassware is arranged on dusty shelves that reach from floor to ceiling. ♦ M-Sa 2:30-6:45PM; closed 15 July-Aug. 13 Rue des Francs-Bourgeois. Métro: St.-Paul. 42.78.77.00

18 Jean-Pierre De Castro Antique silver and silver-plated articles such as champagne buckets, candelabras, and sugar tongs are the specialties of this busy boutique. Forks and spoons are displayed by the basketful and sold by the kilogram. ♦ M 2-7PM; Tu-Sa 10:30AM-7PM; Su 11AM-7PM. 17 Rue des Francs-Bourgeois. Métro: St.-Paul. 42.72.04.00

18 Les Bourgeoises ★★$$ Dining here on the baked St. Marcellin cheese on toast, fresh raviolis stuffed with herbed cheese, lamb stew with coriander and ginger, or Indian specialties such as chicken tandoori is like dining in the living room of owner **Martine Robin's** grandmother, and for good reason: the oil paintings, chairs, and tables all come from his grandparents' antique shop. The homemade raspberry liqueur aging in a jar by the front window is, unfortunately, purely decorative. ♦ Tu-Sa noon-2PM, 8-11PM. 12 Rue des Francs-Bourgeois. Reservations recommended. Métro: St.-Paul. 42.72.48.30

19 Galerie Gourmande ★★$ Armed with a secret 1912 recipe and the darkest chocolate bars, this tea salon concocts the best hot chocolate in the Marais. The decor is simple yet classic: blond wood chairs, white tablecloths, and a vase of red roses on each table. Fare includes light lunches, fresh pastas, and tarts. ♦ Tu-Su noon-7PM. 38 Rue de Sévigné. Métro: St.-Paul. 42.74.48.40

20 Dattes et Noix ★$ This tea salon caters to a young artistic clientele; it is decorated with white tile floors, peach walls, and a photo exhibition that features a new artist every month. A friendly snack bar also offers homemade tarts, some 20 flavors of prize-winning Motta Carte d'Or ice cream, delicious lunches of smoked salmon, and fresh pastas. ♦ Daily 11:30AM-3:30PM (F 7:30PM-midnight for couscous). 4 Rue du Parc-Royal. Métro: St.-Paul. 48.87.88.94

Maison SUBA

21 Maison Suba A stone's throw from the Place des Vosges you will find a shop full of delicious red pepper conserves and oak-smoked Hungarian sausages. Don't pass up the Tokaji wine, so loved by **King George V,** the father of **Queen Elizabeth II,** that he ordered it in industrial quantities. ♦ Tu-Sa 9AM-1PM, 3-7PM; closed in Aug. 11 Rue de Sévigné. Métro: St.-Paul. 48.87.46.06

21 Carnavalet Hôtel et Musée The laughing carnival mask sculpted in stone above the gate (facing the Rue des Francs-Bourgeois) of this splendid mansion is a misleading visual pun: this 16th-century building does not conceal a midway of clowns or a family of dancing bears. A truer clue to the building's contents is found in the ship (the symbol of Paris) on the gate (illustrated above). In 1880 the Hôtel Carnavalet was put into service as the Historical Museum of the City of Paris, and today vividly displays four centuries (1500-1900) of Paris life. The Hôtel Carnavalet's original 1540 design is attributed to **Pierre Lescot,** who was then architect of the Louvre. The *hôtel* (mansion) was spruced up in 1655 by **François Mansart,** the architect memorialized by the term *mansard* roofs. The building's name evolved from an early owner's name, the widow of the Breton **Sire de Kernevency,** whose surname Parisians constantly mispronounced and permanently corrupted to its present form.

Restaurants/Nightlife: Red
Shops/ 🌳 Outdoors: Green
Hotels: Blue
Sights/Culture: Black

Ground Floor

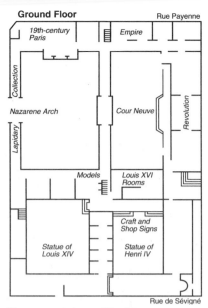

Rue Payenne

- 19th-century Paris
- Empire
- Collection
- Nazarene Arch
- Cour Neuve
- Lapidary
- Revolution
- Models
- Louis XVI Rooms
- Craft and Shop Signs
- Statue of Louis XIV
- Statue of Henri IV

Rue de Sévigné

The museum has something for everyone, even the most fidgety youngster. On the ground floor is an entire roomful of old metal shop signs and 18th-century billboards, dating from an age of mass illiteracy. The baker advertised himself with a golden sheaf of wheat, the butcher with a suckling pig, and the locksmith with an ornate iron key. There is also a lively show-and-tell description of the French Revolution; the royal family's itemized laundry bill; the young dauphin's penmanship book; the rope ladder used by a political prisoner to escape from the Bastille; a model of the guillotine; a pair of drums banged by the Revolutionaries; a *Who's Who* of the Revolution in portraits (from crazed **Marat** to stern **Robespierre**); and, finally, perhaps foreshadowing the end of the Reign of Terror, the penknife **Napoléon Bonaparte** used during the Egyptian campaign.

Second Floor

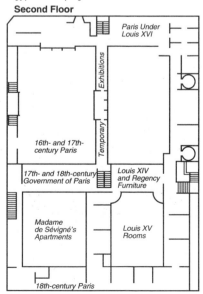

- Paris Under Louis XVI
- Exhibitions
- Temporary
- 16th- and 17th-century Paris
- 17th- and 18th-century Government of Paris
- Louis XIV and Regency Furniture
- Madame de Sévigné's Apartments
- Louis XV Rooms
- 18th-century Paris

On the second floor are exhibitions of fashionable furnishings from the reigns of the last Bourbon kings (**Louis XIV, Louis XV,** and **Louis XVI**) and salon murals by **Jean-Honoré Fragonard** and **François Boucher,** and also the apartments of **Madame de Sévigné** (1626-96). This "Grande Dame of the Marais" (who was born, baptized, and married in the district) lived at the Hôtel Carnavalet for the last 19 years of her life. Here she entertained the greatest thinkers of the day and, in her famous *Lettres,* inscribed her witty, incisive observations of the court of Louis XIV. Her association with the royals was not forgotten by well-read Revolutionary hotheads, who a century later exhumed her remains, beheaded the corpse, and triumphantly paraded through Paris with her skull. On your way out, catch Louis XIV, looking rather silly decked out as a Roman general with a wig (the **Antoine Coysevox** courtyard statue was brought here from its former home, the Hôtel de Ville), and be certain to pass by the current exhibition rooms on the ground floor. ♦ Admission. Tu-Su 10AM-5:40PM. 23 Rue de Sévigné. Métros: Chemin-Vert, St.-Paul. 42.72.21.13

22 Rue Pavée The construction of one of the city's first paved (*pavée*) streets was a pioneer achievement in the 14th century, when the

city's sinking muddy roads also served as open sewers and pigsties. ♦ Métro: St.-Paul

22 Bibliothèque Historique de la Ville de Paris Designed in 1611 by **Baptiste du Cerceau,** the **Hôtel Lamoignon** (pictured above) has, since 1969, housed the Historical Library of Paris and is a mecca for French historians. The mansion was originally the property of **Diane de France,** the bastard daughter of **Henri II.** As the story goes, young Henri, while traveling in Italy, was in hot pursuit of the **Duchess of Angoulême.** When she refused to leave her house, he burned it down and had her kidnapped and taken to France. Out of their tumultuous union, Diane was born. At age seven, she was legally adopted by the king and given all the rights of nobility, among them this mansion, where she lived until her death at age 82.

This was the city's first private mansion and is adorned with a colossal order of Italianate pilasters. The low triangular pediment is embellished by a stag with antlers, a tribute, naturally, to **Diana,** goddess of the hunt. On a rainy day, the library is one of the best places in Paris to read about Paris. Once in the courtyard, bear right, up the steps to the reading-room door. If you manage to convince the guard you are a visiting scholar, he will give you a reader's card. Take a seat at one of the long wooden tables and gaze up at the gilded beams, one of which is ornamented with a painting of Diana and the hunt. ♦ M-Sa 9:30AM-6PM; closed holidays. 24 Rue Pavée. Métro: St.-Paul. 42.74.44.44

23 Synagogue The sinuous facade of the only synagogue (1913) designed by **Hector Guimard,** the Art Nouveau architect best known for his sculptural métro entrances, suggests an open book, perhaps the Torah. ♦ Services on Saturday. 10 Rue Pavée. Métro: St.-Paul

24 Rue des Rosiers *Rosiers* means rosebushes and refers to the roses that bloomed nearby within the old medieval city wall, but the fragrances wafting along this narrow, crooked street today are anything but floral. Scents of

Marais & Les Halles

hot pastrami, steaming borscht, chopped chicken livers, and fresh matzos emanate from the kosher butcher shops, delicatessens, and bakeries that line this street, the *Platzel* of the Jewish quarter since the Middle Ages. The adjoining **Rue des Ecouffes** takes its name from the Lombardian pawnbrokers who were derided as *écouffes,* French for kite, a rapacious bird. A terribly haunting souvenir of the district's history was a plaque that until recently hung outside an elementary school on the street. It read: "165 Jewish children from this school, deported to Germany during World War II, were exterminated in Nazi camps. Never forget." Down this street the Nazis and Vichy French marched and dragged away 75,000 Jews to concentration camps. In **Jo Goldenberg,** the most famous delicatessen on the street, there occurred a more recent tragedy: on 9 August 1982, masked gunmen killed six customers. The PLO took credit, and the gunmen were never caught. ♦ Métro: St.-Paul

The 283-member Senate, France's equivalent of the House of Lords, can be overruled at any time by the National Assembly. If the president of the Republic dies in office, however, the constitution provides the president of the Senate with the authority to take over the president's responsibilities pending a presidential election, which must be held within 35 days. Ever since World War II, in referendum after referendum, the French have unsuccessfully tried to abolish this elitist provision.

The original Raspail métro entrance, a 1900 Art Nouveau masterpiece by Hector Guimard, is on display at New York's Museum of Modern Art.

24 Le Loir dans la Théière ★★$ With its flea-market furniture, sprung-out sofas, wooden tables, and raffish air, this comfortable tea salon could be in Seattle or Berkeley. The name, "Dormouse in the Teapot," recalls *Alice in Wonderland,* as does the mural of other characters from the **Lewis Carroll** fantasy. The light tasty salads and fine homemade cakes and tarts are very real. ♦ M-Sa noon-7PM; Su 11AM-7PM. 3 Rue des Rosiers. No credit cards. Métro: St.-Paul. 42.72.90.61

24 Jo Goldenberg ★★$$ The sweet aroma of spiced meat, the clatter of dishes, and, particularly on Sunday afternoon, the babble of strong, animated voices fill this Jewish delicatessen/restaurant. Try the *foie haché* (chopped liver), *poisson farci* (gefilte fish), Cracovian sausages, and strudel, washed down with a cold Pilsen. ♦ Daily 8:30AM-11PM; closed Yom Kippur. 7 Rue des Rosiers. Reservations recommended. Métro: St.-Paul. 48.87.20.16, 48.87.70.39

24 Le Roi du Falaffel-Rosiers Alimentation ★$ North African grocers offer hummus, Israeli dishes, and falafel sandwiches to go. ♦ M-F, Su 10AM-8:30PM; M-F, Su 10AM-10PM in winter. 34 Rue des Rosiers. Métro: St.-Paul. 48.87.63.60

25 Le Loft A faint fragrance of fresh polish permeates this three-story warehouse of English antique imports. French Anglophiles shop here for old pine towel rails and three-door wardrobes. ♦ M-Sa 10AM-7PM. 17bis Rue Pavée. Métro: St.-Paul. 48.87.46.50

26 Smart/Société des Métiers d'Art Handpainted tiles and ceramics by a score of French craftspeople scattered from Alsace to Provence are sold here. You can reconstruct the Place des Vosges in terra-cotta tile miniatures of the 17th-century town houses or assemble a fantasy Gallic village with postage stamp-sized tiles of a French bakery, café, butcher shop, pharmacy, school, and church. Other items on Smart's bestseller list are Marseillaise tarot cards in tile, and brass European faucets. A victim of its own success, it is now open only by appointment. ♦ 22 Rue des Francs-Bourgeois. Métro: St.-Paul. 42.77.41.24

26 Marais Plus ★$ An inventive array of kiwi, pear, and apple-custard tarts, the sound of pianist Keith Jarrett on the stereo, and the gentle chirping of canaries combine to make this bookstore/tea salon a tranquil oasis on a busy street. Among its eclectic literary offerings are recent museum catalogs, biographies of modern artists (Paul Klee to Gustav Klimt), and books on art and Paris. Ask about the activities of the **Cultural Center of the Marais.** ♦ M-Sa 9AM-midnight; Su 9AM-8PM. 20 Rue des Francs-Bourgeois. Métro: St.-Paul. 48.87.01.40

27 Musée Cognacq-Jay A marvelously complete collection of 18th-century art, acquired by the husband-and-wife team of **Louise Jay** and **Ernest Cognacq,** who created the Samaritaine department stores and boasted of never having set foot in the Louvre. The collection was moved to the five-story, 16th-century **Hôtel Donon,** and the works of **Boucher, Tiepolo, Watteau, Fragonard, Greuze, La Tour, Rembrandt, Gainsborough,** and **Reynolds** are as well-displayed here as they were in their old home on Boulevard des Capucines. There's also a remarkable set of perfume cases and snuffboxes and **Meissen** porcelain statuettes. ♦ Admission. Tu-Su 10AM-5:40PM. 8 Rue Elzévir. Métro: St. Paul. 40.27.07.21

28 Maison Mansart The ground floor of the house **François Mansart** built for himself (and inhabited until his death in 1666) now houses **Alain Thiollier's** stark, high-ceilinged gallery, which exhibits contemporary art from Chinese landscapes to abstract lithographs. Thiollier's mother lives upstairs in Mansart's old flat, and on the second floor is a strange Positivist chapel (with an altar inscribed to "Humanism") built by a Brazilian follower of French Positivist **Auguste Comte.** The chapel has yet to be opened to the public, but inquire about the occasional string-quartet concerts. ♦ Tu-Su 3-7PM. Métro: St.-Paul. 45.74.45.90

28 Lutherie **François Perrin** buys, sells, makes, and restores violins, violas, bows, guitars, harps, and old instruments in these quarters of the **Hôtel de Savourny.** ♦ M-F 9:30AM-noon, 1:30-5PM; Sa 9:30AM-12:30PM, 2:30-7PM. 4 Rue Elzévir. Métro: St.-Paul. 42.77.68.42

29 Musée Bricard et Musée de la Serrure (Lock and Metalwork Museum) Everything from Roman door knockers to medieval cuckold-prevention devices (iron chastity belts) can be found in this quirky museum of locksmithing, housed in the **Hôtel Libéral Bruant.** Architect Bruant built this mansion as his personal residence, and it remains his most important work after the **Hôtel des Invalides** and the **Salpêtrière** chapel. ♦ Admission. Tu-Sa 2-5PM; closed in Aug and one week at Christmas. 1 Rue de la Perle. Métros: Chemin-Vert, St.-Paul. 42.77.79.62

The name Picasso was derived from *picazo,* which means magpie, a bird that scavenges anything that catches its eye.

Restaurants/Nightlife: Red   Hotels: Blue
Shops/ 🌳 Outdoors: Green   Sights/Culture: Black

30 Musée Picasso The museum was opened by French **President François Mitterrand** on 23 September 1985. It had taken two other French presidents, five ministers of culture,

and 11 years to establish. In the first month alone, it received 80,000 visitors.

"Give me a museum and I'll fill it up," said **Pablo Picasso,** perhaps the 20th century's most important and prolific painter. His wish was granted posthumously in the form of the **Hôtel Salé.** The man who epitomized outlaw modernism yet preferred ancient houses would have been happy with this 17th-century building. Today the mansion enshrines the artist's collection of his own works, the largest in the world: 203 paintings, 158 sculptures, 16 collages, 29 relief paintings, 88 ceramics, 30 sketchbooks, more than 1,500 drawings, and numerous prints, including the *Vollard Suite,* his Neoclassical etchings created in the 1920s. The museum also houses Picasso's personal art collection, including works by **Matisse, Renoir, Cézanne, Braque, Balthus,** and **Le Douanier Rousseau.**

In December 1912 at the age of 31, Picasso began to hoard his own work. He wrote his dealer, **Daniel Henry Kahnweiler,** that he would keep five paintings a year, as well as his self-portraits, family portraits, and most of his sculpture. For 70 years Picasso also made a habit of holding on to the works he painted during the week of his birthday, 25 October.

When Picasso died on 8 April 1973 with no will, France's tax collectors were quick to pounce on his estate. In lieu of $65 million in inheritance taxes, Picasso's heirs donated one quarter of his collection to the state. **Dominique Bozo** (former chief curator of the Museum of Modern Art at the Pompidou Center) and a team of Picasso experts carved up the artist's pie for France. Ironically, as late as 1945, France owned only three Picassos in public collections, a handful far outnumbered by the many in the possession of the Museum of Modern Art in New York.

The Hôtel Salé has but a few of Picasso's masterpieces: *Still Life with Caned Chair, Two Women Running on Beach*, and the Neoclassical *Pipes of Pan* among them. However, his collection is exhibited chronologically, and the work affords an extraordinary odyssey through the artist's growth and psyche. Furthermore, revealing Picasso memorabilia are sprinkled throughout the museum: photos of Picasso at bullfights, posing on the beach with a fig leaf, hoisting a bull's skull at the beach of Golfe-Juan, playing with his children, and consorting with friends such as **Jean Cocteau** and **Max Jacob.**

Throughout the museum are portraits of the women in Picasso's life: **Olga Kokhlova,** the Russian dancer; **Marie-Thérèse Walter,** the 17-year-old earth mother; **Dora Maar,** the intellectual; **Françoise Gilot,** the painter; and

Marais & Les Halles

his widow, **Jacqueline.** Picasso wrote: "1935-1939 was the worst time of my life." But it was the best time for his art. During those years, he broke with Olga, fathered a child with Marie-Thérèse, and then turned to Dora Maar. The pictures he produced in that period are particularly violent, such as *Cat Seizing a Bird* and the grotesque feminine figure of *Woman in a Red Chair.* Personal anguish mixed with outrage at Franco's butchery in Picasso's native Spain is expressed in his surreal print *The Dream and Lie of Franco,* which presages the theme and force of his masterwork, *Guernica.*

You could spend the entire day wandering through the museum, but if it's 11:30AM and you've got a 1PM lunch date, it is best to concentrate on the second-floor collection, then sample the sculpture in the basement on your way out. Here are a few highlights: **Room 1** brings you face-to-face with one of his Blue Period masterpieces, the wintery 1901 *Self-Portrait at Age 20,* gaunt in a mangy beard and an overcoat to ward off the drafts that doubtlessly plagued his bohemian existence. The influences of **Toulouse-Lautrec** and **van Gogh** are particularly evident in the Expressionist deathbed portrait of the poet **Casagemas. Rooms 2** and **3** contain sketches and drawings inspired by **Cézanne's** geometrical style and by the primitive sculpture from Africa and New Caledonia that so fascinated Picasso and ultimately led to the creation of his masterpiece, *Les Demoiselles d'Avignon.* **Room 4,** especially his *Still Life with Caned Chair,* portrays his years of cubist inquiry (1909-1917) with

Georges Braque. The next several rooms feature his paper collages and three-dimensional paintings made of cigar-box wood, newspapers, and metal shards. Musical instruments, such as guitars and mandolins, recur throughout Picasso's work, but as he once told a friend: "Music has never interested me." It was the womanly shape of the guitar rather than its sound that sparked his imagination. **Room 5** contains the best of the 60 works in Picasso's collection: masterpieces by **Matisse, Braque, Rousseau,** and **Cézanne.** Of the latter, Picasso told the photographer **Brassai** in 1943: "Do I know Cézanne! He's my one and only master."

The museum crescendos in **Room 6** with paintings from his classical period, *La Lecture de la Lettre* and *The Pipes of Pan.* The minuscule side room (**6B**) is devoted entirely to Picasso's theater and costume designs, created in collaboration with **Cocteau, Massine, Stravinsky,** and **Diaghilev.** Near the end of his life, Picasso's art became childlike and cartoonish. The last painting in the collection, dated 14 April 1972, is called *Young Painter,* a sketchy thing of a smiling dauber. In his final years the artist confessed, "It has taken all my life to learn how to paint like a child again." Picasso's playfulness is perhaps most evident in his sculpture, which is fashioned from an amusing assortment of odds and ends. En route to the exit, descend into the museum's basement to find his sculpture collection, with originals of his celebrated monkey, goat, and skipping girl.

Hôtel Salé was built from 1655 to 1659 by architect **Jean Bouillier** for **Pierre Aubert de Fontenay,** a man who got rich collecting taxes on salt (hence *Salé*) for the king. With the fall of **Nicolas Fouquet** (1615-1680), **Louis XIV's** greedy finance minister, Aubert lost his job, his house, and finally, in 1668, his life.

Later the Hôtel Salé was leased to the embassy of the Venetian Republic and the naval minister of **Louis XVI.** After the Revolution, in 1793, it became a boys school (**Balzac** studied here), a science laboratory, and, from 1887 to 1964, an exhibition hall for a bronze foundry. After Picasso's death, Minister of Culture **Michel Guy** secured a 99-year lease on the building from the City of Paris, and the government spent some 65 million francs on its restoration.

Roland Simounet, winner of the 1977 Grand Prix for Architecture, was selected to design the museum. Simounet's plan preserved the architectural integrity of the building while doubling its interior space from 3,000 to 6,000 square meters. A design detail lost on most visitors: the museum's extraordinary benches, tables, and light fixtures were fashioned by the late **Diego Giacometti,** brother of artist **Alberto.** ◆ Admission. M, Th-Su 9AM-5PM (ticket window closes at 4:30PM); W 9AM-10PM (ticket window closes at 9:15PM). 5 Rue de Thorigny. Métros: St.-Paul, St.-Sébastien-Froissart. 42.71.25.21

Within the Musée Picasso:
Museum Restaurant ★$ Above the museum book and print shop is a small, attractive tea salon serving salads, quiche, soups, grilled salmon, and fruit tarts. ◆ M, W-Su 9:15AM-5PM. 42.71.25.21

31 A l'Image du Grenier sur l'Eau Brothers **Yves** and **Sylvain Di Maria** have spent the last decade assembling this extraordinary collection of more than one million vintage postcards of locales from Avignon to Zaire and a universe of images in between, each one for sale. They also carry French publicity photos from the 1950s and the same turn-of-the-century aristocratic illustrations that decorate the walls of Maxim's. ♦ M-F 10AM-6:30PM; Sa 2-6PM. 45 Rue des Francs-Bourgeois. Métro: St.-Paul. 42.71.02.31

31 Janine Kaganski Exquisite 18th-century handpainted wedding chests and armoires from France, Austria, and the Rhine Valley are presented in this shop. ♦ M-Sa 11AM-6:30PM; Su by appointment. 41 Rue des Francs-Bourgeois. Métro: St.-Paul. 48.87.94.73

32 Le Fax Here you'll find everything to gratify your Filofax fetish. The famous pocket-size, three-ring English notebooks come in myriad styles, from black leather to herringbone tweed, and with notepaper in every hue. Also in stock are sheaves of maps, calendars, and metric conversion charts to store in your portable file cabinet. ♦ M-Sa 11AM-7PM; closed in Aug. 32 Rue des Francs-Bourgeois. Métro: St.-Paul. 42.78.67.87

33 Finkelsztajn Since 1851 a Jewish bakery has operated at this address, and today **Sacha Finkelsztajn** carries on the tradition, making the tastiest Jewish pastry on the block. Her cheesecake is the richest this side of Manhattan's Second Avenue. The affable baker offers newcomers a free taste of her Polish herrings, chicken livers, and eggplant purée. ♦ W-Su 9:30AM-1:30PM, 3-7:30PM; closed 1 July-mid Aug, one week in winter. 27 Rue des Rosiers. Métro: St.-Paul. 42.72.78.91

Gourmet Take-Away

Whether you're purchasing hors d'oeuvres for the holidays or preparing a romantic picnic for two, here's where you can buy some of France's finest food:

Beauvilliers Celebrate the holidays with delicacies from this superb spot in Montmartre. 52 Rue Lamarck, 75018 Paris; 42.54.54.42.

Fauchon This renowned St.-Honoré supermarket can fulfill all your gastronomic needs. 24 Place de la Madeleine, 75008 Paris; 47.42.60.11.

Guy Savoy Near the Arc de Triomphe, this famous restaurant makes excellent foie gras. 18 Rue Troyon, 75017 Paris; 43.80.40.61.

Lenotre Foie gras and *bûches de Noël* (traditional French cakes shaped like Yule logs) are among the holiday specialties at this shop in St.-Germain. 44 Rue d'Auteuill, 75016 Paris; 45.24.52.52.

La Maison du Champagne All the top brands and many others are carried by this 16th-arrondissement shop. 48 Rue des Belles Feuilles, 75016 Paris; 47.27.58.23.

Vigneau-Desmarets An excellent St.-Germain address for turkey and *poulet de bresse* (guinea hen). 107 Rue de Sèvres, 75006 Paris; 45.48.04.73.

Vignon Wonderful *boudin blanc* (white sausage) with truffles is available at this Champs-Elysées restaurant. 14 Rue Marbeuf, 75008 Paris; 47.20.24.26.

34 Jules des Prés The most extraordinary dried flower arrangements in Europe are created here. The hyperaffluent clientele, which includes designers **Christian Lacroix, Karl Lagerfeld,** and **Christian Dior,** doesn't flinch at spending $1,200 on a basket of cinnamon sticks, bay leaves, and juniper berries. After all, it is an investment and doesn't wilt or need watering. ♦ M-Sa 11AM-7PM. 46 Rue du Roi-de-Sicile. Métro: St.-Paul. 48.04.79.49

35 Le Bistrot Russe ★$ Despite the restaurant's name, the chef is Polish and the customers are Eastern European émigrés, local merchants, and an occasional *Herald Tribune* art critic. Not to be missed are the blinis with smoked salmon and stroganoff. ♦ M 8-11:30PM; Tu-Th noon-2PM, 8-11:30PM; F noon-2PM, 8PM-midnight; Sa 8PM-midnight; closed first two weeks of Aug. 31 Rue Vieille-du-Temple. Reservations recommended at lunch. Métro: Hôtel-de-Ville. 42.71.08.39

35 Au Petit Fer à Cheval ★★★$ Named after its 1903 marble-topped horseshoe *(fer à cheval)* bar, this neighborhood café offers lunchtime *plats du jour* in its back room, where one of the booths is an old wooden métro seat. ♦ M-F 9AM-1:30AM; Sa-Su 11:30AM-1:30AM. 30 Rue Vieille-du-Temple. Métro: Hôtel-de-Ville. 42.72.47.47

36 Hôtel des Ambassadeurs de Hollande When this Baroque mansion (built in 1660) was quizzically named, there were no Dutch ambassadors to France, and none have ever lived here. Subsequently rebuilt by **Pierre Cottard,** the *hôtel* housed its most famous resident, **Caron de Beaumarchais,** author of *The Marriage of Figaro* and *The Barber of Seville.* The great wooden doors are embellished by what looks like howling Medusas or perhaps a pair of baritones warming up. ♦ 47 Rue Vieille-du-Temple. Métro: St.-Paul

37 Picard Surgelés Who said the French are all food snobs? The brave new world of French frozen food is displayed in this chilly, sterile mart (one of a chain of stores in Paris) that sells microwave ovens and anything you might want to defrost in them. Press your nose against the glass, watch Parisians wheel shopping carts around yellow, blue, and red freezers looking for tonight's TV dinner, and ask yourself what Julia Child would say. ♦ M-W, F-Su 9AM-7:30PM; Th 9AM-8PM. 48 Rue des Francs-Bourgeois. Métro: Rambuteau. 42.72.17.83

37 Le Dômarais ★$$/$$$ Covered by a glass rotunda, sumptuously adorned with scarlet walls and bronze statues, this trading house-turned-restaurant oozes romance. Tucked away on a quiet courtyard, it provides the perfect setting for an intimate dinner. ♦ M, Sa-Su 7:30-10:30PM; Tu-F 12:15-2PM, 7:30-10:30PM. 53bis Rue des Francs-Bourgeois. Reservations recommended. Métro: Rambuteau. 42.74.54.17

37 Crédit Municipal de Paris Paris' first municipal pawnshop is still a place for hocking ("putting it on the nail," as the French say). Auctions, especially for jewelry, are frequent and well-attended; check the notices posted outside. ♦ 55 Rue des Francs-Bourgeois. Métro: Rambuteau. 42.71.25.43

37 Archives Nationales/Musée de l'Histoire de France The letters of **Joan of Arc** and **Voltaire,** the wills of **Louis XIV** and **Napoléon I,** a papyrus signed by Merovingian **King Dagobert** (622-638), the Edict of Nantes, the Declaration of the Rights of Man, and six billion other documents are stored on 175 miles of shelves in this admirable 18th-century mansion, the former **Hôtel Soubise.** Even if you have no interest in scrapbook French history, the museum's fortified turrets, colonnaded courtyard (72 Corinthian columns in all), and the riot of rococo in the **Oval Salon** (with its eight famous paintings by **Charles Natoire** depicting the *Loves of Psyche*) make a visit worthwhile. Designed by **Alexis Delamaier** for **François de Rohan,** the prince of Soubise, the ornate interior (1739) was engineered by **Germain Boffrand,** a pupil of François Mansart. Boffrand hired the best artists of the day, among them **François Boucher** and Natoire, to decorate the *hôtel.* The archives, housed in the Hôtel Soubise

Marais & Les Halles

since 1808, began taking over the adjacent **Hôtel de Rohan** in 1927. ♦ Admission. M-F 9AM-5PM. 60 Rue des Francs-Bourgeois. Métros: Hôtel-de-Ville, Rambuteau. 40.27.60.00

38 Hôtel de Rohan In 1705 the son of **François de Rohan,** prince-bishop of Strasbourg, commissioned **Alexis Delamaier** to build a mansion opposite the **Hôtel Soubise,** where his parents lived. In the courtyard to the right, above the entrance to the former stables, is one of the masterpieces of 18th-century French sculpture: **Robert Le Lorrain's** superb relief-sculpture *The Watering of the Horses of the Sun.* The building sometimes houses temporary exhibitions. ♦ 87 Rue Vieille-du-Temple. Métro: Rambuteau

39 Rue des Archives For generations, the lower section of this street bore the name *Rue ou Dieu fut boulli* (The street where God was boiled) after the legend of the money-lender who stabbed a communion wafer with his knife, then threw it into a steaming pot, where to his astonishment it began to bleed. ♦ Métro: Hôtel-de-Ville

39 Musée de la Chasse et de la Nature (Museum of the Hunt) Housed in a portion of the **Hôtel de Guénégaud** (1654) designed by **François Mansart,** this museum presents three floors full of hunting paraphernalia, and related items, including: crossbows, muskets, game trophies, whole stuffed animals, and paintings of hunting dogs and animals by the likes of **Rubens** and **Brueghel.** Among the most lavish paeans to the slaughter are the paintings of

Desportes, the court artist employed by Louis XIV to portray the royal hunts at Versailles. A favorite of children. ♦ Admission. M, W-Su 10AM-12:30PM, 1:30-5:30PM. 60 Rue des Archives. Métros: Hôtel-de-Ville, Rambuteau 42.72.86.43

Les Halles

The area known as *Les Halles* (the marketplace) take its name from the great wholesale food market that began here in 1100. The market operated until the mid-1970s, when it was moved to Rungis near Orly Airport, leaving behind *le trou* (the hole, which later was filled by an underground shopping mall known as the **Forum des Halles**) and a perimeter consisting of the **St.-Eustache Church** and several old all-night restaurants serving onion soup and pig's trotters. As recently as a few decades ago, it was occupied by a run-down garment district and slum that stretched between the St.-Merri Church and the old food market. The opening of the Forum des Halles and the **Georges Pompidou Center** in the late 1970s brought new commercial life into the area (as well as architectural controversy). Retired food vendors now share their turf with hordes of tourists, mall-bound French youths, and upscale professionals who come to soak up the local color.

The inclined plaza west of the Georges Pompidou Center is now home to an impromptu circus of folksingers, hypnotists, kerosene garglers, sword-swallowers, Hare Krishnas, rowdies, acrobats, jugglers, and (may you be forewarned) purse snatchers and panhandlers who prey on gawking tourists.

40 Gambrinus A beer drinkers' paradise that offers 400 kinds of brew-to-go from 34 countries and 200 sorts of whiskey, enough to please the sophisticated sipper or the gargantuan guzzler. ♦ M 3-8PM; Tu, Th-F 11AM-1:30PM, 3-8PM; W 11AM-1:30PM, 3-10PM; Sa 9AM-1:30PM, 3-8PM. 13-15 Rue des Blancs-Manteaux. Métro: Rambuteau. 42.76.03.52

41 Rue de la Verrerie This narrow street, which takes its name from the 11th-century glassblowers guild, is where **Jacquemin Gringoneur** once lived. He invented playing cards to amuse **King Charles VI** ("The Beloved"), who ruled from 1380-1422. ♦ Métro: Hôtel-de-Ville

42 Lescene-Dura Since 1875 this sprawling wine-lover's warehouse has been offering all manner of oenological paraphernalia, from corkscrews to champagne buckets. ♦ Tu-Sa 9:30AM-1PM, 2-7PM; closed two weeks in Aug. 63 Rue de la Verrerie. Métro: Hôtel-de-Ville. 42.72.08.74

43 Vieux Marais $$ A 30-room hotel redecorated with Chinese carpets and floral wallpaper, wherein a warm welcome always awaits. ♦ 8 Rue du Plâtre. Métro: Rambuteau. 42.78.47.22

44 The Studio ★★$$ A Tex-Mex canteen that in the adjoining dance studio courtyard, throws the hottest Fourth of July party in Paris. ♦ M-F 7:30PM-1AM; Sa-Su 12:30-3P, 7:30PM-1AM. 41 Rue du Temple. Métro: Rambuteau. 42.74.10.38

45 Café de la Cité ★★$ No wider than a bowling alley, this café/luncheonette has become one of the most popular pit stops in the area. Decorated with wooden pinwheel fans and prints of old Breton sailing vessels (the owner comes from Brittany), this is where you can get tasty *plats du jour,* and the management boasts that you can order, eat, and head out the door in less than 30 minutes. ♦ M-Sa 9AM-11:30PM. 22 Rue Rambuteau. Reservations required for dinner. Métro: Rambuteau. 42.78.56.36

46 Musée de la Musique Mécanique A private collection featuring more than one hundred music machines, from mechanized trumpets to the curious pianola for which **Debussy** and **Stravinsky** composed some works. ♦ Admission. Sa-Su, holidays 2-7PM. Impasse Berthaud. Métro: Rambuteau. 42.71.99.54

46 Galerie Daniel Templon Modeled after New York's SoHo galleries, Daniel Templon helped launch conceptual art, language art, and a good deal of the "Support Surface" movement in France. ♦ Tu-F 10AM-1PM, 2:30-7PM; Sa 10AM-7PM; closed in Aug. 30 Rue Beaubourg. Métro: Rambuteau. 42.72.14.10

47 Le Tango To dance here cheek-to-cheek among Brylcreem dandies and perfumed widows is to enter a time warp that leads back to 1906, when the tango first hit Paris. Calypsos, salsas, beguines—any beat but disco are danced to all night long. Authentic and cheap. ♦ W-Sa 11PM-5AM. 13 Rue au Maire. Métro: Arts-et-Métiers. 42.72.17.78

48 Rue du Vert-Bois The remains of the walls of **St.-Martin-des-Champs** date from 1270. An inflammatory letter from **Victor Hugo** is said to have saved the wall from demolition. ♦ Métro: Temple

49 Musée National des Techniques This extraordinary collection of 80,000 machines traces the evolution of science from the 16th century onward. Housed in an Orwellian juxtaposition of religion and technology, part of the museum is in the remains of the **St.-Martin-des-Champs** priory, one of the finest naves to survive the Middle Ages. In the museum you will see the clockwork dulcimer-player of **Marie Antoinette, Pascal's** adding machine, **Foucault's** pendulum, and the **Lumière** brothers' first magic lantern. The mechanically bent will be in heaven, especially at 2:30PM the first Wednesday of each month, when the machines are set in motion. ♦ Admission. Tu-Su 10AM-5:30PM; closed holidays; free on Sunday. 270 Rue St.-Martin. Métros: Réaumur-Sebastopol, Stras-bourg-St.-Denis. 40.27.23.75

50 St.-Nicolas-des-Champs Construction on this church began in the 12th century, and it has acquired distinguished features throughout the ages: a flamboyant Gothic facade, a Renaissance doorway, and many 17th-, 18th-, and 19th-century paintings. ♦ M-Sa 9AM-7PM; Su 9:30AM-noon. 254 Rue St.-Martin. Métro: Arts-et-Métiers. 42.72.92.54

51 Galerie Yvon Lambert Works by **Lewitt, Twombly, Oppenheim, Schnabel, Blais, Combas,** and **Christo** are showcased here. ♦ Tu-F 10AM-1PM, 2:30-7PM; Sa 10AM-7PM; closed in Aug. 5 Rue du Grenier-St.-Lazare. Métro: Rambuteau. 42.71.09.33

51 Ambassade d'Auvergne ★★$$/$$$ Run by Italian **Joseph Petrucci** and his Auvergnat wife, this rustic restaurant is adorned with flickering oil lamps, a roaring fire, and cured hams dangling from heavy wood beams. Hearty *Massif Central* cuisine is served here, from *loulus* (pot-au-feu) and *loujus* (roast suckling pig) to lentil cassoulet and blood sausage with chestnuts. ♦ Daily 7:30-11:30PM. 22 Rue du Grenier-St.-Lazare. Reservations recommended. Métro: Rambuteau. 42.72.31.22

The Bastille's Bustling Bistros

The area around the Bastille, rejuvenated by the relatively new opera house and scores of art galleries, is called the SoHo of Paris. Formerly a working-class haven for painters and other bohemians, the neighborhood has undergone a mind-boggling transformation. The once seedy

Marais & Les Halles

Rue de Lappe, just off the Place de la Bastille, is now dubbed "the trendiest street in Paris." Quite a change from 1944, when Somerset Maugham wrote in *The Razor's Edge* that even as you enter Rue de Lappe, "you get the impression of sordid lust." Back in the 1930s, the street was filled with *bougnats,* Auvergnat dispensaries of wine and coal. Nowadays, however, the streets are replete with oh-so-trendy bars and cafés, including these favorites:

Le Bar a Nenette ★★$ At the turn of the century this friendly café was a traditional Auvergnat *bougnat.* The original woodstove, still in working order, has become the café's centerpiece and is surrounded with artists and antique dealers dining on hearty salads and light meals. Oddly delicious, the café's Auvergne cheese platter is served Provençal style, drenched in olive oil and fresh herbs. ♦ M-F 10AM-1AM; Sa 6PM-1AM. 26bis Rue de Lappe. Métro: Bastille. 48.07.08.18

Café Iguana ★$ This corner bar has a woody interior and the muddiest draft Guinness this side of Dublin. ♦ Daily 9AM-2AM. 15 Rue de la Roquette. Métro: Bastille. 40.21.39.99

L'Entre-Pots ★$$ A dark cavernous bar whose decor is a credible rendition of Paris in the 1940s. Hip French students sip expensive American cocktails and lip sync to booming Otis Redding and Madonna tunes. ♦ Daily 7PM-2AM. 14 Rue de Charonne. Métro: Bastille. 48.66.57.04

La Palette Bastille ★★$ Like its artsy namesake on the Rue de Seine, this corner café is an architectural jewel. It opened in 1907 as a bistro/billiard hall and retains the original Eiffel-era girders, carved wood panels, and peeling gold-leaf lettering. Have a *pastis* on the terrace and luxuriate in the faded fin de siècle elegance. ♦ Daily 7AM-2AM. 116 Avenue Ledru Rollin. Métro: Bastille. 47.00.34.39

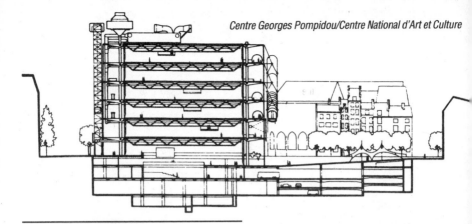

ESPACE VIT'HALLES

52 Espace Vit'Halles This popular health club, started in 1983 by French Olympic wrestler **Christophe Andanson** and his wife, **Claudy,**

Marais & Les Halles

has become one of the hottest underground (in a literal sense) singles spots in the district. Among the more than one thousand members are Pompidou Center staffers flocking to aerobics classes and young Bourse financiers pumping iron as a respite from lusting after gold. The clean and affordable facilities include a sauna, Jacuzzi, tanning rooms, bodybuilding equipment, and juice bar. Memberships are available for one day, one week, and longer. ♦ M-F 9AM-10PM; Sa 11AM-7PM; Su 11AM-3PM. 48 Rue Rambuteau. Métro: Rambuteau. 42.77.21.71

53 Defender of Time Inspired by the Rathaus clock in Munich, the one-ton **Jacques Monestier** kinetic sculpture (1975) in oxidized brass sends a sword-brandishing warrior to do battle with a bird, a crab, and a dragon (representing the three elements: air, water, and earth). As every hour strikes, one of the beasts attacks, and at noon, 6PM, and 10PM, the Defender of Time is forced to take on all the creatures at once, always emerging victorious. A bit kitschy (as is this whole mini-shopping mall, the **Quartier de l'Horloge**), but young children love it. ♦ Rue Brantome. Métro: Rambuteau

Faubourg means literally false town or suburb and usually denotes the extension of a Parisian street beyond the old city walls. Hence, Rue St.- Honoré turns into Faubourg-St.-Honoré and Rue St.-Antoine becomes Faubourg-St.-Antoine after reaching the Bastille.

Restaurants/Nightlife: Red   Hotels: Blue
Shops/ 🌳 Outdoors: Green   Sights/Culture: Black

54 Centre Georges Pompidou/Centre National d'Art et Culture Critics took to calling the five-story jumble of glass and steel the "gasworks" and wondered "who forgot to take the scaffolding down?" Still, this surrealistic Tinkertoy of modern culture is the biggest attraction in Paris, outdrawing both the Louvre and the Eiffel Tower. One million people visited in 1977 during the first seven weeks it was open; more than half the visitors are under age 25. Created at the behest of then **President Georges Pompidou** (1911-1974) and designed by Italian **Renzo Piano** and Englishman **Richard Rogers** (whose proposal was selected from among a field of 681), the revolutionary (some say revolting) structure houses a modern art museum, the city's largest public library (with more than half a million books), one of the world's most advanced computer music centers, a language library, a children's theater and dance workshop, and a fifth-floor restaurant with a four-star view. Pompidou, who was a patron of modern art as well as a politician, is immortalized by **Victor Vasarely** in a hexagonal portrait that hangs on the ground floor.

The high-tech design concept of the center celebrates the building's working functional parts (heating ducts, ventilator shafts, stairways, and elevators) by brightly color-coding them: red means vertical circulation, green means water, blue is for air, yellow for electricity, and white for structure. An escalator in a Plexiglas tube snakes up the front of the Pompidou. Even if you aren't moved by the **Salvador Dalí** portrait of **Lenin** dancing on piano keys, which is exhibited on the fourth floor, you should still ride up and, once there, scan one of the city's best-loved vistas, the view over the Right Bank rooftops. Unfortunately, innovation and popularity carry a price: the Pompidou is showing wear and tear in tarnished steel, peeling paint, and shredded carpets. Architects blame not just the crowds but the design. "To put the bones and intestines outside the skin," said one, "is to invite health problems." ♦ M, W-F noon-10PM; Sa-Su 10AM-10PM. Métros: Châtelet-Les Halles, Hôtel-de-Ville, Rambuteau. 42.77.12.33

Within the Centre Georges Pompidou:

Musée d'Art Moderne The third and fourth floors of the Pompidou Center houses one of the world's largest collections of modern and contemporary art. Beginning with **Rousseau's** *Snake Charmer* and ending with the museum's up-to-the-minute acquisitions, the collection includes works by the greatest artists of the 20th century: **Picasso, Bonnard, Matisse, Kandinsky, Mondrian, Chagall, Pollock, Magritte, Calder, Moore,** and **Bacon.** Exhibitions are splendidly mounted. ◆ Admission; free on Sunday 10AM-2PM

Cinémathèque Française This famous film archive and cinema, located on the fifth floor, presents three international classics daily. The cinémathèque's other auditorium is at the National Cinema Museum in the **Palais de Chaillot** (Place du Trocadéro, 45.53.74.39), where there is also an exhibition of movie memorabilia, such as dresses worn by **Greta Garbo,** the tunic **Rudolph Valentino** wore in *The Sheik,* and one of the robots from the 1926 **Fritz Lang** film *Metropolis.*

55 IRCAM (Contemporary Institute of Musical and Acoustic Research) One of the world's most advanced computer music centers is located at the bottom of what looks like another métro entrance on the Place Igor-Stravinsky. Toiling away in IRCAM's underground reaches, **Pierre Boulez's** studio of composers and electronic engineers is creating the music of the future. You can take in one of the frequent lectures or a concert performed by **L'Ensemble Intercontemporain.** ◆ Admission by application only. 31 Rue St.-Merri. Métro: Hôtel-de-Ville. 42.77.12.33

55 Rites of Spring Fountain A fantastic and frivolous ballet of animals, serpents, and musical notes floats in this kinetic fountain created by **Niki de Saint-Phalle** and **Jean Tinguely,** making this a great spot for an urban picnic. ◆ Place Igor-Stravinsky. Métros: Châtelet-Les Halles, Hôtel-de-Ville

55 Benoît ★★$$/$$$ You need not take the train to Lyon to savor blood sausage with apples and roast potatoes, ducklings with turnips, or mussel soup. A stone's throw from the Tour St.-Jacques (pictured above), this attractive 1912 bistro is frequented by families in the evening. ◆ M-F noon-2PM, 8-10:15PM; closed four weeks in Aug. 20 Rue St.-Martin. Reservations required. No credit cards. Métro: Châtelet-Les Halles. 42.72.25.76

55 Café Beaubourg ★★$ This more intellectual cousin of Café Costes offers a vantage point on the local wildlife roaming around the Pompidou Center. Palatable sandwiches, daily copies of *Le Monde* and *Liberation,* the occasional volume of Rimbaud, and a stray cat to lend a personal style to another **Philippe Starck** creation. ◆ Daily 8AM-2AM. 100 Rue St.-Martin. Métro: Rambuteau. 48.87.63.96

56 Hôtel St.-Merri $ A quirky 13-room hostelry is attached to the medieval **St.-Merri Church.** Specializing in irreligious caprice, this hotel uses communion rails as bannisters and has a room with a flying buttress and another with a confessional-as-clothespress. ◆ 78 Rue de la Verrerie. Métro: Hôtel-de-Ville. 42.78.14.15

57 Aux Délices de Chine ★$/$$ Lacquered duck, stuffed pigeon with swallow's nest, and Chinese hot pot are **Victor** and **Suzanne Chau's** specialties. The decor is nothing fancy, unlike some of the dishes that are so elaborate they must be ordered 48 hours in advance. Fine, if your stomach can plan that

Marais & Les Halles

far ahead, but there are also items on the menu that do not demand such gastronomic premeditation. ◆ M-Sa noon-2:30PM, 7-10:45PM. 26 Rue des Lombards. Reservations recommended. Métro: Châtelet-Les Halles. 42.78.38.62

58 Rue Quincampoix The Scottish financier **John Law** founded a bank on this street in 1719 after he became France's comptroller general, prompting a brief rash of speculation in this part of the city. In more recent times, the street has been a sanctuary for *les femmes de la nuit,* women photographed so remarkably by **Brassai** in the early 1930s. ◆ Métro: Rambuteau

58 Pacific Palisades ★★$$ A Les Halles imitation of Californian nouvelle cuisine is served by French waiters who act like they just stepped off the beach at Malibu. In summer, the terrace is splendid. Any season of the year, the piano bar downstairs is smoky and the crowd trendy. ◆ Daily 10AM-2AM. 51 Rue Quincampoix. Reservations recommended. Métro: Rambuteau. 42.74.01.17

58 46 Rue Quincampoix A complex containing a cinema, theater, and the Cultural Center of Yugoslavia. Don't miss the startling entryway sculpture of an army of nudes bursting through the seams in the wall. ◆ Métro: Rambuteau

58 Galerie Jean Fournier The ideal art dealer, Jean Fournier is always amenable to showing and discussing his selections. American artists include **Sam Francis, Shirley Jaffe,** and **Joan Mitchell.** The gallery includes a bookstore specializing in painting as well as ancient and contemporary art. ♦ M-Sa 10AM-1PM, 2-7PM; closed in Aug. 44 Rue Quincampoix. Métro: Rambuteau. 42.77.32.31

58 Galerie Zabriskie This is Paris' outpost of New York's first-rate Fifth Avenue photo gallery. ♦ Tu-Sa 11AM-7PM; closed in Aug. 37 Rue Quincampoix. Métro: Rambuteau. 42.72.35.47

59 Galerie Alain Blondel Born of the ashes of the defunct Luxembourg Gallery, the Blondel gallery features early 20th-century works, large canvases from the 1930s, trompe l'oeil, and realism. ♦ Tu-F 11AM-7PM; Sa 2-7PM. 4 Rue Aubry-le-Boucher. Métro: Rambuteau. 42.73.66.67

60 Café Astaire ★$ This crowded New York-style café serves sandwiches, salads, and fresh fruit juice while Tina Turner and David Bowie videos play on TV. There's a good brunch on Saturday and Sunday. ♦ Daily noon-2AM. 147 Rue St.-Martin. Métro: Rambuteau. 42.78.83.50

60 Passage Molière For now, this ramshackle 19th-century alley with its tiny one-room flats and cheap tailor shops offers a glimpse, in contrast to the glitter and glamor of Les Halles, of

Marais & Les Halles

what the Beaubourg quarter was like before it got malled. ♦ Métro: Rambuteau

60 Clair Obscur A whimsical bookstore/gallery specializing in marionettes, Venetian masks, and books on theater and cinema. Ask the owner to crank up the mechanical performing circus, complete with lion tamer, acrobats, and hypnotist. ♦ M-Su 11AM-7:30PM. 161 Rue St.-Martin. Métro: Rambuteau. 48.87.78.58

61 Porte St.-Denis At the intersection of Rue St.-Denis and Boulevard Bonne-Nouvelle stands this consciously Roman-style triumphal arch celebrating **Louis XIV's** victorious battles in Flanders and the Rhineland. **François Blondel** modeled the gigantic arch after the Arch of Titus in Rome; **Charles Le Brun's** allegorical sculptured adornments were inspired by the reliefs on Trajan's Column. ♦ Métro: Strasbourg-St.-Denis

62 Porte St.-Martin In 1674 **Pierre Bullet** constructed this arch after plans made by **François Blondel** for Porte St.-Denis (pictured below). These two triumphal arches, astride the most important routes leading to the north, were erected by the Sun King to announce the grandeur of the French capital to visitors at the very time he had moved to Versailles and was tearing down the 13th-century city wall. ♦ Métro: Strasbourg-St.-Denis

63 Duthilleul et Minart For more than a century, this store has sold uniforms and work clothes, from waiters' aprons to chefs' toques, plus an array of uniquely French occupational garb. This is a great spot for gifts, too, such as the popular French watchmakers' smocks. ♦ M-Sa 9AM-7PM. 14 Rue Turbigo. Métros: Etienne-Marcel, Les Halles. 42.33.44.36

64 Saint-Leu-Saint-Gilles A 14th-century church of interest less for its unimposing exterior than for its unusual interior. On a street epitomizing voyeurism, the glass doors of the church appropriately provide their own peep show of medieval architecture. ♦ M 5-10PM; Tu-F 1-10PM; Sa 1:30-10PM; Su 10AM-12:30PM. 92 Rue St.-Denis. Métro: Les Halles

65 Rue St.-Denis Once the route by which France's kings entered Paris to be crowned and exited to be buried in the basilica at St.-Denis, this street now unfurls a lurid panoply of Parisian sleaze: peep shows, prostitutes, and fast-food joints such as the **Love Burger.** ♦ Métro: Les Halles

65 Aux Deux Saules ★★$ The Two Willows, a remnant of old Les Halles in a wasteland of gaudy neon-splashed sex shops, offers simple fare such as onion soup, sausages, *pommes frites*, and cheap wine served on outdoor wooden tables. Inside are gorgeous ceramic murals. ♦ M, W-Su noon-midnight. 91 Rue St.-Denis. Métro: Les Halles. 42.36.46.57

66 Rue de la Cossonnerie On this 13th-century street, **Giovanni Boccacio** (1313-1375), the man who was considered one of the founders of the Italian Renaissance, was born. He was the author of *Filocopo*, the first European novel. ♦ Métro: Les Halles

67 Au Père Tranquille ★$ French teenagers wearing penny loafers and fake American varsity-letter jackets crowd this late-night corner café. On a warm evening, order a Kir on the terrace while you sit and watch the Les Halles parade pass by. **e.e. cummings** set Act III of his play *Him* here. ♦ Daily 8AM-2AM. 16 Rue Pierre-Lescot. Métro: Les Halles. 45.08.00.34

67 Le Bon Pêcheur ★$ When the adolescents at Au Père Tranquille grow up, they graduate to this smoky café across the street. Le Bon Pêcheur is decorated with orange neon lights, mirrored columns, a zinc bar, and maps of Brazil on the wall. It offers salsa on the stereo, *caipirinha* (the fiery Brazilian drink), and quiche lorraine for the hungry. ♦ Daily 8AM-2AM. 9 Rue des Pêcheurs. Métro: Les Halles. 42.36.91.88

68 Chez Vong aux Halles ★★$$/$$$ Refined Cantonese and Szechuan dishes may be found in the company of excellent French wines at this attractive Chinese bistro. Dim sum, beef in oyster sauce, and lacquered pigeon are good choices. ♦ M-Sa noon-2:30PM, 7PM-12:30AM. 10 Rue de la Grande-Truar.derie. Reservations recommended. Métro: Les Halles. 40.39.99.89

69 Joe Allen ★$$ One of the most popular restaurants in Les Halles, this is a replica of its Los Angeles and Manhattan namesakes, right down to the old photographs on the dark brick walls. The menu, also a replica, offers spareribs, chili con carne, black bean soup, and apple pie. Terribly American, or at least the beautiful Parisians think so. ♦ Daily noon-2AM. 30 Rue Pierre-Lescot. Métro: Les Halles. 42.36.70.13

70 Chez Pierrot ★★★$$$ Walk through the doors of this bistro and you'll find yourself back in the old Les Halles market days. It's been decorated in period and everything is done to excess. A cornucopia of hors d'oeuvres is followed by grilled kidneys and marinated mackerel. Customers prefer cheese to desserts, insists Pierrot's owner, so they can order another hearty Bordeaux. ♦ M-F noon-2:30PM, 8-10:30PM; closed in July. 18 Rue Etienne-Marcel. Métro: Etienne-Marcel. 45.08.05.48

71 Pharamond ★★$$/$$$ Try the *tripe à la mode de Caen,* cooked in apple cider in classic Normandy fashion and served in old-fashioned charcoal-fired brass braziers. Nobody simmers it better. ♦ M 7:30-10:45PM; Tu-Sa noon-2:15PM, 7:30-10:45PM; closed in July. 24 Rue de la Grande-Truanderie. Reservations required. Métro: Les Halles. 42.33.00.72, 42.36.51.29

71 Batifol ★$/$$ While the pre-WWII decor remains, the Royal Mondétour and the beloved Bonnenfant family, alas, are no longer. They have been replaced by more professional (and regrettably more mercenary) *patrons* who turn out acceptable, affordable bistro fare (hot chèvre salad, pot au feu, coq au vin, and *tarte tartin* with Calvados), but rush diners in the interest of squeezing in a second and sometimes even a third seating each night. ♦ Daily 11AM-1AM. 14 Rue Mondétour. Reservations recommended. Métro: Les Halles. 42.36.85.50, 42.36.85.51

71 Les Bains-Douches ★$$$ Architectural whiz kid **Philippe Starck** transformed these old public Turkish baths with their 1900 facade into one of the trendiest discos and restaurants in Les Halles. What would former patron of these baths **Marcel Proust** have to say? ♦ Restaurant: daily 9PM-4AM. Disco: daily 11PM-dawn. 7 Rue de la Cossonnerie. Métro: Etienne-Marcel. 48.87.01.80

72 Forum des Halles Architect **Victor Baltard's** 12 marvelous 19th-century iron-and-glass food halls were torn down in the 1970s after the 800-year-old wholesale market was moved near Orly Airport in 1969. In its place, architects **Claude Vasconi** and **Georges Pencreach** designed a four-level underground shopping mall along the lines of an inverted hollow pyramid. This crater of consumerism is a labyrinth of walkways, cinemas, snack bars, cafés, 12 restaurants, more than 200 boutiques (the most chic of which are on the top levels), and a branch of **FNAC,** a popular hang-out where French teenagers congregate to buy concert tickets and peruse the latest *bande-dessinées* (hardcover comic books). According to a survey conducted by the McDonald's here, 80,000 pedestrians walk past its doors every day.

Recently, a Japanese insurance company dished out more than $80 million for a 32.7 percent stake in the Forum, which will earn it one-third of the annual rent paid by the Forum's shops and movie theaters ($463 million in 1988 alone). Beneath the forum is the **Châtelet-Les Halles** métro station, the world's largest underground train station, giving direct access to the métro, the RER (to Charles de Gaulle Airport), and to various underground parking lots. ♦ Rues Rambuteau,

Pierre Lescot Berger, and Les Halles Garden. Métro: Châtelet-Les Halles

Within the Forum des Halles:

Jacques Cousteau's Parc Oceanique
This 90-minute educational "sea voyage" includes a walk through a whale's stomach and a sound-and-light tour of the ocean floor. Kids love it. ♦ Admission. Tu, Th 10AM-5:30PM; W,F-Su 10AM-7PM (daily 10AM-7PM during school vacations). Level three of the Grande Galerie. 40.26.13.78

72 Kiosque-Théâtre A kiosk in the Châtelet-Les Halles métro station sells half-price tickets to theater, dance, music hall, concert, café theater, and, occasionally, opera events, on the day of performance. ♦ Daily 1-8PM. Métro: Châtelet-Lés Halles

73 Café Costes ★★★$ What Café Flore was to St.-Germain-des-Prés in the 1950s, this is to Les Halles in the 1990s. Intelligent, elegant, and chic, Café Costes is one of the city's most talked-about night spots and the flagship of a whole new generation of Paris cafés. Owner **Jean-Louis Costes** hired architectural designer **Philippe Starck,** whose work is definitely worth viewing (including the space-age bathrooms) before sitting down to sip your Blue Lagoon. ♦ Daily 8AM-2AM. Square des Innocents. No credit cards. Métro: Châtelet-Les Halles. 45.08.54.39

In 18th-century France the terms *livre* and *franc* were interchangeable. There were approximately 23 livres to the pound sterling, which was the currency generally referred to by Americans. A livre in 1776 roughly equaled one dollar today.

73 Innocents Fountain During the 16th century, Les Halles fishmongers and butchers alike drew their water from this fountain, which was commissioned by **Henri II** and designed by **Pierre Lescot** in 1547. An important architectural relic of early Renaissance Paris, it stands on the site of what was once the overcrowded, foul-smelling **Church of the Innocents** cemetery. In 1786 the church was razed and the skeletons of its many inhabitants were transported to a quarry, which was then most appropriately renamed the **Catacombs.** Later, during WWII, the Catacombs was the macabre setting for the headquarters of the French Resistance. (Catacombs: Admission. Tu-F 2-4PM; Sa-Su

9-11AM, 2-4PM. Guided tours W 2:35PM. 1 Place Denfert-Rochereau. Métro: Denfert-Rochereau. 43.22.47.63.) Today, the area surrounding the Innocents Fountain is the haunt of tattooed lowlifes and indigent backpackers poring over out-of-print copies of *Europe on $5 a Day.* ♦ Square des Innocents. Métro: Les Halles

74 Les Trottoirs de Buenos Aires The most authentic tango music in town is played here, as evidenced by the largely South American clientele. It's guaranteed to be crowded after 11PM, so call and reserve a table. Reasonably priced tango classes (private as well as group instruction) with Uruguayan and Spanish dance teachers are offered each evening before the club opens. (If you're looking for a night of tango and salsa dancing, however, try **Le Tango.**) ♦ Shows: Tu-Sa 9:30PM. Classes: Tu, Th by appointment; W 5:30-6:30PM; F 5:30-7:30PM; Sa 1:30-4:30PM. 37 Rue des Lombards. Reservations recommended. Métro: Châtelet-Les Halles. 40.26.28.58

74 Au Diable des Lombards ★$/$$ A trendy bistro serving cheeseburgers, rabbit terrine, and homemade ice cream, Au Diable is run by **Alain Eclache.** ♦ Daily 11AM-1AM; closed Christmas Eve. 64 Rue des Lombards. Métro: Châtelet-Les Halles. 42.33.81.84

75 Ducs d'Anjou $$ This small, 30-room hotel sits just off the charming Place Ste.-Opportune. Rooms on the courtyard are somber. ♦ 1 Rue Ste.-Opportune. Métro: Châtelet-Les Halles. 42.36.92.24

75 Via Diffusion Design superstar **Philippe Starck** fashioned this stunningly sleek, simple gallery, which exhibits the most innovative in French furniture, and lighting designs galore. The office of Valorisation de l'Innovation dans l'Ameublement (VIA), a trade association promoting contemporary French design worldwide, is upstairs. ♦ M-Sa 10:30AM-7PM; closed in Aug. 8-10 Place Ste.-Opportune. Métro: Châtelet-Les Halles. 43.29.39.36

76 Rue de la Ferronnerie Here **King Henri IV** was murdered in his carriage on 14 May 1610 as he passed along Ironmongers Row. His assassin, **Ravaillac,** was subsequently quartered by four horses in the Place de Grève, today called Place de l'Hôtel-de-Ville. ♦ Métro: Châtelet-Les Halles

76 Papeterie Moderne If you've got enough patience to sort through this store's marvelous hodgepodge of old Parisian signage (for streets, butcher shops, bakeries, and the like), you can take home a fine souvenir. A copy of anything in the store may be ordered; allow ten days for pickup. ♦ M-Th, Sa 7:30AM-noon, 1-8PM; F 10:30AM-noon, 1-8PM; closed two weeks in summer. 12 Rue de la Ferronnerie. Métro: Châtelet-Les Halles. 42.36.21.72

77 Novotel Paris Les Halles $$ This sprawling 300-room Postmodern hostelry of glass and zinc borders the oppressive Forum des Halles shopping complex. One of the chain's many hotels in the Paris region, it is popular with whirlwind tourists and businesspeople. ♦ 8 Place Marguerite-de-Navarre. Métro: Châtelet-Les Halles. 42.21.31.31

78 Les Bouchons $$ In the cellar of an unremarkable restaurant with the same name is a former cork factory turned into a blues and jazz club. ♦ Restaurant: M-F noon-3PM, 8PM-1AM; Sa-Su brunch noon-5PM. Jazz: daily 10:30PM-1:30AM. 19 Rue des Halles. Métro: Les Halles. 42.33.28.73

79 La Tour de Montlhèry ★★$$ The owner, **Jacques,** with his white apron and 1890s moustache, serves his loyal clientele of wine merchants, advertising executives, and visiting English novelists stick-to-the-ribs specialties such as stuffed cabbage, mutton with beans, and steak with shallots. Old friends find this a nice place to meet over a bottle of Brouilly. ♦ M-F 24 hrs (Sa until 7AM); closed mid-July through mid-Aug. 5 Rue des Prouvaires. Métro: Les Halles. 42.36.21.82

80 Le Samovar ★$$ Beef stroganoff, Siberian *pelmeni,* Caucasian shashlik, blinis, and vodka accompanied after dark by the balalaika. How Russian can you get? ♦ M-F noon-2PM, 8:30PM-2AM; Sa 8:30PM-2AM; closed in Aug. 14 Rue Sauval. Reservations recommended. Métros: Les Halles, Louvre. 40.26.77.79

81 Rue Montorgueil A lively market street where Paris chefs have continued to shop despite the demolition of the old Les Halles markets. Begins at the Rue Rambuteau. ◆ Market: Tu-Su 6AM-1PM. Métro: Les Halles

81 L'Escargot Montorgueil ★★★$$$ One of the most authentic displays of 1830s decor in Paris, the restaurant has a black-and-gilt facade, enormous cut-glass mirrors, tulip chandeliers, and red banquettes. The old cooking allegory gracing the wall came from the dining room of actress **Sarah Bernhardt.** The champagne comes in carafes; the escargots come in mint, curry, fennel, or *à la bourguignonne;* and the customers come from the Maxim's, Lasserre, Grand Véfour, Tour d'Argent class. Small wonder. The restaurant is run by **Mademoiselle Saladin-Terrail,** the sister of **Claude Terrail,** owner of La Tour d'Argent. ◆ Tu-Su 12:30-2:30PM, 8PM-12:30AM. 38 Rue Montorgueil. Reservations recommended. Métro: Les Halles. 42.36.83.51

81 Les Halles Garden The razing of the Les Halles market left 106 acres of open space, which has now been transformed into a tree-lined garden and children's playground in the shadow of St.-Eustache Church. Beneath this urban wilderness is **Paul Chemetov's** subterranean sports and culture complex that includes a gymnasium, radio station, billiard hall, art gallery, record-lending library, performing-arts conservatory, and a learning center offering instruction on anything from cooking to magic tricks and bridge. ◆ Olympic swimming pool: Admission. 10 Place de la Rotonde. M 11:30AM-8PM; Tu, Th-F 11:30AM-10PM; W 10AM-7PM; Sa-Su 9AM-5PM. Métro: Les Halles

82 St.-Eustache Church This massive amalgam of Gothic flying buttresses, rose windows, and flamboyant vaulting with a Renaissance facade was built in 1640 to rival Notre-Dame. While its dimensions are enormous (346 feet long with a 112-foot-high nave), the church is better known for its musical legacy than architectural grandeur. The

Marais & Les Halles

Berlioz *Te Deum* and **Liszt** *Grand Mass* were first performed here, composer **Jean-Philippe Rameau** is buried in this church. The Christmas offering of the impressive 8,000-pipe organ and talented church choir at midnight Mass outshines even the Notre-Dame's. Notable treasures of plastic arts in the church are the **Rubens** *Pilgrims at Emmaus,* the **Pigalle** statue of the Virgin, and a colorful sculpted scene honoring the vegetable vendors forced out of Les Halles in 1969.

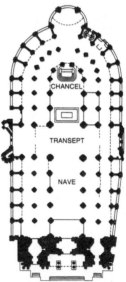

The church is dedicated to **Saint Eustache,** a second-century Roman general who

converted to Christianity when, like Saint Hubert, he saw a vision of the cross poised between the antlers of a stag. (A sculpted stag's head and cross are beneath the gable in the church's Renaissance transept facade.) Saint Eustache, as the story goes, was gruesomely martyred; he was roasted alive inside an immense bronze bull with his wife and children. This was once the parish church for the merchants of Les Halles and the nobility from the nearby Louvre and Palais Royal. It hosted the infant baptisms of **Cardinal Richelieu, Jean-Baptiste Poquelin (Molière)**, and **Madame de Pompadour**, as well as the funerals of fabulist **Jean de La Fontaine, Colbert** (prime minister of **Louis XIV**), Molière, and Revolutionary orator **Mirabeau**. During the Revolution the St.-Eustache Church was vandalized and renamed the "Temple of Agriculture," doubtless in honor of its proximity to the Les Halles market. ♦ M-Sa 8:30AM-7PM; Su 8:30AM-12:30PM, 3-7PM. A 45-minute tour is available Sunday at 3PM. 2 Rue du Jour. Métro: Les Halles

Within St.-Eustache Church:

Crypt Ste.-Agnès An improbable nightclub in the basement of St.-Eustache. Spo-

radic concerts feature everything from bluegrass and Brazilian to chamber music. Look for the doorway decorated with a stone sea serpent. For upcoming events, check listings in *Pariscope*. ♦ Cover charge. Enter at 1 Rue Montmartre. Métro: Les Halles

83 Le Cochon à l'Oreille ★★$ An authentic turn-of-the-century working-class bar/café that's adorned with beautiful ceramic murals. Butchers, foie gras wholesalers, local merchants, and paunchy men of indefinite occupation wearing blue coveralls hang out here. They come for their coffee and Calvados before dawn or to share a *pastis* at the crowded zinc bar in the afternoon. ♦ M-Sa 7AM-7PM. 15 Rue Montmartre. No credit cards. Métro: Les Halles. 42.36.07.56

84 agnès b. Cheerful striped cotton T-shirts, chic silk blouses, pajamas, and skirts. In her three outlets along Rue du Jour, one each for children, men, and women, agnès b. comfortably and colorfully outfits the 1990s generation. Her trademark cotton cardigans with mother-of-pearl snaps in countless colors are de rigeur Parisienne attire. ♦ M noon-7:30PM; Tu-Sa 10:30AM-7:30PM. 3 Rue du Jour. Métro: Les Halles. 42.33.04.13

84 Au Pied de Cochon ★$$ This nostalgic all-night onion soup restaurant specializes in *fruits de mer* (chilled shellfish), pig's trotters (hence the restaurant's name), and an overrated onion soup *gratiné*. A favorite of local night owls at 4AM, but otherwise it's a tourist mecca. Oysters of a dozen varieties are washed down with champagne at the bar for a Parisian version of Sunday brunch. Service is as poky as the snails are delicious. ♦ Open daily 24 hrs. 6 Rue Coquillière. Métro: Les Halles. 42.36.11.75

Furniture Fantastique

Haute-couture furniture houses in Paris are open to the public (unlike in America), and showcase stores devoted to the work of avant-garde designers are becoming as popular for furniture as for fashion. Hot spots for top-of-the-line French furnishings include the following:

Ecart Opened by Andrée Putman in 1978, this shop offers re-editions of furniture by such 20th-century designers as Robert Mallet-Stevens and Eileen Gray, as well as new designs. ♦ M-Sa 9AM-6PM. 111 Rue St.-Antoine. Métro: St.-Paul. 42.78.88.35

Edifice Philippe Starck got his start in this showroom, and his iconoclastic design spirit lives on in the work of such young designers as Marie-Christine Dorner and Shiro Kuramata. ♦ M-Sa 10AM-7PM. 27bis Boulevard Raspail. Métro: Sèvres-Babylon. 45.48.53.60

Galerie Agora Owner Claude Lévy-Soussan sponsors competitions and promotes classic contemporary designs in the sleekest showroom in Paris. Take a look at the garden in back. ♦ M-F 9AM-6:30PM; Sa 10AM-1PM, 2:30-6:30PM. 28 Rue de Berri. Métro: George V. 43.59.78.01

Mobilier International A pioneer of importing and marketing 20th-century design since 1950, this company features the work of French designer Jean-Michel Wilmotte, as well as other European designers and such 20th-century design doyens as Charles Eames. ♦ M-F 9:30AM-12:30PM, 2-4:30PM. 166 Rue du Faubourg-St.-Honoré. Métro: St.-Philippe-du-Roule. 43.59.08.40

Neotu This is the place for whimsical furniture-as-sculpture, where any material is fair game, from bags of stones to molded plastic. ♦ M-Sa 11AM-1PM, 2-7PM. 25 Rue du Renard. Métros: Hôtel-de-Ville, Rambuteau. 42.78.91.83

Via Diffusion The Valorisation de l'Innovation dans l'Ameublement (VIA), is a joint venture between the government and the furniture industry to promote experimental designs. ♦ See page 100 for additional information.

84 Au Cochon d'Or ★★$$ An authentic hold-over from old Les Halles days, this small, friendly, lace-curtained bistro serves classic *la moelle au pochet* and grilled beef accompanied by the best french fries in Paris. ◆ M-F noon-2:30PM, 7:30-10:30PM; Sa 7:30-10:30PM. 31 Rue du Jour. Reservations recommended. Métro: Les Halles. 42.36.38.31

84 L'Epi d'Or ★★$$ A humble 1950s Les Halles standby serving honest *pomme de ris de veau en cocotte,* salt pork and lentils, and unsophisticated Rhones and Bordeaux. ◆ M-F noon-3PM, 7PM-midnight; Sa 7PM-1AM; hours may change in Aug. 25 Rue Jean-Jacques-Rousseau. Reservations recommended. Métro: Les Halles. 42.36.38.12

85 La Chambre de Commerce One of the few buildings to escape the Les Halles demolition, the Commercial Exchange (built in 1887) is a graceful birthday cake of iron and glass. Not to be confused with the **Bourse des Valeurs,** the Roman temple to the north that houses the Paris Stock Exchange, here brokers in wheat, sugar, and other commodities do their trading. Beside the Chambre de Commerce is a 101-foot classical column, topped with what appears to be a giant iron birdcage. This curiosity, called the **Horoscope Tower,** was once attached to the **Hôtel de la Reine** of **Catherine de Médici** and accommodated her stargazing astrologer, **Ruggieri,** during the late 16th century. ◆ Reception/information: M-F 8AM-7:30PM. 42.89.70.00

86 Le Pavillon Baltard ★$ An Alsatian brasserie serving *choucroute* (sauerkraut) with your choice of fish, pork, calf's head, or stuffed pig's tail. Nouvelle cuisine this ain't. Plan a long stroll after dinner. ◆ Daily noon-3PM, 7PM-1AM. 9 Rue Coquillière. Reservations recommended. Métro: Les Halles. 42.36.22.00

87 Dehillerin Half warehouse, half hardware store, this family-run kitchen emporium has been supplying the great chefs of Europe with cooking vessels and utensils since 1820. Dehillerin even furnishes the French Army with cast-iron frying pans, boxwood knives, spatulas, and the wire skimmers known as "spiders." And they mail-order to civilians anywhere in the world. Dehillerin also happens to be the city's leading specialist in retinning copper pots. The salespeople speak broken English. ◆ M-Sa 8AM-12:30PM, 2-6PM. 18-20 Rue Coquillière and 51 Rue Jean-Jacques-Rousseau. Métros: Les Halles, Louvre. 42.36.53.13

88 La Cloche des Halles ★★$ This wine bar, named after the *cloche* (bronze bell) that for decades signaled the opening and closing of the Les Halles market, offers not only superb Sancerres, Morgons, and Côtes-de-Brouillys, but scrumptious plates of baked country ham, assorted regional cheeses, chicken-liver pâté, and homemade fruit tarts. Crowded with local merchants, journalists, and the folks in dark suits from the Bourse and Banque de France up the street. ◆ M-F 8AM-10PM; Sa 10AM-6PM. 28 Rue Coquillière. No credit cards. Métros: Les Halles, Louvre. 42.36.93.89

88 Gérard Besson ★★$$/$$$ One of the neighborhood's finest lunch menus. Begin with owner/chef Besson's thick fish soup, followed by roast Bresse chicken with mushrooms. For dessert, try the *biscuit glacé à la framboise.* The detailed wine list is strong on Bordeaux. ◆ M-F noon-2PM, 7:30-10:30PM; closed two weeks in July. 5 Rue du Coq-Héron. Reservations recommended. Métros: Louvre, Palais-Royal. 42.33.14.74

88 La Coutellerie Suisse You can't miss this consummate cutlery shop with its giant red Swiss Army knife splayed open in the window. ◆ M-F 9AM-noon, 2-6PM; closed in Aug. 44 Rue Coquillière. Métro: Les Halles. 42.33.20.92

88 La Fermette du Sud-Ouest ★★$$/$$$ Jacky Mayer reigns supreme over this countrified restaurant. La Fermette is famous for homemade *boudin* (blood sausage) with onions in sautéed potatoes, cassoulet, magnificent entrecôtes, and hearty Cahors wines. ◆ M-Sa noon-2PM, 7:30-10:30PM; closed in Aug. 31 Rue Coquillière. Reservations recommended. Métro: Châtelet-Les Halles. 42.36.73.55

89 Banque de France The mansion, which became home to the Bank of France in 1812 by order of **Napoléon,** was originally built for the

Comte de Toulouse, the son of **Louis XIV** and **Mademoiselle de Montespan.** Among its lavish treasures is a first-class work of art, *Fête à Saint Cloud,* which many art historians say is the best of **Fragonard's** landscape paintings. That huge (seven- by ten-foot) canvas hangs in the private office of the governor of the bank. Therefore, unless you have specific business with the governor, you will have to content yourself with the sight of smaller Fragonards down the street at the Louvre. ◆ 39 Rue Croix-des-Petits-Champs. Métro: Louvre

Napoléon, or, more correctly, Bonaparte, as he was then known, first came to national attention at the seige of Toulon, where his bravery and innovative use of artillery caught the attention of Robespierre's younger brother. Born in Corsica, Napoléon had a sensational career—the most stunning of the 19th century. His rise from relative obscurity to emperor of all Europe was made possible by the Revolution; indeed, he often said he was its heir. By a coup d'état in 1799, he made himself the Republic's First Consul and, soon afterwards, First Consul for life. In 1804 he had himself crowned emperor.

By law in Paris, prostitutes have to stand absolutely still, and their potential clients must make the first gesture.

Never say *Je suis pleine* after one of those enormous Parisian meals, especially if you're a woman. Literally, the words mean "I am full," but idiomatically it is a rather vulgar way of declaring that you are pregnant.

Restaurants/Nightlife: Red   **Hotels:** Blue
Shops/ 🌳 Outdoors: Green   **Sights/Culture:** Black

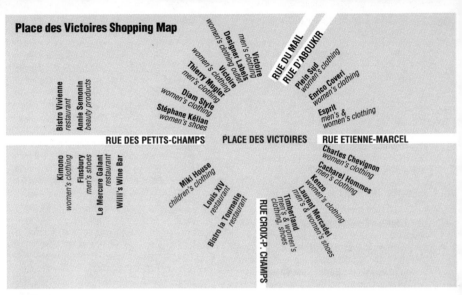

Place des Victoires Shopping Map

Victoire men's clothing

Designer Labels women's clothing outlet

Victoire women's clothing

Thierry Mugler men's clothing

Diam Style women's clothing

Stéphane Kélian women's shoes

Bistro Vivienne restaurant

Annie Semonin beauty products

RUE DU MAIL

RUE D'ABOUKIR

Plein Sud women's clothing

Enrico Coveri women's clothing

Esprit men's & women's clothing

RUE DES PETITS-CHAMPS

PLACE DES VICTOIRES

RUE ETIENNE-MARCEL

Charles Chevignon women's clothing

Cacharel Hommes men's clothing

Kenzo women's clothing

Laurent Mercadel men's & women's shoes

Timberland men's & women's clothing, shoes

Kimono women's shoes

Finsbury men's shoes

Le Mercure Galant restaurant

Willi's Wine Bar

Miki House children's clothing

Louis XIV restaurant

Bistro la Tournelle restaurant

RUE CROIX-P. CHAMPS

90 Place des Victoires Like the Place Vendôme, this circle of noble, uniform mansions was designed by **Jules Hardouin-Mansart** to celebrate a triumph of **Louis XIV,** this time the Treaty of Nimegen that marked his victory over Spain, Holland, Piedmont, and Germany. The square originally housed a gilded bronze statue (1686) portraying the king being crowned by a goddess of victory, with four bound warriors at his feet representing the conquered nations. Destroyed during the Revolution, the first statue was replaced in 1822 with the **Astyanax Bosio** equestrian version of Louis XIV that proudly rears here today. During the 19th century, the Place des Victoires fell into ruin and its buildings were converted into tradesmen's shops. A recent restoration has turned the square into the Right Bank's hub of high fashion. ♦ Métro: Bourse

91 Marithé and François Girbaud These two young designers, who have totally revolutionized casual wear in France, are responsible for ten clothing lines (Closed, Maillotparty, Montagnes, and Fôrets) for men, women, and children. Everything is here in this three-floor high-tech loft. ♦ M 11AM-7PM; Tu-Sa 10AM-7PM. 38 Rue Etienne-Marcel. Métros: Etienne-Marcel, Les Halles. 42.33.54.69

92 Lina's ★★★$ This airy sandwich bar with its ochre walls, blond-wood trim, and acres of windows is the perfect vantage point for spying on the chic fashion show that promenades in the vicinity of the Place des Victoires. Behind the counter, statuesque men in white shirts and smart neckties offer delicious shrimp-avocado, pastrami, and smoked-salmon sandwiches on crusty country bread (*pain pavé*). ♦ M-Sa 10:30AM-5PM. 50 Rue Etienne-Marcel. Métro: Louvre. 42.21.16.14

93 Au Panetier Lebon A Belle Epoque bakery selling hundreds of crispy sourdough baguettes daily, all fresh from the wood-fired oven of **Bernard Lebon.** ♦ M-F 8AM-7PM. 10 Place des Petits-Pères. Métro Bourse. 42.60.90.23

93 Notre-Dame-des-Victoires Based on the plans of **Pierre Le Muet,** architect **Sylvain Cartaud** completed this rather undistinguished church in 1740, whose name commemorates the **Louis XIII** trouncing of the Protestants in 1628 La Rochelle. Inside the church are a bust (1702) of the composer **Jean-Baptiste Lully,** who lived down the street at **45 Rue des Petits-Champs,** and an estimated 30,000 tablets blanketing the walls. ♦ M-F 7:30AM-7PM; Sa 8:30AM-12:15PM, 2:30-7:15PM; Su 8:30AM-12:15PM, 4-7:15PM. Place des Petits-Pères. Métro: Bour

93 Chez Georges ★★$$/$$$ Handwritten menus, beveled mirrors, waitresses in black dresses, and an honest platter of beefsteak and fries are all the hallmarks of this classic Parisian bistro. ♦ M-Sa 12:15-2:15PM, 7:15-9:30PM; closed three weeks in Aug. 1 Rue du Mail. Reservations recommended. Métro: Sentier. 42.60.07.11

94 Victoire Come here to find out what's new in the current fashion scene. Victoire takes pride in being the very first specialty store to discover new Paris talent. ♦ M-Sa 9:30AM-7PM. 10-12 Place des Victoires. Métros: Bourse, Pyramides. 42.61.09.02

94 Kenzo This appealing, natural-wood boutique has some of the most fanciful fashions and friendliest sales help in town. For the young at heart: menswear downstairs, ladieswear upstairs. ♦ M 11AM-7PM; Tu-Sa 10AM-7PM. 3 Place des Victoires. Métros: Bourse, Pyramides. 40.39.72.00

94 Cacharel Company founder **Jean Bosquet** has long since moved into politics. Nevertheless, the design flame continues with the sensible sportswear and cotton paisley print fabrics in collaboration with Liberty of London. Menswear is in the basement. (Ladieswear is sold nearby at 49 Ave Etienne-Marcel.) ♦ M 11AM-7PM; Tu-Sa 10AM-7PM. 5 Place des Victoires. Métros: Bourse, Pyramides. 42.33.29.88

94 Louis XIV ★★$$/$$$ This old bistro in the prettiest building in the Place des Victoires serves generous portions of traditional Burgundy and Lyon dishes such as dandelion greens with bacon, rabbit in mustard sauce, and beef Bourguignonne. The house Beaujolais comes in pitchers, the pickles in large vats, and a mammoth help-yourself block of butter is passed from table to table. The lunch crowd consists of reporters, bankers, brokers, and fashionable types fueling up to shop at Kenzo and the other smart boutiques on the square. In good weather, reserve a sidewalk table and enjoy the view of Louis XIV, majestic on horseback. ♦ M-F noon-2:30PM, 7:30-10:30PM; closed in Aug. 1bis Place des Victoires. Reservations required. Métro: Bourse. 40.26.20.81

95 Legrand This renowned wineshop's bright red Belle Epoque facade, glass candy jars out front on the sidewalk, and ceiling covered in corks are a joy to behold. For three generations, the Legrand family has run this *épicerie* stocked with a knowing selection of wine, chocolate, tea, coffee, and jam. **Francine Legrand,** the daughter of the late **Lucien,** has a passion for younger, undiscovered (and less expensive) wines from France's smaller vineyards in Burgundy and Bordeaux. Ask her to recommend one: she loves to chat. ♦ Tu-F 8:30AM-7:30PM; Sa 8:30AM-1PM, 3-7PM. 1 Rue de la Banque. Métro: Bourse. 42.60.07.12

France's Revolutionary Timeline: 1787 to 1804

Pre-Revolutionary Period (January 1787-May 1789)

February 1787: Louis XVI's realm is in dire financial straits; the First Assembly of Notables refuses to be taxed to raise money.

May 1788: Law courts *(parlements)* refuse to tax privileged orders.

June-July 1788: Revolt of the nobility.

August 1788: Louis XVI calls a meeting of the Estates-General.

January 1789: Sieyès pamphlet, "What is the Third Estate?"

From the Estates-General to the Fall of the Bastille (May 1789-July 1789)

17 June 1789: The Third Estate declares itself the National Assembly.

20 June 1789: The Tennis Court Oath (the National Assembly swears not to disband until a constitution is adopted).

23 June 1789: Louis XVI refuses to recognize the National Assembly; he holds a session of the Estates-General.

27 June 1789: The king orders the first two estates to join the National Assembly.

11 July 1789: Dismissal of Jacques Necker.

14 July 1789: Fall of the Bastille.

The Constituent Assembly (July 1789-September 1791)

17 July 1789: Capitulation of Louis XVI to Paris. The beginning of the Constituent Assembly, the new legislative body that emerged from the National Assembly.

July-August 1789: Massive peasant rebellion called the Great Fear.

4-11 August 1789: Constituent Assembly abolishes feudalism.

26 August 1789: Declaration of the Rights of Man and of the Citizen is adopted by the Constituent Assembly.

5-6 October 1789: Women march to Versailles and bring the king and his family back to Paris.

19 October 1789: Constituent Assembly also relocates to Paris.

2 November 1789: All church property is confiscated.

13 February 1790: All religious orders are abolished.

19 June 1790: Every hereditary title is abolished.

12 July 1790: The church is made subservient to the State.

20-25 July 1791: Louis XVI is captured at the border town of Varennes while trying to flee France. He is returned to Paris.

17 July 1791: Petitioners in the Champ-de-Mars demanding Louis XVI's abdication are attacked; about 50 are killed.

3 September 1791: The new constitution is proclaimed.

14 September 1791: Louis XVI accepts the constitution and is restored to power.

The Legislative Assembly (October 1791-September 1792)

1 October 1791: The new Legislative assembly meets under the new constitution. Former members of the Constituent Assembly are prohibited from sitting in the new assembly.

20 April 1792: After long debates, war is declared against the king of Bohemia-Hungary.

20 June 1792: Crowds invade Tuileries Palace to intimidate the king into accepting Revolutionary legislation. He refuses.

28 July 1792: A manifesto by the Duke of Brunswick, commanding general of the Austro-Prussian Army, is distributed in Paris. It threatens those refusing to obey Louis XVI.

10 August 1792: Attack on Tuileries, de facto end of the monarchy.

13 August 1792: The royal family is imprisoned in the Temple Tower by the Commune.

19 August 1792: Lafayette defects and is imprisoned in Austria. Prussian troops and French émigrés invade France.

Marais & Les Halles

2-7 September 1792: Prison massacres take place in Paris.

20 September 1792: The Prussian advance is halted at the Battle of Valmy.

The Convention Assembly (September 1792-October 1795)

From the Republic to the Terror (September 1792-June 1793)

21 September 1792: The First Republic is proclaimed. The Convention Assembly replaces the Legislative Assembly.

21 January 1793: After months of debate, a trial and a condemnation. Louis XVI is executed.

1 February 1793: The Convention Assembly declares war on Great Britain.

24 February 1793: Military conscription is decreed.

March 1793: Royalist-Catholic rebellion (or counter-revolution) breaks out in the Vendée.

5 April 1793: General Dumouriez deserts to the Austrians.

6 April 1793: The Committee of Public Safety is decreed.

The Terror (June 1793-July 1794)

31 May-2 June 1793: Twenty-nine Girondin deputies are purged from the Convention Assembly.

24 June 1793: The "Jacobin" constitution is completed (adopted on 4 August but never applied).

27 July 1793: Robespierre is elected to the Committee of Public Safety.

27 August 1793: Touloun, the French naval headquarters for the Mediterranean, falls to the British.

4-5 September 1793: The Hébertist uprising in Paris forces emergency measures on the Convention Assembly. The constitution is suspended.

17 September 1793: Law of Suspects is decreed.

4 December 1793: Law of Frimaire centralizes all activities of the Revolutionary Government.

26 February-3 March 1794: The Laws of Ventôse authorize the seizure and redistribution of the property belonging to the suspects.

March 1794: Execution of the Hébertists.

April 1794: Execution of the Dantonists.

4 June 1794: Robespierre elected president of the Convention.

10 June 1794: Law of 22 Prairial is decreed, inaugurating the final phase of the Terror.

26 June 1794: Battle of Fleurus liberates Belgium from the Austrians and ends the foreign military threat to the Revolution.

27 July 1794: Fall of Robespierre. He is executed the next day.

After Robespierre's Fall (July 1794-October 1795)

18 September 1794: Church and State are separated.

12 November 1794: Paris' Jacobin Club is closed.

22 August 1795: A new constitution is approved; it provides for a Directory government.

5 October 1795: Napoléon puts down a royalist revolt in Paris.

26 October 1795: Napoléon is named commander-in-chief of all armies in France.

From the Directory to the Empire (October 1795-December 1804)

27 October 1795: Directory government succeeds the Convention.

2 March 1796: Napoléon named commander-in-chief of the French Army in Italy.

1 July 1798: Napoléon launches his Egyptian campaign.

1 August 1798: Nelson defeats the French fleet at Aboukir Bay.

16 October 1799: Napoléon arrives in Paris.

9-10 November 1799: Napoléon's coup d'état. He becomes First Consul of the Consulate government.

15 December 1799: Constitution of the Consulate is issued.

2 December 1804: Napoléon is crowned emperor in the Notre-Dame Cathedral. End of the First French Republic.

—David P. Jordan
Reprinted with permission from *France Magazine*

Louvre & Champs-Elysées

This superlative stroll includes the largest museum in the Western world (the **Louvre**), the world's most famous boulevard (the **Champs-Elysées**), the most ancient monument in Paris (the 3,300-year-old Egyptian **Obelisk of Luxor**), the best 360-degree view of Paris (from **La Samaritaine's** rooftop café), the grandest hotels (the **Meurice, Crillon,** and **George V**), the city's oldest métro station (**Franklin-D.-Roosevelt**), the most elegant tea salon (**Angélina**), the best English paperback bookshop (**W.H. Smith and Son**), one of the world's most magnificent squares (**Place de la Concorde**), the largest concert hall in Paris (**Théâtre du Châlet**), the "hautest" of haute couture (along **Avenue Montaigne**), the sexiest cabaret in Paris (**Crazy Horse Saloon**), the city's best restaurant (**Taillevent**), and the world's biggest triumphal arch (**L'Arc de Triomphe**). That's a lot to take in for one day, so get an early start, put on your most comfortable shoes, and *bon courage*—that's French for "keep a stiff upper lip."

Monday may be the best day to follow this walk, for it's the only day the **Hôtel de Ville** (City Hall) is open and the lines at the Louvre Museum slack off (on Sunday, when admission to the Louvre is free, it's a mob scene). Monday is also discount night at the cinemas on the Champs-Elysées. Begin your tour with the Hôtel de Ville, then pass along the Seine by the pet and plant shops on **Quai de la Mégisserie** and stop for morning coffee and a spectacular city panorama atop La Samaritaine department store. Next comes the Louvre Museum. Ask someone to hold your place in the museum's ticket line so you can run across the street to peek at the Louis XIV royal pew in the artists' church of **St.-Germain-l'Auxerrois.** Then prepare yourself for a two- to three-hour whirlwind tour of the history of Western art that includes those three remarkable Mediterranean ladies: *Venus de Milo, Winged Victory of Samothrace,* and *Mona Lisa.* After the Louvre take a break at the nearby **Tuileries Gardens,** then either splurge for lunch at Gaston Lenôtre's **Le Pavillon Elysée** or join the fashion models with fierce sweet cravings who order the Mont Blanc dessert at Angélina. En route to Place de la Concorde, you might stop at W.H. Smith and Son for the latest *New Yorker* or an English novel to read on the plane home.

From the base of the Obelisk of Luxor, it is a mile to the Arc de Triomphe. If you need motivation to keep walking, consider the delights that lie ahead: the Vermeer and Rembrandt paintings at the **Petit Palais,** chef Deligne's hot oysters with truffles at Taillevent, and perhaps even a feast for the eyes—a strip-tease artist at the famous Crazy Horse Saloon. The eastern half of the Champs-Elysées is bordered by gardens (designed by **André Le Nôtre,** a gardener for Louis XIV, who also landscaped Versailles) that have not changed since novelist **Marcel Proust** played there as a child. On the right, you pass behind three fine properties: the **British Embassy,** the **Japanese Embassy,** and the **Palais de l'Elysée.** At **Rond Point,** a round-

about in the east end of the Champs-Elysées, shoppers should veer left to Avenue Montaigne, the high-fashion row, while art buffs and stamp collectors will

want to go directly to the galleries on **Avenue Matignon** and to the stamp stalls on **Avenue Gabriel.**

The last stretch of the Champs-Elysées, which leads up to Napoléon's triumphal arch, is meant to be strolled in the evening when the city lights are glittering, upholding the reputation of Paris as the "City of Light." High rollers will have a cocktail on the terrace at **Fouquet's,** and dinner at **Taillevent, Chiberta,** or, perhaps, upstairs at **Lasserre,** where the ceiling rolls back for stargazing between courses. Those who are on a tighter budget might catch a first-run movie at the **Gaumont,** jazz at the **Blue Note,** or a Beckett play at the **Théâtre Renaud Barrault,** and then enjoy a late-night raclette (melted cheese on bread) at **La Boutique à Sandwiches** or a light Danish meal at **Olsson's.** When the day's strolling is over, you may feel like you've ridden in the Tour de France, the world's greatest bicycle race, which finishes each July on the Champs-Elysées, where you too will complete your one-day Tour de Paris.

1 Place de l'Hôtel-de-Ville The present seat of the Paris city government, this square is where **Etienne Marcel,** one of the first mayors of Paris, established his city council in 1357. Marcel incited a mob to rise against the monarchy and storm the royal palace on **Ile de la Cité.** The next year, Marcel was killed—not by the king, but by his fellow Parisians. Centered in the granite on the square is the image of a boat, the city symbol, adopted from the 13th-century coat of arms of the Boatmen's Guild.
♦ Métro: Hôtel-de-Ville

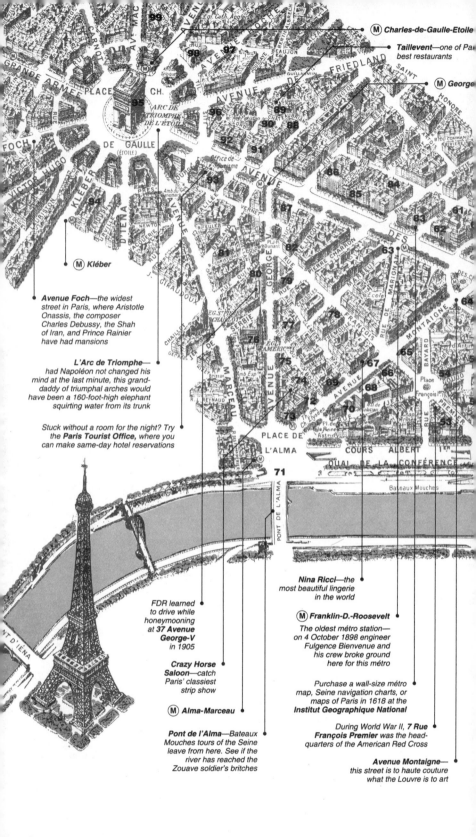

M Charles-de-Gaulle-Etoile

Taillevent—one of Pa best restaurants

M George

Avenue Foch—the widest street in Paris, where Aristotle Onassis, the composer Charles Debussy, the Shah of Iran, and Prince Rainier have had mansions

L'Arc de Triomphe— had Napoléon not changed his mind at the last minute, this grand-daddy of triumphal arches would have been a 160-foot-high elephant squirting water from its trunk

Stuck without a room for the night? Try the **Paris Tourist Office,** where you can make same-day hotel reservations

M Kléber

Nina Ricci—the most beautiful lingerie in the world

M Franklin-D.-Roosevelt

The oldest métro station— on 4 October 1898 engineer Fulgence Bienvenue and his crew broke ground here for this métro

FDR learned to drive while honeymooning at **37 Avenue George-V** in 1905

Crazy Horse Saloon—catch Paris' classiest strip show

M Alma-Marceau

Pont de l'Alma—Bateaux Mouches tours of the Seine leave from here. See if the river has reached the Zouave soldier's britches

Purchase a wall-size métro map, Seine navigation charts, or maps of Paris in 1618 at the **Institut Geographique National**

During World War II, **7 Rue François Premier** was the head-quarters of the American Red Cross

Avenue Montaigne— this street is to haute couture what the Louvre is to art

M = *Métro*

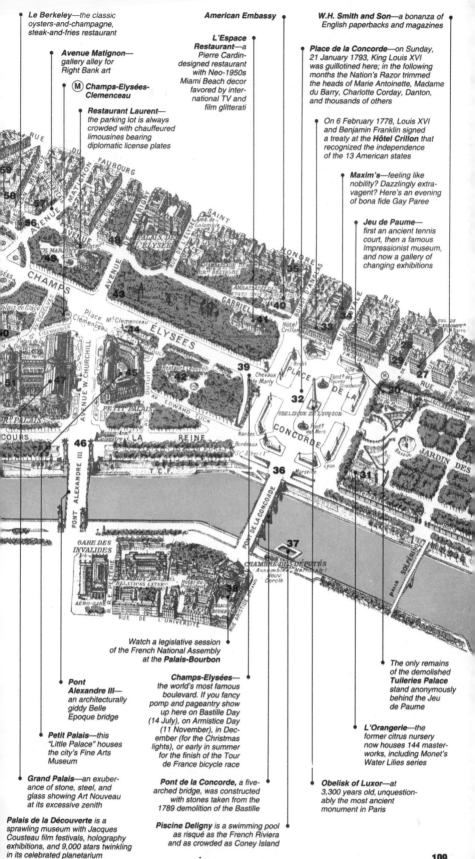

Le Berkeley—the classic oysters-and-champagne, steak-and-fries restaurant

Avenue Matignon— gallery alley for Right Bank art

Ⓜ Champs-Elysées-Clemenceau

Restaurant Laurent— the parking lot is always crowded with chauffeured limousines bearing diplomatic license plates

American Embassy

L'Espace Restaurant—a Pierre Cardin-designed restaurant with Neo-1950s Miami Beach decor favored by international TV and film glitterati

W.H. Smith and Son—a bonanza of English paperbacks and magazines

Place de la Concorde—on Sunday, 21 January 1793, King Louis XVI was guillotined here; in the following months the Nation's Razor trimmed the heads of Marie Antoinette, Madame du Barry, Charlotte Corday, Danton, and thousands of others

On 6 February 1778, Louis XVI and Benjamin Franklin signed a treaty at the Hôtel Crillon that recognized the independence of the 13 American states

Maxim's—feeling like nobility? Dazzlingly extravagent? Here's an evening of bona fide Gay Paree

Jeu de Paume— first an ancient tennis court, then a famous Impressionist museum, and now a gallery of changing exhibitions

Watch a legislative session of the French National Assembly at the Palais-Bourbon

Pont Alexandre III— an architecturally giddy Belle Epoque bridge

Petit Palais—this "Little Palace" houses the city's Fine Arts Museum

Grand Palais—an exuberance of stone, steel, and glass showing Art Nouveau at its excessive zenith

Palais de la Découverte is a sprawling museum with Jacques Cousteau film festivals, holography exhibitions, and 9,000 stars twinkling in its celebrated planetarium

Champs-Elysées— the world's most famous boulevard. If you fancy pomp and pageantry show up here on Bastille Day (14 July), on Armistice Day (11 November), in December (for the Christmas lights), or early in summer for the finish of the Tour de France bicycle race

Pont de la Concorde, a five-arched bridge, was constructed with stones taken from the 1789 demolition of the Bastille

Piscine Deligny is a swimming pool as risqué as the French Riviera and as raucous as Coney Island

The only remains of the demolished Tuileries Palace stand anonymously behind the Jeu de Paume

L'Orangerie—the former citrus nursery now houses 144 masterworks, including Monet's Water Lilies series

Obelisk of Luxor—at 3,300 years old, unquestionably the most ancient monument in Paris

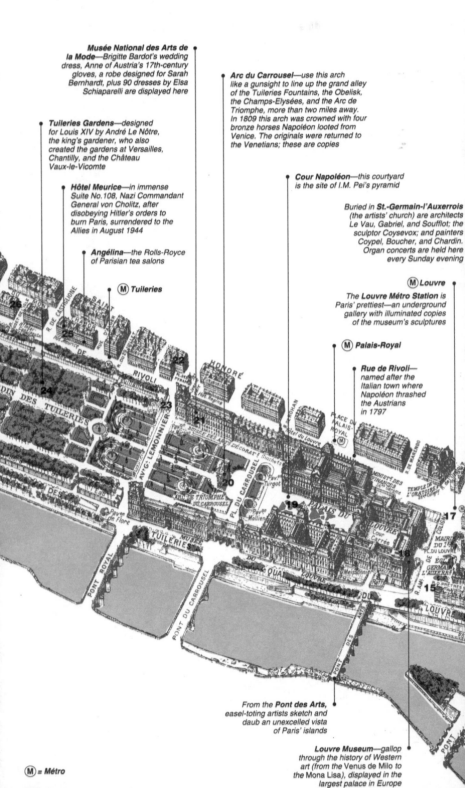

Musée National des Arts de la Mode—Brigitte Bardot's wedding dress, Anne of Austria's 17th-century gloves, a robe designed for Sarah Bernhardt, plus 90 dresses by Elsa Schiaparelli are displayed here

Tuileries Gardens—designed for Louis XIV by André Le Nôtre, the king's gardener, who also created the gardens at Versailles, Chantilly, and the Château Vaux-le-Vicomte

Hôtel Meurice—in immense Suite No.108, Nazi Commandant General von Cholitz, after disobeying Hitler's orders to burn Paris, surrendered to the Allies in August 1944

Angélina—the Rolls-Royce of Parisian tea salons

(M) **Tuileries**

Arc du Carrousel—use this arch like a gunsight to line up the grand alley of the Tuileries Fountains, the Obelisk, the Champs-Elysées, and the Arc de Triomphe, more than two miles away. In 1809 this arch was crowned with four bronze horses Napoléon looted from Venice. The originals were returned to the Venetians; these are copies

Cour Napoléon—this courtyard is the site of I.M. Pei's pyramid

Buried in **St.-Germain-l'Auxerrois** (the artists' church) are architects Le Vau, Gabriel, and Soufflot; the sculptor Coysevox; and painters Coypel, Boucher, and Chardin. Organ concerts are held here every Sunday evening

(M) **Louvre**

The **Louvre Métro Station** is Paris' prettiest—an underground gallery with illuminated copies of the museum's sculptures

(M) **Palais-Royal**

Rue de Rivoli—named after the Italian town where Napoléon thrashed the Austrians in 1797

From the **Pont des Arts**, easel-toting artists sketch and daub an unexcelled vista of Paris' islands

Louvre Museum—gallop through the history of Western art (from the Venus de Milo to the Mona Lisa), displayed in the largest palace in Europe

(M) = **Métro**

2 Hôtel de Ville The City Hall is another example of late 19th-century architectural eclecticism. Part Renaissance palace, part Belle Epoque fantasy, its exterior is lavished with 146 statues, among them bronze effigies of the sentries who patrolled the perimeter of the city wall during the Middle Ages. Visitors on guided tours of the **State Rooms** are shown the splendid staircase by **Philibert Delorme,** murals by **Puvis de Chavannes,** and a lesser-known **Rodin** sculpture, *La République.*
♦ Tours: M 10:30AM, starting from the information desk at 29 Rue de Rivoli, but call ahead the previous Friday to confirm hours. Métro: Hôtel-de-Ville. 42.76.40.40

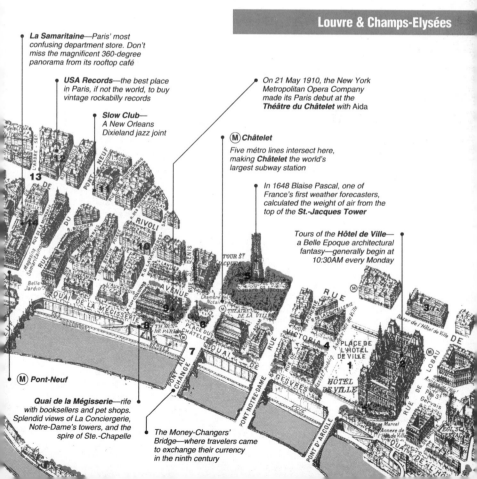

La Samaritaine—Paris' most confusing department store. Don't miss the magnificent 360-degree panorama from its rooftop café

USA Records—the best place in Paris, if not the world, to buy vintage rockabilly records

Slow Club—A New Orleans Dixieland jazz joint

On 21 May 1910, the New York Metropolitan Opera Company made its Paris debut at the *Théâtre du Châtelet* with Aida

Ⓜ *Châtelet*

Five métro lines intersect here, making *Châtelet* the world's largest subway station

In 1648 Blaise Pascal, one of France's first weather forecasters, calculated the weight of air from the top of the *St.-Jacques Tower*

Tours of the *Hôtel de Ville*—a Belle Epoque architectural fantasy—generally begin at 10:30AM every Monday

Ⓜ *Pont-Neuf*

Quai de la Mégisserie—rife with booksellers and pet shops. Splendid views of La Conciergerie, Notre-Dame's towers, and the spire of Ste.-Chapelle

The Money-Changers' Bridge—where travelers came to exchange their currency in the ninth century

A L'OLIVIER

2 A l'Olivier Founded in 1860, this shop still sells every oil imaginable—hazelnut oil for vinaigrettes, almond-honey oil shampoo, and apricot-nut oil for massages. Tarragon mustard and dried figs are also sold. The classic bottles alone are worth taking home, and the giant pottery casks for olive oil are not to be missed. ◆ Tu-Sa 9:30AM-1PM, 2-7PM. 23 Rue de Rivoli. Métro: Hôtel de Ville. 48.04.86.59

3 Bazaar de l'Hôtel-de-Ville Need a floor sander or new drapes for your hotel room? A spare tire for your rented car? BHV is every Parisian's hardware store, with five floors replete with the wherewithal to do it yourself. This is a veritable paradise for Monsieur Fix-It. ◆ M-Tu, Th-Sa 9AM-7PM; W 9AM-10PM. 52-64 Rue de Rivoli. Métro: Hôtel-de-Ville. 42.74.90.00

4 Avenue Victoria One of the shortest streets in Paris. This avenue doesn't commemorate any military victory, but rather the royal visit of the dowager **Queen of England** to Paris. ◆ Métro: Hôtel-de-Ville

Louvre & Champs-Elysées

5 Tour St.-Jacques This 1522 architectural anomaly was the Gothic belfry of **St.-Jacques,** a church that was destroyed in 1802; the tower (see the illustration on page 97) was spared as a factory for manufacturing lead musket balls. Cast your eyes up and you will see meteorological equipment lurking among the gargoyles. The tower now doubles as a weather station, appropriately enough, for at the tower's base is a statue of **Blaise Pascal** (1623-1662), one of France's first weather forecasters. In 1648, at the top of this very tower, he used a barometer to calculate the weight of air. ◆ Métro: Châtelet-Les Halles

One look at the kamikaze traffic around the Arc de Triomphe or Place de la Concorde and you'll have a better idea of why France leads the Mediterranean in traffic fatalities. According to Pierre Karli, noted Parisian brain specialist and author of the book *L'Homme Aggressif,* French drivers use their automobiles to express their high opinion of themselves and their low opinion of others. In 1988, 1,600 pedestrians were killed and 30,000 were injured; half of those accidents occurred on or within a few meters of a pedestrian crossing.

Caricature played an important political role during the French Revolution, often serving as a primary means of public communication. The different parties fought for public support through the often colorful drawings and etchings.

Restaurants/Nightlife: Red
Shops/ 🌳 Outdoors: Green
Hotels: Blue
Sights/Culture: Black

6 Place du Châtelet Named after a fortress and prison that once stood on this site, Châtelet is the principal crossroads of Paris, a hub of east-west and north-south traffic. The **Châtelet Fountain** in the center of the square, flanked by French sphinxes, was designed in 1808 to celebrate the triumphant Egyptian campaign of **Napoléon.** Below grade, five métro lines intersect, making Châtelet-Les Halles the world's largest underground station. ◆ Métro: Châtelet Les Halles

6 Théâtre de la Ville de Paris Formerly the **Sarah Bernhardt Theatre,** this mid-19th-century stage is now devoted to contemporary dance, jazz, and classical theater, but still preserves the dressing room of the "Divine Sarah" ◆ Box office: M, Su 11AM-6PM; Tu-Sa 9AM-8PM. 2 Place du Châtelet. Métro: Châtelet-Les Halles. 42.74.22.77

7 Pont au Change The **Money-Changers' Bridge** was the ninth-century forerunner of American Express: a spot where travelers and foreigners came to change money. Today this Second-Empire bridge is flanked by identical state-owned theaters, both built by architect **Davioud** in 1862. ◆ Métro: Châtelet-Les Halles

8 Quai de la Mégisserie Once a malodorous *mégisserie* (sheepskin tannery), today this spot is rife with booksellers, pet shops, fish-tackle dealers, and plant stores where mice and goldfish are sold alongside dahlias and fertilizer. The cacophony of the parakeets, turkeys, and guinea fowls, whose cages clutter the pavement, vies pleasantly with that of the automobile traffic nearby. Even if you don't fancy housepets or have a green thumb, this delightful stroll will treat you to splendid views of **La Conciergerie,** the towers of **Notre-Dame,** and the spire of **Ste.-Chapelle.** ◆ Métro: Châtelet-Les Halles

9 Théâtre du Châtelet This third-largest auditorium in Paris, after the **Bastille Opéra** and the **Palais des Congrès,** was built in 1862. Seating half as many people as the Paris Opéra, the theater is primarily a venue for operas, ballets, and symphonies. On 21 May 1910, the **New York**

Metropolitan Opera Company made its Paris debut here with *Aida*. **Toscanini** conducted, **Caruso** sang, and the audience, which included most of the French diplomatic corps, the **Vanderbilts**, and **Louis Cartier** (who estimated that more than $3 million worth of jewelry was worn that evening), went wild. ♦ Box office: daily 11AM-7PM. 1 Place du Châtelet. Métro: Châtelet-Les Halles. 40.28.28.28

10 Le Petit Opportun This popular jazz club headlines such names as **Clark Terry**, **Slide Hampton**, and **Pepper Adams**. But don't expect the cloud of cigarette smoke that usually hangs around jazz nightclubs: smoking is not permitted during performances. Buy your tickets at least a half hour in advance. ♦ Shows: daily 8:30PM and 11PM. 15 Rue des Lavandières-Ste.-Opportune. No credit cards. Métro: Châtelet-Les Halles. 42.36.01.36

10 Grand Hôtel de Champagne $$ Small, comfortable rooms characterize this hotel, which is a short walk from the Place du Châtelet, the Louvre, Ste.-Chapelle, Notre-Dame, and the Ile de la Cité. ♦ 17 Rue Jean-Lantier. Métro: Châtelet-Les Halles. 42.36.60.00

11 Slow Club Dixieland jazz is alive and well in Paris. ♦ Tu-Th 9:30PM-2:30AM; F 9:30PM-3AM; Sa 9:30PM-4AM. 130 Rue de Rivoli. No credit cards. Métros: Châtelet-Les Halles, Pont-Neuf. 42.33.84.30

12 Chez la Vieille ★★$$/$$$ Chef **Adrienne Biasin** prepares a cuisine reminiscent of the kitchen of a French country grandmother: pork liver pâté or sautéed chicken livers, followed by sautéed lamb, veal Marengo, her special peasant pot-au-feu, and, for dessert, a traditional chocolate mousse or chocolate cake. ♦ Daily noon-2PM; closed in Aug. 37 Rue de l'Arbre-Sec. Métros: Louvre, Pont-Neuf. 42.60.15.78

12 USA Records This is the best place in Paris—perhaps in Europe—to buy vintage rockabilly, plus rock 'n' roll, oldies, and blues from the 1950s and 1960s. ♦ M-Sa 10:30AM-1:30PM, 3-7PM. 50 Rue de l'Arbre-Sec. Métros: Louvre, Pont-Neuf. 42.97.42.35

13 Rue de l'Arbre-Sec This short street is long and rich in history. At **No. 4** (formerly the Hôtel des Mousquetaires, now **La Samaritaine** department store) lived **d'Artagnan** of the **Three Musketeers;** at **No. 52** is the **Hôtel de Trudon**, the former home of Louis XV's wine steward; nearby is the **Hôtel de François Barnon**, named after Louis XIV's barber. The name *arbre-sec* (which literally means dry tree) suggests that a gibbet once stood in the street. ♦ Métro: Pont-Neuf

14 La Samaritaine One of the city's oldest department stores and possibly its most confusing, La Samaritaine takes its name from an old Pont-Neuf water pump decorated with an image of the woman of Samaria offering Jesus a drink of water. Today the store sprawls through four grand old buildings offering everything from pop psychiatry books to kitchen sinks, and at bargain prices. Its best deal, however, is the rooftop view. On a pleasant summer day, walk into **Store No. 2**

(designed by **F. Jourdan**) and ride the elevator to the ninth floor. Sip a *café crème* or *citron pressé*, then mount the stairs and enjoy a 360-degree panorama of Paris annotated by a ceramic legend that locates points of interest. ♦ Store: M, W-Th, Sa 9:30AM-7PM; Tu, F 9:30AM-8:30PM. The café is open the same hours in the summer months. 19 Rue de la Monnaie. Métro: Pont-Neuf. 40.41.20.20

Pâtisserie
St=Germain=l'Auxerrois

15 Pâtisserie St.-Germain-l'Auxerrois This one-hundred-year-old pastry shop and tea salon, elegant with crystal chandeliers, gilded pillars, and marble tables, makes all its sweets and ice creams in a basement factory. Be sure to buy a few treats to munch on while you wait in the Louvre ticket line. Try the chocolate pastries (*le Chasseur* or *la Nocturne*) or a flaky *palmier* and *tuile*. ♦ Tu-Su 9AM-7:30PM; closed two weeks in Aug, two weeks in Sep. 2 Rue de l'Admiral-de-Coligny. No credit cards. Métros: Louvre, Pont-Neuf. 45.08.19.18

16 Place du Louvre In 52 BC, between the present site of the Louvre and St.-Germain-l'Auxerrois, **Labienus**, a lieutenant of Caesar, bivouacked here with his troops before capturing the settlement of **Lutetia**. ♦ Métros: Louvre, Pont-Neuf

Louvre & Champs-Elysées

16 St.-Germain-l'Auxerrois On Saint Bartholomew's Day (24 August) in 1572, at the orders of **Catherine de Médici** and **Charles IX,** the pealing bells of St.-Germain-l'Auxerrois (illustrated above) signaled the beginning of a brutal religious massacre. Some 3,000 Huguenots, Protestant wedding guests of **Henri de Navarre** and **Marguerite de Valois**, were slain in their beds. The 38-bell carillon in the Neo-Gothic tower is the only truly ancient one in Paris. (All the others were melted down during the Revolution.) The bells still ring out every Wednesday, a grave reminder of the massacre.

The gargoyle-laden edifice that was designed in 1220 by **Jean Gaussel** takes its name from **Saint Germain,** the bishop of Auxerre (378-448). This good saint claimed **Saint**

Patrick of Ireland, **Saint Illtyd** of Wales, and **Sainte Geneviève** of Paris among his students. When **Louis XIV** and his court moved to Versailles, the artists colony he had established there took over the Louvre, and St.-Germain-l'Auxerrois became its parish church.

Among the luminaries buried here are architects **Louis Le Vau, Jacques-Ange Gabriel,** and **Jacques-Germain Soufflot;** the sculptor **Antoine Coysevox;** and painters **Nöel Coypel, François Boucher,** and **Jean-Baptiste Chardin.** Every Ash Wednesday a service is held to pray for artists throughout the world who will die in the coming year. Royalists flock here annually to a Mass said for **Louis XVI** on the anniversary of his 21 January 1793 execution. Be sure to notice the ornately canopied and sculpted oak bench on the right side of the aisle and imagine Louis XIV and his family contemplating the sermon, enthroned in this red-velvet pew designed in 1682 by painter **Charles Le Brun.** ♦ Daily 8:30AM-8:30PM. Organ recitals: Su 5PM. Bells: W 1:30PM. 2 Place du Louvre. Métros: Louvre, Pont-Neuf. 42.60.13.96

17 Louvre Métro Station The platform is a museum in itself, with softly illuminated copies of the sculptures found aboveground in the Louvre. This and the **Varenne Métro Station** (with replicas of **Rodin** sculptures) are two of the prettiest in Paris.

17 Rue de Rivoli On this arcaded street (pictured above), an incongruous mix of luxury hotels and tacky souvenir shops lies demurely behind a graceful but rather monotonous First-Empire colonnade designed by **Charles Percier** and **Pierre Fontaine** in 1811 at the behest of **Napoléon.** The street was named after an Italian town where the emperor thrashed the Austrians in 1797. Strict rules pertaining to the arcades forbade leasing shops to any entrepreneur using ovens or metal tools, thus excluding such artisanal riffraff as bakers, butchers, and their like.

18 Louvre Museum The Louvre is the single largest building in Paris, the largest palace in Europe, the largest museum in the Western world, and probably the most dominating symbol of art and culture the world has ever known. "I never knew what a palace was until I had a glimpse of the Louvre," said 19th-century American author **Nathaniel Hawthorne.** It has 224 halls, and its enormous **Grande Galerie** is longer than three football fields. It took seven centuries to build, spanning the lives of 17 monarchs and countless architects.

The Louvre Museum's Floor Plans

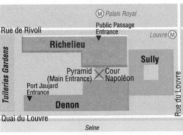

Denon Wing:
Sculptures
Painting
Greek, Etruscan,
and Roman
Antiquities
Graphic Arts

Sully Wing:
Oriental and
Egyptian Antiquities
French Paintings
Objects of Art
Medieval Louvre
Louvre History

Richelieu Wing:
Renovation in
process. Opening
scheduled for
the museum's
bicentenary in
1993.

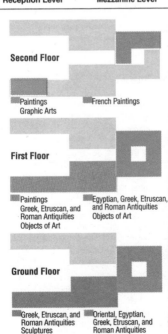

114

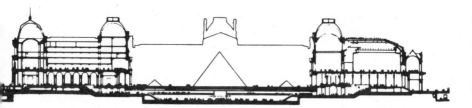

History

The origin of the word *louvre*, though obscure, is believed to be a derivation of the Old French word *louverie*, which meant wolf lodge; from a corruption of the word *l'oeuvre*, meaning a work of art; or from an Old Flemish word meaning fortress. In 1190 **King Philippe Auguste** began surrounding Paris with a 30-foot-high city wall that included the fortified Louvre. More than three centuries later, **François I** agreed to live in this fortress at the request of Parisian citizens who had ransomed him from captivity in Italy. In 1527 he tore down most of the old structure, and by 1546 he had constructed the **Cour Carrée** (Square Court).

In 1578 **Catherine de Médici** built a new palace, the **Tuileries,** at the far end of the present Louvre. The two palaces were joined by **Henri IV,** who created a number of apartments in the **Long Gallery** for the use of court painters and their families in 1608. This same Henri was stabbed by an assassin in 1610 and became the only king to die within the Louvre's walls. **Colbert,** a minister of finance to **Louis XIV,** hired the Roman architect **Bernini** to redesign the Louvre. When Bernini suggested knocking the whole place down and starting from scratch, Colbert sent the famous Roman packing. Louis XIV proceeded to reconstruct the Cour Carrée to his own tastes, consulting with the architect **Le Vau,** the painter **Le Brun,** and **Claude Perrault,** a Parisian physician whose brother Charles was the author of *Puss 'n Boots.* After renovating the Louvre, Louis XIV established an art colony there with painters such as **Coustou, Boucher,** and **Coypel.** Louis XIV left Paris for Versailles in 1678, and without royal occupants, the palace fell into disrepair. Overrun by freeloaders and squatters, it soon became a slum, and a shantytown of bars and whorehouses sprang up outside its walls.

Louis XVI was narrowly dissuaded from tearing it down, and shortly before he and **Marie Antoinette** were beheaded in 1793, he magnanimously put some of the royal art collection on display, thus reviving the Louvre's function as a gallery. Following his rise to power, **Napoléon** moved into

the Tuileries Palace and built **Rue de Rivoli** for quick access to the Louvre. (Napoléon also built the **Arc du Carrousel,** which he crowned with the famous bronze horses of San Marco that were plundered from Venice during one of his military campaigns. After Waterloo, the horses and other looted works of art were returned to their owners.) During the Second Empire, Napoléon's nephew **Napoléon III** and **Baron Georges-Eugene Haussmann,** the radical urban planner, completed the Louvre (or so they thought) by building the **North Wing** and the **Flore** and **Marsan** pavilions now adjoining the main palace to the Tuileries.

Collection

The Louvre's art collection began with 12 paintings, including works by **Titian, Raphael,** and **Leonardo da Vinci** that **François I** had looted from Italy (François knew what he was doing; he not only took the *Mona Lisa,* but also the man who had painted it). By the time of **Louis XIV** (who reigned from 1643 to 1715), the royal collection numbered more than 2,500 items. Until the Revolution, works in the Louvre were strictly

for the pleasure of the kings and their courtiers. In 1793, after nearly burning the Louvre to the ground, the Revolutionaries opened the collection to the masses. Today the Louvre possesses more than 400,000 works of art. Only a fraction of these are on exhibit at any given time. In a morning's hoofing, however, you can see many of the Louvre's greatest hits: the *Venus de Milo,* the *Winged Victory of Samothrace, Mona Lisa,* the Crown Jewels, the David Galleries, *Eagle of Sugerius,* Giudia—Law Code of Hammurabi, the Rubens Gallery, Michelangelo's *Slaves,* the *Seated Scribe,* and other highlights of art history.

The Louvre's collection is divided into seven categories: Greek and Roman Antiquities, Oriental Antiquities, Egyptian Antiquities, Sculptures, Objets d'Art, Paintings, and Drawings. Although Greco-Roman, Egyptian, and Oriental Antiquities warrant at the very least a quick look, the Louvre's richest collection consists of paintings.

Louvre Pyramid Adding to the Louvre Museum building seems to be an irresistible French pastime. Per the designs of Chinese-American architect **I.M. Pei,** now topping the **Cour Napoléon** (Napoléon Court) is a 70.5-foot-tall glass pyramid, flanked by three smaller pyramids, a series of fountains, reflecting pools, and a bronze replica of the **Bernini** statue of **Louis XI.** The largest pyramid serves as the central entrance to the museum and as an enormous skylight above a 70,000-square-foot underground cavern.

The pyramid officially opened in April 1989, and its underground space contains an auditorium, an area for temporary art shows, and an exhibition of the 12th-century fortress that was unearthed prior to the pyramid's controversial construction, as well as ticket offices, conference rooms, laboratories, and museum shops. Tunnels lead from under the pyramid to each side of the U-shaped Louvre.

Traditionalists fear this latest addition has marred the Louvre's grandeur with a sort of Hyatt Regency chrome glitz. **Michel Guy,** cultural minister under former French **President Giscard d'Estaing,** said Pei's pyramids turn the Louvre into a "cultural drugstore that looks like an airport." However, since the completion of the Louvre pyramids, the design has garnered ardent supporters as well, and, lest we forget, the Eiffel Tower was also first greeted with guffaws.

Eventually, the **Richelieu Wing,** which was once occupied by France's Finance Ministry,

Louvre & Champs-Elysées

will be connected to the existing museum, increasing exhibition space by nearly 80 percent. This second stage of the grand Louvre project will be completed by 1993, in time to honor the bicentennial of the creation of a public museum in a palace that had housed the kings of France since the 14th century.

Excavations At the same time **President François Mitterrand** approved the Pei pyramid project, he also set aside close to $2 million for an immense archaeological excavation of the Louvre's courtyard. This ambitious project brought 70 archaeologists to supervise the dig in the **Cour Napoléon** and expose the ancient dungeons of the **King Philippe Auguste** fortress. More than 11 million objects were retrieved, ranging from Chinese porcelain imported during the Ming Dynasty to coins from the first century AD and an eighth-century human skeleton.The pyramid allows visitors to descend to the 12th-century dungeons and to view about 10,000 of the objects uncovered in the dig. In mid-1990 Pei, Cobb, Freed, and Partners began work on a large underground parking garage and bus station that will connect directly to the large pyramid. Aboveground will be a sculpture garden with trees, grass, and 18 **Maillol** sculptures.

A few words of advice for touring the Louvre: **1.** Don't even think about trying to see the museum's entire collection—or even half of it—in one day. Visit your favorite artworks the first time around, and come back for more

another day. **2.** In the summer or other high-season months count on a half-hour wait to buy tickets. **3.** Wear comfortable shoes. Check your coat as you enter, but in winter keep a sweater handy because the museum is drafty. **4.** Guided tours in English leave every 20 minutes from the ground-floor information stand. **5.** When fatigue sets in, take a break in the museum cafeteria. If you lunch outside the Louvre and decide to re-enter, you'll need to buy a new ticket. **6.** Certain exhibitions (for example the Crown Jewels, Assyrian Gallery, and 16th-century Dutch and Flemish paintings) close during the lunch hour (noon-2PM) and when there is a shortage of museum guards. ♦ Museum: M, Th-Su 9AM-6PM; W 9AM-9:45PM. Bookstores and postcard shops: M, W-Su 9:30AM-5PM. Place du Carrousel. Métro: Louvre; 42.60.39.26

Within the Louvre Museum:

Cour Carrée The **Carrée Courtyard** in the Louvre becomes a chic circus during the fall and spring, when more than 50 fashion designers parade their ready-to-wear collections through a campaign headquarters of striped tents set up here. An international array of beauties and beasts gathers. ♦ Check at the information stand for a schedule of events

Le Grand Louvre ★★★$$$ An exceptional restaurant by any standard, Le Grand Louvre is run by **André Daguin,** the chef and proprietor of the Hôtel de France, 64 kilometers (40 miles west of Toulouse in Auch. Gascon specialties include foie gras, goose, confit, and prune ice cream. Light fare and desserts are offered at the afternoon tea. ♦ M, W-Su noon-1:30PM, 7-9:45PM. 40.20.53.41

19 Cour Napoléon Under **King Philippe Auguste,** the **Napoléon Courtyard** was a patch of sparsely populated farmland. Over time, it sprouted a church, charity school, meat market, a menagerie for wild animals, the castle kitchens, and a street for prostitutes frequented by soldiers from the castle garrison. **Napoléon III** leveled the houses and paved over the courtyard in the late-19th century. ♦ Métro: Louvre

20 Place du Carrousel The square was named to commemorate a *carrousel* (equestrian gala) held by **King Louis XIV** and his court in June 1662 to honor the birth of the king's first child. More than 15,000 spectators watched the king lead a thundering brigade of horsemen dressed as Romans, sporting golden helmets with red plumes, gold breastplates, and red stockings. ♦ Métro: Louvre

During the 15th century, Paris was essentially three separate cities: the Ville (with the Louvre on the Right Bank), Cité (with Notre-Dame on the Island), and the Université (with the Sorbonne on the Left Bank).

The best bird's-eye views of Paris are from the Eiffel Tower, the 56th floor of the Montparnasse Tower, the café on the tenth floor of La Samaritaine, Notre-Dame's south tower, and the dome of Sacré-Coeur in Montmartre.

Restaurants/Nightlife: Red   **Hotels:** Blue
Shops/ 🌳Outdoors: Green   **Sights/Culture:** Black

116

20 Arc du Carrousel This marble arch with pink pillars was built in 1808 by **Napoléon** to celebrate **Austerlitz** and other military victories. It was then crowned with four splendid bronze horses Napoléon had looted from Venice; originally, the horses had stood in the **Temple of the Sun** at Corinth. In 1815, with the fall of Napoléon, Italy recovered the masterworks and copies were placed on top of the **Carousel Arch.** The arch can be used like a gunsight to line up the grand alley of the **Tuileries Fountains,** the Egyptian **Obelisk of Luxor** in the Place de la Concorde (a half mile to the west), the **Champs-Elysées,** and the **Arc de Triomphe,** more than two miles away. ♦ Métro: Louvre

21 Musée des Arts Décoratifs Exhibiting furnishings that date from the period of **Louis XVI** through the 19th century, the **Museum of Decorative Arts** is something of a composite mansion, with rooms taken wholesale from different periods. Amid too much wallpaper and too many bowlegged chairs from Versailles, the patient and searching eye will discover singular treasures such as a **Tiepolo** painting, an exquisitely carved floral boiserie (woodwork) by **Oudry,** and hunting scenes by **Desportes.** ♦ Admission. W-Sa 12:30-6PM; Su noon-6PM. 107 Rue de Rivoli. Métro: Palais-Royal. 42.60.32.14

21 Musée National des Arts de la Mode Located in the Louvre's **Pavillon de Marsan,** the **Fashion Museum's** sleek and chic collection consists of some 10,000 costumes dating back to the 16th century. Among the highlights of the collection are the 17th-century gloves worn by **Anne of Austria, Brigitte Bardot's** wedding dress (made by **Jacques Esterel** in 1958), a robe designed for **Sarah Bernhardt,** and the gown worn by the **Empress Eugénie** to please **Napoléon III** when he returned from a hard day of empire-building. To enjoy everything the museum has to offer, take the elevator to the fifth floor and walk down; the view of the **Tuileries Gardens** from the top is spectacular. The museum boutique sells, among other things, a beret with an instruction sheet showing four ways to wear the classic French headgear. ♦ Admission. M, W-Sa 12:30-6PM; Su 11AM-6PM. 109 Rue de Rivoli. Métro: Palais-Royal. 42.60.32.14

22 Jeanne d'Arc This gilded equestrian statue by 19th-century sculptor **Frémiet** honors **Joan of Arc** (1412-1431), the French national hero and Roman Catholic saint. Born during the **Hundred Years' War** (1337-1453), this charismatic peasant girl claimed she heard the voices of saints urging her to save France from the English. The saints (or whatever) enabled her to convince the **Dauphin Charles VII** to provide her with troops. Under Joan's generalship, the troops took back Orléans and routed the English forces in the Loire. In 1429, during an unsuccessful attempt to liberate Paris from the occupying English army, Joan stationed a cannon on Butte St.-Roch (leveled some three centuries ago to landfill the Champ-de-Mars) to attack the St.-Honoré Gate (which is now 163 Rue St.-Honoré). A year later Joan of Arc was captured, and the following year she was convicted of witchcraft and heresy, then burned at the stake in Rouen. She was canonized in 1920, and today France honors her with a national holiday. Several years ago, Parisian medical students went on strike and, as part of their protest, wrapped statues throughout Paris with bandages. Joan of Arc was given special treatment: full-length plaster casts on both her legs. ♦ Place des Pyramides. Métro: Tuileries

23 Tuileries Palace Designed in 1564 by **Philibert Delorme,** this palace stood until 1884. It connected the two corner pavilions of the

Louvre (paralleling what is today **Avenue du Général Lemonnier**) and took its name from the *tuile* (tile) factories that had previously stood on the site. **Catherine de Médici,** who built Tuileries, moved out after her astrologer, **Ruggieri,** told her she would die close to St.-Germain. (Tuileries was in the parish of St.-Germain-l'Auxerrois.) Catherine therefore built another palace near what is today the **Bourse du Commerce** (Commercial Stock Exchange), and there she died. As for Ruggieri's prediction: the priest who administered the last rites to Catherine de Médici was named **Julien de St.-Germain.**

Napoléon's second wife gave birth in the Tuileries Palace to a short-lived imperial heir, **l'Aiglon,** who was named the king of Rome. Other subsequent royal residents included **Charles X** and **Louis-Philippe,** who ruled from 1831 to 1848 and was popularly known as the Grocers' King for his custom of carving the Sunday roast himself. In 1871, during the **Siege of Paris,** the Communards set Tuileries Palace afire. It burned for three days while the Louvre Museum staff worked frantically to save the collections. The palace was razed between 1882 and 1884. A single bay of the old Tuileries Palace was preserved and stands unmarked in a remote corner of the Tuileries Gardens behind the Jeu de Paume. ♦ Métro: Tuileries

24 Tuileries Gardens The gardens, which are scheduled to soon undergo a $50 million facelift, were designed in 1649 for **Louis XIV** by **André Le Nôtre,** the king's gardener, who was born in a cottage on the royal grounds. Le Nôtre also designed the gardens at **Versailles, Chantilly,** and the **Château Vaux-le-Vicomte.** The Tuileries' violent past during the Revolution seems scarcely possible when you stroll through the manicured hedges and lawns near the 18 bronze nudes by **Aristide Maillol.** Old ladies feed the pigeons while threadbare African immigrants loft mechanical birds into the air in hope of attracting a sale. Kids race sailboats on the fountain under the watchful eyes of their governesses. You will also find four refreshment stands, a small merry-go-round, a swing set, and subdued pony rides for children.

From the upper terrace of the gardens is a splendid view of the Seine, the new **Musée d'Orsay,** and the **Legion d'Honneur,** which was begun by **Napoléon** to laud French accomplishment. Farther in the distance, you can glimpse the stern **Chambres des Députés,** France's congress. The Tuileries terrace has become a well-known spot for gay men to frequent. ♦ Métro: Tuileries

25 Hôtel Meurice $$$$ Heads of state, vacationing or exiled, have always favored the Meurice. **Alphonse XIII** of Spain stayed for years in Suite

112, and **Salvador Dalí** made the Royal Suite his Paris home for 30 years. During WWII, the Meurice served as Nazi headquarters. There, in August 1944, in the immense Suite 108, **Commandant General von Cholitz,** after disobeying Hitler's orders to burn Paris, surrendered to the Allies.

Since 1816, when the hotel opened, its list of famous American visitors has included **Herman Melville, Henry James, Henry Wadsworth Longfellow,** and **Wilbur** and **Orville Wright,** who stayed here in 1907 while trying to sell their airplane to the French. (The Wrights used the familiar argument that their invention was the weapon to end all wars. The French military didn't bite on that hopeless chestnut, but the public was captivated by the Wrights' biplane, which they had shipped all the way to Paris from Dayton, Ohio.) Tea in the **Salon Pompadour** next to the Meurice's charming bar is a discreet pleasure, especially in the late afternoon after the pianist tunes up. Note: Owners of dogs must pay for bunking their pets in the hotel, while children under six cost their parents no extra charge. ♦ 228 Rue de Rivoli. Métros: Tuileries, Concorde. 42.60.38.60

25 Galignani The classic French bookstore is sprinkled liberally with selections in English, Italian, and Spanish. ♦ M-Sa 10AM-7PM. 224 Rue de Rivoli. Métros: Tuileries, Concorde. 42.60.76.07

ANGELINA

25 Angélina ★★★$/$$ The Rolls-Royce of Parisian tea salons, Angélina originally went by the name **Rumpelmayer's.** It was founded in 1903 on the former site of the king's stables. Amid marble pedestal tables, landscapes by **Lorrant-Heilbronn,** red carpet, and gilt decor, Angélina's overworked waitresses deliver justly celebrated pastries, sumptuous hot chocolate, and *Mont Blanc,* a weighty concoction of chestnut cream purée (a favorite of the **Aga Khan**). The whipped cream is fresh and the ice water is served on silver trays. In spring and autumn, strive to get a table near **Rue de Rivoli,** where you can watch the flurry of top models and fashion designers returning from the ready-to-wear collections. ♦ Daily 9:30AM-7PM; closed three weeks in Aug. 226 Rue de Rivoli. Métros: Concorde, Tuileries. 42.60.82.00

26 Inter-Continental $$$$ With more than 500 rooms, the Inter-Continental is one of the largest luxury hotels in the world, but size has not swamped its considerable charm or its lovely central courtyard. Designed in 1878 by **Charles Garnier** (who built the **Paris Opéra** and the **Grand Hôtel**), the hotel has three salons (classified as historical landmarks) where the fanciest receptions in town are hosted, including the haute couture collections of **Yves Saint Laurent, Guy Laroche,** and **Jean Patou.** The Inter-Continental has always drawn a varied clientele: **Victor Hugo** and the **Empress Eugénie** liked it, and so does **Jerry Lewis.** *Saturday Night Fever* fans will enjoy the **Estrela,** the hotel's Brazilian-style disco. ♦ 3 Rue de Castiglione. Métros: Concorde, Tuileries. 44.77.11.11

Within the Inter-Continental:

La Terrasse Fleurie ★★$$/$$$ This pleasant garden atrium offers a delicious lamb and *tabouleh* salad or mousseline of rabbit in mustard, among other entrées. Save room for the delicious desserts. No dogs are allowed. ♦ Daily noon-3PM, 7-11PM. 44.77.11.11

Café Tuileries ★$$ Simple cuisine is served at reasonable prices. ♦ Daily 6AM-11PM. 44.77.11.11

Bar du Lobby The celebrity-studded bar is paneled in dark wood and softly lighted with Tiffany lamps. ♦ Daily 9AM-midnight; closed July and Aug. 44.77.11.11

27 W.H. Smith and Son A bonanza of English paperbacks and magazines is carried here. ♦ M, W-Sa 9:30AM-7PM; Tu 10AM-7PM. 248 Rue de Rivoli. Métro: Concorde. 42.60.37.97

28 Lescure ★★$$ This unspoiled bistro serves duck with cabbage, rabbit and olives, beef Bourguignonne, dandelion green salad, and delicious tarts. ♦ M-F noon-2:15PM, 7-10:15PM; Sa noon-2:15PM; closed 1-28 Aug 23 Dec-1 Jan. 7 Rue de Mondovi. Reservations recommended. Métro: Concorde. 42.60.18.91

29 Hôtel Talleyrand Designed by **Gabriel,** the architect for **Louis XV,** and **Chalgrin,** who built the Arc de Triomphe, this *hôtel* was originally the residence of diplomat par excellence **Charles-Maurice de Talleyrand-Périgord** and subsequently housed **Czar Alexander I,** several French **Rothschilds,** and, during WWII, the German Navy, which kept prisoners of war in the cellars. Today this historic building houses the US cultural and information services, best known among traveling Americans as the office where you replace lost or stolen passports. ♦ Rue de Mondovi (Rue de Rivoli). Métro: Concorde. 42.61.80.75

30 Jeu de Paume Museum Built in 1853 by **Napoléon III,** the Jeu de Paume has nothing to do with *jus de pomme* (apple juice). Its name refers to a racket game (see below). From 1947 until 1986, the museum contained many French Impressionist masterpieces and was the most visited museum in the world relative to its size. The collection has moved across the river to St.-Germain's **Musée d'Orsay** (see page 52), and the Jeu de Paume has recently renovated and reopened to host changing exhibitions by contemporary artists. On the terrace to the south of the museum is a monument to **Charles Perrault,** the 17th-century fabulist who convinced **Colbert** to make the Tuileries public. ♦ M, W-Su 9:45AM-5:15PM; closed holidays. Jardin des Tuileries, Place de la Concorde. Métro: Concorde. 42.60.12.07

30 Octagonal Fountain and Statues Between the **Jeu de Paume** and **L'Orangerie** are 18th-century statues representing the Nile, the Tiber, the Loire and Loiret, the Marne, and, of course, the Seine rivers. On the right is a modest bust of **André Le Nôtre,** the landscape architect. The Tuileries is framed from the west by two winged horses by **Coysevox,** erected in 1719. The first human ascent in a hydrogen balloon, on 1 December 1783, was launched beside the octagonal fountain. The flight was made by physician **J.A.C. Charles** and his mechanic, **Noel Robert.** Thousands packed the park to watch the historic flight; among the

From Monks to McEnroe—Tennis Has Come a Long Way

The French court game *jeu de paume,* the complicated progenitor of modern lawn tennis, originated when bored 13th-century French monks swatted a wad of rags around a monastery courtyard with their bare hands (*jeu de paume* literally means "a game of the palm"). By the 17th century, it was played with a racket and had become the French national game: Paris alone had 250 courts. The dashing François I constructed a court in the Louvre as well as a floating tennis court on his 2,000-ton warship *La Grande Françoise.*

The kings and nobles who played it used lopsided rackets to send the balls ricocheting off the wall, floor, and sloping gallery roof, or sailing over a net that sagged like a hammock. Points were awarded for swatting balls through portals and striking bells in windows. It was life-size pinball, high-speed chess, and racketball in a Gothic cathedral all wrapped into one. A player had 40 different surfaces to bounce a ball off of, and the ball often traveled in excess of 120 miles per hour.

At its toughest, the royal tennis game proved to be a killer workout for overzealous sovereigns. Half a dozen kings expired from sheer exhaustion and pneumonia after ferocious jeu de paume matches. Another crowned casualty of the game was the affable but maladroit King Charles VIII, who keeled over shortly after a head-on collision with the lintel of the tennis-court door in his château at Amboise.

Jeu de paume became wildly popular and was repeatedly banned by nobles convinced that tennis-playing merchants and yeomen were neglecting their work and the country's defense. In spite of the prohibition, the craze raged on in hundreds of underground *tripots*—athletic speakeasies notorious for bootlegged tennis equipment, cheap wine, and reckless games of chance. (To this day, when the French gamble away their paychecks, they still curse: *"J'ai paumé."*)

In the France of Louis XIV, the game's popularity began to suffer as a consequence of increasingly repressive legislation and the king's indifference to the sport (he, after all, was a billiards man). Eventually jeu de paume courts were transformed into playhouses or public meeting places. In fact, a meeting

held on 20 June 1789 in the court at Versailles changed the course of French history. Deputies of the Third Estate assembled there and took the historic oath that sparked the French Revolution. More than a century later, in 1907, another group of revolutionaries, the painters called Impressionists, commandeered the city's last two royal jeu de paume courts in the Tuileries Gardens to use them as a gallery for their canvases.

Modern tennis owes a great debt to jeu de paume. The very name tennis comes from the traditional warning *Tenez* (Take heed), which French monks shouted before each *serve*—another term added later to the game by nobles who felt it was beneath them to start a game themselves (they ordered a servant to toss the first ball, and then the nobles would join in).

Known as court tennis in the United States, the game is frequently referred to by English purists as "real tennis" or "Tennis with a capital T" to distinguish it from that slam-bang adulteration played at Flushing Meadows and Wimbledon. Although it originated in France, jeu de paume today is unquestionably Anglo-Saxon. Of the world's 34 courts currently in use, Britain boasts 19, the United States 9, and Australia 4. Only two courts remain in France, one in Bordeaux, and one in Paris at the Société Sportive de Jeu de Paume et de Racquets on Rue Lauriston. To catch a glimpse of the ancient game, stop by the club in the late afternoon or evening when the French and American businesspeople from the fashionable 16th arrondissement stop on their way home to play a friendly set.

spectators were **Benjamin Franklin** and the French philosopher **Denis Diderot,** who instantly conjectured that one day human beings might go to the moon. The hot-air balloon rose more than 2,000 feet and carried its passengers safely 25 miles to the north of Paris. Now, every New Year's Day, the celebrity-studded **Paris-Dakar** overland motor race across Europe and North Africa begins here. ♦ Métro: Concorde

31 L'Orangerie This former citrus nursery is the permanent home of the **Walter-Guillaume** collection of paintings, including 144 masterworks by such artists as **Renoir, Monet, Cézanne, Soutine, Picasso, Derain,** and **Matisse.** The artists best represented are Pierre-Auguste Renoir (24 works) and André Derain (28 paintings). The Cézannes are exceptional, particularly *Apples and Biscuits,* whose audacious composition is held together by a severe drawer latch placed dead center in the picture.

On the lower floor, mounted on curved panels, are Claude Monet's eight giant waterlily murals, *Les Nymphéas.* Monet's visual kingdom was centered at his house and gardens in Giverny near Paris (see "Day Trips," page 191). ♦ Admission. M, W-Su 9:45AM-5:15PM. Jardin des Tuileries, Place de la Concorde. Métro: Concorde. 42.97.48.16

Louvre & Champs-Elysées

32 Place de la Concorde The largest square in Paris, covering 21 acres, was a swamp until royal architect **Jacques-Ange Gabriel** was asked by **Louis XV** to find a setting appropriate for an equestrian statue of the king himself. The statue, which was removed during the Revolution, lasted here less than 20 years. On Sunday, 21 January 1793, the guillotine was set up on the Place de la Concorde's west side, near the spot where the statue of **Brest** sculpted by **Cortot** stands today. That done, **Louis XVI** was beheaded, and the 13-month **Reign of Terror** began. Among its thousands of victims were **Marie Antoinette, Madame du Barry, Charlotte Corday,** and **Danton**. On the evening of 28 July 1794, more than 1,300 townspeople gathered here to watch the execution of **Robespierre.** During the Revolution, no fewer than 1,343 victims were executed on the **Place de la Revolution** (as it was known then), and the square reeked so of gore that herds of oxen balked at crossing it. ♦ Métro: Concorde

32 Obelisk of Luxor This 3,300-year-old, 220-ton Egyptian obelisk is unquestionably the oldest monument in Paris. Originally erected around the 13th century BC, the 76-foot-tall monument was a gift to **Louis Philippe** from **Mohammed Ali Pasha,** who was viceroy of Egypt in 1831. (He also gave **Queen Victoria** a slightly shorter obelisk taken from Heliopolis, **Cleopatra's Needle.**) The Paris obelisk, which replaced the eques-

trian statue of **Louis XV** that was removed during the Revolution, had been taken from the ruins of the Temple of Luxor. (The Louvre has a marvelous set of four sun-worshipping baboons that came from the temple.)

The pink-granite obelisk traveled 600 miles by barge down the Nile to Alexandria, was towed across the Mediterranean and Atlantic, carted through Normandy, and finally erected at Place de la Concorde in 1836, ending a political squabble over whose monument should adorn the square dedicated to neither a French king nor Napoléon's army. The designs on the pedestal are meant to illustrate the technological wizardry involved in the obelisk's journey from Egypt to Paris. Visitors to this square should be forewarned: a Frenchman behind the wheel of his Citroën regards pedestrians as an affront to masculinity and personal honor, so those crossing the Place de la Concorde on foot may be risking their life. But go ahead; you only live once (however briefly), and the obelisk is worth a close look. What's more, the island surrounding it provides an unobstructed view up the length of the Champs-Elysées. Cross at the light! ♦ Métro: Concorde

32 Sculpture and Fountains Defining **Gabriel's** original octagonal square are several groups of statuary, allegories of **Bordeaux, Brest, Lille, Marseilles, Nantes, Rouen,** and **Strasbourg** (a lovely French actress of the day modeled for the last). Believe it or not, the tiny two-room pavilions underneath the statues were once rented out as dwellings. North and south of the obelisk stand two fountains, one representing *Maritime Navigation* and the other *River Navigation.* The latter, ironically, is the farthest from the Seine. The sea nymphs and water gods adorning the fountains were replicated from fountains in St. Peter's Square in Rome. ♦ Métro: Concorde

33 North Facade of Place de la Concorde When royal architect **Jacques-Ange Gabriel** designed the **Place de la Concorde,** he made sure that buildings would face only its north side, and in 1757, work began on the two matching Neoclassical north facades separated down the middle by Rue Royale. The facade's design was borrowed from the **Louvre Colonnades,** which Gabriel himself had restored. The **Hôtel de la Marine,** part of the facade east of Rue Royale, was intended to be lodging for foreign ambassadors, but became first a royal-furniture storehouse, and then, in 1792, the **Admiralty** (now known as the Ministry of the Navy). The building on the opposite corner is now occupied by the prestigious **French Automobile Club** and the very elegant **Hôtel Crillon.** On 6 February 1778, however, the Crillon was where **Louis XVI** and American diplomats (including **Benjamin Franklin**) signed the Treaty of Friendship and Trade, which recognized the independence of the 13 American states. ♦ Métro: Concorde

Restaurants/Nightlife: Red	Hotels: Blue
Shops/ ♠Outdoors: Green	Sights/Culture: Black

33 Hôtel Crillon $$$$ One of the swankest hotels in Paris. The building's facade was designed in 1758 by **Jacques-Ange Gabriel** for the **Count of Crillon.** The family managed to hold onto the property right through the Revolution, in spite of having the guillotine set up practically on its doorstep. And today the Crillon is the last of the grand four-star hotels in Paris that is still one-hundred percent French-owned. Should you decide that the kids don't really need to go to college after all, rent one of the three royal suites (Red, White, or Blue) and enjoy some of the best views in Paris of the Place de la Concorde, the Seine, and the Eiffel Tower. The management has recently opened the **Marie Antoinette Apartment** (room rates quoted on request), where the queen is said to have taken her music lessons. Among the famous American couples who have romanced in the Crillon: **Mary Pickford** and **Douglas Fairbanks,** who stopped here during their 1920 honeymoon; and newspaper magnate **William Randolph Hearst** and his girlfriend, **Marion Davies.** The hotel's proximity to the American and British embassies assures a clientele of well-bred Anglo-Americans, diplomats, royalty, and wealthy foreigners. ♦ 10 Place de la Concorde. Métro: Concorde. 42.65.24.24

Within the Hôtel Crillon:

Ambassadeurs Restaurant ★★$$$$ Innovative chef **Christian Constant's** restaurant features a savory *St. Pierre, agneau de Pauillac,* and a tasty chocolate *mousse à l'orange.* ♦ Daily noon-2:30PM, 7-10PM. Reservations required. 42.65.24.24

Obelisk ★$$/$$$ Serving delicious pastas and regional cheeses, this restaurant offers meals suitable for lighter appetites and slimmer purses. ♦ M-F noon-2:30PM, 7-10:30PM; Sa noon-2:30PM; closed in Aug. Reservations recommended. 42.65.24.24

Bar du Crillon ★$$ International journalists and visiting diplomats often stop here for a glass of champagne before dinner. Its hot *feuilletés* (croissantlike pastries) are great snacks. ♦ Daily noon-1:30AM. 42.65.24.24

34 Maxim's ★★★$$$ Paris without Maxim's? *Pas possible.* Where would all those rich business executives lunch? And where would the bona fide blue bloods, glitzy jet-setters, and fashionably late diners find such a Belle Epoque setting? Maxim's has given the royal treatment to **Edward VIII** of England and **Leopold II** of Belgium, as well as to prominent Americans such as **John Paul Getty, Jackie Onassis,** and **Elizabeth Taylor.** Not everyone is admitted to the **Pierre Cardin** landmark that has since been cloned in New York, Mexico, Tokyo, Singapore, Beijing, and soon in Moscow. If you are allowed to pass through the doors, expect unsurpassed champagne and service, disappointing food, and a splendid and expensive Parisian evening. ♦ Daily 12:30-2:30PM, 7:30-1AM; hours change July-Aug. 3 Rue Royale. Reservations required. Métro: Concorde. 42.65.27.94

35 Au Bain Marie This elegant housewares shop sells such articles as silver asparagus tongs, crystal carafes, and other signatures of refinement. ♦ M-Sa 10AM-7PM. 10 Rue Boissy-d'Anglas. Métro: Concorde. 42.66.59.74

36 Pont de la Concorde This five-arched bridge designed in 1791 by civil engineer **Jean Rodolphe Perronet** is constructed in part with stone souvenirs from the 1789 storming and demolition of the Bastille, legend holds, so people could forever trample the ruins of the old fortress. ♦ Métro: Concorde

37 Piscine Deligny The best outdoor swimming pool in Paris, this sunbather's paradise floats on a 19th-century double-deck barge in the Seine. A pleasure dome as risqué as the French Riviera and as crowded as Coney Island, the Piscine Deligny has several snack

Louvre & Champs-Elysées

bars, Ping-Pong tables, and a sailing school. Towels and swimsuits are available for rent. ♦ Daily 8:30AM-7:30PM, Apr-Sep. Quai Anatole-France. Métro: Chambres-des-Députés. 45.51.72.15, 45.55.51.62 (restaurant)

38 Palais-Bourbon The French home of the **National Assembly** was constructed in 1728 by the **Duchess of Bourbon,** one of **Louis XIV's** daughters. In 1807 **Povet** designed the mansion's facade for Napoléon in the Greek-Revival style, to mirror the **Madeleine** across the river; it now houses the **Chamber of Deputies** (the lower house of the French Parliament). Nearly 500 deputies convene in a chamber decorated in crimson and gold and adorned with a large Napoleonic eagle (however, republicanism has since whittled that symbol down to a cock). Even the president of France is denied entrance into this exclusive club's assemblies. Ordinary people, however, can watch sessions from a public gallery (provided they are among the first in line, tag along with a journalist, or have a pass signed by a deputy). If you tour the building (which also requires written permission), don't miss the **Delacroix** allegorical *History of Civilization* on the library ceiling. To attend an assembly debate, write (while it's in session) to: Assemblée Nationale, 33 Quai d'Orsay, 75007 Paris. To tour the building, write to: Administrative Office, 126 Rue de l'Université, 75007 Paris. ♦ Entrance on Quai d'Orsay. Métro: Chambre-des-Députés. 42.97.64.08

121

The Restaurant: A Revolutionary Invention

During the French Revolution, food was so scarce that most people were far more concerned with sheer survival than they were with gastronomy. Never before had the humble potato, introduced to the Court of Versailles by Parmentier on 25 August 1785, been so revered. And Parisians were in no condition to appreciate the inadvertent humor of Marie Antoinette's legendary suggestion that they eat cake if they had no bread. Of course, "the baker, the baker's wife, and the baker's son" (a reference to the royal family) did not survive the Revolution.

Far from being a mere digression in culinary history, however, the Revolution did much to determine its course. It interrupted an unprecedented refinement in taste and decorative arts, and as soon as the initial turmoil subsided, frustrations that had been mounting amid deprivation gave way to an explosion of culinary creativity that would last throughout the 1800s. In a broad sense, the Revolutionary period was a crucial stage in the evolution of taste and in the creation of restaurants as we know them today.

The cuisine of the *Ancien Régime* (see "Revolutionary Expressions" on page 133) was legendary for its heaviness. Rousseau, who apparently wished only for a simple chervil omelet, complained in his *Confessions* of the overly elaborate dishes his patrons lavished upon him. Diderot, completely exhausted by the Baron d'Holbach's dinner parties, used to tell about taking walks to aid digestion, "if such a thing

Louvre & Champs-Elysées

was possible." Twenty-odd courses of rich foods could weaken even the heartiest resolve.

Under the circumstances, the time was ripe to impose what was then referred to as *la cuisine moderne*. The luminaries of the day felt that cooking, like the other arts, should contribute to the march of progress. Food became less rich, and those who could afford it hired a cook.

Then everything grew complicated. The cookbook appeared, later to evolve into a particularly prolific literary genre. The chef's métier became so specialized that besides the cuisiner himself, there was also the *pâtissièr* and the *rôtisseur*. A major turning point came when the art of cooking emerged from the kitchens of private mansions to reach the general public in the form of a restaurant.

Under the Ancien Régime, post houses, taverns, inns, and cafés throughout France offered hazardous fare, often in conditions of dubious cleanliness. The first true restaurant was the illustrious Beauvilliers, established in 1782. It boasted elegant dining rooms, a large wine cellar, and excellent cuisine. For more than 20 years, high-society dinners would consider this address *sans pareil*. Even today, the restaurant on Butte Montmartre puts on grandiose airs.

Another major event of the time was the appearance of the first literary cafés. As author Gérard-Georges Lemaire wrote, these cafés revolutionized the spread of ideas. Paris had 2,000 cafés before the Revolution began; that number doubled by the early 1800s.

Coffee had just been introduced from the French West Indies, and cafés quickly came into vogue, animated by enlightened thinkers from dawn till dark. Lampoons and other rags made the rounds and were posted on the ceramic stove of the most famous café of all, Le Procope, which is still in business on Rue de l'Ancienne Comédie in Paris. The Café Anglais on Quai de Conti relayed political sparks originating in England, and activities at the cafés tucked under the arches of the Palais Royal created a veritable political powder keg. Speakers stood on tabletops, and journalists drifted from one place to another.

These cafés took on distinct personalities. Le Procope was the haunt of Danton and Marat; the Café de Foy was frequented first by the aristocrats and then by the Jacobins; and the terrifying *tricoteuses,* the radical women who took their knitting to the Convention deliberations, gathered at the Café des Feuillants. As for Robespierre, he enjoyed playing chess at the Café de la Régence.

Meanwhile, the provinces were braving drought and food shortages. The masses were convinced that the Duc d'Orléans and hoarders hoping to make big profits wanted to starve them, and there was talk of a "famine pact." Fortunately, the Revolutionaries had no objection to importing foreign wheat, and the return to more normal harvests in 1790 and 1791 tided them over until 1793. In these times of domestic insurrection and foreign wars, the Convention passed rationing measures, legislated price ceilings on basic foods (illicit price hikes were punishable by death), and instituted a bread card. Even the idea of a "civic fast" was considered, and the Revolutionaries planted vegetables in the Tuileries and Luxembourg gardens—more a symbolic statement than an effective solution to the hunger problem.

As supplies of the most basic ingredients dwindled, the idea of the civic banquet was born—ancestor of both the republican banquet and the soup kitchen. A certain Monsieur de Saint-Ange believed that all the bourgeois of Paris should serve an open-house meal in front of their residences as a grand community gesture in observance of the fall of the Bastille. This would give them the opportunity to feed the poor while demonstrating their Republican zeal. These civic banquets were held in 1794, but an atmosphere of suspicion prevailed. People worried about how their neighbors would judge them: too much generosity could be suspect, and too little could be interpreted as a lack of Revolutionary enthusiasm.

During Thermidor, the Revolutionary period marking the end of the Reign of Terror, signs of the good life reappeared in Paris. The Viscount Paul de Barras, who had a hand in the coup ousting Robespierre, resumed hosting his legendary feasts, and chefs unemployed since the Ancien Régime went back to work. But the Revolution continued to influence cuisine. For example, a well-known lobster dish was named after Victorien Sardou's play *Thermidor,* which apparently opened and closed on the same night, 24 January 1894. "But lobster thermidor," says chef and author Craig Claiborne, "is still a running hit."

—Alexandre Lazareff
Reprinted with permission from *France Magazine*

39 Horses of Marly These rearing marble horses (entitled *Africans Mastering the Numidian Horses*) were sculpted by **Nicolas** and **Guillaume Coustou.** They guard the entrance to the **Champs-Elysées** and were taken from the **Château de Marly** (the **Louis XIV** château that was destroyed in the Revolution) and brought to Paris in 1795. Sixteen live horses dragged the stone effigies to Paris in five hours, a transportation feat considered so marvelous that the vehicle in which they were carried is on exhibition in the **Conservatoire des Arts et Métiers.** ♦ Métro: Chambre-des-Députés

39 Champs-Elysées The world's most famous boulevard was formerly a forsaken marshland, unsafe after dark, until 1616, when **Marie de Médici,** the wife of **Henri IV,** decided to turn it into a fashionable carriage-drive, the **Cours-la-Reine** (Queen's Way). A half-century later, master landscaper **André Le Nôtre** planted double rows of chestnut trees along this wide avenue and renamed it the **Elysian Fields.** In 1724 the boulevard was extended to the top of the **Butte de Chaillot.** During the Second Empire, architect **Jacques Soufflot** leveled it by 16 feet to ease the climb for carriage-horses.

Since its creation, the Champs-Elysées has always been the place to promenade. Processions marking the liberation of Paris (26 August 1944), the student-worker demonstra-

tions (30 May 1968), and the silent march after the death of **Charles de Gaulle** (12 November 1970) all made their way down the Champs-Elysées. If you fancy pomp and pageantry, show up here on Bastille Day (14 July), when the jets of the French Air Force streak over the Champs-Elysées at low altitude; Armistice Day (11 November), when the president lays a wreath on the **Tomb of the Unknown Soldier;** the finish of the grueling three-week Tour de France bicycle race in July; and at Christmastime, when the avenue's trees twinkle with tiny white lights. The eastern half of the Champs-Elysées, from **Place de la Concorde** to **Rond Point,** is bordered by lush gardens of azaleas and mature chestnut trees where **Marcel Proust** played as a child. Within the garden today are a number of theaters (the **Théâtre de Marigny** and **Théâtre Renauld Barrault**) and

Louvre & Champs-Elysées

exclusive restaurants with pretty garden terraces, such as **Laurent, L'Espace,** and **Le Pavillon Elysée.** The western half of the avenue, between **Rond Point** and **Place de l'Etoile,** has lost its aristocratic sheen; today it is a crowded commercial strip of banks, airline offices, cinemas, outdoor cafés, fast-food parlors, and emporia selling perfume and Ray Ban sunglasses. ♦ Métros: Concorde, Champs-Elysée-Clemeneau, Franklin-D.-Roosevelt, George-V, Charles-de-Gaulle-Etoile

40 American Embassy Designed in 1933 by the New York firm **Delano and Aldrich** and flanked by two bald eagles in stone, the embassy and nearby consulate are staffed by about 500 Americans working for an alphabet soup of agencies including the IRS, CIA, FBI, and, of course, the departments of defense, state, agriculture, and commerce. ♦ Rue de Boissy-d'Anglas (Ave Gabriel). Métro: Concorde

41 L'Espace Restaurant ★★$$ This **Pierre Cardin**-designed restaurant furnished in neo-1950s Miami Beach (floral beach parasols and plastic chairs) serves a dandy buffet of 110 entrées and 40 desserts. It is a favorite with international TV and film glitterati, whose autographed photos festoon the walls. **Liza Minelli, Richard Gere, Brigitte Bardot,** and **Arletty** have all passed through at one time or another. There's dining on the garden terrace in summer and a Sunday brunch. ♦ Daily noon-3PM, 8:30PM-1AM; closed Sunday evenings in winter. 1 Ave Gabriel. Reservations recommended. Métro: Concorde. 42.66.11.70

42 Ledoyen ★★$$$$ During the reign of **Louis XVI** (1774-1792), this restaurant (pictured below) was a country inn and dairy bar serving fresh milk to travelers. Dinner here on the south side of the Champs-Elysées can still seem pleasantly bucolic. **Régine,** the reigning queen of Paris nightlife, recently bought and redecorated the historic restaurant. The menu

Louvre & Champs-Elysées

is Mediterranean-influenced: zucchini flowers with truffles, shellfish ratatouille, and *millefeuille* of polenta and lobster. Within months of its 1988 opening, Ledoyen had earned its first Michelin star. ♦ M-Sa noon-2:30PM, 8-10:30PM. Carré des Champs-Elysées. Jacket and tie required. Reservations required. Métro: Franklin-D.-Roosevelt. 47.42.23.23

43 Le Pavillon Elysée ★★$$$$ In a **Louis XVI** pavilion that has served dinners to a range of notables from **Edward VII** to **Toulouse-Lautrec,** the celebrated pastry chef **Gaston**

Lenôtre offers delectable meals topped off with his pièces de résistance: marvelous desserts. On the ground floor is the less expensive **Les Jardines de Lenôtre** (★★$$$), which opens onto a garden terrace where lunch is served in the summer. ♦ Le Pavillon: M-Sa 8-10:30PM. Les Jardines: M-F 12:15-2:30PM; closed in Aug. 10 Ave des Champs-Elysées (in the Carré Marigny). Métro: Champs-Elysées-Clemenceau. 42.65.85.10

44 Statue of Clemenceau **Georges Clemenceau** (1841-1929) was the outspoken French politician who at the end of WWI helped form a coalition government to rally French morale and fight the Germans. Sculptor **François Cogne** has captured Clemenceau's trademarks in bronze: the walrus mustache, high leather boots, walking stick, and wool scarf flapping in the wind. ♦ Place Clemenceau. Métro: Champs-Elysées-Clemenceau

45 Petit Palais This little turn-of-the-century palace houses the city's **Fine Arts Museum,** with a collection specializing in 19th-century French painters such as **Delacroix, Courbet, Monet, Cézanne,** and **Bonnard.** The architect, **Charles Girault,** crowned the building with a graceful cupola and decorated its two wings with Ionic columns and rococo embellishments. ♦ Admission. Tu-Su 10AM-5:40PM. Ave Winston-Churchill. Métro: Champs-Elysées-Clemenceau. 42.65.12.73

46 Pont Alexandre III Between the **Invalides** and the **Grand Palais** is an elegant Belle Epoque bridge embodying the architectural giddiness that celebrated the French spirit of ingenuity and optimism at the turn of the century. The Pont Alexandre III is encrusted with every Greco-Roman frippery in the book: man-size cupids, lavish garlands, huge golden statues of Pegasus and Renown, prides of lions, and reams of trumpets, tridents, shells, and shields. Built to commemorate the 1892 French-Russian alliance, the bridge bears the Russian and French coats of arms side-by-side and teams a sculptural allegory of the Seine with one of the Neva. ♦ Métro: Champs-Elysées-Clemenceau

Ledoyen

47 Grand Palais Along with the **Pont Alexandre III** and the **Petit Palais,** this exuberant stone, steel, and glass structure is an Art Nouveau creation at its excessive zenith. The Grand Palais and Petit Palais were built for the Universal Exhibition of 1900, the first world's fair in Paris. Famous for its domed and vaulted glass roof and superb staircase, the Grand Palais was designed by three architects: **Henri Deglane** built the principal facade; **Albert Thomas** the rear facade; and **Louis-Albert Louvet** the rest. With 54,000 square feet of floor space (equivalent to nearly 14 basketball courts), the Grand Palais is used for book fairs, car shows, and blockbuster art exhibitions. It has hosted major retrospectives of **Picasso, Léger, Chagall, Cézanne,** and **Manet.** ◆ Admission. Open only for special exhibitions and salons. Check hours in *Pariscope.* Ave Winston-Churchill. Métro: Champs-Elysées-Clemenceau. 42.89.23.13

48 1 Avenue de Marigny In 1954, when American novelist **John Steinbeck** and his family moved into this house, he described it in a letter to **Richard Rodgers** and **Oscar Hammerstein:** "It is next to the Rothschilds and across the street from the president of France. How's that for an address for a Salinas kid?" ◆ Métro: Champs-Elysées-Clemenceau

49 Restaurant Laurent ★★$$$ Just down the street from the official residence of the French president, this restaurant's parking lot is always crowded with chauffeured limousines bearing diplomatic license plates. Laurent is known for its lovely garden terrace, impeccable service, and nouvelle bourgeoisie cuisine, which includes lobster soup with cucumber rinds, roulade of smoked and raw salmon, and New York sirloin steak. The excellent wine list is overseen by the aptly named **Philippe Bourguignon.** ◆ M-F noon-2:30PM, 7:30-11PM; Sa 7:30-11PM. 41 Ave Gabriel. Jacket and tie required. Reservations required. Métro: Champs-Elysées-Clemenceau. 47.23.79.18

49 Résidence Maxim's $$$$ Near the intersection of the Champs-Elysées and the Place de la Concorde, **Pierre Cardin** has created an Art Nouveau architectural confection that accommodates visiting executives and sheiks for anywhere from $345 to $6,900 per night, depending on whether you prefer, say, the **Sarah Bernhardt** bed or the **Toulouse-Lautrec** painting in your room. Decisions, decisions. ◆ 42 Ave Gabriel. Métro: Franklin-D.-Roosevelt. 45.61.96.33

50 Théâtre Renaud Barrault After moving from the old Gare d'Orsay, the renowned theater company of **Jean-Louis Barrault** and **Madeleine Renaud** has taken up residence on the Champs-Elysées and performs everything from **Aristophanes** to **Pierre Corneille** and **Samuel Beckett.** Brief, often bravura programs take place every Sunday at 11AM from October through May. ◆ Box office: M-Sa 11AM-6PM. Ave Franklin-D.-Roosevelt. Métros: Champs-Elysées-Clemenceau, Franklin-D.-Roosevelt. 42.56.70.80 (information), 42.56.60.70 (reservations)

Within the Théâtre Renaud Barrault:

Théâtre du Rond-Point Restaurant ★$$ On the lower level of the prestigious theater, this restaurant serves reasonably priced lunch, dinner, and tea. Dine on the delightful terrace in summer. ◆ Daily noon-midnight; closed in August if no plays are showing. Reservations recommended. 42.56.23.01

51 Palais de la Découverte The western part of the Grand Palais houses a sprawling science museum with Jacques Cousteau festivals, holography exhibitions, 9,000 stars twinkling on the ceiling of its celebrated planetarium, and daily demonstrations on everything from ants to astronomy. Kids love the Madagascar agates and, of course, metal replicas of dinosaurs. Much of the museum is being moved to the new **Cité des Sciences** at **Porte de la Villette** (see "Additional Highlights" on page 185). ◆ Admission. Tu-Su 10AM-8PM. Ave Franklin-D.-Roosevelt. Métro: Franklin-D.-Roosevelt. 43.59.18.21

52 France Amérique If you want to give a party during your Paris stay and insist on nothing less than a Second-Empire town house for your surroundings, consider the France Amérique, which rents its three Louis XVI rooms (200 square meters) for festivities lasting just until midnight. Have your catering prepared by **Angélina** for the perfect lavish

Louvre & Champs-Elysées

bash. ◆ 9 Ave Franklin-D.-Roosevelt. Métro: Franklin-D.-Roosevelt. 43.59.51.00, 42.25.98.27

52 Lasserre ★★★$$$$ In the same luxurious league (and price range) as the Tour d'Argent and the Grand Véfour, Lasserre is famous for its caviar, 1930s oceanliner decor, and service bordering on perfection. Owner **René Lasserre** got his start in the restaurant business washing dishes at the age of 13. Located in a small town house, Lasserre's main dining room is reached by a velvet-lined elevator. In warm weather, the ceiling, painted by **Touchagues,** rolls away to admit the stars and a little cool air. Lasserre's masterpieces from a rather traditional repertoire include: Belon oysters, *canard à l'orange,* sea bass with sorrel, and crêpes Grand Marnier. The restaurant's wine cellar has 140,000 bottles. ◆ M 7:30-10:30PM; Tu-Sa 12:30-2:15PM, 7:30-10:30PM; closed in Aug. 17 Ave Franklin-D.-Roosevelt. Reservations required. Métro: Franklin-D.-Roosevelt. 43.59.53.43

The pyramid designed by I.M. Pei isn't the first to grace the Cour Napoléon. After the murder of Marat, his corpse, along with his writing desk and the bathtub where he met his demise, were placed in a wooden pyramid that stood near the Carousel Arch. The macabre monument has since been removed.

Restaurants/Nightlife: Red   **Hotels:** Blue
Shops/ ◆Outdoors: Green   **Sights/Culture:** Black

53 7 Rue François I During WWII, this building, formerly the **Hôtel du Palais,** was the headquarters of the **American Red Cross.** It was here that American poet **e.e. cummings,** a volunteer ambulance driver, spent a glorious May in 1917 detached from his unit. This act of independence resulted, through a tragicomic series of events, in his spending six months in a French prison, an experience that provided cummings with ample material for *The Enormous Room,* published in 1922. ♦ Métro: Franklin-D.-Roosevelt

54 San Régis $$$$ This sophisticated and discreet little Paris hotel has hosted **Gene Kelly, James Mason, Raquel Welch,** and **Lauren Bacall.** It's decorated with fine antiques and paintings and sits close (but not too close) to the Champs-Elysées. ♦ 12 Rue Jean-Goujon. Métro: Franklin-D.-Roosevelt. 43.59.41.90

55 25 Avenue Franklin-D.-Roosevelt From 1862 until the end of the Civil War, **John Slidell,** the Confederate commissioner to France, spent his time in a vain attempt to gain diplomatic recognition and financial support for the Southern cause. After the Confederacy's defeat, Slidell chose to remain in this house in Paris. ♦ Métro: Franklin-D.-Roosevelt

56 Avenue Matignon This is gallery alley for Right Bank art and antiques. Take note of the stamp-collectors market along this street and

Louvre & Champs-Elysées

the connecting **Avenue Gabriel.** ♦ Stamp market: Th, Sa-Su, holidays. Métro: Franklin-D.-Roosevelt

56 Le Berkeley ★$$ This classic oysters-and-champagne, steak-and-fries restaurant features the red decor (and high prices) of a first-class dining car. ♦ Daily 8AM-2AM. 7 Ave Matignon. Reservations recommended. Métro: Franklin-D.-Roosevelt. 42.25.47.79, 42.25.72.25

57 Artcurial This sprawling three-story complex of galleries has an extraordinary bookstore for art lovers in the middle. ♦ Tu-Sa 10:30AM-7:15PM; closed three weeks in Aug. 9 Ave Matignon. Métro: Franklin-D.-Roosevelt. 42.99.16.16

58 La Place Boisterous Parisian university students dance to very loud music until the very wee hours at this popular nightclub (formerly Le Privé). ♦ Daily midnight-exhaustion. 12 Rue de Ponthieu. Métro: Franklin-D.-Roosevelt. 42.25.51.70

59 Le Boeuf sur le Toit ★★★$$/$$$ This is the sixth and fanciest of **Jean-Paul Boucher's** marvelous group of old brasseries that includes Chez Flo, Julien, Terminus Nord, Vaudeville, and La Coupole. Note the superb Art Deco interior. ♦ Daily noon-2AM. 34 Rue du Colisée. Reservations recommended. Métro: Franklin-D.-Roosevelt. 43.59.83.80

60 Jadis et Gourmande This is a chocolate-lover's sweet dream. ♦ M 1-7PM; Tu-Sa 9:30AM-7PM. 49bis Ave Franklin-D.-Roosevelt. Métro: Franklin-D.-Roosevelt. 42.25.06.04

61 Lamazère ★★$$$/$$$$ Monsieur Lamazère, a former magician from Pigalle, no longer finds rabbits in top hats but performs some rather nifty culinary tricks, like keeping truffles fresh year-round and serving some of the best cassoulet and Landes foie gras in town. Takeout service is available. ♦ M-Sa noon-2:30PM, 7:30-11PM. 23 Rue de Ponthieu. Métro: Franklin-D.-Roosevelt. 43.59.66.66

62 Colisée $$$ The hotel rooms are embellished with quilted bedspreads and bamboo furniture. The room numbers of the largest suites end in 8. ♦ 6 Rue du Colisée. Métro: Franklin-D.-Roosevelt. 43.59.95.25

62 La Boutique à Sandwiches ★★$/$$ Stop here for the perfect late-night snack: all-you-can-eat Swiss raclette. This crowded two-story restaurant/snack bar also serves 40 kinds of sandwiches, as well as Welsh rabbit, ravioli, corned beef, *pickelfleisch,* and strudel. Better yet, it's a great value. ♦ Restaurant: daily 11:45AM-11:30PM. Snack bar: M-Sa 11:45AM-1AM. 12 Rue du Colisée. Reservations recommended. Métro: Franklin-D.-Roosevelt. 45.59.56.69

63 Franklin-D.-Roosevelt Métro Station This is the oldest métro station in Paris. On 4 October 1898 men with picks and shovels began digging a labyrinth beneath the city as directed by engineer **Fulgence Bienvenue.** Thus began the Parisian underground railway, or *métro* (short for *métropolitain*). Every day the métro trains travel the equivalent of three times around the world; since its opening in 1900, the métro has carried a number of passengers equivalent to more than 20 times the world's population.

64 Avenue Montaigne This street is to haute couture what the Louvre is to art . The swank avenue is lined with high-fashion temples (Christian Dior, Nina Ricci, Jean-Louis Scherrer, Valentino, Ungaro, and Laroche). You will also find the **Canadian Embassy,** the luxurious **Plaza Athénée** hotel, and two smart theaters (the **Comédie des Champs-Elysées** and the **Théâtre des Champs-Elysées**).

65 Chanel The dashing and successful Chanel collections are displayed here to their best advantage: a setting of crisp white walls, gleaming mirrors, and spacious dressing rooms, all overseen by attractive salespeople. ♦ M-F 9:30AM-6:30PM; Sa 10AM-6:30PM. 42 Ave Montaigne. Métro: Alma-Marceau. 47.23.74.12

66 Christian Dior In 1949 Dior signed the first designer licensing contract (for stockings), planning the day when women would be able to dress in his wares from top to toe. A stop in this three-floor, gray-and-white complex, which sells dresses, furs, jewelry, and gifts, makes that more than possible. ♦ M, Sa 10AM-6:30PM; Tu-F 9:30AM-6:30PM. 30 Ave Montaigne. Métro: Franklin-D.-Roosevelt. 40.73.54.40

66 **26 Avenue Montaigne** In 1857, when he was 14, **Henry James** moved here with his family. ♦ Métro: Franklin-D.-Roosevelt

67 **Nina Ricci** Perhaps the most beautiful lingerie in the world, plus a stylish array of dresses, scarves, scents, and jewelry. The **Ricci Club,** an elegant wood-paneled menswear shop, is next door at 19 Rue François I. ♦ M-Sa 10AM-6:30PM. 39 Ave Montaigne. Métro: Franklin-D.-Roosevelt. 47.23.78.88

68 **Isabel Canovas** Looking for something special to consolidate your look? This shop is the last word in accessories. ♦ M-Sa 10AM-7PM. 16 Ave Montaigne. Métro: Franklin-D.-Roosevelt. 47.20.10.80

68 **Bar des Théâtres** ★★$$ The noisy bar/restaurant is patronized by theater critics before, bored ticket holders during, and bushed actors after the theater. The fare is simple: steak, Welsh rabbit, osso buco, and the like. It's a favorite lunch spot of film director **Roman Polanski.** ♦ Daily 6PM-2:30AM. 6 Ave Montaigne. Métro: Franklin-D.-Roosevelt. 47.23.34.63

69 **Plaza Athénée** $$$$ The Plaza Athénée has long enjoyed its reputation as the most fashionable palace hotel in Paris, largely because its **Relais Plaza** restaurant remains the favorite lunchtime hangout of Paris couturiers. In fact, when the great designer **Pierre Balmain** died, the hotel management retired his table. The select out-of-town clientele includes the likes of **Rockefellers** and rich Brazilians. There's a lavishness of flowers, and, indeed, the hotel staff boasts that the monthly florist's bill is higher than the electric bill. In 1918 West Point graduate **Captain George Patton** stayed here on his errand to France: learning to fence at the French Military Academy in Saumur. In this hotel, Patton discussed the use of tanks and combat with another young officer, the 28-year-old **Charles de Gaulle.** ♦ 25 Ave Montaigne. Métro: Franklin-D.-Roosevelt. 47.23.78.33

Within the Plaza Athénée:

Relais Plaza ★$$/$$$ For a late-night, after-theater meal, try the filets of *sôle boccador* or braised beef in aspic, accompanied by a good house wine. ♦ Daily 11AM-1AM. 47.23.78.33

Bar Anglais ★$$ After a performance at the **Théâtre des Champs-Elysées,** the concert crowd may come to this night spot and mix with the South American night owls staying at the hotel. ♦ Daily 11AM-1AM. Piano bar after 11PM. 47.23.78.33

Régence-Plaza ★★$$$/$$$$ The most expensive of the hotel's restaurants is peopled, as a rule, by the rich and famous. The *sôle Reine Astrid,* lobster filet, and the crêpes Montaigne are house specialties. **Patrick Jeanne,** the restaurant's manager, has mastered the art of mingling the stars and the not-yet-famous so that everyone can get a look at everyone else and see how the other half lives. ♦ Daily 12:30-2:30PM, 7:30-10:30PM. Reservations recommended. 47.23.78.33

70 **2 Avenue Montaigne** Back when this was the **Hôtel Elysée-Bellevue, Sinclair Lewis** passed the winter of 1924 here writing *Arrowsmith.* ♦ Métro: Alma-Marceau

71 **Pont de l'Alma** The Pont de l'Alma, built in 1855 to honor the first French victory in the **Crimean War** (1854), is decorated with a statue of a Zouave soldier that acts as a high-water marker. During the flood of 1910, the Seine reached his chin. ♦ Métro: Alma-Marceau

72 **15 Montaigne, Maison Blanche** ★★★$$$$ Fresh from the success of the trendy original Maison Blanche, **René Duran** has taken over an even trendier spot atop the Théâtre des Champs-Elysées and redecorated the space in fashionable monochromes. The culinary magic includes *croustillant d'anchois* (whole-grain toast infused with tomatoes and topped with anchovies and sea salt), oyster-stuffed cabbage, and braised veal with fresh pasta. ♦ Daily noon-2:30PM, 8PM-12:30AM. 15 Ave Montaigne. Métro: Alma-Marceau. 47.23.55.99

72 **Théâtre des Champs-Elysées** Here, on 29 May 1913, the **Ballet Russe** of **Sergei Diaghilev** first performed to the music of the **Stravinsky** piece *Le Sacré du Printemps.* Riots followed a performance shocking in its originality and modernity. Diaghilev, Stravinsky, **Nijinsky,** and **Cocteau** fled the mobs for the Bois de Boulogne and drove around while

Diaghilev wept. This theater was one of the first buildings of reinforced concrete in Paris and the city's main concert hall. It was designed by **Auguste Perret,** who was later hired to reconstruct the entire port city of Le Havre after WWII.

American footnotes: On 2 October 1925, **John Dos Passos** painted the stage set, **Sidney Bechet** played clarinet, and **Josephine Baker** danced to "Yes, Sir That's My Baby" for the opening here of *La Revue Nègre.* In May 1927 a **Charles Lindbergh** autograph sold for $1,500 at an auction held here (the name of his plane, *The Spirit of St. Louis,* pleased the French, who associated it not with Missouri, but with the saintliest of their line of kings); on 16 April 1928, the **Gershwins** attended the opening of a performance of *La Rhapsodie en Bleu* by the Ballet Russe. ♦ Box office: M-F 2-5PM; closed holidays. 15 Ave Montaigne. Métro: Alma-Marceau. 47.20.36.37

73 **Avenue George V** Along this grand avenue named after the English king, you will find the spired 19th-century Gothic **American Episcopal Cathedral;** the salons of Givenchy, Balenciaga, and Nina Ricci; the **Chinese** and **Mexican** embassies; two swank hotels (**George V** and **Prince de Galles**); the **Crazy Horse Saloon,** with its sophisticated girlie shows; and the **Place de l'Alma** whence the *Bateaux Mouches* (tour boats) and evening dinner cruises embark on their tour of the Seine.

73 Le Bistrot de Marius ★★$$$ Pagnol's Marius may have run away to sea, but this chef appears to have just returned. In a warm, Provençal decor, the menu revolves around the freshest of seafood, from baby clams on a bed of spinach to *daurade grillé*, a sumptuous sea bream. ◆ Daily noon-2:30PM, 7PM-midnight. 6 Ave George-V. Métro: Alma-Marceau. 40.70.11.76

73 Marius et Janette ★★$$$/$$$$ For a taste of some of the finest Provençal cuisine available in Paris, try this gracious seafood restaurant that has long been a favorite stop along Avenue George-V. Chef **Bernard Valeuet** serves classic bouillabaisse, lobster salad, fried smelts, *loup grillé*, and a selection of dishes representative of the western maritime provinces. ◆ Daily noon-2:30PM, 7-11PM. 4 Ave George-V. Reservations recommended. Métro: Alma-Marceau. 47.23.41.88, 47.23.84.36

74 Crazy Horse Saloon The Saloon's upscale strip show is a knowing display of naughtiness featuring 16 gorgeous (mostly British), uniform (5 feet, 4 inches tall) lasses with silly stage names such as *Bianca Sundae, Ivy Speculation, Rita Cadillac,* and *Pompea Mackintosh.* The impresario of the Crazy Horse is former antique dealer **Alain Bernardin,** but the unseen star of the show is his lighting designer, who strobes, tints, patterns, and spotlights dancers with erotic flair. ◆ Shows:

Louvre & Champs-Elysées

M-F, Su 9PM, 11:35PM; Sa 8PM, 10PM, 12:50AM. 12 Ave George-V. Métro: Alma-Marceau. 47.23.32.32

74 Hôtel de la Trémoille $$$$ This hotel is a bit of *Vieux France* in the heart of the high-fashion district. Do your shopping at Christian Dior or Nina Ricci in the afternoon, then dine here and charge your meal to your room at the nearby **Plaza Athénée,** which is under the same ownership. ◆ 14 Rue de la Trémoille. Métros: Franklin-D.-Roosevelt, Alma-Marceau. 47.23.34.20

75 Chez Edgar ★$/$$ This noisy restaurant thronged with politicians, journalists, and actors serves meals to fit any pocketbook. Try the red *mullet au pistou,* salmon tartare, fresh pastas, pot-au-feu, or fresh shellfish. ◆ M-F noon-3 PM, 7:15-11:15PM. 4 Rue Marbeuf. Reservations recommended. Métro: Alma-Marceau. 47.20.51.15

76 American Cathedral On 6 July 1905, one hundred years after his death, a service was held here for **John Paul Jones,** naval hero of the American Revolution, and more than 500 Americans attended. Afterward, his casket was taken to Annapolis, Maryland. ◆ M-F 9AM-12:30PM, 2-5PM; Sa 9AM-noon. 23 Ave George-V. Métro: Alma-Marceau. 47.20.17.92

77 24 Rue du Boccador In the late 1940s this apartment building was rife with movie stars such as **Brigitte Bardot,** Ivy League CIA agents posing as novelists, and legitimate American writers, including **Theodore H. White, Art Buchwald,** and **Irwin Shaw.** This is where White, after working for six years as *Time* magazine's Beijing bureau chief, wrote his Pulitzer Prize-winning WWII novel, *The Mountain Road.* In a fifth-floor studio, Buchwald wrote his *Paris After Dark* column for the *Herald Tribune,* and Shaw, in much grander digs, completed his best-selling novel *The Young Lions,* which was published in 1948. ◆ Métro: Alma-Marceau

78 Claridge-Bellman $$$ Redecorated with antiques, paintings, 17th-century tapestries, Chinese vases, and other costly objets d'art, this posh hotel is home to the Italian couturiers during the fashion collections. Reserve well in advance. ◆ 37 Rue François I. Métro: Franklin-D.-Roosevelt. 47.23.54.42

Within the Claridge-Bellman hotel:

Relais Bellman ★$$ This restaurant and English bar is frequented by reporters from *Paris-Match* and the television station Europe 1. ◆ Daily 24 hours. Reservations required. 47.23.54.42

78 Chez André ★★$$ Unchanged since 1938, this bistro bustles at lunchtime with the dressed-for-success crowd from the Champs-Elysées and matronly waitresses loping through with hot plates of poached haddock and short ribs. Also recommended are roast leg of lamb with mashed potatoes, sponge cake with rum sauce, and the affordable house Muscadet and red Graves. ◆ Daily noon-1AM. 12 Rue Marbeuf. Reservations recommended. Métro: Franklin-D.-Roosevelt. 47.20.59.57

79 American Pershing Hall ★$ The restaurant of the American Legion's Paris Post #1 is patronized largely by over-the-hill Legionnaires, sometimes dressed in tattered uniforms and apparently ready to re-enlist. It's open to members and American citizens. ◆ Post: daily 11AM-midnight. Restaurant: daily noon-3PM, 7-11PM. 49 Rue Pierre-Charron. Métro: Franklin-D.-Roosevelt. 42.25.81.22, 42.25.38.17

80 George V $$$$ **Art Buchwald** put it this way: "Paris without the George V would be Cleveland." Whether or not you agree, the George V hotel has something special to offer, and not just its red-leather elevator. **François Dupré,**

who owned the hotel from its opening in 1928 until 1968, amassed a vast collection of antique furniture, Baroque statues, Louis XIV tapestries (the value of these alone is estimated at $6 million), and paintings (among them, *Vase de Roses* by **Renoir**), that still decorates the public and private rooms. The George V has long attracted the greats of every field. **Duke Ellington** stayed here in 1933 while he was performing at the Salle Pleyel. He wrote in his memoirs that he spent a long time trying to get out of his suite: apparently, it was so enormous, with doors opening onto other rooms or closets, that it took a while to locate the exit. ♦ 31 Ave George-V. Métro: George-V. 47.23.54.00

Within the George V hotel:

Les Princes ★★$$$/$$$$ The menu at this elegant restaurant runs from the delicate (filet of sole with spring truffles) to the hearty (salt pork with lentils). ♦ Daily 7-11AM, 12:30-2:30PM, 7:30-10:30PM. Reservations required. 47.23.54.00

Bar du George V ★$$ This bar has a glorious but too rarefied atmosphere. ♦ Daily 11AM-2AM. 47.23.54.00

Le Grill A fine place for snacks. ♦ Daily 7AM-1AM. 47.23.54.00

80 **37 Avenue George-V** On their honeymoon in 1905, **Franklin** and **Eleanor Roosevelt** visited Franklin's aunt, **Deborah Delano,** who had an apartment at this address. She used to take the newlyweds driving; indeed it was in the **Bois de Boulogne** that FDR learned to drive. ♦ Métro: George-V

80 **François I** $$$ This luxurious little hotel off the Champs-Elysées features a tasteful Art Deco interior. ♦ 7 Rue Magellan. Métro: George-V. 47.23.44.04

81 **16 Rue Christophe-Colomb** In 1898 **Henry Adams,** grandson of **John Quincy Adams** and professor of history at Harvard University, stayed in several rooms in this building while reading medieval manuscripts for his study, *Mont-Saint-Michel and Chartres.* ♦ Métro: George-V

82 **L'Ecluse II** ★★$$ The second of this chain of classy wine bars offers vintage Bordeaux and light meals of smoked salmon, carpaccio, and goat cheese. ♦ Daily noon-1:30AM. 64 Rue François I. Métro: George-V. 47.20.77.09

83 **Institut Geographique National** The French counterpart of the **National Geographic Society** in Washington, DC, is a cartographer's heaven, selling maps of the entire universe (at least that which is recognized by the French) and more. You may purchase wall-size maps of the Paris métro, navigation charts for the Seine, infrared satellite photos of France, 1618 city maps of Paris, and four-by-four-foot color aerial photographs of 164 square-mile sectors of downtown Paris so detailed you can make out pedestrians on the Champs-Elysées. ♦ M-F 8AM-6:50PM; Sa 10AM-12:30PM, 1:45-5:20PM. 107 Rue La Boétie. Métro: Franklin-D.-Roosevelt. 42.25.87.90

83 **Virgin Records' Megastore** This majestic music shop looks like a **Cecil B. DeMille** movie set, complete with a monumental marble staircase. Its various levels are replete with a mind-bending selection of records, CDs, tapes, and videos (in English and French), as well as books on music and stereo equipment. ♦ M-Th, Su 10AM-midnight; F-Sa 10AM-1AM. 52-60 Ave des Champs-Elysées. Métro: Franklin-D.-Roosevelt. 40.74.06.48

84 **Régine's** The notorious queen of Paris nightlife, Régine puts in only rare appearances at her enticing, dimly lit private club off the Champs-Elysées, but the Ritz/Tour d'Argent/Maxim's crowd keeps coming back nevertheless. ♦ Daily 11PM-dawn. 49 Rue de Ponthieu. Métro: Franklin-D.-Roosevelt. 43.59.21.13

84 **Gymnase Club** The largest health club in Paris offers five floors of aerobics studios, body-building equipment, saunas, Jacuzzis, a solarium, and a juice bar. ♦ M-F 7:30AM-10PM; Sa 9AM-8PM. 55bis Rue de Ponthieu. Métro: Franklin-D.-Roosevelt. 45.62.99.76

85 **Guerlain** You must reserve at least eight days in advance if you wish to visit this Regency-paneled beauty salon and undergo the royal treatment from the perfumed ladies in pink. ♦ M-Sa 9AM-6:45PM. 68 Ave des Champs-Elysées. Métro: George-V. 43.59.31.10

85 **Club Méditerranée** Club Med, a chain of swinging summer camps, was started in the

Louvre & Champs-Elysées

1950s by a French tent salesman. Today it is the world's fifth-largest hotel group, and its owner, **Gilbert Trigano,** is one of France's most prominent businesspeople. ♦ M-Sa 10AM-7:30PM. 90 Ave des Champs-Elysées. Métro: George-V. 42.96.10.00

86 **1 Rue de Berri** On 17 October 1785, 42-year-old **Thomas Jefferson** succeeded **Benjamin Franklin** as minister to France and moved into this mansion, the **Hôtel de Langeac,** designed by architect **Jean Chalgrin.** Jefferson made this his home for the next four years. ♦ Métro: George-V

86 **Lancaster** $$$$ This first-class hotel has an atmosphere more like a rustic private house than a grand hostelry. **Helen Keller** stayed here in 1937, **John Steinbeck** in 1954, and a continuing parade of American luminaries since then. ♦ 7 Rue de Berri. Métros: George-V, St.-Philippe-du-Roule. 43.59.90.43

Fouquet's

87 **Fouquet's** ★★★$$$/$$$$ Irish writer **James Joyce** dined most every night at this old high-priced café/restaurant that has become a watering hole for show-biz celebrities, glamour girls, and rubberneckers. American novelist **Ernest Hemingway** may have liberated the Ritz bar after WWII, but sexism still reigns at Fouquet's bar. For the last 80 years, a

sign at its seven-stool bar has read: *Les dames seules ne sont pas admises au bar,* which translates without much grace to "No single women allowed!" The maître d', one **Monsieur Casanova,** offers the spurious consolation that the house rule is for the ladies' own protection. ♦ Daily 7AM-2AM. 99 Ave des Champs-Elysées. Reservations recommended. Métro: George-V. 47.23.70.60

88 Résidence Lord Byron $$$ This comfortably classy small hotel lacks the pretensions of the grander hotels in town. ♦ 5 Rue Châteaubriand. Métros: Etoile, George-V. 43.59.89.98

89 Taillevent ★★★$$$$ As close as a restaurant comes to perfection. **Jean-Claude Vrinat,** the owner and idea man, and chef **Claude Deligne** have made this establishment (dare we say it?) the best restaurant in Paris. Named after **Guillaume Tirel** (a.k.a. Taillevent, the 14th-century royal cook who wrote the first treatise on French cooking), the restaurant, set in a town house with high ceilings, oak-paneled walls, and Louis XV furniture, has the feel of a grand bourgeois private club. Taillevent's innovative signature dishes include *fruits de mer* with truffles and pistachios, langoustines with fresh pasta, Barbary duck, veal kidneys, and almond ice cream. The wine list draws on a cellar of 130,000 bottles ranging from collector's items such as the Laffite-Rothschild 1806 to a less risky and far less expensive Château Haut Brion. Taillevent

Louvre & Champs-Elysées

is the perfect restaurant for a first-class business lunch or that once-in-a-lifetime dining experience. ♦ M-F 12:30-2PM, 7:30-9:30PM; closed one week in February, four weeks beginning the end of July. 15 Rue Lamennais. Reservations required well in advance. Métro: Etoile. 45.63.39.94, 45.61.12.90

90 Hôtel de Vigny $$$$ This could be the best new little hotel in Paris. It features sumptuous wood paneling, a lobby resembling a private London club, and bright and airy rooms that are royally furnished with antiques, puffy down comforters, and private Jacuzzis. ♦ 9-11 Rue Balzac. Métros: Georges-V, Charles-de-gaulle-Etoile. 40.75.04.39

91 Lido The largest cabaret in Paris, this lavish extravaganza outglitters Las Vegas with its $2.5-million stage set and famous **Bluebell Girls,** whose dance numbers are choreographed by computer. Dazzling special effects include a safari number (two elephants making a ponderous circuit of the stage), a sea battle, a dolphin-filled swimming pool, and a skating rink rising out of the floor. Throw in a few jugglers, acrobats, and bare-breasted dancers decorously lowered from the ceiling and you have your basic night at the Lido. It's always packed with Japanese tourists, car salesmen, and sailors on leave. ♦ Shows: daily 10PM, midnight. Doors open at 8PM. 116bis Ave des Champs-Elysées. Métro: George-V. 40.76.56.10

91 Burger King ★★$ This bustling establishment (one of 12 in Paris) serves traditional American cuisine, called *le fast food,* to hom sick Yankees and a young and foolish intern tional clientele. *Spécialités de la maison* incl *Le Whopper avec fromage, les frites, et le m shake.* Note the bronze plaque marking the s where on Bastille Day of 1985 more Whoppe were sold than in any other Burger King in th world. ♦ M-Th, Su 11AM-1AM; F-Sa 11AM-2AM. 122 Ave des Champs-Elysées. No cre cards. Métro: George-V

92 La Boutique Flora Danica ★★$$/$$$ T enjoyments of Danish dining—pickled herri eel, marinated salmon, shrimp salad, roast with onions, Tuborg on tap, and the flakiest pastries around—abound in this informal lu cheonette with blond-wood tables and chee abstract art. In summer, meals are served in umbrella-shaded courtyard. ♦ Take-out: M-4-10PM; Su 4-8PM. Degustation: daily noor 11PM. Restaurant: daily noon-2:30PM, 7-11PM. 142 Ave des Champs-Elysées. Métro Charles-de-Gaulle-Etoile. 43.59.20.41

The Guillotine

"The king heard his sentence with remarkable equa nimity. They offered him a coat; he said: 'I don't ne it.' He wore a brown jacket, black breeches, white stockings, and a white flannel waistcoat. He climbe into the carriage, a green one. He sat at the back w his confessor; two gendarmes sat in front. He read some psalms.... The steps of the scaffold were extremely steep. The king leaned on the priest. On th last step, he escaped, as it were, from his confesso and ran to the far end of the scaffold. He was very flushed; he gazed down at the square, waiting for t drums to cease beating for a moment. Voices calle out to the executioners: 'Do your duty!' Four of ther seized him: while they were binding him he let out dreadful cry."

—Michelet on the execution of Louis

93 Copenhague ★★$$$ Upstairs from **La Boutique Flora Danica,** this restaurant serves slightly higher-priced Danish cuisine. ♦ M-Sa noon-2:30PM, 7:15-10:30PM; closed in Aug, first week in Jan. 142 Ave des Champs-Elysées. Métro: Charles-de-Gaulle-Etoile. 43.59.20.41

93 Office du Tourisme de Paris Home of the city's official tourist bureau, here you can find free maps, sightseeing information, and for tourists stuck without a room for the night, same-day hotel reservations. ♦ Daily 9AM-8PM. 127 Ave des Champs-Elysées. Métros: Charles-de-Gaulle-Etoile, George-V. 47.23.61.72

93 Drugstore des Champs-Elysées ★★$/$$ This drugstore sells not only aspirin and Band-Aid bandages, but gourmet groceries, quick brasserie meals, wristwatches, banana splits, and Cuban cigars. ♦ Daily 9AM-2AM. Restaurant: daily 8:30AM-2AM. 133 Ave des Champs-Elysées. Métro: Charles-de-Gaulle-Etoile. 47.23.54.34

93 133 Avenue des Champs-Elysées After WWII, **General Dwight D. Eisenhower,** supreme commander of the Allied Forces in Europe, had his headquarters here in what was the old **Hôtel Astoria.** He asked for a room with a view of the **Arc de Triomphe,** his favorite structure in Paris. ♦ Métro: Charles-de-Gaulle-Etoile

94 Raphael $$$$ This luxurious lodging with Oriental carpets, marble floors, and Louis XVI furniture attracts Italian and American movie stars. ♦ 17 Ave Kléber. Métros: Charles-de-Gaulle-Etoile, Kléber. 45.02.16.00

95 Place Charles-de-Gaulle This square was created in 1854 by **Baron Haussmann** when he added another seven avenues to the existing five to create a 12-pointed star. The area is a total snarl of traffic. Of the avenues beginning here, **Avenue Foch** is the widest (120 meters, or 390 feet) in Paris. It has always been the street where the rich and famous, such as **Aristotle Onassis,** the divine **Maria Callas,** the composer **Claude Debussy,** the **Shah of Iran,** and **Prince Rainier** of Monaco, have had their mansions. Avenue Foch leads to the **Bois de Boulogne,** a 2,000-acre park. ♦ Métro: Charles-de-Gaulle-Etoile

95 L'Arc de Triomphe If the **Emperor Napoléon** hadn't changed his mind in the nick of time, Parisians would be staring not at this magnificent arch, but at a 160-foot-high elephant squirting water from its trunk. The decision was so close that a model of the elephant was made and stood for a while at the Place de la Bastille. In the end, Napoléon chose the more tasteful triumphal arch to honor his army's victory at the **Battle of Austerlitz.** (And the story is that the sun sets exactly along this axis on 2 December, the anniversary of that victory.) This granddaddy of triumphal arches is 164 feet high and 148 feet wide.

Construction of the arch began in 1806, and the walls had scarcely risen above the ground by the time Napoléon divorced the childless

Louvre & Champs-Elysées

L'Arc de Triomphe

Empress Josephine and wed **Princess Marie-Louise** of Austria in 1810. As a result, the bridal procession passed through a fake arch of canvas, hastily constructed for the occasion by the architect **Chalgrin.** The arch was not completed until 1836, well after Napoléon's downfall, and only four years before the chariot bearing his body would pass beneath the arch on its way to the **Invalides.** On 14 July 1919, victorious French soldiers, led by their generals, marched through the arch. The following month, pilot **Sergeant Godefroy** flew a plane with a wingspan of nine meters (29 feet) through the 15-meter-wide (48 feet) arch. On 11 November 1920 the body of the **Unknown Soldier** was laid in state to commemorate the dead soldiers of WWI. The eternal flame at the tomb (first kindled in 1923) is lit each evening at 6:30PM. (A crudely irreverent Frenchman once cooked an omelet over the flame.) On 26 August 1944, after the Germans had been routed from the capital, **General Charles de Gaulle** led a jubilant crowd to the arch, then walked down the Champs-Elysées to Notre-Dame, where the famous **Te Deum Mass** was celebrated in thanksgiving. On state occasions, an enormous French flag hangs inside the arch.

It would be suicide to cross the **Place Charles-de-Gaulle** on foot (cars have a hard enough time). However, you can reach the arch by the underground passage. Then, an

Louvre & Champs-Elysées

elevator, or 284 steps, will take you (during daylight hours only) to the platform at the top of the arch, which affords a magnificent panorama of Paris. ♦ Métro: Charles-de-Gaulle-Etoile

La Marseillaise

On the Arc de Triomphe:

Departure of the Volunteers Known as *La Marseillaise,* this sculpture (pictured above) by **Rude** is the arch's most inspired and noteworthy stonework. (It is on the right when your back is to the Champs-Elysées.) In 1916,

on the day the **Battle of Verdun** started, the sword brandished by the figure representing the Republic in the sculpture broke and fell off. The disarmed sculpture was immediately hidden to conceal the accident from the superstitious, who might have seen it as a bad omen.

96 Chiberta ★★$$$$ The most chic nouvelle-cuisine restaurant in Paris is made even more hip by its Art Deco decor. Chef **Jean-Michel Bédier** offers seasonal specialties such as wild mushroom fricassee, truffle-and-parsley ravioli in autumn, and salmon with fresh artichokes and asparagus come spring. ♦ M-F noon-2PM 7:30-10:30PM; closed in Aug, 25 Dec-1 Jan. 3 Rue Arsène-Houssaye. Reservations recommended. Métro: Charles-de-Gaulle-Etoile. 45.63.77.90

97 Royal Monceau $$$$ The Italian Ciga hotel chain funneled $15 million into renovating the rooms, which apparently have something to please everyone from **Alexander Haig** to the rock group **The Police.** The saunas, steam rooms, herbal massages, and low-cal restaurant at the adjoining **Thermes Health Spa** are open to hotel clients. ♦ 35-39 Ave Hoche. Métro: Ternes. 45.61.98.00

98 14 Rue de Tilsitt It was April of 1925: *The Great Gatsby* was selling briskly and American novelist **F. Scott Fitzgerald** was at the height of his fame. He and his wife, **Zelda,** took an apartment at this address. At that time, Fitzgerald's drunken binges began. There were times when he would stumble into the Paris bureau of the *Chicago Tribune* and **William L. Shirer** and **James Thurber** would have to pack him home in a taxi to deeper ignominies ahead. ♦ Métro: Charles-de-Gaulle-Etoile

99 Guy Savoy ★★★$$$/$$$$ A shining star in the Parisian culinary firmament found this setting to match his enormous talent. Not so long ago chef Savoy took over the spacious quarter of **Maguy** and **Gilbert Le Coze** (who moved their famous fish restaurant Le Bernardin to Manhattan). Try the sardine and red mullet marinade, smoked eel with green beans in an onion sauce, and the *fondant au chocolat.* ♦ M-F noon-2:30PM, 7:30-10:30PM. 18 Rue Troyon. Reservations recommended. Métro: Charles-de-Gaulle-Etoile. 43.80.40.61

99 L'Etoile Verte ★★$ This small, inexpensive neighborhood restaurant serves traditional French fare nonstop from midday to night. The waitresses can be gruff, but at these prices, politeness is perhaps too much to expect. Enjoy such fundamental cuisine as coq au vin, sautéed veal, and châteaubriand Béarnaise. ♦ Daily 11AM-3PM, 6:30-11PM. 13 Rue Brey. Métro: Charles-de-Gaulle-Etoile. 43.80.69.34

"The French do not go to priests, doctors, or psychiatrists to talk over their problems. They sit over a cup of coffee or a glass of wine and talk to each other."

Eric Sevareid, "Town Meeting of the World," CBS-TV (1 March 196

Restaurants/Nightlife: Red   **Hotels:** Blue
Shops/ ♥ Outdoors: Green   **Sights/Culture:** Black

Revolutionary Expressions

Ancien Régime:
General term for the government and society of France before the French Revolution. Often rendered in English as "Old Regime."

Bastille:
Originally a fortress guarding eastern Paris, the Bastille was transformed into a royal prison by Cardinal Richelieu in the 17th century and acquired its sinister reputation under Louis XIV. In the 18th century several critics of the government—including Voltaire—were imprisoned there.

Commune of Paris:
The municipal government of Paris organized after the fall of the Bastille was largely composed of extremist revolutionaries who supported Robespierre. The Commune exerted great influence on the various national assemblies, but it was finally dissolved after Robespierre's fall.

Département:
The Constituent Assembly organized France into 83 approximately equal units called *départements*, which replaced the provinces of the Ancien Régime.

Empire:
The First French Empire was created in 1804 when Napoléon formally destroyed the Republic and had himself crowned emperor.

Guillotine:
A beheading device proposed by Dr. Joseph Guillotin in 1791 as an instantaneous and thus more humane instrument of death (see the illustration on page 130). It was adopted for all capital crimes in 1792. It is not true that Dr. Guillotin was the victim of the machine that bears his name; he died in his bed in 1814 at age 76.

Liberté, Egalité, Fraternité:
The slogan of the French Revolution. As the politics of the Revolution changed, different elements of the slogan were given more or less weight. Fraternity, for example, was especially stressed during the First Republic, when the Paris Commune played an important role.

Marianne:
The female allegorical figure of the First Republic, which was adopted in 1797. There is a complicated history of the transformations imposed on the image of Marianne; actress Catherine Deneuve served as the Marianne model for years. Marianne appears on numerous French postage stamps.

La Marseillaise:
Declared the national anthem in 1795 (and again in 1879), this martial song, whose words were written by Claude-Joseph Roget de Lisle, was first sung by the Army of the Rhine, but it was brought to Paris by volunteer troops from Marseilles.

Palais Royal:
This was once the palace of the Orléans branch of the royal family, first cousins to the Bourbons. The Duc d'Orléans rented out space under the elegant colonnade of his palace, and the place became a notorious haunt of gamblers, prostitutes, and, during the Revolution, political agitators.

Sans-Culottes:
Literally means "without culottes" (the knickers worn with silk stockings and pumps that were favored by the aristocracy). Originally the term designated the artisans and the working class, who wore trousers rather than culottes. As the Revolution became increasingly democratic, the term lost its pejorative sense and became an assertion of pride by those who espoused popular or radical politics.

Louvre & Champs-Elysées

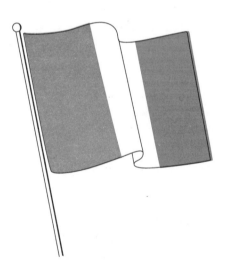

Tricolore:
Taking its colors from the red, white, and blue *cocarde* (rosette), the tricolor flag with three vertical bands was adopted in 1790. With the exception of the Restoration (of the Bourbons, 1815–1830), all French governments have used the *tricolore* as the nation's flag.

—David P. Jordan

Reprinted with permission from *France Magazine*

133

Bests

Patricia Wells
Restaurant Critic, *International Herald Tribune*

Jogging in the **Parc de Monceau** before 9AM anytime of the year—as long as it's not raining.

Riding around Paris with friends in a comfortable car driven by someone else on a snowy evening just before Christmas, and circling the **Rond Point**, driving down **Avenue Montaigne** with Christmas lights gleaming, and crossing over to the Left Bank for dinner at the Eiffel Tower restaurant, **Jules Verne.**

Walking through **Place des Vosges** after midnight with friends, especially on the night of a full moon, after a happy evening together.

The luxury of spending a morning alone, slowly examining the wonders of the **Musée des Arts Décoratifs.**

Enjoying a Friday night dinner at **Jamin,** and a Sunday night dinner at **L'Ami Louis.**

A stroll through the **Marché aux Puces** at Porte de Clignancourt on a sunny afternoon.

Breakfast at **Ladurée** with anyone I love.

Wandering down any market street when the first-of-the-season asparagus, cherries, and melons are being sold.

Stopping at the cheese shop, **La Ferme St.-Hubert,** for some *Beaufort d'Alpage.*

Louvre & Champs-Elysées

The best chocolate in the world is from **Bernachon** in Lyon—only a two-hour train ride away.

Landing at **Charles de Gaulle** airport after being away from Paris for more than two weeks.

Frank Mielert
General Manager, Grand Hôtel Inter-Continental

Favorite deluxe hotels: **Le Bristol** and the **Concorde-Lafayette** (outstanding values for the money).

Favorite small hotel: **L'Hôtel.**

Favorite restaurants: **Le Dodin-Bouffant** for the best food and wine in Paris for a reasonable price, and **Pavillon des Princes** on Avenue de la Porte d'Auteuil.

Favorite places for drinks: **Bar du Grand Hôtel** and **Harry's Bar.**

Most French citizens prefer leg of lamb over any other main course. But a staggering 32 percent choose mixed salad and another 21 percent choose pasta as their favorite dish, over traditional cassoulets, stews, sausages, and beans. When asked to select from a list of food what they would miss most if it became unavailable, two-thirds said bread, and only one in 10 said they would miss red wine—for many a symbol of *la vie francaise.* While McDonald's and Burger King do a booming business in this culinary capital, only one in 200 French people admit to eating *le fast food.* When presented with a list of "luxury" gifts, 58 percent chose dinner with friends in a four-star restaurant, and 13 percent preferred to devour the complete works of Marcel Proust.

Claude Terrail
Owner, La Tour d'Argent restaurant

Place des Vosges, which represents so much of the history of France.

Walking through the **Marais** and the **Ile St.-Louis.**

Place de la Concorde at dawn and the view from the **Carrousel** all the way up the **Champs-Elysées** to **Place d'Etoile**—when one is accompanied by a beautiful woman.

My three favorite churches: **Notre-Dame, Ste.-Clotilde, Ste.-Geneviève.**

Paris' greatest monument is the **Seine.**

I love the brasseries because there is no jealousy about tables, just a kind of peace hard to find in other public places. At **Lipp,** for example, even the politicians refrain from quarreling.

Oysters and crab at **La Coupole** on a late Sunday night.

Drinking downstairs and dining upstairs at **Castel's.**

Zipping about Paris on a motorcycle, and window-shopping in fair weather.

Hubert de Givenchy
Fashion Designer

I don't have the time to wait three weeks for a reservation at some of the more famous restaurants in Paris, but I like good food and a pleasant atmosphere. I find them both at **Le Quai Voltaire, Caviar Kaspia, Chez Gildo** (for Italian cuisine) on Rue de Grenelle, **Le Stresa** (for the prosciutto and asparagus) on Rue Chambiges, **L'Orangerie** on a Sunday night, and **Au Cochon d'Or.**

Jean Castel
Owner of Castel's Restaurant and Nightclub

St.-Germain-des-Prés and **St.-Sulpice** churches.

The magic triangle: **Lipp, Flore,** and the **Deux Magots** cafés.

Place de Furstemberg, the **Cour de Rohan,** the antique shops, art galleries, bookstores, small hotels, and the inhabitants.

My part of Paris; the **sixth arrondissement.**

Peter C. Balas
President, Inter-Continental Hotels, Europe/Middle East

Favorite deluxe hotel: **Hôtel Meurice.**

Favorite small hotel: **Hôtel de Castille** on Rue Cambon.

Favorite hotel restaurant: **Opéra Restaurant** at the **Grand Hôtel** on Rue Scribe.

Favorite restaurant in Paris: **L'Ami Louis** bistro on Rue Vert-Bois.

Favorite place for drinks: **Maxim's** upstairs bar.

According to the French Perfume Committee, the French use an average of two-and-a-half bars of soap per person per year. They lag behind the Italians, who use more than three bars, the Germans, who use four, and the British, who use five.

Steven Spurrier
Wine Merchant; Author

Taking a taxi along the Right Bank quai to my flat in the Bastille and passing Ile de la Cité and Ile St.-Louis. There is no other view in the world quite like it.

Walking in the evening from my office to **Place de la Concorde** with all its illuminated globes and seeing the **Eiffel Tower** lit up in the distance.

The métro is the best in the world. The Paris stations are not as deep as London's and the cars here are bigger and cleaner. In London I ride the underground for convenience. In Paris it's for sheer pleasure.

Chez Joséphine, a restaurant where everyone eats seriously without being boring about it. Order anything on the menu with truffles when they are in season. The wine list is wonderful.

Alain Dutournier's **Au Trou Gascon.**

Le Rubis, always jammed with customers. The smoked ham and tartines are wonderful. I prefer the white wines that are bought directly from the producers. The reds can be a bit thick.

Willi's Wine Bar with its magnificent wine list, especially the Rhones.

Caviar Kaspia, because it is near my office and it makes me feel rich when I eat caviar and drink champagne there, although I feel poor when I get the bill.

Le Cherche Midi for Italian home cooking and the best hors d'oeuvres in Paris (somehow, even in the middle of winter, the tomatoes and basil are always fresh).

Café de la Nouvelle Mairie for its rigorous selection of Loire Valley wines. It is run by a working-class Frenchman who does it all himself. One-hundred percent better than L'Ecluse.

Looking in the store windows of men's shops, knowing I can buy better and cheaper in London.

The **Picasso Museum, Musée d'Orsay,** and dropping into the **Carnavalet Museum** to see the old working sign collection.

My favorite walk is from **Place des Victoires** through **Palais Royal** and the **Louvre,** across the **Seine,** down **Ile de la Cité** and **Ile St.-Louis,** across **Pont Sully** to **Bastille,** past **Place des Vosges,** up Rue des Francs-Bourgeois by the **Beaubourg,** and back to Place des Victoires. I know I miss Montmartre, Montparnasse, and all the rest of Paris, but if I had to choose, I'd pick this walk.

La Coupole, because it's always fun, the service is excellent, and anyone can get in, be they *clochard* or *duchesse*. When I've rung up half a dozen restaurants that are booked, I always seem to end up here.

The ease with which one can get out of Paris and into the French countryside (the traffic coming back on Sunday nights, however, is terrible).

The French, who are more friendly than people give them credit for. You may have to make more of an effort to prove yourself, but the effort is richly repaid. The secret in a conversation with a French person is to talk about *him* or *her* rather than yourself.

Pierre Salinger
ABC News, European Correspondent

The view of the **Eiffel Tower** from my office window.

A twilight trip on the **Seine,** riding on a *bateau mouche.*

Dinner at the **Jules Verne** restaurant in the Eiffel Tower.

Lunch at the **Espadon Grill** at the **Ritz.**

Visiting the **Georges Pompidou Center** in Beaubourg.

Sunday lunch at **Brasserie Lipp.**

Walking with my dog, Marmelade, in the **Bois de Boulogne** in fair weather.

Purchasing a good seat at the **Longchamp Racetrack** during the Arc de Triomphe race in the Bois de Boulogne on the first Sunday of October.

A trip to the airport without a traffic jam.

Soft-boiled eggs and purée of truffles at **Faugeron,** anytime.

A hamburger at **Burger King** on the **Champs-Elysées.**

Marcel Marceau
Mime

L'Auvergnat 1900 and **Etoile d'Asie** on Rue Jean-Mermoz.

The **Théâtre des Champs-Elysées.**

Louvre & Champs-Elysées

Linda Duchin
Director of Special Projects, Cinecom Films

The children's puppet show in the Luxembourg Gardens, where the kids sit in front and the grownups in back. The children scream and yell at the puppets and then the candy lady comes to serve them.

The magic show and room of mirrors (**Palais de Mirage**) at the **Musée Grevin,** where palm trees and other bizarre objects descend from the ceiling and are reflected thousands of times, transporting you on a wonderfully funky journey to exotic locales.

The **Hammam de la Mosquée de Paris** on Rue Geoffroy St.-Hilaire, which is the closest you can ever come to the ambience of a harem. Step out of the baths and into an Arab tearoom that serves a fresh mint brew and Oriental pastries.

The taxidermy at **Deyrolle,** my favorite store, on Rue du Bac.

The **Clown Bar** near the Cirque d'Hiver with its fabulous Belle Epoque tiles of circus scenes and photographs of circus performers.

Eating passion-fruit ice cream at **Berthillon.**

The **Pagoda Cinema** in St.-Germain; exquisite Oriental interior.

Ste.-Chapelle, the rose garden of the **Bagatelle, Place des Vosges, Bofinger, Le Train Bleu, Giverny,** and **Vaux-le-Vicomte.**

The annual **Fête de Musique** in June, when there is dancing in the streets all night long and music in the most beautiful places.

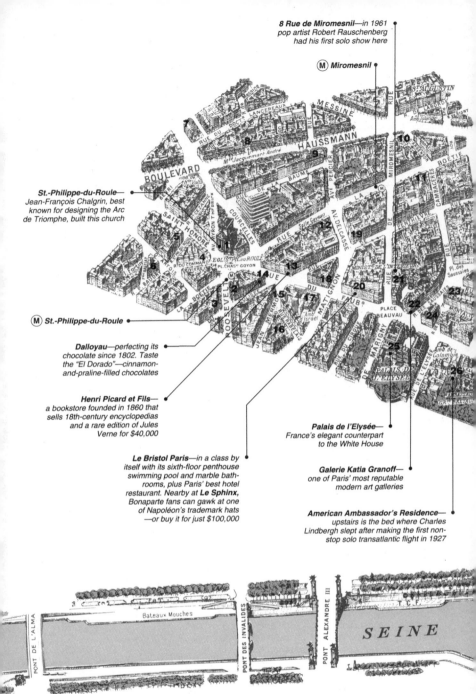

8 Rue de Miromesnil—in 1961 pop artist Robert Rauschenberg had his first solo show here

Ⓜ **Miromesnil** •

St.-Philippe-du-Roule—Jean-François Chalgrin, best known for designing the Arc de Triomphe, built this church

Ⓜ **St.-Philippe-du-Roule** •

Dalloyau—perfecting its chocolate since 1802. Taste the "El Dorado"—cinnamon-and-praline-filled chocolates

Henri Picard et Fils—a bookstore founded in 1860 that sells 18th-century encyclopedias and a rare edition of Jules Verne for $40,000

Le Bristol Paris—in a class by itself with its sixth-floor penthouse swimming pool and marble bathrooms, plus Paris' best hotel restaurant. Nearby at **Le Sphinx**, Bonaparte fans can gawk at one of Napoléon's trademark hats —or buy it for just $100,000

Palais de l'Elysée—France's elegant counterpart to the White House

Galerie Katia Granoff—one of Paris' most reputable modern art galleries

American Ambassador's Residence—upstairs is the bed where Charles Lindbergh slept after making the first non-stop solo transatlantic flight in 1927

St.-Honoré

Move over Fifth Avenue and Rodeo Drive. The **Faubourg-St.-Honoré**, named after the patron saint of pastry chefs, takes the cake as the world's most glamorous shopping district. *La plus haute* of international haute couture is here en masse: Christian Dior, Yves Saint Laurent, Lanvin, Gucci, Hermès, Pierre Cardin, Guy Laroche, Ungaro, Courrèges, Jean-Paul Gaultier, and countless purveyors of such extravagances as diamonds, crystal, silver, mink, caviar, truffles, and champagne.

Lanvin—for women's scarves, perfume, haute couture, and prêt-à-porter

Hermès—the most celebrated leather-goods emporium in the world

British Embassy

Chapelle Expiatoire—where victims of the Revolution (Marie Antoinette, Louis XVI, and Charlotte Corday) are interred

Place de la Madeleine—specialty food shops to spoil the spoiled; a lively flower market blossoms Tuesday through Sunday

Marquise de Sévigné—superlative macaroons and hot chocolate

American Express

Café de la Paix—a historical landmark once frequented by Salvador Dalí, Harry Truman, Maurice Chevalier, and Maria Callas

Charles Garnier's famous **Opéra**—don't miss the white marble Grand Staircase and Marc Chagall's 1964 ceiling masterpiece

(M) **Concorde**

Lucas-Carton—four-star nouvelle cuisine by superstar chef Alain Senderens

28 Rue Boissy-d'Anglas—site of the old *Le Bœuf sur le Toit*, a famous avant-garde nightclub

Carita—a lavish hair salon whose clients include Catherine Deneuve, Paloma Picasso, and French rocker Johnny Hallyday

Place Vendôme—home of the Hôtel Ritz and one of the world's greatest concentrations of jewelers, perfumeries, and banks

Cadolle—a lingerie shop run by a descendant of the woman who reportedly invented the brassiere

(M) **Tuileries**

(M) **Opéra**

(M) **Pyramides**

Scribe—this deluxe hotel served as the Allied Forces' press headquarters at the end of World War II

(M) = Métro

137

Chartier—*a cavernous Belle Epoque soup kitchen with pinwheel fans, surly waiters, and reasonable prices*

Ⓜ *Richelieu-Drouot*

Ⓜ *4-Septembre*

Ⓜ *Bourse*

Bibliothèque Nationale—*look through the glass door of the Second Empire reading room at the breathtaking domed ceiling by Labrouste*

Les Passages—*on a rainy day chart a walk through the interconnecting turn-of-the-century tunnels*

Willi's Wine Bar—*one of Paris' most elegant watering holes bustles nonstop*

Le Grand Véfour—*a favorite Parisian restaurant where Napoléon courted Josephine, Victor Hugo romanticized, and Colette and Jean Cocteau, who lived nearby, enjoyed regular repasts*

Robert Capia—*Catherine Deneuve's favorite antique store*

Chez Nous—*Paris' best jock bar and restaurant is run by ex-rugby player Gilbert Ghiraldi*

Ⓜ *Pyramides*

Manufacture Nationale de Sèvres—*the famous Sèvres porcelain factory's showroom*

Ⓜ *Palais-Royal*

Comédie Française—*where Molière and the divine Sarah Bernhardt once performed*

Palais Royal Garden—*a six-acre enclave of flowering serenity perfect for picnics*

Chez Pauline—*a relaxed restaurant serving French classics*

Ⓜ *= Mé*

This walk includes other dazzlements as well. There is a small, remarkable art collection at the **Musée Jacquemart-André;** several architectural jewels, including **St.-Roch** (the city's finest Baroque church), the splendid **Palais Royal** and its gardens, and the vaulted reading room of the **Bibliothèque Nationale;** the city's two most important theaters, the **Paris Opéra** and **Comédie Française;** and several grand hotels, such as **Le Bristol, St.-James et Albany,** and the **Hôtel Ritz,** whose name is synonymous with luxury. Rue du Faubourg-St.-Honoré is made for that favorite Parisian pastime, *flânerie élégante* (tasteful loitering).

The St.-Honoré walk is best taken on a weekday from Tuesday through Friday, since many shops and exhibits are closed on Monday, and the streets are crowded on weekends. Start with an early-bird pastry and coffee at one of the Right Bank's finest bakeries, **Boulangerie St.-Philippe** (open at 7:30AM), and continue down Rue du Faubourg-St.-Honoré to the street's most fashionable stretch, which lies between the presidential **Palais de l'Elysée** at Avenue Matignon and Rue Royale. Those getting a slow jump on the day might consider visiting **Le Val d'Or,** a popular neighborhood wine bar, where an elite crowd stands *tuer le ver* (killing the worm) with a mid-morning Bordeaux. While lovers of the Italian Renaissance keep their date with **Donatello, Botticelli,** and **Titian** at the Musée Jacquemart-André, serious shoppers will head down past embassy row (where the American, British, and Japanese ambassadors hang their hats) and make a mandatory stop at **Hermès,** the world-famous leather and accessories shop.

As you pass onto Rue Royale, which starts at legendary **Maxim's** and ends near **Fauchon** (the "millionaires' supermarket"), you will look upon the finest in antiques, tapestries, jewelry, and silver. By midday you will have reached **Place de la Madeleine.**

Survey the plaza and whet your appetite with the truffles at **La Maison de la Truffe,** chocolates at **Marquise de Sévigné,** and the cheese at **La Ferme St.-Hubert.** When you're finished with those delicacies, why not splurge your life's savings on the four-star nouvelle cuisine at **Lucas-Carton** or on a feast of caviar and champagne at **Caviar Kaspia?** If, however, you're down to your last few francs, settle for a modest, though tasty, repast at **Ladurée** or **L'Ecluse.** Those feeling brash and regal by turns could knock back a shot of one of the 156 whiskies sold at **Harry's Bar** and weave into **Charvet** to buy a cravat, as **Edward VII** was in the habit of doing not so long ago.

While your partner is changing money at **American Express,** line up for tickets inside the Paris Opéra, Charles Garnier's architectural birthday cake also known as the Opéra Garnier. If you're an antique hound, **Le Louvre des Antiquaires** (240 dealers under one roof) is the place for you. Otherwise, go gape at the Bibliothèque Nationale's reading room or watch (as did everyone from Louis XIV to Colette) the sun set on the gardens of the Palais Royal. Dinnertime already? Consider the best (and most expensive) sushi in Paris at **Issé,** a hearty cassoulet at the **Globe d'Or,** or an Alsatian specialty at **La Providence.** Or go for broke at **Le Grand Véfour.** Nightlife in the neighborhood might consist of polishing your French at the Comédie Française, a night at the Opéra, taking in a movie on Boulevard Haussmann, or an evening of people-watching on the terrace of **Café de la Paix.** You can start burning off the day's calories by returning to the beginning of the walk and dancing till dawn at **Keur Samba.**

1 St.-Philippe-du-Roule Before Jean-François Chalgrin (better known for his Arc de Triomphe) built this church, its parishioners prayed in the chapel of a local leprosy asylum. The floor plan, three aisles divided by two rows of fluted Ionic columns, resembles that of the early Christian basilicas. ◆ 153 Rue du Faubourg-St.-Honoré. Métro: St.-Philippe-du-Roule

2 Le Val d'Or ★★★$ On the ground floor of the St.-Honoré's most popular wine bar you'll find all the ingredients for a great quick lunch: quiche, charcuterie, perhaps the best sandwiches in Paris, and, of course, wines admi-

rably selected by **Monsieur Rongier.** Downstairs, for those with leisure to dine, there's a hearty beef Bourguignonne. Try the Côtes-du-Brouilly and Côtes-du-Rhône, and, in November, the new Beaujolais, the best of which Rongier somehow always manages to snag. Under the exceedingly civil house rules, wine must be ordered by the bottle, but you pay only for what you drink. Lunchtime is the liveliest time. ◆ M-F 7:30AM-9PM; Sa 9AM-6PM; closed Christmas Day and New Year's Day. 28 Ave Franklin-D.-Roosevelt. Métro: St.-Philippe-du-Roule. 43.59.95.81

3 Keur Samba This nightclub uncorks around 2AM when actors, models, musicians, and diplomats of every stripe and color push their way past **Kane** at the door and into this black-upholstered, after-hours playpen. Located near Régine's and Elysée Matignon. ◆ Cover. Daily midnight-7AM. 79 Rue La Boétie. Métro: St.-Philippe-du-Roule. 43.59.03.10

4 Boulangerie St.-Philippe ★★$/$$ This bakery's luncheonette (beside the crowded bread counter) features *foie de veau à la* *vapeur,* delicious house terrines, grilled meats, and wine by the glass. Order one of the eclairs, a slice of lime tart, or *tarte tatin* for dessert and find out why the bakery is always crowded. ♦ M-F, Su 7:30AM-7:30PM. 73 Ave Franklin-D.-Roosevelt. Métro: St.-Philippe-du-Roule. 43.59.78.76

4 Lord Sandwich ★★$$ Umpteen varieties of sandwiches are served on pita bread or rye. Rich brownies, berry tarts, and apple cider as well. It's crowded, but pleasantly so. ♦ M-F 9AM-5PM. 134 Rue du Faubourg-St.-Honoré. No credit cards. Métros: Miromesnil, St.-Philippe-du-Roule. 42.56.41.68

4 Cailleux This shop is full of works primarily by 18th-century artists: drawings and paintings by the likes of **Watteau, Boucher,** and **Fragonard.** ♦ M-F 9AM-noon, 2-6PM; closed in Aug. 136 Rue du Faubourg-St.-Honoré. Métro: St.-Philippe-du-Roule. 43.59.25.24

5 Bradford $$ A surprising oasis of calm and friendliness wedged in between the harried Champs-Elysées and Rue du Faubourg-St.-Honoré. Rooms are spick-and-span and even big enough to dance in. ♦ 10 Rue St.-Philippe-du-Roule. Métro: St.-Philippe-du-Roule. 43.59.24.20, 42.25.43.71

5 La Poularde Landaise ★$$/$$$ A midwinter-night's dream: flickering firelight plays over the dark

St.-Honoré

beams of this restaurant, which serves full-bodied cuisine and regional wines from southwest France. Best bets include *pleurote* mushrooms with garlic, *confit de canard,* and, for dessert, *tarte tatin.* ♦ M-F noon-3PM, 7-10PM. 4 Rue St.-Philippe-du-Roule. Reservations recommended. Métro: St.-Philippe-du-Roule. 43.59.20.25

6 L'Artois ★★$$ A popular bistro rife with gray-suited business types who come for the sole Isidore (baked with white wine, tomatoes, and shallots), that old standby coq au vin, and the homemade desserts. ♦ M-F 12:15-2:30PM, 7-10:30PM; closed one month in the summer. 13 Rue d'Artois. Reservations recommended. Métros: Franklin-D.-Roosevelt, St.-Philippe-du-Roule. 42.25.01.10

7 C.T. Loo and Co. Located in a fantastic three-story salmon pagoda equipped with a Chinese elevator, **Michael Bosc's** Asian art gallery displays and traffics in Orientalia from lacquered hardwood furniture from the Ming Dynasty to 13th-century Nepalese sculpture. ♦ M-Sa 10:30AM-12:30PM, 2:30-6:30PM; closed in Aug. 48 Rue de Courcelles. Métro: Miromesnil. 45.62.53.15, 42.25.17.23

8 Musée Jacquemart-André Originally this Neoclassical building was the private residence of banker **Edouard André** and artist **Nélie Jacquemart.** The couple poured considerable wealth into their exquisite collection of art, which now belongs to the **Institut de France.** Among the Italian Renaissance and French 18th-century art still at home here are works by **Donatello, Botticelli, Tintoretto, Titian, Bernini, Watteau, Fragonard, Tiepolo, Rembrandt, Reynolds,** and **Murillo,** as well as four **Gobelins** tapestries. ♦ Free. M, Th-Su 11AM-6PM; Tu 1-6PM; W 11AM-10PM. 158 Blvd Haussmann. Métro: Miromesnil. 45.62.39.94

9 Ma Bourgogne ★$$ The owner of this reputable wine bar, **Louis Prin,** won the coveted *Meilleur Pot* award in 1962 and is known for his hot daily lunch specials. ♦ M-F 7AM-8:30PM. 133 Blvd Haussmann. Reservations recommended for lunch. Métro: Miromesnil. 45.63.50.61, 45.63.56.62

10 Le Marcande ★★$$$/$$$$ Chef **Thierry Lemoine** allows the visitor not only a view of a charming courtyard, but of himself at work in the kitchen (separated by a glass partition), where he prepares such dishes as crayfish, gazpacho, pigeon in a rhubarb glaze, and a delicious chocolate cake with mint. ♦ M-F noon-2PM, 8-10PM; closed three weeks in Aug. 52 Rue Miromesnil. Reservations recommended. Métro: Miromesnil. 42.65.19.14

10 René-Gérard Saint-Ouen Instead of clay, this artist shapes bread dough into a loaf for any whim or occasion: elephants, chickens, half-moons, bicycles, even the Eiffel Tower. Your imagination sets the limit. If you can't bring yourself to eat these yeasty works of art, brush on some varnish and hang them in the kitchen. ♦ M-Sa 8AM-7PM. 111 Blvd Haussmann. Métro: Miromesnil. 42.65.06.25

11 19 Rue La Boétie The 13-year-old **Henry James** developed an addiction to the croissants sold across the street when he lived here from 1856 to 1857. ♦ Métro: St.-Philippe-du-Roule

12 45 Rue La Boétie Here in the **Salle Gaveau,** in June 1921, Harvard's glee club became the first American glee club to sing in France. ♦ Métro: St.-Philippe-du-Roule

13 Henri Picard et Fils Founded in 1860, this exquisite bookstore deals in treasures such as **Diderot's** 35-volume, 18th-century encyclopedia; *Democracy in America* by **Alexis de Tocqueville;** and a rare 47-volume edition of **Jules Verne's** work worth $40,000. ♦ M-Sa 10AM-12:30PM, 2-7PM; closed in Aug. 126 Rue du Faubourg-St.-Honoré. Métro: St.-Philippe-du-Roule. 43.59.28.11

In 1789 the population of Paris was 650,000—about the same as San Francisco's today.

14 Dalloyau This dessert shop has been perfecting its chocolate since 1802. Sunday-morning lines bear witness to the best croissants in town. Sample the El Dorado (cinnamon-and-praline-filled chocolates) or a *gâteau mogador* (a confection of chocolate cake and chocolate mousse with a racing stripe of raspberry jam), or its best-selling Opéra, with layer upon layer of differently textured chocolate. ♦ Daily 9AM-9PM. 101 Rue du Faubourg-St.-Honoré. Métro: St.-Philippe-du-Roule. 43.59.18.10

15 Chez Germain ★$/$$ An inexpensive bistro serving quick lunches to the models, fashion designers, and art dealers who work in the neighborhood. Sample the *petit salé aux lentilles, blanquette de veau,* and steak in Roquefort sauce. ♦ M-F noon-2PM, 8-9:30PM. 19 Rue Jean-Mermoz. Reservations recommended for lunch. Métro: Franklin-D.-Roosevelt. 43.59.29.24

16 Au Petit Montmorency ★★★$$$ The culinary whimsy of chef **Daniel Bouché** lures back chic customers again and again. Here you'll find such offbeat specialties as baked hare with truffles, *foie gras de canard au caramel poivre,* warm truffle salad, and, for dessert, hot hazelnut soufflé. ♦ M-F noon-3PM, 7:30-10:15PM; closed in Aug. Reservations recommended. 5 Rue Rabelais. Métros: Franklin-D.-Roosevelt, St.-Philippe-du-Roule. 42.25.11.19

17 83 Rue du Faubourg-St.-Honoré Around 1840 **William Thackeray** took a small pied-à-terre here. ♦ Métro: St.-Philippe-du-Roule

18 Jullien Cornic This prestigious shop is a Circe's Isle to connoisseurs and collectors of art books. Among its allures are beautifully bound catalogs of the oeuvres of artists as diverse as **Edouard Manet** and **Norman Rockwell,** and an eclectic assortment of books on interior design, architecture, and fashion (everything on the rag trade from Balmain to buttons). An annex around the corner specializes in rare art books. ♦ M-F 9AM-1PM, 2-6PM. 118 Rue du Faubourg-St.-Honoré; Annex: 29 Ave Matignon. Métro: St.-Philippe-du-Roule. 42.68.10.10

19 Trompe-l'Oeil On the corner of Rue de Penthièvre and Avenue Delcassé, a man gazes from his balcony at a bronze nude as two doves flutter away, casting shadows on the walls. Painted by artist **Rieti** in 1985, this trompe l'oeil enlivens an otherwise unremarkable intersection. ♦ Métros: Miromesnil, St.-Philippe-du-Roule

---

Paris is full of archaeological digs in progress. Interested volunteers should contact the Direction des Antiquités de l'Ile-de-France, Fouille du Louvre, Donjon du Vieux-Fort, Château de Vincennes, 94300 Vincennes.

Restaurants/Nightlife: Red   **Hotels:** Blue
Shops/ 🌳 Outdoors: Green   **Sights/Culture:** Black

20 Le Bristol Paris $$$$ One of the last and perhaps the most prestigious of Paris' grand hotels, the Bristol caters to the diplomats and dignitaries who conduct business down the street at the Elysée Palace. Features such as the sixth-floor penthouse swimming pool and marble bathrooms place the Bristol in a class by itself. This sumptuous hotel boasts of having had **Ulysses S. Grant** as a guest in the fall of 1887. **Sinclair Lewis** lived here in 1925, the year he won the Pulitzer Prize (which he declined to accept) for his novel *Arrowsmith.* And, in 1975, the celebration of **Josephine Baker's** 50th anniversary in show business was held in this hotel. ♦ 112 Rue du Faubourg-St.-Honoré. Métros: Champs-Elysées-Clemenceau, Miromesnil, St.-Philippe-du-Roule. 42.66.91.45

Within Le Bristol Paris:

Le Bristol ★★$$$/$$$$ Chef **Emile Tabourdiau** provides refined nouvelle cuisine that suits the elegance of the restaurant's Regency wood-paneled decor. Le Bristol is one of the very few Paris hotel restaurants that has been awarded two Michelin stars. ♦ Daily 12:30-2:30PM, 7-10:30PM. Reservations recommended. 42.66.91.45

St.-Honoré

Bar du Bristol ★★$$ Don't order lemonade from this barkeep: **Michel** is vice president of the French Association of Bartenders. Try the *Nathaly* (a drink named after Michel's daughter, with Grand Marnier, white Martini vermouth, cognac, and raspberry brandy). ♦ Daily 11AM-1:30AM

20 Le Sphinx Together with its sister shop, **L'Aigle Imperiale** (around the corner at 3 Rue de Miromesnil, 42.65.27.33), Le Sphinx has one of the city's largest collections of antique weapons and Napoleonic memorabilia. Here you will find portraits of the emperor, a bottle of 1811 cognac he never got around to drinking, and one of Napoléon's trademark hats enshrined in a glass case. Le Sphinx's proprietor, **Pierre de Souzy,** will part with the latter item for a mere $100,000. ♦ M-Sa 10:30AM-1PM, 2-7PM. 104 Rue du Faubourg-St.-Honoré. Métro: St.-Philippe-du-Roule. 42.65.90.96

21 Arts et Marine A veritable armada of handcrafted models of wooden sailing vessels floats before your eyes. Among the replicas are a sleek 1830 slave ship, Napoléon's 1811 ceremonial barge, and the *USS Constitution.* Also for sale are old brass compasses, ivory-clad binoculars, and a great many frigates in bottles. Sufficient nauticalia, in short, to salt up any landlubber. ♦ M-F 11AM-7PM; closed in Aug. 8 Rue de Miromesnil. Métro: Miromesnil. 42.65.27.85

21 8 Rue de Miromesnil In May 1961 pop artist **Robert Rauschenberg's** first solo show was held here and received rave reviews. ♦ Métro: Miromesnil

22 Hôtel de Beauvau **Le Camus de Mezières** designed this mansion for **Prince Charles de Beauvau,** but the Revolution transferred it to the hands of the state. The Ministry of the Interior has resided behind its ornate iron gates since 1861. ♦ 96 Rue du Faubourg-St.-Honoré. Métro: St.-Philippe-du-Roule

22 Galerie Katia Granoff One of the city's most reputable modern art galleries. ♦ M 2-7PM; Tu-F noon-7PM; Sa noon-1PM, 2:30-7PM. 92 Rue du Faubourg-St.-Honoré. Métro: St.-Philippe-du-Roule. 42.65.24.41

23 Au Vieux Saussaies This shop trades in 18th- and 19th-century silver—from sugar bowls to samovars, evening bags to champagne ice buckets. You will find top-name *orfevrerie* here at lower prices than at some of the other dealers. ♦ Tu-Sa 11AM-7PM. 14 Rue des Saussaies. Métro: St.-Philippe-du-Roule. 42.65.32.71

24 Muriel A remnant of Old Paris, this is one of the few remaining boutiques that sells only gloves. ♦ M-Sa 10AM-6:30PM, Sep-June; Tu-Sa 10AM-6:30PM, July-Aug; closed one or two weeks in Aug. 4 Rue des Saussaies. Métro: St.-Philippe-du-Roule. 42.65.95.34

St.-Honoré

25 Palais de l'Elysée The most famous address on Rue du Faubourg-St.-Honoré, if not all of France, is this country's counterpart of the White House. Built in 1718 to a design by **Molet,** the Elysée Palace has been the official residence of the French president since 1873. The public is not admitted, but you can glimpse at the dignified facade through the gateway. The palace was purchased in 1753 by **Madame de Pompadour, Louis XV's** rich and spoiled mistress, who hired the architects **Lassurance, de Boucher,** and

de Van Lee to expand her palace and extend the gardens to the Champs-Elysées. Expropriated to serve as a government printing office (for the *Bulletin des Lois*) and dance hall during the Revolution, the mansion became a hideaway for the **Empress Joséphine** after she was divorced by **Napoléon.** At one time, the Elysée Palace was known as the **Hameau Chantilly** and was the site of a restaurant and fairgrounds run by an ice cream maker named **Velloni.** On 22 June 1815 Napoléon signed his second abdication here. Subsequently, the **Duke of Wellington** and Russian **Czar Alexander I** stayed here. The history is rather confusing but worth a pause. ♦ 55 Rue du Faubourg-St.-Honoré. Métro: St.-Philippe-du-Roule

26 American Ambassador's Residence In the 19th century the **Hôtel de Pontalba** was owned by financier and art collector **Baron Edmond de Rothschild.** (When the baron died in 1934 at the age of 89, he left 3,000 drawings and 43,000 postage stamps to the Louvre.) The US government had the good taste to rent the *hôtel particulier* from **Baron Maurice de Rothschild** to serve as the residence of the American ambassador. The 40-room, 13-bathroom building is not open to the public, but if you are invited for dinner by the ambassador, you will see the original **Oudry** wood paneling and paintings by **John Singer Sargent, Cézanne,** and **van Gogh.** In one of the upstairs guest rooms is the bed where **Charles Lindbergh** slept after completing the first nonstop solo flight across the Atlantic on 21 May 1927. ♦ 41 Rue du Faubourg-St.-Honoré. Métro: St.-Philippe-du-Roule

27 British Embassy The lovely **Hôtel de Charost,** built by **Mazarin** in 1720, was bought by **Napoléon's** pet sister, **Pauline,** who after a tumultuous series of loves and marriages, became the **Princess Borghese.** In 1815, after Waterloo, the princess sold her **Palais Borghese** to George III of England, who turned it into his nation's embassy. Upstairs is Pauline's bed with gilded curtains descending from the talons of a Napoleonic eagle. The building is not open to the public. ♦ 39 Rue du Faubourg-St.-Honoré. Métro: Concorde

Palais de l'Elysée

Rue du Faubourg-St.-Honoré Shopping Map

RUE DU CIRQUE
Pierre Cardin
women's clothing

AVENUE DE MARIGNY
Palais de l'Elysée

RUE DE L'ELYSEE
Leon Vissot
furs
Alimia
women's clothing
Jean Lupu
antiques
Hiroko Koshino
women's clothing
British Embassy
Espace Pierre Cardin
women's clothing
Lancôme
cosmetics
Gucci
leather goods
Ted Lapidus
women's clothing
Cartier
jewelry

Karl Lagerfeld
women's clothing

RUE BOISSY D'ANGLAS
Lanvin
men's & women's clothing
Istante
women's clothing
Carita
beauty products
La Baggagerie
leather goods
Hanae Mori
women's clothing
Jaeger
women's clothing
Igin
women's clothing

RUE ROYALE

RUE DE MIROMESNIL
Perrin
antiques
Armorial
leather goods
Galerie Katia Granoff
contemporary art

RUE DES SAUSSAIES
Stéphane Kélian
women's shoes
Lilane Romi
women's evening wear
Jean-Louis Scherrer
women's clothing
Louis Féraud
women's clothing
Popoff & Cie
porcelain, paintings
S.L. Dupont
pens, watches, fine gifts
Marina
baby clothes, shoes
Maxim's
women's clothing

RUE DE DURAS
Burma
jewelry
Le Tanneur
leather goods
Sonia Rykiel
women's clothing
Arfan
jewelry
Etro
men's & women's clothing
Gianni Versace
women's clothing
Zilli
men's clothing

RUE D'AGUESSEAU
Chloé
women's clothing
Ungaro
women's clothing
Au Vieux Venise
antiques
Fratelli Rossetti
men's & women's shoes
Rety
women's & children's clothing
Cour aux Antiquaires
antiques
La Fontaine Dauphin
optician
Parfumerie Douglas International
beauty products
Cassandre
women's clothing, leather goods
Courrèges
women's clothing

RUE D'ANJOU
Maxandre
women's clothing
Hôtel de Castiglione
Yves Saint Laurent
men's & women's clothing
Jun Ashida
women's clothing
Yves Saint Laurent
women's accessories
Guy Laroche
women's clothing
Givenchy
women's clothing
Hermès
leather goods, scarves, saddlery

RUE BOISSY D'ANGLAS
Lanvin
men's & women's clothing
Maurice Segoura
art, antiques
Eva Segoura
objets d'art
André Chékière
men's clothing
Charles Jourdan
men's & women's shoes
Aldebert
jewelry
Benetton
men's, women's, & children's clothing
Gucci
leather goods

RUE ROYALE

(Side label: RUE DU FAUBOURG-ST.-HONORE)

---

27 33 Rue du Faubourg-St.-Honoré Built by the architect **Grandhomme** in 1714, this house was the home of **Duc Decres,** who was minister of the French Navy until 1820, when a bomb hidden beneath his bed dealt him a mortal wound. For seven subsequent years, it housed the Russian Embassy, until it was sold to **Nathaniel Rothschild.** In 1918 the house was born anew as **Cercle de l'Union Interalliée,** a swank international businessmen's club. ♦ Métro: Concorde

27 Japanese Embassy In 1718 **Lassurance** built this *hôtel* for **Louis Blouin,** confidant and premier *valet de chambre* of **Louis XIV. Napoléon's** sister and brother lived here, as did the king of Bavaria. Currently, it's the Japanese ambassador's turn. ♦ 31 Rue du Faubourg-St.-Honoré. Métro: Concorde

28 Georges Bernard Antiquités Sate that craving to magnify, measure, and modify. Bernard, co-author of a book on corkscrews, specializes in old scientific instruments. ♦ M-Sa 10:30AM-6:30PM; closed two weeks in Aug. 1 Rue d'Anjou. Métro: Concorde. 42.65.23.83

29 Castiglione $$$ This hotel's high prices are in keeping with its choice location amid the splendorous boutiques. Unfortunately, a mod-

St.-Honoré

ern face-lift has left it a hostelry in search of character. ♦ 38-40 Rue du Faubourg-St.-Honoré. Métro: Concorde. 42.65.07.50

29 Hermès Started in 1837 as a saddle store by **Thierry Hermès,** *artisan d'élite,* this is perhaps the most celebrated leather-goods emporium in the world. Having outlasted the age of the horse and carriage, Hermès now furnishes the leather fittings for Lear jets. Its bags are considered necessities, not accessories. Hermès gloves are unsurpassed in craftsmanship, and its signature scarves are huge and tend toward horsey designs. Hermès' scarves come in more than 200 styles, the most popular of which is the Brides de Gala, and more than a half-million of these silken trifles are sold every year. ♦ M-Sa 10AM-1PM, 2:15-6:30PM, July-Aug; M, Sa 10AM-1PM, 2:15-6:30PM, Tu-F 10AM-6:30PM, Sep-June. 24 Rue du Faubourg-St.-Honoré. Métro: Concorde. 40.17.47.17

Within Hermès:

Hermès Museum On the top floor is a private museum displaying old saddles, ornamented trunks, and even **Napoléon's** stirrups. ♦ For admission, write in advance to the store manager: Hermès, 24 Rue de Faubourg-St.-Honoré, Paris 75008

John Lobb On the second floor is the Paris branch of the super-reputable London shoe- and boot-maker. Join the ranks of other satisfied Lobb alumni: **Lyndon Johnson,** the **Shah of Iran, Gary Cooper,** and the **Duke of Edinburgh.** Stop in to be measured heel to toe, after which one of Lobb's cobblers will fashion two wooden lasts (one for each foot) on which to model your shoes. In the nearby studio, the skins are cut and stitched, and in one month (first-time customers must wait a year), this labor will have produced a noble pair of handmade shoes sure to last at least a decade— and all for a mere $2,000 per pair. ♦ M, Sa 10AM-1PM, 2:15-6:30PM; Tu-F 10AM-6:30PM; closed in Aug. 24 Rue du Faubourg-St.-Honoré. Métro: Concorde. 42.65.24.45

30 28 Rue Boissy-d'Anglas The site of **Le Boeuf sur le Toit,** the famous avant-garde nightclub whose 10 January 1922 inaugural party thrown by **Jean Cocteau** was attended by **Constantin Brancusi, Pablo Picasso,** and **Max Beerbohm,** among others. Leading the club's orchestra that night was **Vance Lowry,** a black American saxophonist who was partially responsible for introducing the French to jazz and the music of **George Gershwin.**
♦ Métro: Concorde

St.-Honoré

LANVIN

31 Lanvin For women's scarves, perfumes, haute couture, and prêt-à-porter. ♦ M-Sa 9:30AM-6:30PM. 22 Rue du Faubourg-St.-Honoré. Métro: Concorde. 42.65.14.40

31 Charles Jourdan Forty years ago, celebrated Monsieur Jourdan became the first cobbler to use glue instead of nails to hold his shoes together: the result was the first truly delicate feminine footwear. ♦ M-Sa 9:45AM-7PM. 12 Rue du Faubourg-St.-Honoré. Métro: Concorde. 42.65.35.22

31 Gucci A four-floor marble palazzo filled with the trademark Gucci red and green. ♦ M-Sa 9:30AM-1PM, 2-6:30PM. 21 Rue Royal and 350 Rue du Faubourg St.-Honoré. Métro: Concorde. 42.96.83.27

32 15 Rue du Faubourg-St.-Honoré In 1804 **Claude Rouget de Lisle,** composer of the *Marseillaise,* lived here, and after him, **Felix,** hairdresser to **Empress Eugénie.** (She was so superstitious she had the number 13 removed from the Faubourg address.) ♦ Métro: Concorde

32 Carita A lavishly decorated trendsetting hair salon (whose clients have included **Catherine Deneuve, Paloma Picasso,** and French rocker **Johnny Hallyday**) with a relaxed, down-to-earth staff. There are separate entrances fo men and women. The salon is also noted for its skin-care treatments. ♦ Tu-Sa 9AM-7PM. 11 Rue du Faubourg-St.-Honoré. Métro: Concorde. 42.65.79.00 (women), 42.65.10.70 (men)

32 5 Rue du Faubourg-St.-Honoré The once-popular puffy pompadour hairstyle burgeoned here in the salon of coiffeur **Henri de Bysterveld.** ♦ Métro: Concorde

33 Lachaume The city's oldest and most exquisite florist has catered to haute couturiers and well-heeled clientele (who can afford long-stemmed red roses in December) since 1845. Gaze into the shop window at the gorgeous bunches of tulips and orchids; it will cure your midwinter blues. ♦ M-F 9AM-7PM; Sa 9AM-6PM; closed in Aug. 10 Rue Royale. Métro: Concorde. 42.60.59.74, 42.60.57.26

33 Christofle Want to make your little one's first baby tooth even more precious? How about encasing it in silver? Nothing is impossible for Christofle, the shop that has provided silver-plating services for more than a century. Christofle also features a fine selection of antique gold, as well as the stunning yellow and blue tableware **Claude Monet** designed for his house at Giverny. Peek into the museum at the same address. ♦ M 9:30AM-1PM, 2-6:30PM, Tu-Sa 9:30AM-6:30PM, Oct-May; M 9:30AM-1PM, 2-7PM, Tu-Sa 9:30AM-7PM, June-Sep. 9 Rue Royale. Métro: Concorde. 49.33.43.00

34 Ladurée ★★★$ This *salon de thé* par excellence is posh and ultra-Parisian but not snobbish. The heavenly taste of the croissants in this elegant turn-of-the-century café is ample reason for taking breakfast here. Habitués recommend *financiers* (almond cakes), chocolate macaroons, babas au rhum, and *royals* (almond biscuits with a dash of chocolate or mocha). Don't miss the painting of the roly-poly, rosy-cheeked cherub-turned-pastry chef on the downstairs ceiling. ♦ M-Sa 8:30AM-7PM; closed in Aug. 16 Rue Royale. Métro: Concorde. 42.60.21.79

34 La Maison du Valais ★★$$ A Swiss and Alpine chalet, this restaurant serves *à volonté* (all you can eat) raclette (melted cheese served with potatoes, cornichons, and onions), delectable fondues, assortments of thinly sliced charcuteries, and cool Fendant wine brought to you by cheerful waiters. Heartening in winter when you fancy a ski weekend in the mountains but haven't time to escape the rainy gray northern skies of Paris. ♦ M-Sa 12:15-11PM (tea salon 3-7:15PM); closed the first three weeks in Aug. Reservations recommended, especially in winter. 20 Rue Royale. Métro: Madeleine. 42.60.23.75, 42.60.22.72

Place de la Madeleine Shopping Map

Rodier
men's & women's clothing
Hôtel Opal
Jacadi
children's clothing
Obrey
jewelry
Emerich Meerson
watches
Pullman Tourisme
travel agency
Gérard Pasquier
women's clothing
Coralie
women's shoes
Hôtel Madeleine Plaza
Café Madeleine
restaurant & café
Nicolas
wine, liquors
Hédiard
restaurant, specialty foods
Maison de la Truffe
specialty foods
Créplet-Brussol
fromagerie
Caviar Kaspia
Russian restaurant
Cerruti
women's clothing
René Furterer
beauty products
L'Ecluse
wine bar
Mieux Vivre
health products
Baccarat
crystal
Cerruti
men's clothing

RUE TRONCHET

PLACE DE LA MADELEINE

Bruce & Scott
men's & women's clothing
Hôtel Tronchet
Salavin
chocolates
La Carpe
fine housewares, gifts
La Baggagerie
luggage
Marcelle Griffin
women's clothing
Lasserre
women's clothing
Simy
women's clothing
Carel
women's shoes
Descamps
linens
Erés
women's clothing
Fauchon
specialty foods
Racine
interiors
Gaudin
men's & women's shoes
Racine Club
men's clothing
Racine Gallery
old maps, model boats
Etablissments Porcher
bathroom interiors

CITE BERRYER

Façonable
men's clothing
Lufthansa
airline company
Villeroy & Boch
china, porcelain
Gucci
men's & women's accessories
RUE ST.-HONORE

RUE ROYALE

Mario Valentino
men's clothing
Rodier
men's & women's clothing
Carel
men's & women's shoes
Delvaux
tableware, porcelain
Ladurée
restaurant, tea salon
Wempe
jewelry
RUE ST.-HONORE

Aurele
women's shoes
Rubén Heurgon
jewelry
Cristal Lalique
crystal
Christofle
silverware
Maxim's Fleurs
florist
Maxim's
restaurant

Oréale
cosmetics
Lachaume
florist
Royal Quartz
watches
Perrin
jewelry
M. Grunspan
antiques
Fred
jewelry

---

35 Cité Berryer The alley, formerly an open-air market, has been classified as a historic monument. ♦ Between Rue Royale and Rue Boissy d'Anglas. Métros: Concorde, Madeleine

35 Le Moulin du Village ★★$$ In the Cité Berryer, nicely tucked away from the traffic on Rue Royale, sits this peaceful little restaurant. Dining on the terrace in the summer is wonderful, and rare wines are available year-round. English wine czar **Steven Spurrier** and **Mark Williamson** of Willi's Wine Bar are part-

owners of the restaurant. ♦ M-F noon-2:30PM, 7-11PM. Cité Berryer, 23-25 Rue Royale. Reservations recommended. Métro: Concorde. 42.65.08.47, 42.65.10.72

35 Blue Fox Bar ★★$/$$ If you don't want dinner intruding upon your wine, skip Le Moulin du Village next door and spend the evening in this chic yet comfortable wine bar. ♦ M-F noon-11PM. Cité Berryer, 25 Rue Royale. Métro: Concorde. 42.65.08.47, 42.65.10.72

36 Place de la Madeleine Around the edges of this square, the heart of luxury noshing in Paris, are specialty shops to spoil the spoiled (see the shopping map at left). Amid the fumes of buses and a more-or-less perpetual rush hour, a lively flower market blossoms just east of the **Madeleine** church. Here, at her funeral in 1975, **Josephine Baker,** having already received the Legion d'Honneur and the Medaille de la Résistance, became the first American woman ever to be honored with a 21-gun salute. ♦ Flower market: Tu-Su 6AM-3PM. Métro: Madeleine. No phone

36 Kiosque-Théâtre In the Place de la Madeleine is a kiosk that sells half-price tickets to theater, dance, music hall, concert, café theater, and, occasionally, opera events on the day of performance. During the first two years of operation it sold 140,600 tickets. (Another kiosk is located inside the Châtelet-Les Halles métro station.) ♦ Tu-Sa 12:30-8PM; Su 12:30-4PM. Métro: Madeleine. No phone

36 Public Lavatory Even if nature isn't calling, look for a sign that reads: "Hommes et Dames

---

St.-Honoré

W.C." It will lead you underground to an elegant 1905 facility with Art Nouveau wood paneling, stained glass, and tilework built by **Etablissements Porcher,** now one of the largest plumbing suppliers in France. ♦ Métro: Madeleine

36 Peny The coconut cake, *croque monsieur*, yellow umbrellas, and pavement tables at Peny are summertime favorites with Americans in Paris. ♦ Daily 7AM-9PM. 3 Place de la Madeleine. Métro: Madeleine. 42.65.06.75

36 Lucas-Carton ★★★★$$$$ The nouvelle cuisine of superstar chef **Alain Senderens,** who left the celebrated L'Archestrate to take over the Lucas-Carton kitchen, is better (and more expensive) than ever. Lucas-Carton, with its gorgeous Majorelle Belle Epoque maple and sycamore woodwork, is one of the Parisian capitals of nouvelle cuisine. Try the delicious foie gras in steamed cabbage, duck roasted with honey and spices, raviolis filled with clams, fig and cinnamon tarts, and a bittersweet chocolate soufflé. ♦ M-F noon-2:30PM, 8-10:30PM; closed three weeks in Aug, two weeks over Christmas. 9 Place de la Madeleine. Reservations required. Métro: Madeleine. 42.65.22.90

Restaurants/Nightlife: Red
Shops/ ♥Outdoors: Green

Hotels: Blue
Sights/Culture: Black

Madeleine

36 Madeleine The Madeleine's 28 monumental steps rise to meet 52 immense Corinthian columns, defining an edifice that dominates the hub of the financial district. However, the building has always been an architectural orphan. Begun as a church in 1764 under the reign of **Louis XV** and modeled after a Greek temple, the Madeleine has, at various times in its turbulent past, been slated to become a bank, parliament building, theater, stock exchange, banquet hall, and yet another temple to glorify **Napoléon's** army (as if

St.-Honoré

the Arc de Triomphe and the Invalides were not enough). In 1837 the windowless structure, designed by **Pierre Vignon** and **Jean-Jacques Huvé,** was selected to be the capital's first railway station but was consecrated as a church dedicated to Saint Mary Magdalene five years later.

Not a single cross adorns the pediments of this church, and its rose marble and gilt interior is surprisingly sensual. The imposing bronze door portraying the *Ten Commandments* is by **Lemaire,** and his gigantic *Last Judgment* on the south pediment is the largest work of its kind in the world (and it contains one of the chubbiest Christs in Europe). On the north side of the church, the inscription beneath a headless statue of **Saint Luke** reads: "On 30 May 1918, a German shell struck the church of the Madeleine and decapitated this statue." The splendid organ was played by **Saint-Saëns,** and the *Funeral March* of **Chopin** debuted here as the composer himself was laid to rest. The grandest funeral ever accorded an American in Paris was that of **Josephine Baker,** held in the Madeleine on 15 April 1975. ♦ M-Sa 7AM-7PM; Su 8AM-1:30PM, 3:30-7PM. Place de la Madeleine. Métro: Madeleine

37 Au Verger de la Madeleine Since 1936 this has remained one of Paris' finest family operated *épiceries.* **Jean-Pierre Legras** will help you find an old Sauterne bottled in the year you were born, married, or made your first trip to Paris. ♦ M-Sa 10AM-1:30PM, 3-8PM. 4 Blvd Malesherbes. Métro: Madeleine. 42.65.51.99

38 L'Ecluse ★★★$ One of a chain of six wine bars selling marvelous old Bordeaux by the glass. Lively, fashionable, affordable, and ideal for people-watching. ♦ M-Sa noon-12:30AM. 15 Place de la Madeleine. Métro: Madeleine. 42.65.34.69

38 Caviar Kaspia ★★★$$$ Besides purveying the finest in Russian and Iranian caviars, this chic little upstairs restaurant adorned in Czarist turquoise and overlooking Place de la Madeleine offers vodka, aquavit, and blinis languidly draped with slices of smoked salmon. The shop downstairs sells all the makings for your own Russian dinner. Worth a detour. ♦ Restaurant: M-Sa 11:30AM-12:30AM. Store: M-Sa 9AM-12:30AM. 17 Place de la Madeleine. Métro: Madeleine. 42.65.33.52

The phrase *Les Grands Boulevards* refers to a series of broad boulevards running between the Opéra and the Place de la République or the Bastille, including the boulevards Poissonnière, Montmartre, Bonne-Nouvelle, St.-Martin, St.-Denis, du Temple, Filles du Calvaire, Beaumarchais, des Capucines, and des Italiens. Built under Louis XIV, the boulevards came into their heyday under Baron Haussmann, who expanded them and built elegant and fashionable blocks of theaters. At the cafés on the boulevards, immortal stars such as Maurice Chevalier and Edith Piaf got their starts. Today the grand boulevards, sadly, are lined with kung fu movie theaters, discount stores, and fast-food joints.

38 La Maison de la Truffe Brooklyn delicatessens never looked like this. A fancy place specializing in black gold (fresh truffles, in season from November through the end of February) and most any other edible delicacy your gourmand's heart could desire, from foie gras to creamy liqueurs and *vieux alcools*. ♦ M-Sa 9AM-8PM. 19 Place de la Madeleine. Métro: Madeleine. 42.65.53.22

38 La Cave d'Hédiard Perhaps the grandest selection of Bordeaux wines in Paris, but the privilege of choosing something from it may cost you dearly. Armagnac, calvados, and cognac are sold, as well. ♦ M-Sa 9:30AM-7:30PM. 21 Place de la Madeleine. Métro: Madeleine. 42.66.04.84

38 Hédiard Recent renovations have diminished the Old World charm of this specialty shop. **Marcel Proust** once lingered here, surveying Hédiard's exotic selection of Asian and African delicacies: spices, oils, vinegars, 30 blends of tea, freshly roasted coffee beans, baskets of rare jellies, and old rums. ♦ M-Sa 9:30AM-9PM. 21 Place de la Madeleine. Métro: Madeleine. 42.66.44.36

39 Roblin $$ The English who cross the channel for a weekend of opera and luxurious take-out food from the Place de la Madeleine find refuge in this hotel. ♦ 6 Rue Chauveau-Lagarde. Métro: Madeleine. 42.65.57.00

40 Chapelle Expiatoire This memorial chapel, commissioned by **Louis XVIII** and designed by **Pierre Fontaine,** has become a shrine for French royalists. It was erected in 1815 on the grounds of the cemetery where, among the thousands of other victims of the Revolution, **Marie Antoinette, Louis XVI,** and **Charlotte Corday** lie. In the chapel's right apse is a statue of Louis XVI being ushered into heaven by an angel resembling **Henry Essex Edgeworth,** the friend who accompanied the king to the guillotine. Downstairs, bedecked with wilting flowers, an altar marks the spot where Louis XVI's body was found. ♦ Admission. M-F 10AM-12:45PM, 2-4:45PM, Feb-Mar, Oct; M-F 10AM-12:45PM, 2-5:45PM, Sep; M-F 10AM-12:45PM, 2-4PM, Nov-Jan. 29 Rue Pasquier. Métro: Madeleine

41 Trousselier This *atelier* (studio) has been creating gardens full of lovely silk flowers, all hand-painted, cut, and embossed, since 1885. Trousselier was bought out several years ago by the US Flower Company, which has a second boutique on 28th Street in Manhattan. ♦ M-Sa 10AM-5PM. 73 Blvd Haussmann. Métro: St.-Augustin. 42.66.97.95

42 Aux Tortues Established in 1864 (long before politically correct consumerism), Aux Tortues vends hairbrushes for baby, chess sets, Japanese *netsuke,* picture frames, combs, and carved balls within balls made from tortoise shells. ♦ M-Sa 9:30AM-6:30PM. 55 Blvd Haussmann. Métro: Havre-Caumartin. 42.65.56.74

42 Hôtel Opal $ For the frugal traveler, here's a renovated hotel with doll-size chambers and modern bathrooms that's located behind the Madeleine church. It's a handy place to stay if you love going to the Opéra and shopping in the nearby stores. ♦ 19 Rue Tronchet. Métro: Madeleine. 42.65.77.97

43 La Maison du Miel Run by the **Gallands** family since 1908, this shop is consecrated entirely to honey and products combined with honey, such as soap and oil. There are sample tastings and an array of honeys in miniature jars for the undecided. Don't pass up the *bruyère* (heather) honey. ♦ M 9:30AM-6PM; Tu-Sa 9:30AM-7PM. 24 Rue Vignon. Métro: Madeleine. 47.42.26.70

43 Le Roi du Pot-au-Feu ★★$$ For some warm consolation on a frigid evening, visit this offbeat little bistro with its red-checkered tablecloths and tableside jukeboxes. The specialty is its namesake: pot-au-feu, a marrow-

rich beef broth served with the meat and vegetables that gave up their substance to the pot. ♦ M-Sa noon-10PM. 34 Rue Vignon. Métro: Madeleine. 47.42.37.10

44 La Ferme St.-Hubert A cheese-lover's heaven with 140 different cheeses, La Ferme is known especially for its excellent Roquefort and Beaufort. The **St.-Hubert** restaurant is next door. ♦ Shop: M-Sa 8:30AM-7:30PM. Restaurant: M 11:45AM-3:30PM; Tu-Sa 11:45AM-3:30PM, 6:45-10:30PM. 21 Rue Vignon. Métro: Madeleine. 47.42.79.20

45 Marquise de Sévigné ★★$/$$ The ambience in this combination tea shop/chocolate shop is as unctuous as the rich hot chocolate it serves. ♦ M-Sa 9:30AM-7PM. 32 Place de la Madeleine. Métro: Madeleine. 42.65.19.47

45 Fauchon One look in the Fauchon window tells the story. Inside is a supermarket for millionaires, with every exotic fruit and vegetable on earth artistically arrayed in gorgeous still life. Fauchon is the most famous food shop in town, stocked with more than 20,000 items, from Scottish salmon and chunky peanut butter to Tongonese mangoes. Customers are not allowed to handle any of the merchandise; they pay first and then are presented with their prize at the door. Everything's high-priced.

On-the-spot overindulgence used to mean standing at the store's self-service cafeteria across the street, but to Fauchon fans' delight, a restaurant opened upstairs featuring a view of the illuminated Church of the Madeleine. Chef **Bruno Deligne's** menu includes delicacies such as hot oysters and leeks with truffle sauce, and for lighter summer fare, melon and Sauternes soup. Fauchon will also cater your next cocktail party in Paris. ◆ Store: M-Sa 9:40AM-7PM. Restaurant: M-Sa 12:15-2:30PM, 7:30-10:30PM. 26 Place de la Madeleine. Métro: Madeleine. 47.42.60.11

46 **Bar Romain** ★$$ One of the Right Bank's most handsome bars, with a basement restaurant decorated like a Belle Epoque railroad car. Try the steak tartare or lentils vinaigrette or one of the 350 cocktails. ◆ Restaurant: M-Sa noon-1AM. Bar: M-Sa noon-2AM; closed in Aug. 6 Rue Caumartin. Métros: Madeleine, Opéra. 47.42.98.04

47 **14 Boulevard des Capucines** On 28 December 1895 the brothers **Auguste** and **Louis Lumiere,** inventors of the cinematograph, projected their first public movie here in what was called the **Salon Indien.** ◆ Métro: Opéra

47 **Scribe** $$$ Completely renovated behind its Napoléon III facade, this luxurious hotel was the Allied Forces' press headquarters at the end of WWII. Correspondent **John Dos Passos,** who stayed here, wrote home describing **Charles de Gaulle** after a press conference: "He has two voices, the Sorbonne voice and the *père de famille, Henri Quatre, bonne soupe*

St.-Honoré

kind of voice. There's more to him than we had been led to believe." ◆ 1 Rue Scribe. Métro: Opéra. 47.42.03.40

Café de la Paix

Within the Scribe:

Les Muses ★$$/$$$ Chef **Christian Massaut** proposes entrées such as marinated crayfish, monkfish with saffron, and filet of lamb in pastry. ◆ M-F noon-2:30PM, 7:30-10:30PM. Reservations recommended. 47.42.03.40

Le Bar St.-Laurent ★$$ Business executives habitually gather around the elegant mahogany bar, sipping one of the different Canadian whiskey cocktails offered each day. ◆ Daily 9AM-2AM. 47.42.03.40

48 **Bar du Grand Hôtel** Tucked under the arches of the hotel is this multilevel operagoers' watering hole. ◆ Daily 11AM-midnight. 12 Blvd des Capucines. Métro: Opéra. 42.68.12.13

48 **Olympia Music Hall** Playing here is an obligatory engagement for top pop singers. **Edith Piaf** sang her heart out on this stage. Years later so did a group of Brits named the **Beatles,** who had just launched their first world tour. ◆ 28 Blvd des Capucines. Métro: Madeleine. 47.42.25.49

49 **Grand Hôtel** $$$ Designed in 1860 by **Charles Garnier,** who also designed the Opéra, the 600-room Grand Hôtel is one of Europe's oldest luxury hotels. Although major renovations have stripped away some of its old-fashioned grandeur, the hotel offers such first-class perks as a sauna, tanning rooms, masseuses, and a gymnasium. Its proximity to the Opéra makes it a favorite of visiting divas and prima ballerinas. ◆ 2 Rue Scribe. Métro: Opéra. 40.07.32.32

50 **Café de la Paix** ★★$$/$$$ Looking like a scene painted by Renoir with green-and-white-striped umbrellas, a dance of light, and brightly clothed patrons, this lovely old café (illustrated below) is classified as a historic landmark. **Salvador Dalí** enjoyed it, as did **Harry Truman, Maurice Chevalier, Maria Callas,** and **General Charles de Gaulle,** who ordered a take-out cold plate here on 25 August 1944—the first in liberated Paris. ◆ Daily 10AM-1:30AM. Place de l'Opéra. Métro: Opéra. 42.68.12.13

RESTAURANT

Within the Café de la Paix:

La Terrasse Tradition holds that if you sit on the terrace long enough, you will see someone you know walk by. ♦ Daily 10AM-1:30AM

Relais Capucine This informal restaurant boasts *service rapide permanente*. ♦ Daily noon-1:15AM

50 Place de l'Opéra Six main thoroughfares, bank headquarters, a theater district, and luxury boutiques are the spokes in this imposing hub. Back when the Opéra was indisputably where one scaled the social heights, the *haut monde* and *demimonde* frequented nearby beaneries such as Café de la Paix, Café de Paris, and the Café Riche. ♦ Métro: Opéra

50 Le Restaurant Opéra ★★$$/$$$ Alas, its luscious setting inspires only uneven cuisine. ♦ Daily noon-3PM, 7-11PM. Place de l'Opéra. Reservations recommended. Métro: Opéra. 42.68.12.13

51 Musée Fragonard A museum devoted entirely to perfume, its history, and its objets d'art. ♦ M-Sa 9AM-5:30AM. 9 Rue Scribe. Métro: Opéra.

51 American Express If you did leave home without it, go no farther. Here you will find, under one roof, traveler's checks, a foreign exchange bank, mail pickup, and tour brochures galore. ♦ M-F 9AM-5:30PM; Sa 9AM-5PM (for changing money and sight-seeing tours only). 11 Rue Scribe. Métro: Opéra. 47.77.77.07

52 Paris Opéra An opera house fit for an emperor, the pièce de résistance of **Baron Haussmann's** revamped Paris, and a last hurrah of Second-Empire opulence, this grandiose culture palace was once the world's largest theater, with an area of nearly three acres and a stage vast enough to accommodate 450 performers. Designer **Charles Garnier,** a 35-year-old previously unknown architect, was selected from among 171 other competitors (including the empress' pet architect, **Viollet-le-Duc**).

Garnier's design gave the facade a unique look–with ornate friezes, winged horses, golden garlands, and busts of famous composers. He crowned this architectural exaggeration with a copper-green cupola topped by **Millet's** *Apollo* thrusting his lyre above his head. A golden bust of the author of all this effulgence stands on the Rue Scribe side of the theater. Garnier's orgiastic mishmash of styles (from classical to Baroque) and materials (every possible hue of marble, from green to red and blue) was less than the hit he hoped it would be. The wife of **Napoléon III,** the empress, is said to have barked in disgust at the design, "What is this style supposed to be? It is neither Greek nor Roman nor Louis XIV nor Louis XV!" Searching for a name, Garnier diplomatically replied: "It is Napoléon III, Your Majesty." The Second-Empire version of the Moral Majority was in an uproar over the sensual **Carrier-Belleuse** lamp-bearing statues and the famous sculpted group *La Danse* by **Carpeaux.**

Inside the opera house, however, the effect is eminently upright, even majestic. Even if **Renoir** loathed the opera house, you may find a night here to be worth your while. In addition to presenting the best classical opera and ballet (recently directed by **Rudolph Nureyev**) in Paris, the gold ornaments, allegories in marble, **Chagall** ceilings, and the parade of Parisian society are all good for a gape. Horror-movie fans will be interested to know that the underground grotto where **Leroux's** *Phantom of the Opéra* lurked actually exists. It lies

beneath the Opéra's cellars, an artificial lake that provides water for the city's fire brigade. The less-than-inspired **Opéra Museum** in the **West Pavilion** displays opera and ballet memorabilia (such as the crown **Pavlova** wore when dancing in *Swan Lake* and the ballet slippers and tarot cards of **Nijinsky**). Tickets to

Paris Opéra

performances at the nearby but lesser-known **Opéra Comique** are cheaper and easier to get, and the presentations there are often more amusing. ♦ Admission. Museum: M-Sa 11AM-4PM. Box office: M-Sa 11AM-6:30PM. Place de l'Opéra. Métro: Opéra. 45.24.57.50 (box office)

Within the Paris Opéra:

Grand Foyer and Staircase Of this apotheosis of splendor (pictured above), **Henry James** wrote: "If the world were ever reduced

to the domain of a single gorgeous potentate, the foyer would do very well for his throne room." The Baroque white Carrara marble Grand Staircase with its Algerian onyx balustrade measures 32 feet wide at its center. At the first landing, it bifurcates and sweeps upward in two flights of steps to the second-floor gallery. The Grand Foyer, 175 feet long and decorated with mirrors and allegorical paintings, is encrusted with gilt ornament, and its ceiling glows with Venetian mosaics and colored marble from the island of Murano. The annual **Ecole Polytechnique Ball** and presidential galas are still held here every year. ♦ Daily 11AM-4PM

Auditorium The theater is famous for its six-ton chandelier and five tiers of loges bedecked in red velvet and gold. It is adorned with **Marc Chagall's** 1964 masterpiece (depicting Parisian scenes and images from operas ranging from *Giselle* to *The Magic Flute*). The ceiling is as colorful as the rest of Garnier's palace, yet oddly out of place. Backstage is the **Foyer de la Danse** so often painted by **Edgar Degas.** ♦ Daily 1-2PM

53 Boulevard Haussmann This drab expanse fronted with mammoth department stores becomes festive in December, when it's strung with Christmas lights. In 1784, two months

after his arrival in Paris as American ambassador to France, **Thomas Jefferson** signed a nine-year lease on a new town house located on what is now the north side of Boulevard Haussmann. The meticulous Virginian filled it with furniture, then set about acquiring a collection of paintings, books, and engravings that would eventually adorn his beloved Monticello. History records that during his sojourn in Paris, Jefferson kept a black servant, **James Hemings,** whom he apprenticed to a local caterer, **Combeaux,** perhaps so he could take home some French culinary art along with his other acquisitions.

53 Au Printemps In the 1870s Paris introduced the world to *grands magasins* (department stores, such as La Samaritaine and Bon Marché), and the city's shopping giants have been drawing crowds ever since. Today, two outclass the rest: Les Galeries Lafayette and Au Printemps, right next to each other along the Boulevard Haussmann. These are great places to get a peek at the latest in Parisian fashion as well as some indication of what it costs. Rest your feet and have a cup of tea or a slice of tart in the sixth-floor tea salon beneath Au Printemps' Belle Epoque stained-glass rotunda. If possible, shop on weekday mornings, as afternoons and Saturdays in these stores can resemble a stampede at the Chicago stockyard. ♦ M-Sa 9:45AM-7PM. 64 Blvd Haussmann. Métros: Havre-Caumartin, Opéra. 42.82.50.00

54 Les Galeries Lafayette With its magnificent glass-and-steel dome and Art Nouveau staircase built by the architect **Cahnautin** in 1912, this 10-story department store is classified as a historic monument. More than 10,000 customers visit its fashion department every day. Now there's an added attraction: **Galeries Lafayette Gourmet.** At sit-down counters throughout the food department, you can sample each section's specialty: grilled meats near the butcher, salads in the produce area, etc. And on the top floor there's incomparable browsing and a marvelous vista of the Right Bank's rooftops. ♦ M-Sa 9:30AM-6:45PM. 40 Blvd Haussmann. Métros: Chaussée-d'Antin, Opéra. 42.82.34.56

55 Multistore Opéra Not quite your Main Street soda fountain, this slick and sprawling institution draws more than 20,000 customers a day through its entrances on Boulevard des Capucines and Rue Halévy. They apparently come for the junk shop, jewelry store, and tobacco and gift shops. All those Walgreen-ish things are here: newspapers, makeup, stuffed animals, medicine, and film. The cuisine covers the gamut—from the pizzeria to the chic

L'Ecluse wine bar. Last but not least, for those who have an aversion to French salesclerks, there is a battery of self-service machines: a compact-disc (CD) distributor, while-u-wait business cards, tarot readings, and horoscopes. ♦ Daily 9:30AM-2AM. 6 Blvd des Capucines. Métro: Opéra. No phone

55 8 Boulevard des Capucines It was at this address in 1880, the year of his death, that 61-year-old **Jacques Offenbach** composed his masterpiece *The Tales of Hoffmann.* ♦ Métro: Opéra

55 Le Grand Café ★$ God bless it, one of the few Parisian bistros open 24 hours a day, and serving good seafood to boot. Another haunt of **Oscar Wilde** and now a hangout for journalists, graveyard-shift laborers, and anyone else out walking the streets at the hour of the wolf. ♦ Open daily 24 hrs. 4 Blvd des Capucines. Métro: Opéra. 47.24.75.77

56 Restaurant Drouant ★★$$$/$$$$ At the end of each November since 1903, 10 novelists have met here to award the **Prix Goncourt,** France's prestigious prize for the year's best fiction. (The prize isn't much money, but fame and fortune in the form of lucrative publishing contracts follow.) Selection made, the jury adjourns to the Louis XVI chairs in **Salon 15** (a private third-floor dining room) and addresses a sumptuous repast, which ends traditionally with Reblochon cheese from the Savoy mountains. The specialties of this century-old restaurant are roast pigeon in a potato shell with coral sauce, grilled salmon, and a fine house Muscadet. Drouvant is popular with the elegant crowd from the Opéra. ♦ Restaurant: daily noon-2:30PM, 8-10:30PM. Reservations required. Café: daily noon-2:30PM, 8PM-12:30AM. Place Gaillon. Restaurant reservations required. Métro: 4-Septembre. 42.65.15.16

57 6 Rue Danou **Oliver Wendell Holmes** knew this as the Hotel d'Orient and stayed here when he made a brief trip to Paris in 1886 to meet **Louis Pasteur,** who had just developed the vaccine for rabies. ♦ Métro: Opéra

58 Harry's Bar Opened in 1911, "Sank-Roo-Doe-Noo" (the American pronunciation of the bar's address) really came into its own two years later, when it was purchased from an American jockey by a bartender named **Harry MacElhone.** Here **F. Scott Fitzgerald** stared at the bleary surfaces of successive Scotches and watched the plot lines of his novels take form. At Harry's Bar, **George Gershwin** dreamed up his great fantasy *An American in Paris;* **Ernest Hemingway** dodged swinging fists; **Gloria Swanson** glowed; **Noel Coward** quipped; and **Jean-Paul Sartre,** despite himself, discovered both bourbon and hot dogs. The night before

each US presidential election, the regulars around the bar are polled as to their guess of the outcome; the legendary poll has an uncanny track record for predicting the winner. ♦ Daily 10:30AM-3AM. 5 Rue Danou. Métro: Opéra. 42.61.71.14

59 Rue de la Paix Before 1815 this street was Rue Napoléon, but today for some reason no street, square, or public place in Paris is named after the emperor. ♦ Métro: Opéra

dunhill

59 Alfred Dunhill The Paris branch of a famous English company, this mahogany-paneled shop sells all manner of smoking paraphernalia. Dunhill pipes made from the best French brier, with ebony mouthpieces, are among the world's finest (and most costly). And where else will you find a thujawood cigar box? ♦ M 10:30AM-6:30PM; Tu-Sa 9:30AM-6:30PM. 15 Rue de la Paix. Métro: Opéra. 42.61.57.58

59 Hôtel Westminster $$$ In the 19th century this hotel catered to Americans such as **Hamilton Fish,** who was Secretary of State under **Ulysses S. Grant,** and the family of **Henry James,** who stayed here when the future novelist was 12. ♦ 13 Rue de la Paix. Métro: Opéra. 42.61.57.46

St.-Honoré

Within the Hôtel Westminster:

Bar Les Chenets Frequented by a neighborhood business clientele, this bar specializes in Campari-based cocktails, a misleadingly innocent potable. ♦ Daily 7:20AM-11:30PM. 42.61.57.46

60 35 Boulevard des Capucines This café/restaurant called **Les Impressionistes** is the former site of **Nadar's** photographic studio. At this address on 15 May 1874, one of the worst flops in the history of painting exhibitions took place. A group of fledgling artists, including **Manet, Monet, Sisley, Renoir, Pisarro,** and **Cézanne,** hired the hall to hang their own works. But more than the works were hung: the critics held a lynching. The *Figaro* reviewer, for instance, sneered that the paintings looked like they'd been done by a monkey who'd run off with a paintbox. ♦ Métro: Opéra

61 Family Hôtel $$ This simple family run hotel occupies what was the private residence of **Louis XVI's** minister of finance. It was renovated not too long ago without the loss of charm. Room 51 affords a view of the Vendôme Column. ♦ 35 Rue Cambon. Métro: Concorde. 42.61.54.84

61 Castille $$$ In the thick of commercial Paris, this hotel is patronized mostly by tourists. ♦ 37 Rue Cambon. Métro: Concorde. 42.61.55.20

62 Hôtel Burgundy The last pages of *Look Homeward, Angel* sprang from the fertile imagination of **Thomas Wolfe** here in 1928. ♦ 8 Rue Duphot. Métro: Madeleine

62 29 Rue Cambon Upon his return to Paris in November 1875, young *New York Tribune* correspondent **Henry James** took up residence on the third floor of what is now **Chanel** headquarters. And this is where *The Americans,* his novel set in Paris, was written. ♦ Métro: Concorde

63 Goumard ★★$$$ Fresh shellfish, sea trout, bouillabaisse, and frog legs are a few of the specialties served here. ♦ T-Sa 12:15-2:30PM, 7:15-10:15PM; closed one week in Aug. 17 Rue Duphot. Reservations recommended. Métro: Madeleine. 42.60.36.07

64 Edouard Berck The most renowned stamp dealer in the city. ♦ M-F 9:30AM-1PM, 2:30-6PM; Sa 10:30AM-1PM, 3-6PM. 6 Place de la Madeleine. Métro: Madeleine. 42.60.34.26

St.-Honoré

64 4 Place de la Madeleine Alas, this is no longer the home of **Durand's,** the famous music publisher, where, in 1831, **Liszt** first met **Chopin.** ♦ Métro: Madeleine

64 Au Siamois **Charles Ritz,** a cigar connoisseur, believed the cigars sold here were the finest in Paris. ♦ M-F 8AM-7PM; Sa 8:30AM-7PM; closed first three weeks of Aug. 4 Place de la Madeleine. Métro: Madeleine. 42.60.27.69

65 Au Nain Bleu The Paris equivalent of **F.A.O. Schwarz** sells toys luxurious enough to spoil any child. ♦ M-Sa 9:45AM-6:30PM. 406-410 Rue St.-Honoré. Métro: Concorde. 42.60.39.01

66 Christian Tortu One of the hottest florists in town. Here and at his Left Bank boutique (6 Carrefour de l'Odeon, 43.26.02.56), Tortu creates opulent and original designs with flowers and vegetables. He also sells garden furniture. ♦ M-F 9AM-7PM; Sa 9AM-6PM. 13 Rue St. Florentin. Métro: Concorde. 42.86.94.69

67 Toraya ★★$/$$ In Japanese, *toraya* means "tiger"; for Parisians, it denotes this elegant black-and-gray Japanese tea salon and pastry shop. Dishes include sweet bean noodles, *kuzukiri* (noodles made from jellied arrowroot), and energizing pots of green *ocha* (tea). ♦ M-Sa 10AM-7PM. 10 Rue St.-Florentin. Métro: Concorde. 42.60.13.00

67 Notre-Dame-de-l'Assomption This church, built in 1676, was originally part of a convent where destitute widows and abandoned wives were given shelter; it has served a Polish parish since 1850. The massive cupola on top has been dubbed *le sot dôme* (the silly dome). ♦ 263bis Rue St.-Honoré. Métro: Tuileries

68 Cadolle The lady who is credited with inventing the brassiere in 1900, **Hermine Cadolle,** was the great-grandmother of Cadolle's current proprietor. All manner of deluxe lingerie, French beachwear, and perfume is sold here. ♦ M-Sa 9:30AM-1PM, 2-6:30PM. 14 Rue Cambon. Métro: Concorde. 42.60.94.22

69 France et Choiseul $$$ Franklin and Eleanor Roosevelt stayed in this hotel on their honeymoon in 1905, during which time a clairvoyant told Roosevelt that he'd become president of either the US or the Equitable Life Insurance Company (he wasn't sure which). In 1946, after *The Heart Is a Lonely Hunter* and *Reflections in a Golden Eye* had been published in French, **Carson McCullers** and her husband moved in here. Now the hotel is known for its old-fashioned charm, modern conveniences, small rooms, and courteous staff, which, unfortunately, in peak season seems also to be on holiday. ♦ 239 Rue St.-Honoré. Métros: Concorde, Tuileries. 42.61.54.60

69 Godiva The world-renowned chocolatier takes its name from the 11th-century English noblewoman who sacrificed her modesty and rode naked through the streets of Coventry to plead with her husband, the earl, to reduce taxes on the townsfolk. If these exquisite bonbons had been available then, they might have made a better bribe. ♦ M-Sa 9:30AM-7PM. 237 Rue St.-Honoré. Métros: Concorde, Tuileries. 42.96.44.64

69 Jolly Hôtel Lotti $$$$ This small luxury hotel is favored by British and Italian blue-bloods who are drawn to the large, tastefully decorated rooms, period furniture, and impeccable service. ♦ 7 Rue de Castiglione. Métros: Concorde, Tuileries. 42.60.37.34

Restaurants/Nightlife: Red   Hotels: Blue
Shops/🌳Outdoors: Green   Sights/Culture: Black

The French Revolution has been the subject of more than 200 feature films by directors such as Jean Renoir, Abel Gance, D.W. Griffith, Ettore Scola, and Wajda.

Place Vendôme Shopping Map

RUE DES CAPUCINES		RUE DE CASANOVA
Giorgio Armani		
men's & women's clothing		
Alexandra Reza		
jewelry		**Charvet**
		men's & women's clothing
		Boucheron
		jewelry
Schiaparelli	**PLACE**	**Van Cleef & Arpels**
women's clothing	**VENDOME**	*jewelry*
Ritz Hôtel		**Adelbert Piaget**
Cartier		*jewelry*
jewelry		**Pascal Morabito**
		Chaumet
		fine silver
Hôtel Vendôme		**Reposi**
Morabito		*jewelry*
jewelry, purses		**Giorgio Armani**
		men's clothing
		Gianmaria Buccellati
		fine silver, jewelry
		Huillier
		florist
		les architectes du temps
		jewelry
		Guerlain
		perfume, accessories

(RUE DE LA PAIX — vertical street label)

RUE ST.-HONORE

Godiva		**Annick Goutal**
chocolates		**Rhodes & Brousse**
Le Lotti		*men's clothing*
bar & grill		**Carré des Feuillants**
Diamant Noir		*restaurant*
jewelry		**Kenneth Lane**
Anemoné		*jewelry*
costume jewelry		**British Airways**
Meyrowitz		**Aquascutum**
optician		*men's & women's clothing*
		Luce Brett
		antiques
		Payot
		beauty products

(RUE DE CASTIGLIONE — vertical street label)

RUE DU MONT-THABOR

Hôtel Inter-Continental	**Les Arcades**
Casty	*books*
purses, gifts, jewelry	**Hôtel Meurice**
	(back entrance)
	Swann Pharmacy
	Jacqueline Perès
	women's clothing
	A. Sulka & Company
	men's clothing

70 Carré des Feuillants ★★★$$$$ While Nicole Dutournier minds Au Trou Gascon, their marvelous family restaurant in the 12th arrondissement, her husband, chef **Alain Dutournier,** pioneers this second, fancier, 19th-century-style restaurant near Place Vendôme. His specialty: inventive southwestern-French cuisine such as lobster with white gazpacho, wild hare with truffles, or veal with eggplant in a casserole. Don't skip dessert or his marvelous old cognacs. ♦ M-F noon-2PM, 7:30-10:30PM, Sa 7:30-10:30PM, Sep-June; M-F noon-2PM, 7:30-10:30PM, July-Aug. 14 Rue de Castiglione. Reservations required. Métros: Concorde, Tuileries. 42.86.82.82

71 Place Vendôme Like the **Place de la Concorde, Place des Victoires,** and other magnificent squares, this was conceived as a setting for a royal equestrian statue. The subject was **Louis XIV,** and the sculptor was **François Girardon.** In 1685, to make way for his monument, Louis bought and demolished the **Duke of Vendôme's** town house and the nearby Capucines convent. **Jules Hardouin-Mansart** designed gracefully formal mauve limestone facades with Corinthian pilasters and sculpted masks that were added to the square's periphery in 1715. The "Sun King," a budding real-estate shark, encouraged speculators to buy the lots behind the facades, then hire their own architects to fill in the blanks. During the Revolution the heads of nine victims of the guillotine were displayed here on spikes, and for a while the Place Vendôme was known as the **Place des Piques** (Pike Square).

On 19 June 1792 a huge bonfire in the square incinerated bundles of genealogical documents concerning the French nobility's title deeds. Needless to say, the king's gilt statue didn't survive the mob's wrath, either; it was felled in August of the same year. Today the 440- by 420-foot octagon is characterized by an aloof opulence. It is the home of the **Hôtel Ritz** and of one of the world's greatest concentrations of jewelers, perfumeries, and banks, including Boucheron, Van Cleef & Arpels, Cartier, Chaumet, Schiaparelli, and Guerlain (see shopping map at left). ♦ Métros: Madeleine, Opéra, Tuileries

71 Vendôme Column In place of the toppled statue of **Louis XIV, Napoléon** raised a 144-foot-high bronze monument modeled on Trajan's column in Rome. Made to commemorate Napoléon's military victories in Germany, the Vendôme Column is faced with 378 spiraling sheets of bronze supplied by 1,200 cannons

St.-Honoré

captured from the Austrian and Russian armies defeated at the Battle of Austerlitz in 1805. After the emperor's defeat at Waterloo, the Bourbons mounted their own symbol, the fleur-de-lis, atop the column, commandeering the monument. Along came **Louis Philippe,** and the fleur-de-lis was replaced with a small statue of Napoléon. But on the afternoon of 1 May 1871, the column was toppled again, crashing down along Rue de la Paix and breaking into 30 pieces. This act of destruction was masterminded by the painter **Gustav Courbet** for aesthetic and political reasons. When the Third Republic took power, it ordered Courbet to restore the monument at his own expense. The column was thrust up yet again (this time with Napoléon dressed as Julius Caesar), and Courbet was plunged into bankruptcy. ♦ Métros: Madeleine, Opéra, Tuileries

72 Hôtel Vendôme $$$ Fred Astaire stayed here in 1936 during his time-out from kicking up his heels with Ginger Rogers in *Swing Time* and *Shall We Dance?* Old-fashioned charm, large rooms, and a chic clientele. ♦ 1 Place Vendôme. Métros: Concorde, Madeleine, Tuileries. 42.60.32.84

72 3-5 Place Vendôme This was formerly the **Hôtel Bristol.** From 1890 to 1910, whenever financier and art collector **John Pierpont Morgan** came to Paris, he would stay in the same corner suite in the old hotel, which was run by one of his father's butlers. The building is now owned by **IBM Paris.** ♦ Métro: Madeleine

73 Cartier Since 1847 Cartier has offered the best and the brightest in French bijou, with commensurately dazzling price tags. The tourist discount on gold, however, almost brings those pretty jewels within reach. ♦ M, Sa 10:30AM-7PM, Tu-F 10AM-7PM, Apr-Sep; M, Sa 10:30AM-6:30PM, Tu-F 10AM-6:30PM, Oct-Mar. 7 Place Vendôme. Métro: Madeleine. 42.61.55.55

73 11-13 Place Vendôme This is the **Ministry of Justice,** where, in 1848, the official measure for the meter was set in the facade. ♦ Métro: Madeleine

73 Hôtel Ritz $$$$ Got a special pet chomping at the bit? A pooch who's hard to please? Take it to the Ritz, where even dogs are treated like social lions. The Ritz has been, well, the ritziest hotel in Paris since 1898, when **Cesar Ritz** first took it over. During that time, million-

St.-Honoré

aires, Arab princes, divas, and cinema stars have stayed here. **Marcel Proust** used to arrive sporting lavender gloves and a variety of clothes that never seemed to fit him. **Barbara Hutton** loved it; **Coco Chanel** seemed to have been in residence here forever. There are 440 employees (a third of whom have been here more than a quarter century) catering to the occupants of the hotel's 210 rooms. Sixty of these stalwarts are available for duty as private servants, if your vacation just isn't a vacation without Jeeves. The prices are astronomical but, by all accounts, justified. The suites on the second floor overlooking the Place Vendôme are actually registered with the Bureau of Fine Arts. ♦ 15 Place Vendôme. Métros: Concorde, Tuileries. 42.60.38.30

Within the Hôtel Ritz:

Ritz Espadon ★★★$$$$ The culinary reputation of the hotel's lovely garden restaurant was made from the very start by the presence of that great turn-of-the-century chef, **Escoffier.** He first met **Cesar Ritz** when Ritz was manager of the Grand Hotel in Monte Carlo. Escoffier's celebrated recipe for foie gras in port is still used. Latter-day creations such as grilled turbot with mustard sauce and sea bass with flaming stalks of fennel are equally exquisite. The wine list is nonpareil

and the prices are unsurpassed. ♦ Daily 12:15-10:30PM. Reservations recommended. 42.60.38.30

Ritz Bars Just off Rue Cambon is this more famous little bar, which **Hemingway** "liberated" at the end of WWII. Here the legendary barman **Georges** served drinks to **President Teddy Roosevelt,** just back from an African safari. Other big-time tipplers here were the **Prince of Wales, Greta Garbo, Noel Coward, Douglas Fairbanks, Winston Churchill, J.P. Morgan, Andrew Carnegie, F. Scott Fitzgerald,** and **Marlene Dietrich.** It's still an English-style pub, right down to its tweedy, rubicund patrons. The Vendôme bar has a terrace for drinks or tea in the summer. ♦ Both bars: daily 8AM-1AM. 42.60.38.30

74 Charvet **Edward VII** bought his neckties and cravats here, and so can you. ♦ M-Sa 9:45AM-6:30PM. 28 Place Vendôme. Métro: Opéra. 42.60.30.70

74 Kitty O'Shea's ★$/$$ The most Irish of pubs in Paris serves Guinness, the most Irish of brews, on tap. Popular with businesspeople headquartered around the Opéra. The **John Jameson** restaurant upstairs serves a respectable roast mutton. ♦ M-Th, Su noon-1:30AM; F-Sa noon-2AM; closed one week at Christmas. 10 Rue des Capucines. Reservations recommended. Métros: Madeleine, Opéra. 40.15.00.30, 40.15.08.08

75 16 Place Vendôme Here **Franz Anton Mesmer** (1734-1815), the charlatan Austrian physician who invented mesmerism (later called hypnosis), conducted animal magnetism seminars here wrapped in robes decorated with astrological signs. And in the 1930s **Obelisk Press** had its office at this address. Headed by the Englishman **Jack Kahane,** Obelisk published works that no one else would, such as **Henry Miller's** *Tropic of Cancer,* which appeared in 1934. ♦ Métros: Concorde, Tuileries

75 12 Place Vendôme In 1849 **Frederic Chopin,** Polish composer and pianist, died here at the age of 39. ♦ Métros: Concorde, Tuileries

75 6 Place Vendôme The **Hôtel du Rhin** became the temporary residence of **Napoléon III** during his 1848 presidential campaign. ♦ Métros: Concorde, Tuileries

76 Rue St.-Honoré This ranks as one of the oldest and most historic thoroughfares in Paris. In 1622 **Molière** was born on this street at the corner of Rue Sauval, near Les Halles. On 6 October 1793, a tumbrel traveled down Rue St.-Honoré, carrying a woman whose prison-shorn hair was hidden under a dumpy bonnet. Nearby, **Jacques-Louis David** sketched her as she passed, bequeathing to history a terrifically poignant image of **Marie Antoinette,** her hands tied behind her back, en route to the guillotine. ♦ Métro: Tuileries

Paris remains France's economic and administrative center, with 80 percent of the main offices in the national industries located in the central city.

French Feats: Two Centuries of Discoveries in Science and Technology

1791: Jean-Baptiste Delambre and Pierre Méchain develop the decimal system.

1795: Gaspard Monge creates descriptive geometry.

1800-30: Georges Cuvier and Jean-Baptiste Lamarack develop paleontology.

1811: Bernard Courtois isolates iodine and discovers morphine.

1815: René Laennec invents the stethoscope. Louis-Sebastien Lenormand invents the revolver.

1818: Louis Thenard discovers boron and hydrogen peroxide.

1820: Pierre Pelletier and Joseph Caventou discover quinine.

1829: Louis Braille develops the braille alphabet.

1830: Barthélemy Thimonnier invents the sewing machine.

1834: Jacques Daguerre invents the daguerreotype process for photography.

1852: Léon Foucault invents the gyroscope.

1853: Charles Gerhardt invents aspirin.

1857: Ferdinand Carré invents the mechanical compression refrigerator, capable of producing ice.

1859: Gaston Planté invents the electric storage-cell battery.

1862: Louis Pasteur discovers anaerobic germs and founds the science of microbiology.

1865: Louis Pasteur invents pasteurization.

1867: Aristide Bergès develops the concept of hydroelectric power.

1876: Eugène Woillez invents the iron lung.

1884: Hilaire Chardonnet de Grange invents rayon.

1885: Louis Pasteur develops the rabies vaccine.

1889: André Chantemesse and Fernand Widal develop the typhoid vaccine.

1890: Edouard Branly invents the radio conductor, making wireless telegraph reception possible.

1896: Henri Becquerel discovers radioactivity.

1898: Pierre and Marie Curie discover radium.

1900: Victor Grignard discovers the organomagnesium compounds used for organic synthesis.

1906-23: Albert Calmette and Camille Guérin develop the BCG vaccine (Bacillus Calmette-Guérin) against tuberculosis.

1910: Georges Claude invents the neon lamp.

1920: Jean Perrin outlines the concept of nuclear transmutation.

1924-27: Louis de Broglie discovers the wave nature of the electron and develops wave mechanics.

1934: Frédéric and Irène Joliot-Curie discover artificial radioactivity.

1950: Alfred Kastler discovers optical pumping, permitting the development of lasers and masers.

1952: Félix Trombe invents the solar oven.

1957: Jean Berlin invents the hovercraft.

1961: François Jacob, André Lwoff, and Jacques Monod discover the role of RNA in the transmission of genetic information.

1983: A research team discovers the AIDS virus.

St.-Honoré

1985: Researchers at the Pasteur Institute and the American Department of Health and Human Services invent the AIDS blood-screening test.

1987: Scientists develop RU 486 (the "week-after" birth-control pill).

1989: Astronomers discover a luminous arc in the Abell 370 galaxy cluster. It is a gravitational mirage, the first ever observed in a galaxy cluster.

—Researched by Beth Levin
Reprinted with permission from
France Magazine

76 Chichen-Itza Fine, hand-worked leather bags, briefcases, and wallets fashioned from ostrich, Madagascar crocodile, and the like are sold here. More nonessentials are made from the skins of rare living creatures. ◆ M-F 1-7PM; closed in Aug. 231 Rue St.-Honoré. Métro: Tuileries. 42.60.80.16, 42.60.61.35

76 Royal Saint-Honoré $$ This hotel next door to the Tuileries Gardens has quiet rooms and a refined air. ◆ 13 Rue d'Alger. Métro: Tuileries. 42.60.32.79

76 4 Rue du Mont-Thabor In the summer of 1820, still enjoying the afterglow of the triumphant reception of *Rip Van Winkle* and *The Legend of Sleepy Hollow,* 39-year-old **Washington Irving** moved into an apartment here. Mitigating his pleasure was Irving's unfortunate fear of growing old, the same problem that obsessed old Rip. ◆ Métro: Tuileries

Paris has one physician per 281 residents, ranking it 24th among 82 cities around the world.

77 Selaudoux Patisserie For a kiwi tart or a quick fix of chocolate macaroons, this pastry shop can't be beat, if you can ignore the surly service. ◆ M-Sa 6AM-8PM. 215 Rue St.-Honoré. Métro: Tuileries. 42.97.46.96

78 Tuileries $$ Down a quiet side street, this renovated hotel retains much of its 18th-century charm, plus 20th-century accoutrements: color TVs, minibars, direct-dial phones, and modern conveniences at old-fashioned prices. ◆ 10 Rue St.-Hyacinthe. Métros: Pyramides, Tuileries. 42.61.04.17, 42.61.06.94

78 Chédeville The pâtés and sausages from this busy, popular charcuterie are so good they're served in many of the city's finer restaurants. ◆ M-Sa 9AM-7PM. 12 Rue du Marché-St.-Honoré. Métros: Pyramides, Tuileries. 42.61.11.11

79 Dave ★★★$$$ A hideout for stars such as **George Michael** and **Yves Saint Laurent,** this excellent Sino-Vietnamese restaurant is directed by **Dave,** a sweet but star-struck *maitre d'* who boasts a Polaroid collection of his most famous customers. ◆ M-F noon-2:30PM, 7-11PM; Sa 7-11PM. 39 St.-Roch. Métro: Pyramides. 42.61.49.48

80 Yakitori ★$ Try the morsels of cheese-stuffed pork, teriyaki chicken, and marinated shrimp skewered and grilled *à la Japonaise*. This restaurant is perpetually crowded but worth the effort to grab a seat at

St.-Honoré

the counter and watch the chefs perform. ◆ M-Sa noon-2:15PM, 7-10:45PM. 34 Place du Marché-St.-Honoré. Métro: Pyramides. 42.61.03.54

80 L'Absinthe ★$$/$$$ **Monsieur Malabard's** sophisticated 1900s-style bistro has withstood the test of time, maintaining high quality at moderate prices. Magret de canard, chicken cooked in champagne, fresh salads, and homemade ice creams and sorbets come highly recommended. In summer, request an outdoor table on the square. ◆ M-F noon-2:30PM, 7:45-11:30PM; Sa-Su 8-11:30PM. 24 Place du Marché-St.-Honoré. Reservations recommended. Métro: Pyramides. 42.61.03.32, 42.60.02.45

80 Louise Delpuech A rare, immaculate self-service washeteria run by two redoubtable women inexplicably dubbed *Romeo* and *Juliet* by the neighborhood. Behind their stern scowls lurk hearts of gold. Read the hand-scrawled instructions (in English for Americans) and don't cram your machine too full. Overload and you're in big trouble with this imposing pair, and police headquarters is just across the street. ◆ Daily 8AM-9PM. 24 Place Marché-St.-Honoré. Métro: Pyramides. 42.61.04.49

81 Flo Prestige For the picnicker who enjoys dining *sur l'herbe* and can afford not to bother with preparing the meal. This take-out gourmet deli offers a delectable selection of cheeses, charcuterie, salmon, salads, wines, and pastries of a quality that merits a limo for the tailgate picnic. For a setting, the nearby Tuileries or Palais Royal gardens should do just fine. ◆ Daily 8-11PM. 42 Place du Marché-St.-Honoré. Métro: Pyramides. 42.61.45.46

Brentano's

82 Brentano's For the greatest hits in English literature, try this, one of the best and oldest English-language bookstores in Paris. ◆ M-Sa 10AM-7PM. 37 Ave de l'Opéra. Métros: Opéra, Pyramides. 42.61.52.50

82 Delmonico ★★$$$ At one time the favorite of the **Prince of Wales,** this venerable restaurant has modernized its decor and cuisine. Among chef **Claude Monteil's** offerings are Scottish smoked salmon, sole with fresh pasta and sea urchins, roast wild duck, and a fine coffee soufflé. ◆ M-F noon-2:30PM, 7-10PM. Reservations recommended. 39 Ave de l'Opéra. Métros: Opéra, Pyramides. 42.61.44.26

83 Auberge des Trois Bonheurs ★★$$ Despite the oh-so-French name, classic, elegant Chinese cuisine is what you'll find here. The chef is from Hong Kong and serves specialties such as steamed trout, Peking duck, and jumbo shrimp *à la Cantonaise*. ◆ Daily noon-3PM, 7:15-11:30PM. 280 Rue St.-Honoré. Reservations recommended. Métro: Pyramides. 42.60.43.24

83 Le Ruban Bleu ★★$$$ The maritime decor and blue-ribbon name of this WWII-style restaurant commemorate the record transatlantic crossing by a French vessel called the *Normandie*. The menu is trim and shipshape: grilled chèvre on toast, monkfish in sorrel, and saddle of hare with fresh pasta. ◆ M-F noon-2:30PM. 29 Rue d'Argenteuil. Métro: Pyramides. 42.61.47.53

83 C. Poilly A mom-and-pop charcuterie whose daily luncheon specials draw lines longer (but faster) than those at the bank. For 25 years, jolly Madame and Monsieur Poilly have been dishing up roast pork, mashed potatoes, ravioli, and raspberry tarts. Great for a take-out picnic in the gardens of the Palais Royal. ◆ M-F 9AM-8PM; Sa 10AM-1PM. 256 Rue St.-Honoré. Métro: Palais-Royal. 42.60.62.42

83 Verlet ★★$ Something in the air here shouts "Coffee" with a capital C, though there's more here than just the bean. Amid the open sacks of roasted coffee beans in the window are tins of Ceylonese and Chinese teas and mounds of almonds, dried apricots, and dates, and scattered about are a few precious wooden bistro tables where actors from the nearby Théâtre Français enjoy delicious Viennese pastries in a nonchalant 1930s decor. Mid-afternoon is best for getting a seat. ♦ M-F 9AM-7PM; tea salon noon-6:30PM; closed in Aug. No credit cards. 256 Rue St.-Honoré. Métro: Palais-Royal. 42.60.67.39

84 St.-Roch The bullet holes in this church's facade chronicle one of the most significant military debuts in French history. This is the site of a fierce Revolutionary skirmish that occurred on 5 October 1795, when Royalist troops took a stand on the steps of St.-Roch and were boldly scattered by a then-unknown 27-year-old soldier named **Napoléon Bonaparte.** Ten days later Napoléon was appointed com-mander-in-chief of the home forces. St.-Roch, an architectural mix-and-match, is the city's finest Baroque church and is best known today for its splendid 1752 rococo organ and weekly evening concerts. Built to handle the overflow from St.-Germain-l'Auxerrois, St.-Roch was originally designed by **Jacques Lemercier,** and no less a personage than **Louis XIV** laid its cornerstone in 1653. But it took another century to complete.

Jules Hardouin-Mansart was responsible for the oval **Lady Chapel,** and sculptor **René Charpentier** decorated the edifice in carved imagery. The church is dedicated to an Italian holy man who, accompanied by his dog, ministered to plague victims in the 14th cen-tury. Inside are memorials to the playwright **Corneille,** the philosopher **Diderot,** and Louis XIV's beloved gardener, **Le Nôtre,** whose bust by **Coysevox** is left of the chancel. ♦ M-Sa 8AM-7:15PM; Su 8AM-1PM, 5-7:15PM. 296 Rue St.-Honoré. Métros: Pyramides, Tuileries. 42.60.81.69

84 Gargantua ★★$$$ King Kong could leave here with a full tummy (and an empty pocket-book). The portions are so grand, the food so delicious, the prices, alas, so outrageous. In the rear is a marble lunch counter. Pastries, charcuterie, wines, and salads are packed to go. ♦ Daily 8AM-9PM. 284 Rue St.-Honoré. Métro: Tuileries. 42.60.52.54

85 La Providence ★★$$ Coun-try cuisine with an Alsatian accent is featured at this won-derful little restaurant. Among the daily specialties on its changing menu: *baeckkeefa* (marinated lamb, beef, and pork on a bed of onions and potatoes), lamb chops, broiled goat cheese salad, fresh pear tart, and a light chocolate mousse. A respect-able list of Alsatian wines is offered. Try a Pinot Noir or Gewürztraminer in the Alsatian *winstub* downstairs. ♦ M-F noon-2:30PM, 7:30-11PM. 6 Rue de la Sourdière. Reserva-tions recommended. Métro: Tuileries. 42.60.46.13

85 Tartanous ★★$/$$ For a tasty lunch on the run, try this juice bar/quiche parlor. The quiches are filled with imaginative combina-tions of tastes, such as chicken and carrot with mustard, fennel and mushroom, and *oiseille* and Chavignol cheese. For dessert, try the red and green rhubarb pie or the coconut cream. A horde of well-heeled St.-Honoré office workers and the occasional Birkenstock-shod Califor-nian stopping by for a freshly squeezed carrot-cucumber or orange-grapefruit juice keep this place busy at lunchtime. ♦ M-F 11AM-7PM. 21 Rue St.-Roch. Métro: Tuileries. 42.97.50.40

86 St.-James et Albany $$$$ Portions of this residential hotel date back to the reign of Louis XIV, which is appropriate, since for years its clientele was strictly old European aristocracy. It now offers home-away-from-home suites, duplexes, and studios equipped with kitchen-ettes, so that after stocking up at the garden-floor delicatessen, guests can entertain their friends with crêpe suzettes and a view of the Tuileries. The nicest rooms are nestled in the attic beneath low-beamed ceilings. The hotel incorporates parts of the old **Noailles Man-sion,** where **General Lafayette** married one of the Noailles daughters in 1774. ♦ 202 Rue de Rivoli. Métro: Tuileries. 42.60.31.60

Within St.-James et Albany:

Les Noailles ★$$$ Stroll through the Tuileries with that special blossoming love, then dine tête-à-tête in the courtyard of the elegant Les Noailles. ♦ M-F noon-2:30PM, 7:30-10:30PM. 42.60.31.60

St.-Honoré

Bar St.-James ★$$ This is one of the classi-est snack bars around. Try the club sandwich or cabbage salad with breast of duck. ♦ Daily 10AM-1AM. 42.60.31.60

87 Montana Tuileries $$ Conveniently located near the Tuileries and the St.-Roch church (which has marvelous evening concerts), this small hotel is an isle of economy in an archi-pelago of extravagance. ♦ 12 Rue St.-Roch. Métro: Tuileries. 42.60.35.10

Where Chocolate Lovers Unite

Confessed chocolate addict Maribeth Ricour de Bourgies offers tours of Paris' premier chocolate shops, which include tastings at **Christian Constant** (26 Rue du Bac), **La Maison du Chocolat** (52 Rue François 1er), and **Richarat** (258 Boulevard St.-Germain). The half-day eating excursions are limited to six people (the number of chocolate devotees who can fit into the chauffeured car, naturally). An amaz-ing treat for 400 francs (approximately $64). For more information, call 43.48.85.04.

Restaurants/Nightlife: Red **Hotels:** Blue
Shops/ ♥Outdoors: Green **Sights/Culture:** Black

The average French filmgoer spends 57 francs a year on movies, whereas the average Parisian spends 330 francs.

88 Hôtel Regina $$$ With a splendid view of the Tuileries Gardens, this quiet hotel is furnished with antiques, crystal chandeliers, and a Louis XV-style elevator cage that has been retired from service and put on display in the lobby. ♦ 2 Place des Pyramides. Métros: Tuileries, Pyramides. 42.60.31.10

88 Le Canard Enchaîné France's famous leftist satirical weekly, celebrated for its irreverent cartoons and editorials, makes its home here. The paper specializes in covering scandals and is usually first to the scene of the crime. ♦ 173 Rue St.-Honoré. Métro: Palais-Royal. 42.60.31.36

88 7 Rue de l'Echelle The loveliest of cities can be capricious, as **Mark Twain** found Paris to be when he stayed here at the **Hôtel Normandy** between April and July 1879. Paris scowled, the gray sky poured, and its legendary spring-

St.-Honoré

time never happened. So Twain spent his bleak vacation rereading the doleful *History of the French Revolution* by **Thomas Carlyle** and scribbled what he could. ♦ Métro: Palais-Royal

89 Rue des Italiens Home of the prestigious Parisian daily *Le Monde*. ♦ Métros: 4-Septembre, Richelieu-Drouot

90 Au Petit Riche ★★$ A favorite of journalists, this warm century-old restaurant offers a tasty marinated octopus salad, roast rabbit, hot apple tarts, and carafes of Bourgueil. ♦ M-Sa noon-2:15PM, 7PM-12:15AM. 25 Rue Le Peletier. Reservations recommended. Métro: Le Peletier. 47.70.68.68

91 Hôtel Drouot The closest thing to a Sotheby's in Paris, the Drouot specializes in estate sales and auctions of everything from Cartier jewels, Louis XIV furniture, and African sculpture to baskets of kitchenware and collections of rare illustrated manuscripts. On the top floor, the most valuable objets d'art are overseen by renowned auctioneer **Ader Picard Tajan.** Auctions take place in the afternoons, but it's best to arrive early to scan the merchandise, a great experience in itself. ♦ M-Sa 11AM-6PM. 9 Rue Drouot. Métro: Richelieu-Drouot. 48.00.20.20

92 Chopin $$ At the end of the peaceful Passage Jouffroy (which is classified as a French historic monument), this modest hotel offers small rooms at small rates. ♦ 46 Passage Jouffroy. Métro: Rue Montmartre. 47.70.58.10

93 Chartier ★$ This cavernous turn-of-the-century soup kitchen with pinwheel fans and surly waiters serves better theater than cuisine, but is worth a visit nevertheless. The place is always mobbed with tourists, so get here when the doors open. ♦ Daily 11AM-3PM, 6-9:30PM. 7 Rue du Faubourg-Montmartre. No credit cards. Métro: Rue Montmartre. 47.70.86.29

94 Musée Grevin The city's largest wax museum is populated with distinguished paraffin personalities, including **Charles de Gaulle, Catherine Deneuve, Woody Allen,** and **Yehudi Menuhin.** Children love it. Of late, the museum has become as well known for the chamber music concerts in its small upstairs auditorium as for its wax effigies. ♦ Daily 1-7PM. 10 Blvd Montmartre. Métro: Rue Montmartre. 47.70.85.05

95 Passage des Panoramas Named after two large cylindrical towers on the Boulevard Montmartre in which 19th-century American inventor **Robert Fulton** painted and displayed 18 panoramas, including a portrayal of the burning of Moscow. The French flocked to see the sagas, and, with his profits, Fulton bankrolled his steamboat and submarine schemes. ♦ Métros: Bourse, Rue Montmartre

95 Stern Have your name elegantly engraved on calling cards that can be used for any occasion. ♦ M-F 9:30AM-12:30PM, 1:30-5:30PM. 47 Passage des Panoramas. Métro: Rue Montmartre. 48.08.86.45

95 Aux Lyonnais ★★$$ Long patronized by Bourse des Valeurs traders in the neighborhood, this bistro's reputation is founded on classic, unadventurous cuisine. ♦ M-F 7PM-midnight. 32 Rue St.-Marc. Reservations recommended. Métro: Bourse. 42.96.65.04

96 49 Rue Vivienne On this site stood the **Salle Musard,** an old concert hall wherein **Tom Thumb,** headliner for **P.T. Barnum's** traveling show, performed in 1844. ♦ Métros: Bourse, Richelieu-Drouot

97 La Tour de Jade ★★$/$$ This restaurant, which serves some of the city's best Vietnamese cuisine, was founded by a former minister to Indochina's **Emperor Bao-Dai.** Stuffed duck, lemon chicken, broiled mullet with anchovies, duck with lotus seeds, and pork balls in soy sauce are the highlights. ♦ M-Sa noon-3PM, 7PM-midnight; Su 7PM-midnight. 20 Rue de la Michodière. Reservations recommended. Métro: 4-Septembre. 47.42.07.56

Avenue de l'Opéra was originally called Avenue Napoléon; its name was changed in 1870 after Napoléon III's troups were outfinessed by the Prussians at Sedan, and the monarchy tumbled in the wake of the defeat.

98 Le Vaudeville ★★$$ This vintage 1925 brasserie was rescued from decline and obscurity by brasserie king **Jean-Paul Bucher** and is now packed at lunchtime by execs from the Bourse des Valeurs and Club Med headquarters, and at night by theater patrons. Specialties include: *andouillette,* foie gras, grilled lobster, shellfish (year-round), homemade *saumon rillette,* and a chilled house Reisling. Summer dining is pleasant on the sidewalk. ♦ Daily 11:30AM-3PM, 7PM-2AM. 29 Rue Vivienne. Reservations recommended. Métro: Bourse. 40.20.04.62

99 Bourse des Valeurs **Napoléon** commissioned this "Temple of Money" in 1826, and architect **Alexandre Brogniart** was inspired to adorn it with 64 Corinthian columns. The Stock Exchange's design is epic, and so is the chaos of brokers on the floor. You are welcome to head for the spectators gallery and watch French capitalism at work. On a day of stiff trading, the excitement rivals that of European Cup soccer, and admission is free. ♦ M-F 11AM-2PM. Organized tours: 11:30AM, noon, July-Sep; 11:30AM, noon, 12:30PM, 1PM, Oct-June. 4 Place de la Bourse. Métro: Bourse. 42.33.99.83 (tours), 42.33.99.83 (information)

100 Pile ou Face ★★★$$/$$$ A coin's throw from the Stock Exchange, this intimate restaurant, whose name means heads or tails, serves exquisite nouvelle cuisine without any of the pretentions that normally garnish such food. The owners, **Alain Dumberque** and **Claude Udron,** raise chickens and rabbits on their farm outside Paris, and their refined tastes are exemplified in the delicious *magret de canard, poulet en croute,* rabbit in rosemary, and chocolate cake. The Cahors, Gamay de Touraine, and Moulin de Bellegrave are among the highlights of the rich wine list. A perfect setting for a romantic dinner. ♦ M-F noon-2PM, 8-10PM; closed in Aug. 52bis Rue Notre-Dame-des-Victoires. Reservations required. Métro: Bourse. 42.33.64.33

101 Hollywood Savoy ★★$$/$$$ A restaurant that becomes a nightclub when the Ivy League waiters and waitresses take to the stage and belt out creditable renditions of *Stormy Monday* and other Yankee classics. ♦ M-Sa noon-3PM, 8PM-12:30AM. 44 Rue Notre-Dame-des-Victoires. Reservations recommended. Métro: Bourse. 42.36.16.73

102 Galerie Vivienne From its mosaic floors to the arching glass canopy, the gussied up Galerie Vivienne, established in 1923, is a most fashionable arcade. A myriad of boutiques sells everything from high-tech jewelry and rare books to children's masks and the best brownies in Paris. ♦ Open daily 24 hrs. 6 Rue Vivienne. Métro: Bourse

Within Galerie Vivienne:

Si Tu Veux An old-fashioned toy store where Babar, the universally loved French elephant, comes in plush, plastic, or posters. And enough paper hats and masks are available to regale any six-year-old's kiddie party. ♦ M-Sa 11AM-7PM. 68 Galerie Vivienne. 42.60.59.97

Jean-Paul Gaultier The eye-catching boutique of the young fashion eclectic who brought miniskirts to men and ice cream-cone bras to women. Check out the video screens—on the floor! ♦ M-F 10AM-7PM; Sa 11AM-7PM. 6 Rue Vivienne. 42.86.05.05

Legrand Filles et Fils Out of the back of this Rue de la Banque shop, **Francine Legrand** sells French red wines by the case. Another Legrand wine store is located in the Marais & Les Halles walk (see page 105). ♦ Tu-F 8:30AM-7:30PM; Sa 8:30AM-1PM, 3-7PM. 12 Galerie Vivienne. 42.60.07.12

A Priori Thé ★★$/$$ This tearoom/restaurant was started by three expatriate American women. Wicker chairs and tables and fresh-cut flowers spill into the charming Galerie Vivienne. A creative selection of quiches and salads is served, followed by divine apple crumble and brownies for dessert. The wine list is chosen by **Francine Legrand,** whose wine shop (see entry above) is in the same arcade. ♦ M-Sa noon-6:30PM; Su 1-6PM. 35-37 Galerie Vivienne. 42.97.48.75

St.-Honoré

103 Galerie Colbert Like the adjoining Galerie Vivienne, the Galerie Colbert has recently enjoyed a stylish renaissance. The **Bibliothèque Nationale,** which owns the passage, has spent millions to restore the walkways, glass-roofed rotunda, *faux marble* pillars, and 19th-century bronze fixtures. The library has also installed two museums to house part of its huge collection: a museum of the theater and a museum of sounds and recording (where you can find the voices of **Sarah Bernhardt** and **Captain Dreyfus** among 800,000 other records). Two exhibition halls for prints and photos have also been established. ♦ Daily 8AM-8PM. Entrance on Rue des Petits-Champs. Métros: Bourse, Pyramides

In 1858 a would-be assassin known as Orsini the Carbonaro threw a homemade bomb at a carriage carrying Napoléon III to an opera house. Though the emperor was unharmed, 156 bystanders were killed or injured. With this incident in mind, architect Charles Garnier added a special entrance to his design for another opera house on Rue Auber, which allowed Napoléon III's coach to be driven directly to the level of the dress circle via a curved double ramp into the royal box called the Emperor's Pavilion. Rumor has it that this thoughtful touch helped Garnier's opera design win out over 171 other competing architects.

104 Bibliothèque Nationale In 1537 a copy-
right act was passed to ensure that a copy
of every book published in France would be
housed in a royal library. The result of four
centuries of book and document assembly
is now kept in one of the world's greatest
national libraries, in a building whose architecture is as impressive as its collection.

The library came to occupy its present site
in the 17th century, when **Cardinal Mazarin**

St.-Honoré

merged two of his mansions, the **Hôtel Tubeuf**
and the **Hôtel Chivry.** The collection initially
included 500 pictures and art objects owned
by the cardinal himself. When **Colbert,** finance
minister to **Louis XIV,** moved the library to
his own mansion on Rue Vivienne in 1666,
the collection numbered 200,000 volumes.
In 1720 the library was combined again with
the original Mazarin collection. Today the
library's 68 miles of shelves bend under
the weight of more than nine million books,
including two **Gutenberg** bibles, first editions of
Rabelais, and manuscripts of **Proust** and **Hugo.**
The library received its most dramatic space
in 1854, when the architect **Henri Labrouste**
was commissioned to design a reading room
within the old courtyard of the Palais Mazarin.
The result is the magnificent toplit **Salle des
Imprimés,** which consists of nine square
vaulted bays supported by 16 cast-iron columns and a network of perforated semicircu-
lar iron arches. The room reveals a further
development of ideas Labrouste first explored
in the design of his Bibliothèque Ste.-Gene-
viève, a landmark building that was the first
monumental public edifice to freely employ
iron as both a structural and a decorative ele-
ment. Peek through the glass doors of the

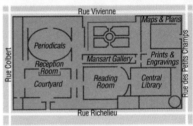

reading room at the Bibliothèque Nationale
(admittance is for members only, although
proof that you're an architect often works)
and admire the beautifully attenuated columns, the gleaming oculi in the ceiling, and
the graceful curves of the iron latticework.
Also be sure to see the **Houdon** statue of
Voltaire in the **Salle d'Honneur** (State Room)
on the ground floor. The philosopher's heart
is ensconced in the pedestal.

The library is divided into 11 departments:
printed books; periodicals and newspapers;
manuscripts; prints and engravings; maps
and plans; medals, coins, and antiques; tech-
nical; audiovisual; arms and weapons; performing arts; and music. ♦ Galleries Mazarin
and Mansart: open for temporary exhibitions.
Musée des Médailles et Antiques: M-Sa 9AM-
4PM. Photo Gallery (4 Rue Louvois): M-Sa
noon-6:30PM. 58 Rue de Richelieu. Métros:
Bourse, Palais-Royal. 47.03.81.26

105 Mercure Galant ★★$$/$$$ Attractive
decor, first-rate service, and specialties such
as homemade duck foie gras, shellfish in puff
pastry, lobster gratin, and lamb marinated in
spicy oil make this a perfect choice for business lunches, among other things. ♦ M-F
noon-2:15PM, 7:30-10:15PM; Sa 7:30-
10:15PM. 15 Rue des Petits-Champs. Reservations recommended. Métros: Bourse,
Pyramides. 42.97.53.85, 42.96.98.89

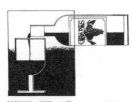

05 Willi's Wine Bar ★★$$ The city's most elegant wine bar bustles nonstop with journalists, lawyers, fashion designers, and the PR crowd who come to partake of 99 French wines and daily specials such as grilled salmon steak, braised oxtail, leg of lamb, pork with fennel, and spinach tarts. The place is run by Willi, the affable Englishman **Mark Williamson,** who knows his Côtes-du-Rhônes. British is spoken here. ♦ Wine bar: M-Sa 11AM-11PM. Restaurant: noon-2:30PM, 7-11PM. 13 Rue des Petits-Champs. Reservations recommended. Métros: Bourse, Pyramides. 42.61.05.09

06 Issé ★★★$$$/$$$$ The city's best (and most expensive) sushi bar also serves impeccable sashimi, grilled salmon, steaming miso soup, red caviar, delectably light tempura, and chirashi, the house specialty. ♦ M, Sa 7-10PM; Tu-F noon-2PM, 7-10PM. 56 Rue Ste.-Anne. Reservations recommended. No credit cards. Métro: Pyramides. 42.96.67.76

07 Pandora ★★$/$$ Behind this chocolate-brown facade is a comfy little tearoom that in summer offers light lunches of cucumbers in yogurt and mint Baltic herring, lemon tarts, and mincemeat pies. Warm winter dishes include chili con carne and chicken *tajine* (stew). ♦ M-F 11:30AM-7PM; closed in Aug. 24 Passage Choiseul. Métro: 4-Septembre. 42.97.56.01

08 Coup de Coeur ★★$$ House specialties in this small, friendly restaurant with modern decor include salmon tartare with chives, *magret de canard,* roasted red mullet filets, and a sinfully delicious chocolate dessert. ♦ M-F noon-2:30PM, 7-10:30PM; Sa 7:30-10:30PM. 19 Rue St.-Augustin. Reservations recommended. Métros: 4-Septembre, Pyramides. 47.03.45.70

ach January Parisians celebrate the Epiphany (*La ête des Rois*) with *galette des rois,* a holiday puff-astry pancake filled with almond paste and a hidden inket. The celebrant Frenchman or woman whose ortion of cake contains the charm is king or queen r the day. The best galettes des rois come from alloyau (101 Rue du Faubourg-St.-Honoré), which as been making kings and queens of the Parisian ite since 1949.

---

estaurants/Nightlife: Red   Hotels: Blue
hops/ 🌳Outdoors: Green   Sights/Culture: Black

109 Bar de l'Entracte ★★$/$$ Tucked in a corner behind the Palais Royal, this amusing restaurant and bar is festooned with old costumes from the theater across the street. Paper currency from all around the world flutters on the ceiling. On a warm summer day, enjoy a glass of cool St. Joseph on the outdoor terrace. ♦ M-Sa 10:30AM-2AM. 47 Rue de Montpensier. No credit cards. Métros: Palais-Royal, Pyramides. 42.97.57.76

110 Le Grand Véfour ★★★$$$/$$$$ A favorite Parisian haunt since the 1760s, this fine restaurant is named after **Jean Véfour,** chef to **Philippe,** the **Duke of Orléans,** who was the gent who voted to send his relative **Louis XVI** to the guillotine and later wound up there himself. Seductively and appropriately time-worn, Le Grand Véfour's Louis XVI-Directoire interior is classified as a historic monument. Here **Napoléon** courted **Josephine, Victor Hugo** romanticized, and **Colette** and **Jean Cocteau,** who lived nearby, enjoyed regular repasts. ♦ M-F 12:30-2:15PM, 7:30-10:15PM; closed in Aug 17. Rue de Beaujolais. Reservations required. Métros: Bourse, Palais-Royal. 42.96.56.27

St.-Honoré

111 Matsuri Sushi ★$$ Customers hunker around a circular bar to snag plates of raw salmon and tuna sailing by on a conveyor belt. To tally the check, waiters simply count the dishes in front of each diner. At lunch, every fifth item is free. So is home delivery throughout the day within Paris city limits. ♦ Restaurant and delivery: M 7-11:30PM; Tu-Th noon-2:30PM, 7-11:30PM. 36 Rue de Richelieu. Métro: Palais-Royal. 42.61.05.73 (reservations), 40.26.12.13 (delivery)

112 Chez Pauline ★★$$$ When tradition works this well, why change? This relaxed restaurant serves French classics such as beef Bourguignonne, *poularde de Bresse*, wild creamed mushrooms with chives, warm foie gras salad, fricassee of sole and crayfish, game in season, and a variety of *plats du jour* such as stuffed cabbage, cassoulet with preserved goose, bacon with lentils, and calf's liver. ♦ M-F 12:30-2:30PM, 7:30-10:30PM; closed surrounding the week of 15 Aug. 5 Rue Villedo. Reservations recommended. Métro: Pyramides. 42.96.20.70, 42.61.79.01

According to the National Wine Bureau, only one French adult in five drinks wine daily, and one in two never touches the stuff.

Palais Royal

113 Molière Fountain The fountain at the junction of Rue de Richelieu and Rue Molière was dedicated in 1773, the centennial of the playwright's death. The monument was designed by **Visconti** and the statue by **Seurre.** Molière's statue is seated atop, pen in hand, flanked on either side by marble statues representing both light and serious comedy, which makes for lofty company altogether. ♦ Métro: Pyramides

113 Juveniles ★★$$ This lively *bistrot à vin* just down the street from the Bibliothèque Nationale is the brainchild of wine-lovers **Mark Williamson** (of Willi's Wine Bar) and his partner, **Tim Johnston.** It's a comfortable spot for noshing on tapas, rabbit pâté, chicken wings, ample sandwiches (chicken salad, beef, and watercress), and afterwards

St.-Honoré

enjoying a slice of their dense, flourless chocolate cake. Wash it all down with an excellent, reasonably priced Bourgueil. ♦ M-Sa noon-11PM. 47 Rue de Richelieu. Métro: Bourse. 42.97.46.49

113 Barrière Poquelin ★★$$/$$$ Serving an original nouvelle cuisine: steamed fish with mushrooms, salmon *unilatérale,* spicy chicken, roast game, and, to top it off, a hot apple tart. ♦ M-F 12:15-2PM, 7:15-10:30PM; Sa 7:15-10:30PM; closed the first three weeks of Aug. 17 Rue Molière. Reservations recommended. Métro: Pyramides. 42.96.22.19

114 La Boutique du Bridgeur The only store in Paris catering strictly to bridge players, this boutique sells bridge tables, scorepads, playing cards, and instruction manuals. If you write in advance, their affiliated bridge club might help find you a partner. ♦ M-F 10AM-6:30PM; Sa 10AM-6PM. 28 Rue de Richelieu. Métro: Palais-Royal. 42.96.25.50

114 L'Incroyable Restaurant ★★$ What's incredible about this seven-table restaurant hidden on a cobbled passage are the generous portions and bargain prices. ♦ M, Sa 11:45AM-2:15PM; Tu-F 11:45AM-2:15PM, 6:30-10:30PM. 26 Rue de Richelieu or 23 Rue Montpensier. No credit cards. Métro: Palais-Royal. 42.96.24.64

115 Palais Royal This six-acre enclave of flowering serenity is completely surrounded by, yet separate from, the urban bustle. Commissioned by **Cardinal Richelieu,** and designed by his architect **Lemercier** in 1642, the palace was christened Palais Royal when **Anne of Austria** temporarily lived here with her son, young **Louis XIV.** In 1780 the property fell into the hands of the shrewd **Philippe, Duke of Orléans,** who embarked on a lucrative and fancy bit of real estate speculation. He hired the architect **Victor Louis** (who built the nearby Théâtre Français) to design a square like Venice's Piazza San Marco, but containing a garden (700 feet by 300 feet), to be faced on three sides with elegant apartments incorporating arcades that had space for 180 shops, which the duke then sold for immense profit. (He also named the bordering streets after his three sons: Valois, Beaujolais, and Montpensier.)

Strolling through the lime-tree groves here became the fashion for French aristocrats as well as for American visitors such as **Thomas Jefferson** and **Washington Irving.** The garden's elegance soon frayed, however, when the profligate Philippe became chronically broke and began renting the galleries to magicians, wax museums, circuses, and brothels. Under his dissolute management, the Palais Royal attracted the Parisian rabble, questionable dandies, and women of easy virtue; soon it became a raffish, depraved enclave. (As late 1804, historians listed the presence of 11 loan sharks, 18 gambling houses, and 17 billiard halls in the palace arcades.) **Marat** referred to the gardens as the "nucleus of the Revolution." Ironically, it was here that **Charlotte Corday** bought the dagger she used to kill Marat. It was also here on 13 July 1789 that **Camille Desmoulins** incited his fellow Parisians to take up arms. Like the Tuileries Palace, the Palais Royal was ransacked during the revolt of 1848; a giant bonfire was kindled in the courtyard with gilt chairs, paintings, and canopies thrown from the windows by the mob. Among the furniture destroyed was the throne on which **Louis Philippe** first sat as king of France.

By the 20th century the luxurious apartments overlooking the gardens housed a number of famous residents: poet and dramatist **Jean**

Cocteau lived here, as did **Colette.** She resided at **9 Rue de Beaujolais** and was often seen writing at her window overlooking the court-yard. Colette died as stylishly as she'd lived: suddenly and painlessly after drinking a glass of champagne. Today the Palais Royal arcades are occupied by curiosity shops sell-ing antiques, old books, cheap jewelry, lead soldiers, medals, and rare stamps. The gar-den is embellished by the fountain where the infant Louis XIV once sailed his toy boats and by two quite modern fountains resembling giant ball bearings. The larger court of the Palais Royal has been the focus of an aesthetic debate reminiscent of the one surrounding the Louvre transformation. Minister of Cul-ture **Jack Lang** initiated a project (conceived by sculptor **Daniel Buren)** that involved the planting of 252 black-and-white striped col-umns, deep pools, and airport lights in the courtyard floor. In the winter of 1986 resi-dents of the palace who objected to the scheme won a court order to temporarily halt construction on the site. The project, how-ever, was completed the following summer. ♦ Métro: Palais-Royal

16 Restaurant Pierre ★★★$$/$$$ In the shadow of the Comédie Française, this res-taurant offers a warm immersion in the mood of France's Massif Central region. Try veal kidneys, *St. Pierre á la rhubarbe,* roast rabbit with mustard sauce, *gratin dauphinois,* a more refined pike with chives, or *estofinade rouergate,* in which the simple codfish achieves transcendence. ♦ M-F noon-2PM, 7-10PM; closed in Aug. 10 Rue de Richelieu. Reservations recommended. Métro: Palais-Royal. 42.96.09.17

16 Montpensier $$ The fact that this hotel was the former residence of a baroness who was a favorite of **Louis XV** explains why it has rooms of varying dimensions and prices. ♦ 12 Rue de Richelieu. Métro: Palais-Royal. 42.96.28.50

16 Dynasty ★★$ This reasonably priced Chi-nese restaurant with pink tablecloths features a menu that's enlivened by several incendiary Vietnamese and Thai specialties. ♦ M-Sa noon-2:30PM, 7:30-11PM. Rue de Richelieu. Métro: Palais-Royal. 42.96.08.92

nspired perhaps by the shopping arcades of Palais Royal and Place des Vosges, Parisians built scores of glass-roofed shopping streets during the sudden urst of consumerism at the beginning of the Indus-rial Revolution. About 24 of these 19th-century galler-es remain today, most of them sadly neglected. Nev-rtheless, there is nothing more pleasant on a rainy day than charting a walk (with a good map of Paris) hat follows these interconnecting chains of tunnels. Dallying en route, you can poke your nose into forgot-en old shops specializing in such things as walking ticks, war medals, meerschaum pipes, antique ameras, and art supplies. Among the passages most likely to spark your imagination are Passage les Panoramas, Galerie Vivienne, Véro-Dodat, ouffroy, and Choiseul.

Voltaire

117 Comédie Française In 1673, while per-forming in his own *Le Malade Imaginaire,* the 51-year-old dramatist **Molière** collapsed onstage and died as the curtain came down. (Legend has it that there were several doctors in the audience who were so enraged by the play's criticism of medicine that they would not treat its dying author.) Seven years later **Louis XIV** founded the Comédie Française with the remaining members of the playwright's troupe. Today it is France's most prestigious theatrical group, residing since the end of the 18th cen-tury in this rather small Doric-style theater de-signed by **Victor Louis.** The company has sur-vived the Bourbon monarchy, the Revolution, two empires, and four republics, and still plays

to packed audiences. After Molière, the theater's most celebrated thespian was the spirited tragic actress **Sarah Bernhardt** (the "Divine Sarah," born **Rosine Bernard** in Paris), who played roles ranging from Cleopatra to Hamlet, thereby reviving Shakespeare in France. Bernhardt was a dynamic, flamboyant sort of character who was fond of saying, even in old age: "Rest? With all eternity before me?"

Today the Comédie Française sticks to serious classical French drama, though not too long ago it conceded the existence of foreign play-wrights. A foyer-bar opens onto a gallery dis-playing busts of famous playwrights. The up-stairs foyer is graced with a notable stone statue of **Voltaire** by **Houdon** and the leather armchair into which Molière collapsed during his last act on stage (illustrated above). ♦ Tours for individuals: third Sunday of each month at 10:15AM starting at the administration entrance on the Place Colette. Tours for groups: second and fourth Sunday of each month (must be reserved three to four months in advance). Box office: daily 11AM-6PM. A special window around the side of the building opens 45 min-utes before the curtain to sell greatly reduced tickets for the night's performance. 2 Rue de Richelieu. Métro: Palais-Royal. 40.15.00.15 (box office), 42.96.10.24 (administration)

118 Place du Théâtre Français/Place André-Malraux In 1874 these two squares were graced by a duo of elegant but simple **Davioud** fountains decorated with bronze nymphs by **Carrier-Belleuse** and **Math Moreau.** ♦ Métros: Palais-Royal, Pyramides

118 Manufacture Nationale de Sèvres This showroom lies adjacent to the famous and venerable (circa 1738) Sèvres porcelain factory. An exhibition of designs ranges from Louis XVI dinner plates to an abstract lamp designed in 1984 by Japanese artist **Asuka Tsu-Boi.** All items sold here are tax-free. ♦ Showroom: Tu-Sa 11AM-6PM. 4 Place André-Malraux. Métro: Palais-Royal. 47.03.40.20

118 Osaka ★★$ An authentic, inexpensive Japanese soup kitchen serving the hundreds of Tokyo tourists who frequent the Opéra-Palais Royal neighborhood. Miso soup, thick with noodles, and pot stickers are the best bets. Next door is a pricey sushi bar and restaurant under the same management. ♦ M-Sa 10AM-8PM. 1 Place André-Malraux. Reservations recommended. Métro: Palais-Royal. 42.60.65.35

118 161 Rue St.-Honoré On this site of the Moroccan Tourist Office once stood the old **St.-Honoré Gate,** where **Jeanne d'Arc** was wounded in the thigh by an English archer in 1429. She was hit while measuring the depth of the moat with her lance in preparation for an assault on the city. ♦ Métro: Palais-Royal

St.-Honoré

119 Hôtel du Louvre $$$ This modern hotel is situated beside the Palais Royal, Tuileries, and Comédie Française, and within walking distance of the Opéra and the Louvre. What more could you ask for? ♦ Place André-Malraux. Métro: Palais-Royal. 42.61.56.01, 42.61.52.52

119 A la Civette For more than two centuries this store has been in the forefront of tobacconists. It was the first shop in Paris to import the fine Montecristo cigar from Cuba. Shelves are cluttered with chewing tobacco, pipes, cigarillos, and stogies to delight the wheeziest connoisseur. ♦ M-Sa 8:30AM-7PM. 157 Rue St.-Honoré. Métro: Palais-Royal. 42.96.04.99

119 Delamain A wonderful old bookshop whose window displays rival museum exhibitions, with everything from 18th-century hand-bound volumes on **King Clovis** to modern editions of **Samuel Beckett.** ♦ M-Sa 10AM-7PM. 155 Rue St.-Honoré. Métro: Palais-Royal. 42.61.48.78

120 Le Louvre des Antiquaires An association of more than 240 antique shops encompasses three floors. You'll find Art Deco prints, period perfume bottles, miniature 16th-century manuscripts, rare Japanese woodcuts, fin-de-siècle dolls and children's clothes, African tribal masks, and Thai Buddhas. One can find any old thing here except a bargain. Be advised that many of these dealers have their main antique shops (generally larger and less expensive) on the Left Bank, so take a card and pay them a visit when you're on the other side of the river. Also, before making a purchase, make sure you understand the complicated regulations concerning the removal of antiques from the country.

This building was formerly the **Grand Hôtel du Louvre,** where **Mark Twain** stayed in 1867. It was here that Twain met the tour guide **Ferguson** who figures in *Innocents Abroad* (1869). ♦ Tu-Su 11AM-7PM. 2 Place du Palais-Royal. Métro: Palais-Royal. 42.97.27.00

121 Passage Véro-Dodat Named after two pork butchers who were here from the start, this covered passageway was the city's first public thoroughfare to be illuminated by gas lighting. ♦ Métros: Louvre, Palais-Royal

121 Robert Capia This antique doll store is a favorite of **Catherine Deneuve.** ♦ M-Sa 10AM-7PM. 24-26 Galerie Véro-Dodat. Métros: Louvre, Palais-Royal. 42.36.25.94

122 Maison Micro A Greek bazaar of produce from Hellas: vats of olives and hot peppers, burlap sacks of whole grains and flour, crates of dried fruits, and barrels of tarama. Step inside and take an Aegean whiff. ♦ M 2-6:45PM; Tu-Sa 8:30AM-12:30PM, 1:30-6:45PM. 142-144 Rue St.-Honoré. Métros: Louvre, Palais-Royal. 42.60.53.02, 42.60.65.17

122 Chez Nous ★$$ The city's best jock bar and restaurant is run by **Gilbert Ghiraldi,** an ex-rugby player. If you manage to out-maneuver the French national rugby team that huddles here, grab a table and order one of chef **Véronique's** Basque specialties. ♦ Daily noon-2:30PM, 7PM-midnight. 150 Rue St.-Honoré. No credit cards. Métros: Louvre, Palais-Royal. 42.60.29.75

122 Le Globe d'Or ★★$$/$$$ This restaurant offers roasted calf's liver under a gravel of coarse black pepper, duck with potatoes, *confit de canard,* and Castelnaudary bean cassoulet—the response of southwestern France to a hearty appetite. ♦ M-F noon-2:30PM, 8-10:30PM. 158 Rue St.-Honoré. Reservations recommended. Métros: Louvre, Palais-Royal. 42.60.23.37

123 115 Rue St.-Honoré Here, two centuries ago, **Count Fersen** bought the invisible ink with which he penned his famous letters to **Marie Antoinette.** ♦ Métro: Louvre

Bests

Bill Murray
Actor and Former Sorbonne Student

The hors d'oeuvres at **L'Impasse.** We used to live just up the street and it was my favorite restaurant, though I never tried the tripe. It doesn't seem fair to ask one stomach to digest another.

Afternoon tea dancing downstairs at **La Coupole;** the **Select** for the best *croque monsieur* served on *pain Poilâne;* the **Passages** (the farther north the better, because the stores get cheaper); the **Parc des Buttes-Chaumont;** the 20th arrondissement, where it gets the most African; the Tunisian temple in the **Parc de Montsouris;** the **Place des Vosges,** where my son always played; the Chinese restaurants in Belleville; and the beekeepers in the **Luxembourg Gardens.**

The **statue of Beaumarchais** near the Bastille. The neighborhood is always dressing him up with funny underwear, painting his lips, and adorning him with a blind-man's cane.

The way the *bateaux mouches* pivot around the Statue of Liberty on the **Seine,** with the **Eiffel Tower** in the background. It's like a panning movie camera.

Richard Reeves
American Author and Columnist

The women. The magic of Paris is that each Parisienne is a work of art, spending, it seems, hours and years making themselves the best they can be.

The movies. There are hundreds of movie screens operating day and night, all chronicled and described weekly in *Pariscope* for just a few francs.

The **Gare de Lyon**—and everything that comes in and goes out of it.

Hôtel Drouot, where every day anything from old Mixmasters to Old Masters is sold on the spot to the highest bidder.

The **St.-Ouen Flea Market** at Porte de Clignancourt. The place where most of Drouot's stuff ends up—at half the price that Americans pay at home.

The bridges, the florists, the **Rodin Museum,** the Sunday market on Rue de Buci near St.-Germain-des-Prés, and the **Luxembourg Gardens.**

Les soldes. The sales in Paris in January and June are the most extraordinary in the world. Advertised even in *Le Monde,* they attract everyone from Saudi princesses to shopgirls looking for 50 to 80 percent off everything.

Small hotels. Why don't America's largest cities have even one good small hotel, when every block in Paris has two?

The **Bazaar de l'Hôtel-de-Ville (BHV)** is my favorite department store in the world. The hardware department alone takes a morning to understand.

Reservations. The French actually honor reservations. Your reserved table is yours and not a commodity to be turned over as many times as possible each night.

Vietnamese restaurants. Perfect (and cheap) relief from the riches of French cuisine. If there is a bad Vietnamese restaurant in Paris, I have yet to find it.

Anne Willan
President of La Varenne Ecole de Cuisine

The triangle in the seventh arrondissement bounded by the Eiffel Tower, Les Invalides, and the air terminal is my home ground. To wander the little back alleys is a constant pleasure, for they shelter traditional artisans—shoemakers, bookbinders, basketweavers—who have been forced off the high-rent main streets.

Rue Augereau and **Rue de l'Exposition** (renamed at the time of the Great Paris Exhibition of 1867) are particularly rich in little restaurants and shops such as **l'Oiseau Bleu** on Rue Augereau, a picture-frame store where you can always find a few bargain items for sale. On Rue Sedillot is **Horlogerie Ancienne,** one of the best menders of antique clocks in Paris. Here, too, you might pick up the occasional timepiece.

In need of refreshment? Pastry chef Denis Ruffel at **Millet,** on Rue St.-Dominique, is renowned beyond the arrondissement for his honey madeleines, flaky croissants, and pain au chocolat, stuffed with not one but two sticks of chocolate. Or pick up a box of his chocolates to take away—they are made on the premises, of course.

For a true bistro meal (my favorite kind), I suggest three possibilities: The **Fontaine de Mars** on Rue St.-Dominique is modest, full of chattering locals, and known for its hot dandelion salad with bacon and its quail with cabbage. Spots farther along the street such as **Thoumieux** are harder and harder to find. Here confit of duck and steak *frites* are best-sellers. Waiters in their shirtsleeves open bottles of house red wine with a conjurer's dexterity, and the noise level reaches a maximum around 11PM. For the very best bistro food I go to **De Chez Eux** on Avenue

St.-Honoré

Lowendaal. It has everything—baskets of dried mountain sausages, homemade terrines, and hors d'oeuvres so copious the dishes must be stacked in towers on the table.

Nicholas Clément
Racehorse Trainer

Hot chocolate and croissants for breakfast in any café.

Visiting boutiques and gadget shops in the **Forum des Halles.**

Châteaubriand with sauce Béarnaise and Bordeaux wine for lunch at **Fouquet's** on the Champs-Elysées.

Going to the latest American film on the Champs-Elysées.

The seafood special for dinner at **Chez Francis** at the Place de l'Alma.

Evenings at **Castel's, Régine's, Palace, Bains-Douches,** and **Calavados.**

And, of course, flat racing on Sunday afternoons at **Longchamp** racetrack in the **Bois de Boulogne,** particularly the big races such as the **Arc de Triomphe** (held the first Sunday in October). Also the **Prix du Jockey Club** race at Chantilly (the first Sunday in June) and the **Prix de Diane Hermes** race at Chantilly (the second Sunday in June).

Montmartre

Crowned with that alabaster wedding-cake church known as **Sacré-Coeur**, Montmartre is the balcony of Paris—half dream, half nightmare. It is a tangle of contradictions: meandering country roads, seedy strip joints, early Christian sites, tourist clichés, sublime vistas, and hidden passages. The butte (which is what Parisians call this storied sandstone height) is geographically the highest point in town (427 feet) and the traditional home of poets, singers, painters, and bohemians of all kinds.

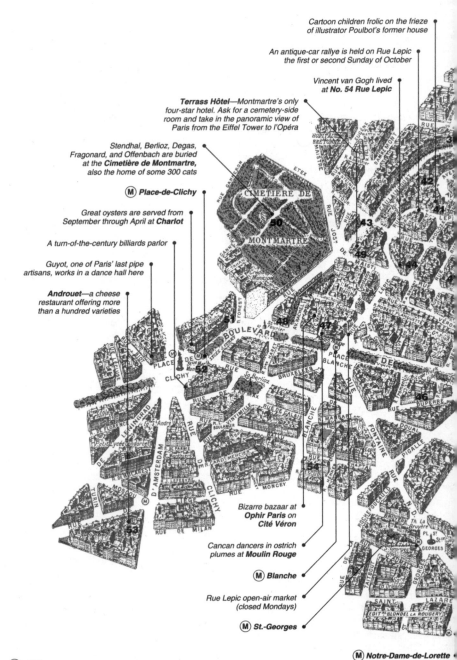

Cartoon children frolic on the frieze of illustrator Poulbot's former house

An antique-car rallye is held on Rue Lepic the first or second Sunday of October

Vincent van Gogh lived at **No. 54 Rue Lepic**

Terrass Hôtel—Montmartre's only four-star hotel. Ask for a cemetery-side room and take in the panoramic view of Paris from the Eiffel Tower to l'Opéra

Stendhal, Berlioz, Degas, Fragonard, and Offenbach are buried at the **Cimetière de Montmartre**, also the home of some 300 cats

Ⓜ **Place-de-Clichy**

Great oysters are served from September through April at **Charlot**

A turn-of-the-century billiards parlor

Guyot, one of Paris' last pipe artisans, works in a dance hall here

Androuet—a cheese restaurant offering more than a hundred varieties

Bizarre bazaar at **Ophir Paris** on **Cité Véron**

Cancan dancers in ostrich plumes at **Moulin Rouge**

Ⓜ **Blanche**

Rue Lepic open-air market (closed Mondays)

Ⓜ **St.-Georges**

Ⓜ = Métro

Ⓜ **Notre-Dame-de-Lorette**

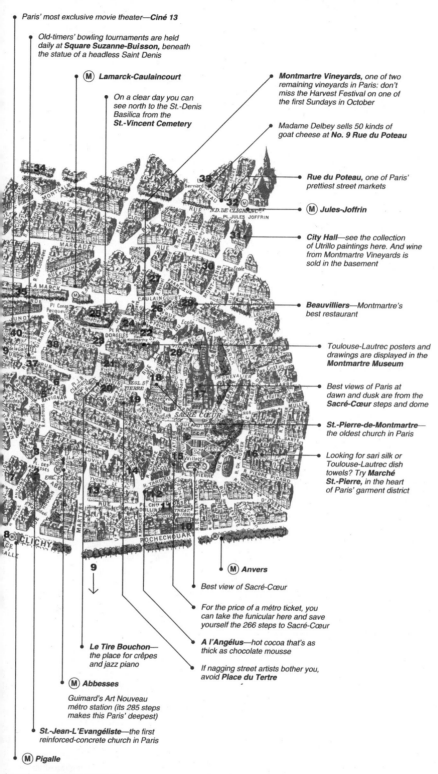

Moulin de la Galette—the last old
windmill in Paris was painted by Renoir

Paris' most exclusive movie theater—**Ciné 13**

Old-timers' bowling tournaments are held
daily at **Square Suzanne-Buisson,** beneath
the statue of a headless Saint Denis

(M) **Lamarck-Caulaincourt**

On a clear day you can
see north to the St.-Denis
Basilica from the
St.-Vincent Cemetery

Montmartre Vineyards, one of two
remaining vineyards in Paris: don't
miss the Harvest Festival on one of
the first Sundays in October

Madame Delbey sells 50 kinds of
goat cheese at **No. 9 Rue du Poteau**

Rue du Poteau, one of Paris'
prettiest street markets

(M) **Jules-Joffrin**

City Hall—see the collection
of Utrillo paintings here. And wine
from Montmartre Vineyards is
sold in the basement

Beauvilliers—Montmartre's
best restaurant

Toulouse-Lautrec posters and
drawings are displayed in the
Montmartre Museum

Best views of Paris at
dawn and dusk are from the
Sacré-Cœur steps and dome

St.-Pierre-de-Montmartre—
the oldest church in Paris

Looking for sari silk or
Toulouse-Lautrec dish
towels? Try **Marché
St.-Pierre,** in the heart
of Paris' garment district

9
↓

(M) **Anvers**

Best view of Sacré-Cœur

For the price of a métro ticket, you
can take the funicular here and save
yourself the 266 steps to Sacré-Cœur

Le Tire Bouchon—
the place for crêpes
and jazz piano

A l'Angélus—hot cocoa that's as
thick as chocolate mousse

If nagging street artists bother you,
avoid **Place du Tertre**

(M) **Abbesses**

Guimard's Art Nouveau
métro station (its 285 steps
makes this Paris' deepest)

St.-Jean-L'Evangéliste—the first
reinforced-concrete church in Paris

(M) **Pigalle**

In an abandoned piano factory at
13 Place Emile-Goudeau, painters
Picasso, Braque, Gris, and Modigliani
fathered the modern-art movement

This walk is best made (rain or shine) on Tuesday, when the museums in the other parts of Paris are closed, or when you feel like fleeing the city for a few hours. Emerging from Hector Guimard's Art Nouveau Abbesses métro station, start the day with café au lait and brioches in one of the cafés along **Rue des Abbesses,** which is crowded with butchers, bakers, and fishmongers from the Rue Lepic street market. Then begin the ascent to **Place du Tertre,** a 14th-century square that in summer is a free-for-all between the street artists, outdoor restaurant waiters, and tourists. The best bets for lunch are crêpes at **Le Tire Bouchon,** fish at **La Crémaillère 1900** on Place du Tertre, or the sublime *foies de volailles* at **L'Assommoir.** After the obligatory pilgrimage to **Sacré-Coeur,** wind down Rue Lepic past the **Moulin de la Galette** until you see the red neon signs of that other temple of folklore, the **Moulin Rouge.** Stay for the cancan show or return to the butte for the evening cabaret at the legendary **Au Lapin Agile.** The métro closes at 12:45AM, but you will find a taxi just down the hill on **Rue Caulaincourt,** the same street taken by revelers in the wine-festival parade held in October.

The name Montmartre has two possible origins: the "Mount of Mercury," to whom a Roman temple on the butte was once dedicated, or the "Mount of Martyrs," commemorating **Saint Denis** (Dionysius), the first bishop of Paris, who, along with the priest **Rusticus** (his own sort of Sancho Panza) and the deacon **Eleutherius,** was tortured and decapitated by the Romans in AD 250. According to the legend, Saint Denis picked up his severed head and carried it 12 miles over the hill. One thousand years later, the Basilica of St.-Denis was built on that hill, where for centuries the kings and queens of France have been buried. (The bishop and deacon did not make the headless trek, and as consolation had streets in Montmartre named after them.)

Montmartre

A lesser-known local martyr was **Pierre-Charles Debray,** the mill owner who during the 1814 invasion of Montmartre by Cossacks was crucified on the blades of his **Moulin de la Galette,** a windmill with a garden tavern and dance hall that a century later would ironically symbolize *Gay Paree* on a **Renoir** canvas. Artists such as Renoir, **van Gogh, Dufy,** and **Utrillo;** poets **Apollinaire, Max Jacob,** and **Jacques Prévert;** and novelist **Boris Vian,** songwriter **Aristide Bruant,** and illustrator **André Gill** all worked in Montmartre. In the late 19th century **Toulouse-Lautrec** sketched the cancan dancers at the Moulin Rouge here, and **Picasso, Braque,** and **Gris,** working out of an abandoned piano factory nearby, gave birth to cubism. Cabarets such as Au Lapin Agile further encouraged *la vie bohème,* and the life was much romanticized by Americans in Paris. Writer **John Roderigo Dos Passos,** for instance, rhapsodized in 1918 that he wanted his heart "to be preserved in a pitcher of *vin de Beaujolais* in the restaurant in Place du Tertre on the summit of Montmartre."

After World War I the artistic center moved to another of the city's seven hills, **Montparnasse,** on the Left Bank. The nightlife, however, remained in Mont-

martre and grew in notoriety. Montmartre reputedly contains the oldest church sanctuary in Paris (St.-Pierre) and was dominated in the 12th century by an abbey run by women. Today the area is best known for women (and men disguised as women) plying an older, less pious profession. Painters may have once scouted out portrait models among the seam-stresses and dancers in **Place Pigalle,** but the seamier live sex shows, porn films, and peep shops took over at the end of World War II. Avoid the crowded butte on weekends. The notable exceptions to this rule are the first Saturday and second Sunday in October, the dates of the local annual wine-harvest festival and the vintage-car rallye, respectively. Both events are worth attending.

1 Abbesses Métro Station Named after *les abbesses,* the nuns who ran the abbey here in the Middle Ages, this métro station is 300 feet below grade, the deepest in Paris. The reason lies in Montmartre's old gypsum mines. Gypsum, a soft stone, was burned to make the internationally famous plaster of Paris used, among other things, to mold busts of George Washington and Thomas Jefferson in the US capitol. Over the years, the growing network of quarry tunnels beneath Montmartre turned the hill, geologically speaking, to Swiss cheese. In the 1840s the mines were closed, but not before 27 houses and several Parisians had disappeared into the void.

The City of Paris is still filling Montmartre's cavities with high-pressure concrete. The métro platform was built at bedrock, precisely 285 steps below **Place des Abbesses.** Take the elevator and save your breath for the Montmartre summit.

The turn-of-the-century exterior of the Abbesses métro station, with its green vinelike, wrought-iron arches and amber lights, is one of the most picturesque in Paris and typifies the early Art Nouveau designs of architect **Hector Guimard.** At first, nationalistic Parisians criticized Guimard's choice of German green and suggested he paint his métro stations *bleu, blanche, et rouge.* His concession to chauvinism was a ship shield (the symbol of the City of Paris) in the middle of the roof, but he stubbornly held his ground on garden green. *Et voila!* (The only other Guimard station that still has its original glass roof is Porte-Dauphine near the Bois de Boulogne.) Ironically, the Abbesses métro entrance is not original to the butte. For decades it stood in front of Hôtel de Ville (city hall), but when **Mayor Jacques Chirac** gussied up the plaza, he banished Guimard's masterpiece to Montmartre. New York's Museum of Modern Art has in its collection an old *Métropolitain* sign and one of these early Guimard arches.

2 St.-Jean-L'Evangéliste Soon after its construction, this Moorish grab bag of architectural tricks (trimmed with what looks like turquoise Art Nouveau jewelry) was rechristened by the neighborhood **Brick St.-John.** Looking amazingly contemporary for an octogenarian, the 1904 church distinguishes itself as the first erected in Paris with reinforced concrete. ♦ M-Sa 8:30AM-noon, 3-7:30PM; Su 8:30AM-noon, 4-7PM. 19-21 Rue des Abbesses. Métro: Abbesses

3 Hôtel Régyn's Montmartre $$ This hotel is in the heart of Montmartre, but otherwise it's nothing fancy. ♦ 18 Place des Abbesses. Métro: Abbesses. 42.54.45.21

4 Gilbert Peyre's Studio This talented metal sculptor with a riotous mustache constructs fantastic contraptions that come to life with the pull of a string or the flick of a switch. Using bicycle chains, coffee cans, camera bellows, and other found objects, Peyre creates whimsical flying machines, trapeze artists, sword swallowers, and other characters to make you giggle. Good luck getting the sword swallower into your suitcase, but stop by anyway to watch Peyre at work. ♦ M-Sa 2-8PM; closed whenever he chooses. 24 Rue Durantin. Métro: Abbesses. 42.64.06.55

4 Place Emile-Goudeau On the former site of a famous *guinguette* (garden tavern) where Parisians came to eat and drink was the famous old piano factory at 13 Place Emile-Goudeau that art historians call the Villa Médici of Modern Art. By the turn of the century this place had attracted poets **Apollinaire** and **Max Jacob,** and other painters **Picasso, Braque, Juan Gris,** and **Modigliani.** Picasso worked here for eight years, painting works such as *Les Demoiselles d'Avignon* (which is now in the collection of New York's Museum of Modern Art, and is often cited as the first example of cubism). This ramshackle building, which had but one water spigot to serve the 40 artists housed here, was ironically dubbed *Bateau Lavoir* after those Renaissance laundry barges inundated with water from the Seine. The original structure burned in 1970, and the City of Paris now rents rebuilt studios (and provides plenty of water) to the far more prosperous, though certainly not more talented, artists of today. ♦ Métro: Abbesses

4 Tim Hôtel $$ Had this two-star hotel been here 70 years ago, you might have asked your neighbors **Pablo Picasso** or **Georges Braque** over for coffee and croissants. ♦ 11 Rue Ravignan (Place Emile-Goudeau). Métro: Abbesses. 42.55.74.79

4 Four Graces Fountain Layered in green paint, this drinking fountain (and 99 other identical ones around Paris) was the gift of **Richard Wallace,** an Englishman who collected 18th-century French art and frequently lamented that it was impossible in his beloved Paris to enjoy a glass of water in a café without paying for it. The metal drinking cup originally attached to it in the 1870s disappeared in the 1950s when the city gave way to sanitation standards. ♦ Rue Ravignan (Place Emile-Goudeau). Métro: Abbesses

5 Relais de la Butte $ Run by a cheerful former barge captain, this restaurant is heavy on the "little old Montmartre" ambience (reminiscent of when Montmartre was a small village) but offers a pot-au-feu, homemade *rillettes*, foie gras, filet of sole with salmon soufflé, and chocolate mousse at bargain prices. ♦ Tu 7PM-midnight; W-Su noon-3PM, 7PM-midnight. 12 Rue Ravignan. Métro: Abbesses. 42.23.94.64

6 Rue de la Mire Getting lost in the twisting streets of Montmartre can be done with the greatest of ease, except on this short pedestrian street. An 18th-century trail marker

(*mire*, hence the street name) points due north. ♦ Métros: Abbesses, Lamarck-Caulaincourt

7 Le Restaurant ★★$$ Modern, minimalist decor complements the array of original and revived cuisine served here: oyster and sorrel omelet, beef marrow tart with red wine sauce, persillade of stuffed squid, and an exquisite crème brûlée. ♦ Tu-Sa noon-2:30PM, 8-10:30PM; closed second half of Aug. 32 Rue Véron. Reservations recommended. Métro: Abbesses. 42.23.06.22

8 Place Pigalle Nineteenth-century sculptor **Jean-Baptiste Pigalle's** celebrated rendering of the Virgin Mary is displayed in **St.-Sulpice,** but his name became synonymous with porn films, sex shops, and prostitutes by dint of being associated with this square. Known as **Pig Alley** to WWII GIs who came stalking the professional wildlife, Place Pigalle has lost many of its hookers to Rue St.-Denis and Bois de Boulogne; these days transvestites predominate. ♦ Métro: Pigalle

Restaurants/Nightlife: Red   **Hotels:** Blue
Shops/ ☞Outdoors: Green   **Sights/Culture:** Black

9 Caravelle $$ This comfortable hotel has 33 air-conditioned, soundproofed rooms. Ask for one in back and avoid the noise of traffic and the electric-guitar store across the street. ♦ 68 Rue des Martyrs. Métro: Pigalle. 48.78.43.31

10 Carlton's $$ Surprise, surprise—there's a three-star hotel amid the strip joints and kung fu cinemas of Pigalle. ♦ 55 Blvd Rochechouart. Métro: Anvers. 42.81.91.00

11 Résidence Charles-Dullin $$ These kitchen-equipped flats, located on a tranquil square, are rented by the night or by the week. ♦ 10 Place Charles-Dullin. Métro: Anvers. 42.57.14.55

11 Théâtre de l'Atelier When this charming theater was first built in 1822 on the cobblestoned square (named in 1957 after actor **Charles Dullin**), it was known for the **Stefan Zweig** adaptation of **Ben Johnson's** *Volpone* and for **L'Opéra Bouffe,** which critics called the best stage performances outside Paris. Today, under the direction of **Pierre Franck,** the theater is truly Parisian, and there isn't a bad red-velvet seat in the house. ♦ Box office: M-Sa 11AM-7PM. 1 Place Charles-Dullin. Métro: Anvers. 46.06.49.24

12 Le Gastelier ★$ The tea salon at the foot of Sacré-Coeur is a perfect luncheon stop before making the final ascent up the white stairs. Try a Milanese tart (spinach, tomato, and cheese) and a dish of fresh mandarin sorbet. Better yet, indulge in a few scoops of nougat ice cream or a plate of macaroons, and then waddle over to the funicular and ride up. ♦ Tu-

Su 8AM-8PM. 1bis Rue Tardieu. Métro: Anvers. 46.06.22.06

12 A l'Angélus ★★$ The path to this nonsmoking neighborhood candy store/tea shop is well worn by schoolchildren and Sacré-Coeur pilgrims alike. The *fait maison* (homemade) bonbons and *Angélus* (almond paste and chocolate mousse) are rich enough to sate any sweet tooth. Try the *Alesien* coffee pralines and the *orangettes*, strips of orange rind dipped into a velvety mixture of melted chocolate and almond chips. And on a drizzling winter afternoon, nothing beats their hot cocoa made from melted chocolate bars. ♦ M-Tu, Th-Su 7:45AM-7:30PM. 1 Rue Tardieu. Métro: Anvers. 46.06.03.75

13 Martyrium Just off the Street of Martyrs, where **Saint Denis** was thought to have been decapitated, is the **Chapel of the Auxiliatrices Order.** In the crypt of an earlier medieval sanctuary on this site, Spaniards **Ignatius Loyola** and **Francis Xavier** founded the mighty Jesuit order on 15 August 1534. ♦ M-W, F-Su 10AM-noon, 3-5PM. 11 Rue Yvonne Le Tac. Métro: Pigalle

14 Wanouchka ★$$ Eastern European immigrants swarm here for classic Polish cuisine (pirogen, blintzes, Baltic herring, and borscht) prepared by chef **Roman Rybicki**, a veteran of the Russian Tea Room in New York. Forget the wine list (when in Warsaw, do as the Poles) and order the plum-and-lemon vodka. ♦ M-Tu, Th-Su 7:30-11PM. 28 Rue la Vieuville. Reservations recommended. No credit cards. Métro: Abbesses. 42.57.36.15

15 Funicular The shortest, steepest métro line in Paris runs every few minutes between **Place Suzanne-Valadon** and the base of **Sacré-Coeur.** While the fitness freaks take the stairs, the rest of us ride up in comfort and enjoy the view, all for the price of a normal métro ticket. ♦ Métro: Anvers

15 Rue Foyatier The most photographed steps in Montmartre, all 266 of them, run from **Rue Azais** down to **Place Suzanne-Valadon** (named after **Utrillo's** mother, a talented painter in her own right). All hell breaks loose here at 4:30PM each day when an elementary school lets out and scores of screaming children with miniature leather briefcases on their backs dart across the square in search of their mothers and fathers —the local butchers, bakers, and souvenirmakers—who have come to walk them home. ♦ Métro: Anvers

MARCHÉ St-PIERRE

16 Marché St.-Pierre Paris' most celebrated discount fabric warehouse is the hub of the city's garment district. In this four-story bazaar, pandemonium reigns over acres of tweed, bolts of polyester, and grab-bag bins of last year's argyle socks. There's something trendy or tacky for everyone: students searching for cheap curtains, Punjabi women rummaging for sari silk, or New Wave couturiers stalking ersatz panther pelts. The costumes of the surly salesclerks range from three-piece suits to studded leather jackets and turquoise tights. The method in this madness? Take it from the top: fifth floor, linens and sheets; fourth floor, lace curtains and duvet covers; third floor, silks, velours, and *incrédibles* (exotic odds and ends); second floor, wools and polyesters; ground floor, a bit of everything. Even if Toulouse-Lautrec dishtowels are not on your shopping list, step inside the market and people-watch; the wildlife here beats the city zoo at the Jardin des Plantes. ♦ M 1:30-6:30PM; Tu-Sa 9:30AM-6:30PM. 2 Rue Charles-Nodier. Métro: Anvers. 46.06.92.25

17 Sacré-Coeur Diocesan architect **Paul Abadie's** Roman-Byzantine marble tribute, universally panned by his peers, has nevertheless become enshrined in the Tourists' Top Ten. The highlight of the church for most people is not its design, but the view from its steps—or even better, from the dome (access through the north aisle) at dusk or dawn. The church is devoted to atonement for the massacre of some 58,000 citizens during the **Franco-Prussian War,** and within its mosaic-encrusted interior you can see priests praying for forgiveness for those war crimes 24 hours a day, a tradition that has been carried on since the church was consecrated more than half a century ago. Begun in 1876, Sacré-Coeur took decades to complete; for the first 15 years of construction, pylons were sunk below grade to stabilize the foundation over the old quarry mines. The towering campanile was added in 1904 by **Lucien Magne;** one of the world's heaviest bells, the 19-ton **Savoyarde,** hangs in the belfry.

From the north side of the dome you can see in the distance the green roof of the basilica built on the site where Saint Denis finally put down his head. A trip to the St.-Denis Basilica is worthwhile (one métro ticket will get you there), if only to see the extraordinary collection of tombs where France buried its kings until the time of the Revolution. Most macabre are the tombs of **Marie de Médici** and **Henri IV,** who lie twice in effigy. On the top they are adorned in their finest Renaissance collars and jewels; below, in marble, are their skeletons eaten away by worms. ♦ Admission for dome. Basilica: daily 6:30AM-11PM. Dome: daily 9AM-7PM in summer, 9AM-6PM in winter. Parvis du Sacré-Coeur. Métros: Abbesses, Anvers

18 St.-Pierre-de-Montmartre An important example of early Gothic architecture, this modest, three-aisled structure was begun 16 years before Notre-Dame and claims to be the oldest sanctuary in Paris (two other churches, St.-Germain-des-Prés and St.-Julien-le-Pauvre, make similar claims). What appears to be a tiny provincial church is all that remains of the original abbey, which was founded in 1134 by **King Louis VI** (the Fat) and his wife, **Queen Adélaide,** who is buried here. The church was dedicated and consecrated by **Pope Eugene III** in 1147. Both **Dante** and **Loyola** worshipped here.

Architecturally, the church is a composite. The vaulted choir assuredly dates from the 12th century (notice the walls buckling beneath the weight of more than 800 years), but archaeologists remain divided over whether the four capitaled columns incorporated in the church came from a Roman temple to Mercury or a Merovingian (AD 500-751) church on the site. The original church windows were shattered at the end of WWII by a bomb intended for a nearby bridge. The new windows, added in 1953 by **Max Ingrand,** closely resemble in style the original Gothic stained glass; the three bronze west doors and the cemetery door depicting the Resurrection are by a contemporary Italian sculptor.

Each Good Friday, the archbishop of Paris carries a crucifix up this Mount of Martyrs to St.-Pierre to perform a stations-of-the-cross ceremony. This church's tiny cemetery is the smallest in Paris, with only 85 occupants, among whom are the sculptor **Pigalle,** the navigator **Bougainville** (after whom the purple flowering creeper is named), and Montmartre's first mayor, **Felix Desportes,** as well as the **Debray** family, the original owners of the **Moulin de la Galette** (the family grave is easy to find: look for the miniature windmill on top). ♦ Church: M-Th, Sa-Su 8:45AM-7PM; F 8:45AM-5PM. Cemetery: open only on All Saints' Day (1 Nov) 7:30AM-6PM. 2 Rue du Mont-Cenis. Métro: Abbesses. 46.06.57.63

19 Place du Tertre Part village carnival, part operetta set, this 14th-century square (*tertre* means hillock or mound) is the hub of Montmartre, where busloads of tourists descend to pay homage to the Unknown Artist's awful landscapes and pathetic paintings of melancholy wide-eyed children. In summer (when the square sprouts parasoled restaurant

tables), white-aproned waiters and hustling artists jealously guard their territories; the daily border wars make for great theater. During the Middle Ages the abbey had a scaffold here to hang anyone who disobeyed their rules, including any vineyard owner on the butte who refused to donate a quarter of the wine he pressed to the ladies of the cloth, *les abbesses.*

The tradition of exhibiting paintings in Place du Tertre comes from the 19th century, but unfortunately the quality of art has changed. Located in front of St.-Pierre-de-Montmartre, the square is hard to miss, though you may leave wishing you had. ♦ Métro: Abbesses

19 Le Clairon des Chasseurs $ In this bustling artists' café, where all the patrons seem to have sketchpads under their arms and charcoal pencils behind their ears, painters gather by the window to case prospective clients in the square. The kitchen performs such improbable feats as ruining a *croque-monsieur* (grilled ham-and-cheese sandwich), and the coffee is as muddy as the canvas of Notre-Dame adorning the rear wall. Nevertheless,

this café scores big points as a refuge. Ironically, the only way to escape the nagging street artists of Place du Tertre is by entering their midst; they come to this café strictly to take a break and won't pester you.
♦ Daily 7AM-3AM. 3 Place du Tertre. Métro: Abbesses. 42.62.40.08

19 La Bohème $$ No-frills traditional French cuisine here means beef Bourguignonne, au gratin potatoes, and apple tarts. The dining room straddles a harshly lit cabaret stage where bored accordion and piano players boom out *chansons de Montmartre*. On weekend afternoons, this is the only music on the square. ♦ M-F 6AM-2AM; Sa-Su 6AM-3:30AM. 2 Place du Tertre. Métro: Abbesses. 46.06.51.69

Montmartre

19 La Mère Catherine ★$$ Founded in 1793 and, as house legend has it, commandeered in 1814 by the Cossacks who overran the Montmartre villagers, this is still the oldest brasserie on Place du Tertre, and the waiters swagger as if to show it. You'll find Belle Epoque reproduction mirrors, red-velvet benches, escargots, rack of lamb, tournedos Rossini (filet of beef cooked in port and foie gras sauce), piano and violin music from the 1920s, and outdoor dining on the terrace.
♦ Daily noon-3PM, 7PM-12:30AM. 6 Place du Tertre. Métro: Abbesses. 46.06.32.69, 42.58.07.42

19 La Crémaillère 1900 ★★$$ This brasserie, with an arbored garden, *fin-de-siècle* decor, and Edith Piaf's greatest hits played nightly on the piano, has a healthy neighborhood clientele. Seafood (fresh oysters, skate and haddock salads, and sole stuffed with shrimp mousse) is the strong suit. ♦ Daily 9AM-12:30AM. 15 Place du Tertre. Métro: Abbesses. 46.06.58.59

20 Le Tire Bouchon ★★$ If you're in the mood for an apricot crêpe or some cider *bouché* garnished with a little "Maple Leaf Rag," go no

farther: this crêperie has a jazz pianist upstairs playing the works of Fats Waller and Scott Joplin, plus a lively cabaret in its crowded basement after 11PM. The decor is reminiscent of an early 1960s Amsterdam jazz dive, with the vintage Coke dispenser, graffiti-scarred beams, and walls papered with posters and press photos of stringy-haired musicians. ♦ Daily 3PM-1AM. 9 Rue Norvins. No credit cards. Métro: Abbesses. 42.55.12.35

20 Au Clair de la Lune ★★$$/$$$ Pierre Roussel, a talented chef, admirably overcomes the restaurant's loud decor with his excellent wine list and in-season specialties. Try the wild boar and girolle mushrooms with a 1978 Château Marbuzet Bordeaux or, if you hit the jackpot last weekend in Deauville, splurge on a rare bottle of the 1975 Château d'Yquem Sauterne to complement your coquilles St.-Jacques in lime sauce. The mustachioed Roussel suggests ending the meal with his pièce de résistance dessert: fresh-mint ice cream in hot chocolate sauce.
♦ M 7-11PM; Tu-Sa noon-1:45PM, 7-11PM. 9 Rue Poulbot. Métro: Abbesses. 42.58.97.03

City Cafés Clear the Air

For those who can't enjoy cuisine under a cloud of cigarette smoke, there are, believe it or not, some restaurants in Paris where smoking is either forbidden or restricted:

Aquarius ★$ Smoke isn't the only thing banned at this vegetarian restaurant in the Marais: there's no meat or alcohol either, and very little atmosphere. Ideal for ascetics or for dessert and tea. ♦ M-Sa noon-10PM. 54 Rue Ste.-Croix de la Bretonnerie. Métro: Hôtel-de-Ville. 48.87.48.71

Aux Deux Canards ★$$/$$$ Traditional cuisine such as duck with candied orange and beef in red wine. More progressive is the policy forbidding smoking. ♦ M-F noon-2:30PM, 7:30-10PM; Sa-Su 7:30-10PM. 8 Rue du Faubourg-Poissonnière. Métro: Bonne-Nouvelle. 47.70.03.23

Chez Nézard ★$ The fare may be unimaginative, but the atmosphere is authentic and there's no smoking at this restaurant, which is more than one hundred years old. ♦ Tu-Su 8:30AM-7:30PM. 3 Rue Notre-Dame-des-Champs. Métro: St.-Placide. 45.48.80.22

La Cour de Rohan ★★$ This tea shop has sweets and light meals. For more information, see page 75.

Mariages Frères ★$ A diplomatic tea shop divided into two rooms, one of which is for nonsmokers. It stocks 350 varieties of tea and offers salmon or duck breast in tea sauce, as well as other light meals and homemade desserts. ♦ Tu-Su 10:30AM-7:30PM. 30 Rue du Bourg-Tibourg. Métro: Hôtel-de-Ville. 42.72.28.11

Tea's Follies ★★$ This tea salon offers more than just fresh air in its nonsmoking room. Try the tuna-and-apple tart or the chicken pie, followed by an almond caramel meringue. ♦ Daily 9AM-9PM. Place Gustave-Toudouze. Métro: St.-Georges. 42.80.08.44

21 L'Auberge de la Bonne Franquette ★$$
This former **van Gogh** studio is now an intentionally rustic restaurant/cabaret serving escargots, *confit de canard,* and choucroute to Japanese, Dutch, and German bus tours. Guitarist **Jack Jacquemin** and accordian player **Jacques Vassart** lead the equivalent of a nightly French hootenanny and hawk their cassettes and records at intermission. The restaurant is so popular on the travel agency circuit it has its own telex number. ♦ Daily noon-3PM, 7-11PM. 18 Rue St.-Rustique. Reservations recommended. Métro: Abbesses. 42.52.02.42; telex: Franket 660094F

22 Montmartre Museum Located just behind 12 Rue Cortot (whose roll call of former tenants includes **Jean Renoir, Maurice Utrillo,** and **Raoul Dufy**), this pleasant little museum is housed in a delightful 17th-century town house called **Le Manoir de Rose de Rosimond,** which is surrounded by two charming gardens. The house was the country residence of **Rosimond,** a 17th-century actor who appeared frequently in the plays of **Molière** and who, like Molière, died while performing *Le Malade Imaginaire.*

The museum's eclectic collection includes caricatures by **Honoré Daumier** and **André Gill,** posters and drawings by **Toulouse-Lautrec,** stunning **Clignancourt** porcelain, and the piano on which **Gustave Charpentier** wrote his opera *Louise* in 1900.

Though it seems outlandish in Paris to visit a museum in order to look at a bistro, the Montmartre Museum displays an entire 19th-century bistro complete with a scalloped zinc bar. The exhibition relates the apocryphal story that the term bistro originated on the butte, where impatient Cossacks used to shout at Montmartre's waiters: *"Bistraou, bistraou!"* (Russian for "Get a move on"). On Wednesday evenings, the **Art et Humour Montmartrois** meets in the museum for poetry readings and art exhibitions; lectures on local culture sponsored by the **Société du Vieux Montmartre** are held Saturday evenings. ♦ Admission. Tu-Sa 2:30-6PM; Su 11AM-6PM. 12 Rue Cortot. Métro: Lamarck-Caulaincourt. 46.06.61.11

22 Montmartre Vineyards This is one of the last two remaining vineyards in Paris. Each year's harvest yields enough grapes for about 500 bottles of red Clos Montmartre wine. The labels are designed by Montmartre artists, and half-bottles are sold each year in the 18th arrondissement's City Hall basement (1 Rue Jules-Joffrin; Métro: Jules-Joffrin; 42.52.42.00). The wine is nothing special, but the harvest fête, the first or second Saturday of October, is not to be missed. Crowds line Rue Lamarck for a celebration that feels like a cross between an academic procession, the Rose Bowl Parade, and Halloween. Participants might include baton twirlers, Auvergnat farmers in wooden clogs, or the mayor's wife picking the first grape. Note the plaque dedicated to **Poulbot,** the popular cartoonist who

prevented the vineyard from being sold to high-rise developers in the 1930s. ♦ Rue des Saules (Rue St.-Vincent). Métro: Lamarck-Caulaincourt

23 La Maison Rose ★$$ **Utrillo** once painted a picture of this pink restaurant and pink it has stayed—even the cutlery. In the summer the tables spill onto Rue de l'Abreuvoir, and if the view doesn't make you dizzy, order escargots in champagne or smoked salmon in vodka to ensure your head spins. ♦ Daily noon-3PM, 7:30-11:30PM. 2 Rue de l'Abreuvoir. Métro: Lamarck-Caulaincourt. 42.57.66.75

24 Au Lapin Agile ★$$ The original **Cabaret des Assassins** was rechristened in 1880 when **André Gill** painted a celebrated rabbit, complete with a red bow tie, bounding from a copper kettle. *Lapin à Gill* (The Rabbit by Gill) became *Lapin Agile* (The Nimble Rabbit), and this famous cabaret turned into a stomping ground for intellectuals and artists who came for poetry readings and folk songs. (In 1985 the French government issued a five-franc stamp of **Utrillo's** oil canvas of the cabaret.) A century later you can still grab a wooden stool, order a Kir, and sing along to those same old songs, as updated by pianist **Yves Robrecht.** Don't miss the 19th-century whimsy in front: a concrete fence made to look like knotty pine. ♦ Tu-Su 9PM-2AM. 22 Rue des Saules. No credit cards. Métro: Lamarck-Caulaincourt. 46.06.85.87

25 St. Vincent Cemetery Musician **Honegger** and painters **Steinlen** and **Utrillo** are buried in Paris' most intellectual cemetery. Enjoy the ivy-covered walls, a tranquil view of **Sacré-Coeur,** and (if you need to get off your feet) south-facing benches that catch the afternoon

sun. The old caretaker is generally helpful but becomes cantankerous between noon and 2PM, when he is emphatically out to lunch. ♦ 15 Mar-5 Nov: daily 8:30AM-6PM. 6 Nov-14 Mar: daily 8:30AM-5:30PM. Square Roland-Dorgelès. Métro: Lamarck-Caulaincourt

26 Au Poulbot Gourmet ★★$$/$$$ Innovative **Jean-Paul Langevin** runs a simple, cozy restaurant decorated with early Montmartre photos and original **Poulbot** illustrations. His specialties are *fait maison foie gras de canard,* escargots with garlic cream and fresh artichokes, and a two-chocolate charlotte with pistachio sauce. ♦ M-Sa noon-2PM, 7:30-10:30PM. 39 Rue Lamarck. Métro: Lamarck-Caulaincourt. 46.06.86.00

27 Musée d'Art Juif If your schedule can coincide with the **Jewish Art Museum's** brief weekly visiting hours, you'll be rewarded by its exhibitions of traditional drawings, crafts, and engravings, and its collection of scale-model synagogues. ♦ Admission. M-Th, Su 3-6PM; closed Aug, Jewish holidays. 42 Rue des Saules. Métro: Lamarck-Caulaincourt. 42.57.84.15

28 24 Rue du Mont-Cenis Composer **Hector Berlioz** lived with his English wife, **Constance Smithson,** from 1834 to 1837 in a house on this site. ♦ Métro: Lamarck-Caulaincourt

EDOUARD CARLIER, A L'ENSEIGNE DU
RESTAURANT
A. BEAUVILLIERS
Officier de Bouche
52, RUE LAMARCK 75018 PARIS
FERMÉ LE DIMANCHE ET LUNDI MIDI
EN
MONT-MARTRE
TÉL.: 42.54.54.42

29 Beauvilliers ★★★$$$ The restaurant's name is borrowed from **Antoine Beauvilliers,** who was *officier de bouche* to gluttonous **Louis XVIII** and founder of the first restaurant in Paris in 1784, but the restaurant itself has a style all its own. **Edouard Carlier** has created one of the most elegant *salons à manger* in Paris. What was once an old bakery is now three intimate Louis-Philippe-style dining rooms. In one of these hang 18th- and 19th-century engravings of the Montmartre windmills and, in another, a portrait gallery of Beauvilliers' contemporaries painted by **Louis-Léopold Boilly** and the like. The dining

Montmartre

rooms are adorned with a profusion of bouquets that are masterpieces themselves. Chef **Michel Deygat** changes the menu weekly. Try the grilled red mullet with pimiento, lamb terrine with thyme, Brittany lobster salad, or duck with passion fruit, and sample the lemon pie in white rum for dessert. Accompany the meal with a white St.-Joseph wine and watch the bill climb like Rue Lepic. ♦ M 7:30-10:30PM; Tu-Sa noon-2PM, 7:30-10:30PM; closed around the first two weeks of Sep. 52 Rue Lamarck. Dinner reservations required. Métro: Lamarck-Caulaincourt. 42.54.54.42

30 Le Château des Seigneurs de Clignancourt Along with the **Church of St.-Pierre,** this is one of the oldest relics of Montmartre's past. In the original manor house was a famous porcelain manufacturer (founded in 1767) that provided **Louis XVIII** with plates and saucers. Regrettably, the early 16th-century house was demolished in 1861, and all that remains is its renovated turret decorating the corner of a modern restaurant. ♦ Rue du Mont-Cenis (Rue Marcadet). Métro: Jules-Joffrin

31 City Hall When artist **Maurice Utrillo** died in 1955, he left two paintings to the local *mairie* (town hall), not as Pablo Picasso did in payment of estate taxes, but simply as a gift. You can still see his collection here; ask the *secrétariat générale* on the second floor. (Half-bottles from the **Montmartre Vineyards** are for sale in the basement.) ♦ 1 Place Jules-Joffrin. Métro: Jules-Joffrin. 42.52.42.00

32 Rue du Poteau Along this street (where **Utrillo** was born in 1883) lies a charming and lively neighborhood market. From behind a fog of simmering choucroute, ruddy-faced women chant *Chaud, chaud, Mesdames! Le boudin noir* (Hot, hot, ladies! Blood sausage). Nearby, their husbands peddle pheasants and Normandy cheeses. Follow your nose left up narrow Rue Duhesme and pass gingerly through the crowd of determined wicker-basket-toting householders who shop with the finesse and subtlety of all-American football players. ♦ Market: M-Sa 6AM-12:30PM, 4-7:30PM; Su 6AM-12:30PM. Métro: Jules-Joffrin

33 Pâtisserie de Montmartre Just north of Place Jules-Joffrin on Rue du Mont-Cenis, you will find heavenly cherry tarts and *Rose-Maries* (brioches filled with almond cream). ♦ M-Sa 9AM-7:30PM; Su 8AM-7:30PM. 81 Rue du Mont-Cenis. Métro: Jules-Joffrin. 46.06.39.28

33 Fromagerie de Montmartre Here **Madame Delbey** offers nearly 50 varieties of goat cheese. ♦ Tu-Sa 8:45AM-12:30PM, 4PM-7:30PM. 9 Rue du Poteau. Métro: Jules-Joffrin. 46.06.26.03

34 Central Hotel $ Hardly what its name suggests, this clean, often noisy hotel is a 15-minute walk from **Sacré-Coeur.** The concierge can be grumpy, but the prices border on philanthropic. ♦ 110 Rue Damrémont. Métros: Lamarck-Caulaincourt, Jules-Joffrin. 42.64.25.75

35 Le Maquis ★★$/$$ This little bistro at the base of Avenue Junot offers light prix-fixe lunches of such dishes as pumpkin soup, leek quiche, and coquilles St.-Jacques. ♦ M-Sa noon-2PM, 8-10:30PM, 15 June-Sep; M-Sa noon-2PM, 8-10PM, winter. 69 Rue Caulaincourt. Métro: Lamarck-Caulaincourt. 42.59.76.07

36 Clodenis ★★$$/$$$ This charming bistro's menu is inspired by seasonal produce. Only the freshest ingredients are used for the crab salad *en chiffonnade,* codfish soufflé with garlic, veal sweetbreads, and homemade pasta. Clodenis is less chic than its main competition, Beauvilliers, and that's reflected in the prices (fortunately). ♦ Tu-Sa noon-2:30PM, 7:30-10:30PM. 57 Rue Caulaincourt. Métro: Lamarck-Caulaincourt. 46.06.20.26

Restaurants/Nightlife: Red   Hotels: Blue
Shops/ ♥ Outdoors: Green   **Sights/Culture: Black**

37 Square Suzanne-Buisson This unexpected little square (named after a WWII Resistance fighter) was once the backyard of the adjoining **Château des Brouillards** (Castle of Fog), an 18th-century mansion turned dance hall. According to religious lore, **Saint Denis** paused here to rinse his severed head. Today a statue of the forlorn-looking bishop surveys neighborhood elders playing an afternoon game of *pétanque,* Lyonnaise-style. The sand bowling alley has stone benches for spectators, and there's no better way to learn about the old Montmartre than eavesdropping on the conversations of these tweed-capped codgers. Admission is free (as is the gossip), and the games gather steam around mid-afternoon. ♦ Daily dawn to dusk. Métro: Lamarck-Caulaincourt

L'ASSOMMOIR

38 L'Assommoir ★★★$$ Montmartre's best bistro takes its name from the **Emile Zola** novel. Proprietor **Philipe Larue,** gourmand and art buff, serves his faithful clientele a flaky *feuilleté de Roquefort, tripes à la mode de Caen, terrine de foies de volailles* (which he makes himself), and *fondant au chocolat* (chocolate cake), the recipe of which he will never divulge. An avid and eclectic art collector, Larue enjoys showing off his latest acquisition, be it an African mask in the dining room or a precious 12th-century Buddha he has hidden away. ♦ Tu-Sa noon-2PM, 8-11PM; Su noon-2PM; closed mid-July through mid-Aug, two weeks at Christmas. 12 Rue Girardon. Reservations recommended. Métro: Lamarck-Caulaincourt. 42.64.55.01

39 Rue Lepic Montmartre's meandering old quarry road is the site of an antique-car rallye held on the first or second Sunday in October. ♦ Métro: Blanche

39 Moulin de la Galette Painted by **Renoir** and many others, this windmill (and its former dance hall) is the best known of the scores of mills that once crowned Montmartre. In the 19th century the Parisian hoi polloi journeyed here on Sunday afternoons with their sweethearts to dance, drink wine, and eat *galettes* (cakes made with flour from the mills). The Moulin de la Galette has a grislier, earlier history as well, dating from the **Franco-Prussian War.** When Montmartre was over-run by 20,000 Silesian soldiers (Cossacks), they crucified the heroic mill owner, **Pierre-Charles Debray,** on the sails of his *moulin.* ♦ 79 Rue Lepic. Métro: Blanche

39 Da Graziano ★$$/$$$ Federighi Graziano's Tuscan restaurant, crowned with an old wind-mill, is frequented by the cinema celebrities who visit the Ciné 13 screening room next door. The carpaccio, San Daniele crêpes, homemade pastas, and light chocolate cake come highly recommended. ♦ Daily 12:15-3PM, 8PM-12:30AM. 83 Rue Lepic. Reservations recommended. Métro: Blanche. 46.06.84.77

39 La Petite Galette $ Right across the street from Montmartre's last old windmill, this bistro affords an inexpensive post-theater stop for a steak and *tarte tatin* (apple pie). The specialties also include foie gras, escargots, *salade aux lardons, rognons de veau,* and salmon-colored *gambas* (shrimp). ♦ Daily 7:30PM-midnight. 86bis Rue Lepic. Métro: Blanche. 42.52.99.72

CINÉ 13

40 Ciné 13 This is the best little projection room in Paris. In 1983 French filmmaker **Claude Lelouch** built this elegant 130-person screening room beside his Montmartre town house. Ciné 13 now draws cinema glitterati such as French film's tough guy **Jean-Paul Belmondo** and American director **Robert Altman,** who comes to screen the rough cuts of his new works. While you may never get to see Altman's rushes, for a reasonable

$80 an hour ($150 after 7PM), you can rent Ciné 13, which is now run by **Martine Lelouch,** Claude's sister, and show home movies if you like. No popcorn is permitted, but the theater can arrange catering. ♦ Call ahead for hours and for screening and catering reservations. 1 Ave Junot. Métro: Lamarck-Caulaincourt. 42.54.15.12

Moulin de la Galette

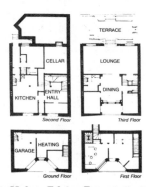

TERRACE

CELLAR · LOUNGE

ENTRY HALL · DINING
KITCHEN

Second Floor · *Third Floor*

GARAGE · HEATING

Ground Floor · *First Floor*

41 Maison Tristan Tzara In the 1920s the Viennese architect **Adolf Loos**, a pioneer of the Modern movement, was the only designer whose work reflected Dadaism. It is not surprising, then, that his "architecture without qualities" should have appealed to the Romanian Dadaist poet **Tristan Tzara,** who brought Loos to Paris with a commission to build this house. Set into a rising embankment, the five-story building has a rigorously symmetrical facade that is punctured by a huge double-height square terrace. The arrangement is a superb example of the Loos predilection for tensely juxtaposed, unadorned cubic forms. The interior is just as eccentrically organized: a patchwork of intersecting split-level spaces, typical of Loos' *raumplan* (room plan), provided Tzara with the sort of ironic, theatrical, and vaguely aggressive setting that befitted a Dadaist artist. ◆ 15 Ave Junot. Métro: Lamarck-Caulaincourt

41 Poulbot's House This is the former residence (1879-1946) of **Francisque Poulbot,** the Montmartre illustrator who drew chubby

Montmartre

little children with cowlicks. Four of his cartoon characters frolic across the tile frieze of the house. In homage to the artist, Montmartre residents still call their children *petits poulbots.* (Near Place du Tertre, you will find a sign at the corner of Norvins and Impasse du Tertre that reads: Drivers go slow. Watch out for the little poulbots.) This local folk hero is also credited with saving **Montmartre Vineyards** and with founding the **Fraternal Association of Wooden Billiard Players,** a faddish Montmartre bar game in which winning is considered immoral (the winner always pays for the drinks). ◆ 13 Ave Junot. Métro: Lamarck-Caulaincourt

41 Hameau des Artistes Behind the gate marked *Interdit* (No Trespassing) are footpaths leading to opulent artists' studios ranging from a gray cement castle to a Tuscan villa. The gate to the **Artists' Hamlet** is open during the day; be adventurous but tactful. ◆ 11 Ave Junot. Métro: Lamarck-Caulaincourt

42 Villa Léandre Down this unexpected country lane leading off Avenue Junot is a hidden village where the eccentric little houses mirror the idiosyncrasies of the artists who have

inhabited them (a ballerina, two successful painters, and a few genuine hermits). It's worth a quick detour. ◆ 25 Ave Junot. Métro: Lamarck-Caulaincourt

43 Toulouse-Lautrec's Studio The innovative graphic artist spent his most productive years (1886-1897) at this studio, just a stroll away from his favorite nocturnal haunts. ◆ 21 Rue Caulaincourt. Métro: Blanche

44 54 Rue Lepic **Vincent van Gogh** and his brother **Theo** lived here. ◆ Métro: Blanche

44 Marché Quatre Saisons Tucked away in this alley of artisans are a woodworker, a marionettemaker, and **Goudji,** an extraordinary Russian jewelry artist. Goudji's primeval designs in gold and silver are exhibited in museums around the world. A graduate of the Tbilisi Beaux Arts School, he fashions his own tools for the hammer-hollowing technique that is his trademark. For a small fortune, you can acquire a piece of his jewelry at **Jansen** on Rue Royal or take a less expensive look at his work on display in the **Musée des Arts Décoratifs** on Rue de Rivoli. ◆ 45 Rue Lepic. Métro: Blanche

45 Résidence Montmartre $$ This hotel, which was recently remodeled, is not far from the Rue Lepic open-air market. ◆ 10 Rue Burq. Métro: Abbesses. 46.06.51.91

46 La Poste ★★$$$ Once the residence of illustrator **Gustave Doré** and *Carmen*-composer **Georges Bizet,** this cavernous *hôtel particulier* (mansion) was turned into a post office after WWII. Restored to its former artistic splendor, La Poste boasts frescoes, colonnades, and caryatids to rival the old Opera Garnier. **Georges Vernotte,** formerly the chef at Beauvilliers in Montmartre, offers seafood specialties such as scallops with lime, New England clam chowder *a la française*, and salmon stuffed with roe. This is gracious, trendy dining at its best, and there's even a piano bar downstairs. ◆ Daily 9PM-midnight. 34 Rue Duperré. Reservations recommended. Métro: Pigalle. 42.80.66.16

47 Moulin Rouge Founded in 1889 (the year the Eiffel Tower was built) and still kicking after all these years, this legendary temple of the risqué proffers all the bare-breasted women, ostrich plumes, rhinestones, and multicolored lights the stage can support. The show recalls the days of the famous cancan dancers: **Jane Avril, Yvette Guilbert, Valentin le Désossé,** and **La Goulue,** who were limned by **Toulouse-Lautrec.** Not long ago, animal-welfare representatives stopped a Moulin number in which a performing dolphin was stealing the show. Dinner is rather expensive and nothing to write home about. ◆ Dinner: daily 8PM. Show: daily 10PM, midnight. 82 Blvd de Clichy (Place Blanche). Métro: Blanche. 46.06.00.19

47 Cité Véron To the left of the Moulin Rouge is this intriguing passageway where the widows of French writers **Jacques Prévert** and **Boris Vian** have made their homes. Along the alley, you will also find a voodoo club; the highbrow

Théâtre Ouvert; the **Boris Vian Foundation,** which is housed in an old hunting lodge and offers exhibitions, dance, and theater classes; and a cluttered warehouse called **Ophir Paris.** This boutique camouflages a back-room treasure trove with racks of cheap Indian imports. Unfortunately, much of the best stuff (19th-century wooden carousel figures, Moulin Rouge stage props, and Balinese shadow puppets) collected by the owners **Jacqueline** and **André Marcovici** is not for sale. ♦ Ophir Paris: M-Th 9AM-noon, 3-5:30PM; F 9AM-noon, 3-4:30PM. Cité Véron. Métro: Blanche. 42.64.58.40, 42.64.42.96

48 Grandgousier ★$$/$$$ Diners get an inspired menu and a warm reception amidst the muted pastoral decor of this elegant restaurant. Don't miss the terrine of leg of lamb with foie gras, quail and foie gras salad, the *panaché* of meats, or any of the luscious desserts, such as nougat ice cream. ♦ M-F 12:30-2PM, 7:30-10PM; Sa 7:30-10PM; closed two weeks in Aug. 17 Ave Rachel. Métro: Blanche. 43.87.66.12

49 Terrass Hôtel $$$ Built in 1912, this is the only four-star hotel in Montmartre; this rating is epitomized by the stellar panorama, taking in the **Opéra, Arc de Triomphe,** and **Eiffel Tower.** Ask to stay on the cemetery side, which in local parlance means a room with a view, unobstructed because you're overlooking the low-rise Montmartre Cemetery. There are plaid carpets, Napoléon III-style wallpaper, and a fireplace in the lobby. ♦ 12-14 Rue Joseph-de-Maistre. Métro: Blanche. 46.06.72.85

50 Cimetière de Montmartre The Montmartre Cemetery is a veritable academy of writers, composers, and painters. Among those at eternal rest here are **Zola, Stendhal, Dumas, Offenbach, Degas,** and **Fragonard,** as is **Greuze,** whose eloquent headstone lauds him for having painted "virtue, friendship, beauty, and innocence, thereby breathing soul into his paintings." Another striking memorial is the **Rude** bronze of a reclining **Cavaignac.** And **Hector Berlioz** lies between his first wife, an English actress, and his second wife, an opera singer. ♦ M-F 8AM-5:30PM, 16 Mar-5 Nov; M-F 8AM-5PM, 6 Nov-15 Mar. 20 Ave Rachel. Métro: Blanche. 43.87.64.24

51 Charlot 1er Merveilles des Mers ★$$/$$$ Some of the freshest oysters, shellfish, and other wonders of the sea are available at this traditional restaurant near the Moulin Rouge. But beware of the steep prices. ♦ Daily noon-3PM, 7PM-1AM; closed 13 July-20 Aug. 128bis Blvd de Clichy. Métro: Place-de-Clichy. 45.22.47.08

52 Place-de-Clichy Stop by the *académie de billard* (pool hall), a converted 1900 stable, and then wander down Rue d'Amsterdam, past carpet shops, used-furniture stores, and homeopathic pharmacies. ♦ Métro: Place-de-Clichy

52 Charlot, Le Roi des Coquillages ★$$/$$$ If you happen to be in Montmartre during the "R" months (the months spelled with the letter R—September through April—denote prime

shellfish season), stop for a no-nonsense lunch of mussels, clams, oysters, and baby shrimp at this restaurant. ♦ Seafood ♦ M-Th noon-3PM, 7PM-midnight; F-Su noon-3PM, 7PM-1AM. 12 Place de Clichy. Métro: Place-de-Clichy. 48.74.49.64

52 Guyot One of Paris' last pipe artisans, **Monsieur Guyot,** works out of the old dance hall where **Mistinguett** made her debut. Selling meticulously crafted brier pipes, he also restores meerschaums. Flatter him by asking about his extraordinary personal pipe collection. ♦ Tu-Sa 10AM-7PM; closed in Aug, 10 days at Easter. 7 Ave de Clichy. Métro: Place-de-Clichy. 43.87.70.88

53 Androuet ★★$$/$$$ This rustic, vaulted salon has been in business since 1909 and sells 30,000 pounds of cheese every month. Try its *dégustation du fromage* (cheese-tasting) of 120 cheeses, accompanied by a salad and a hearty Bordeaux. ♦ Shop: Tu-Sa 10AM-7PM. Restaurant: M-Sa noon-3PM, 6:30-11PM; closed holidays. 41 Rue d'Amsterdam. Métro: Place-de-Clichy. 48.74.26.90 (store), 48.74.26.93 (restaurant)

54 A l'Annexe ★$$ This lively bistro is only a quick stroll away from the glitter of Pigalle. Try the hearty *raie au beurre noir.* ♦ M-F noon-2:30PM, 7-10:30PM; closed Aug. 15 Rue Chaptal. Métro: St.-Georges. 48.74.65.52

Bests

Alain Weill
French Art Dealer

The oldest pot-and-pan maker in Paris: **Establissement Jules Gaillard** on Rue du Faubourg-St.-Denis.

Montmartre

Dinner at **Pouilly-Reuilly,** a great bistro of old times on Rue Joineau.

Lunch or dinner in spring or summertime at **L'Aquitaine** on Rue de Dantzig (Christiane Massia is one of the few women chefs in Paris).

Le Scarlet, the billiard room in the **Grand Hôtel de la Gare St.-Lazare,** which has a great bar with 1940s decor. The owner named it after seeing *Gone with the Wind.*

Late-night eating in 1940s decor at **La Caravelle,** good but not too expensive.

Inside the **Musée de l'Homme** on the Place du Trocadéro is a restaurant called **Le Totem,** where you'll find the most spectacular views of the **Eiffel Tower,** as well as delicious and inexpensive food.

Willi's Wine Bar, by far the best of the city's wine bars.

Record-shopping at **FNAC** on Avenue Wagram; dinner in the summertime at **Les Sportifs** for good food at reasonable prices; dinner while listening to jazz at **Le Bilbouquet;** and dinner at the little Russian restaurant **Karlov** on Rue du Cherche-Midi, which isn't too expensive and has the best Russian musicians in Paris.

For incredible meat, try **Le Gourmet des Ternes** on Boulevard de Courcelles.

For the most beautiful decor, dinner at **Le Grand Véfour.**

Additional Highlights

There are some wonderful spots in Paris that are off the beaten path of the seven city walks in this book. This section features Paris' other major highlights, which include something for everyone: the majestic **Eiffel Tower**, eerie catacombs, famous parks such as **Monceau** and the **Bois de Vincennes**, as well as the high-tech **La Villette** science museum and the fascinating **Musée de la Contrefaçon** (Museum of Forgeries).

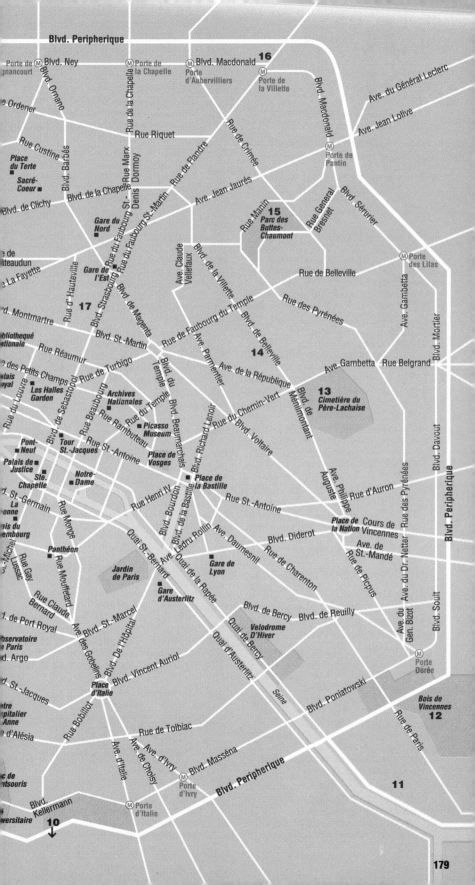

1 Tour Eiffel In 1889 the world was drunk on science. The previous decade had produced one technological marvel after another: the automobile, the telephone, the electric light, and the **Eiffel Tower.** First dubbed a monstrosity, then considered the definitive symbol of Paris, the tower was built to commemorate the centennial of the storming of the Bastille and to stand as the centerpiece of the 1889 International Exhibition of Paris. The now-classic design by **Gustave Eiffel** beat 700 other entries in the design competition. (Among the losers, for obvious reasons, were a giant guillotine and a mammoth lighthouse.) The tower was the tallest structure in the world until 1930, when the title was usurped by the Chrysler Building in New York. Eiffel, the engineer who also designed the iron bones of the Statue of Liberty (undergirding the **Frédéric Bartholdi** copper structure), was himself a diminutive man, only five feet tall.

Spanning 2.5 acres at its base, the tower is made of 15,000 metal parts held together with 2.5 million rivets and covered with 40 tons of paint. A thousand feet high (more than three

Additional Highlights

times the height of the Statue of Liberty), it weighs 7,000 tons and sways no more than 4.5 inches in strong winds. The weight is distributed so elegantly that it exerts no more pressure on the ground per centimeter than does a person seated in a four-legged chair.

When the Eiffel Tower was first completed, much of Paris was unimpressed. Its stark, geometric structure offended the decorative beaux-arts sensibility. Prominent critics, including luminaries such as **Paul Verlaine, Guy de Maupassant,** the younger **Dumas,** and **Emile Zola,** denounced it as the Tower of Babel and a dishonor to Paris. Maupassant used to say he liked to have lunch here because it was the only place in Paris where he didn't have to look at it.

In later years it was discovered the tower could function as the world's largest antenna, and during WWI it became one of France's most vital weapons. Since then, it has served as a radio and meteorological post, and in

1985, was fitted with broadcasting equipment for France's fifth television channel.

Despite these eminently utilitarian applications, the Eiffel Tower's primary effect is to incite the imagination. One man tried to fly from it and was killed when his wings failed him. In 1923 a bicycle-riding journalist careened down the steps to the ground from the top floor. A mountaineer scaled it in 1954, and in 1984 two Englishmen parachuted from it.

In 1980 a nine-year renovation program began, which brought great changes to the tower. About 1,500 tons of extraneous concrete (mostly in the form of concession areas) was removed from the first platform; four new electronic glass elevators and new visitors facilities were installed; and the pavilion housing the tower's restaurant, the **Jules Verne** (★★★$$$), was remodeled. Most dramatic of all, however, is the 292,000-watt interior lighting system inaugurated on New Year's Eve 1986, replacing the old floodlights. The new lights illuminate the entire structure from within, creating a golden tracery against the sky at night. The renovations program was completed in time for the tower's hundredth birthday on the bicentennial of the French Revolution in 1989. ♦ Admission varies for each level. Daily 9:30AM-11PM. Jules Verne restaurant: noon-1:30PM, 7-8:45PM. Métros: Bir-Hakeim, Champ-de-Mars. 45.55.91.11

1 Parc du Champ-de-Mars Named for the god of war, this large rectangular park stretching from the Ecole Militaire to the Eiffel Tower has long been a site of battles, both actual and prospective. Here, in 52 BC, Roman legions defeated the Parisii; in 886 the Parisians beat back the invading Vikings; and, in the early 18th century, when the Champ-de-Mars served as the parade ground for the Ecole Militaire, **Napoléon** drilled with his fellow cadets here.

Now the flowering trees, shrubs, and miniature cascades are the site of pony rides, marionette theaters, organ grinders, occasional parades for children, and fairs and reindeer at Christmastime. You can do most anything in the Champ-de-Mars except have a picnic on the lawns. French grass is sacred grass, and a bluecoat (guard) will appear and order you off before you've even had time to unwrap your salami and uncork the Bordeaux. ♦ Métros: Bir-Hakeim, Champ-de-Mars, Ecole-Militaire

2 Ecole Militaire In an attempt to rival the **Hôtel des Invalides** of **Louis XIV, Louis XV** and his mistress, **Madame de Pompadour,** hired **Jacques-Anges Gabriel,** the architect

who created Place de la Concorde in the 1770s, to design a military school. Unfortunately, money was a problem. It was the inspiration of **Beaumarchais,** who wrote *The Marriage of Figaro* and gave harp lessons to Louis XV's daughters, to pay for the building by authorizing a lottery and a tax on playing cards. The king was convinced, and thus the **Military Academy** (pictured below at left).

Standing at the culmination of the Champ-de-Mars, the Ecole Militaire, with its Corinthian columns, statues, dome, double-columned colonnade, and elegant wrought-iron fence, is considered to be one of Gabriel's masterpieces. Its most famous cadet was **Napoléon Bonaparte.** ♦ Open by appointment only. For more information, write to: Général Direction, Ecole Militaire, 1 Place Joffre, 75007 Paris. Métro: Ecole-Militaire. No phone

3 UNESCO Secretariat This building was designed by architects from three member countries: **Bernard Zehrfuss** of France, **Luigi Nervi** of Italy, and **Marcel Breuer** of the US. When it was built in the late 1950s, the headquarters of the United Nations Educational, Scientific, and Cultural Organization was a hopeful symbol of a new era of international cooperation.

The complex, however, is better known for the works of art it contains than for its architecture or politics. UNESCO headquarters possesses a black metal **Calder** mobile; **Henry Moore's** *Reclining Figure;* two ceramic walls executed by **Artigas** after designs by **Miró;** sculpture by **Giacometti;** and a mural by **Picasso,** appropriately entitled *The Victory of the Forces of Light and Peace over the Powers of Evil and Death.*

Casually visiting UNESCO is somewhat difficult. The security is tight: you'd do best to organize or join a group tour, and even then, bring your passport. ♦ M-F 9AM-6PM. 7 Place de Fontenoy. Métro: Ségur. 45.68.10.00

4 Hôtel des Invalides This monumental group of buildings was built by **Libéral Bruant** on the orders of **Louis XIV** to house the king's old soldiers, many of them invalids who had been reduced to begging or seeking shelter in monasteries. When the *hôtel* was completed in 1676, 6,000 aging pensioners moved in (dozens of old soldiers, many in wheelchairs, still live here). The year after Les Invalides was completed, the "Sun King" (Louis XIV was nicknamed this for his brilliance and his fondness for gold) commissioned a second church for the complex, which was built by **Jules Hardouin-Mansart.** Attached Siamese-twin-style to Bruant's original church (**St.-Louis-des-Invalides**), the **Dome Church** is one of the most magnificent Baroque churches of the *grand siècle.* Its dome is decorated with garlands and crowned with a 351-foot-tall spire.

France's bravest soldiers and greatest warriors are entombed in the Dome Church: **Turenne, Vauban, Duroc, Foch,** and, of

Restaurants/Nightlife: Red   **Hotels:** Blue

Shops/ 🌳 **Outdoors:** Green   **Sights/Culture:** Black

course, **Napoléon.** "I do not think that there is a more impressive sepulchre on earth than that tomb; it is grandly simple," wrote **Theodore Roosevelt** of Napoléon's resting place. "I am not easily awestruck, but it certainly gave me a solemn feeling to look at the plain, red stone bier which contained what had once been the mightiest conqueror the world ever saw."

Concealed by the outward simplicity of red porphyry, Napoléon's remains are contained in seven coffins, one inside the other, made of iron, mahogany, lead, ebony, oak, and marble. Napoléon was originally interred on the island of St. Helena, where he died in 1821. The British finally agreed to repatriate his remains in 1840, thus fulfilling the emperor's wish to be buried "on the banks of the Seine among the people of France whom I have loved so much."

The tomb of Napoléon's son, the emperor of Rome, who died in Vienna at age 21, sounds

181

a morbid footnote to history. In 1940 his remains were given to Paris in a grandiose gesture by a heady **Hitler.** Bruant's church, St.-Louis-des-Invalides, where the occupants of the *hôtel* worshipped, is separated by a glass barrier from the domed edifice. You enter from **Cour d'Honneur.** The tomb's most impressive feature, perhaps, is the collection of captured banners hanging from the upper galleries. Among these tattered mementos of French military victories there is even the red and white flag with the rising sun of Japan, a relic of WWII. In 1837 **Berlioz'** *Requiem* was performed here for the first time.

Cour d'Honneur, an impressive courtyard also designed by Bruant, is where French army officer **Alfred Dreyfus** was publicly disgraced and where **de Gaulle** kissed **Churchill.** The statue of **Napoléon** by **Seurre,** which used to stand on the top of a column in Place Vendôme, now stands in this courtyard. Among the other Napoleonic memorabilia exhibited in Les Invalides: the emperor's death mask, his dinner jacket, and the dog that was his companion during his years on the island of Elba, stuffed for posterity. ♦ Admission. Daily 10AM-5PM (6PM in summer). Place des Invalides. Métros: La Tour-Maubourg, Varenne. 45.55.92.30

4 Musée de l'Armée At the north end of the Invalides complex, the **Army Museum** houses one of the largest collections of military paraphernalia in the world. Swords, guns, armor, flags, and other articles are on display, along with innumerable models, maps, and images that trace the evolution of warfare from prehistoric times until WWII. Understandably, Napoleonic souvenirs are most conspicuous, but there are also intriguing exhibitions of medieval, Renaissance, and oriental militaria. ♦ Admission.

Additional Highlights

Daily 10AM-6PM, Apr-Sep; daily 10AM-5PM, Oct-Mar. Métros: La Tour-Maubourg, Varenne. 45.55.37.70

5 Musée Rodin The **Hôtel de Biron,** which houses the **Rodin Museum,** is a Regency masterpiece of columns and pediments originally built in 1730 by **Jean Aubert** and **Jacques-Anges Gabriel** for a wealthy wigmaker named **Abraham Peyrenc.** It later became the home of the **Duc du Maine,** the illegitimate son of **Louis XIV** and **Madame de Montespan.** In 1753 it was bought by the **Maréchal-Duc de Biron,** who indulged quite a passion for gardening in the years before he went to the guillotine during the Reign of Terror; he spent 200,000 livres each year on tulips alone. During an unfortunate tenure as a convent school, its gold-and-white wood paneling was ripped out by the mother superior: she deemed it too Baroque and materialistic.

In 1908, after the Hôtel de Biron was subdivided into a cluster of artists' studios,

Auguste Rodin (1840-1917) moved in and stayed until his death. His neighbors in the Hôtel included German poet **Rainer Maria Rilke,** French artist **Jean Cocteau,** American dancer **Isadora Duncan,** and French painter **Henri Matisse.**

After you have entered the front door and seen the ground-floor exposition, bear left and gradually spiral up stairs. The works are displayed so you may follow Rodin's career chronologically, beginning with his academic paintings and his sketches in both classic and modern modes. Notice Rodin depicts only right hands, except that of the devil crushing humanity in *The Hand of the Devil.*

The room containing Rodin's *Sculptor with his Muse* also displays several works by **Camille Claudel,** the talented sculptor who became Rodin's muse, model, and lover at the age of 17. Her portrait of Rodin, executed in 1888 at the peak of their affair, when he was nearly 50, reveals a rather cold, small-eyed lover.

Upstairs is a series of studies of **Balzac** created in the early 1890s. In one of them, a bronze, the writer stands stark naked, and is 90-percent paunch. In the final version, which stands at the corner of Rue Vavin and Boulevard Montparnasse, Rodin draped Balzac in a concealing cloak.

The Hôtel de Biron's garden, the third largest of any of the Hôtels in Paris, after those of the **Elysée Palace** and the **Hôtel de Matignon,** provides the setting for Rodin's best-known works. On 30 January 1937, **Helen Keller** visited here and was permitted to touch the sculptures with her hands. Of *The Thinker,* she said: "In every limb I felt the throes of emerging mind." Until recently, across the garden stood the *Six Burghers of Calais,* who surrendered their lives to the English to save their city. Hellen Keller said this heroic and wrenching group was "sadder to touch than a grave." Sadder still, in 1988 a Japanese museum bought the figures for $2.5 million. ♦ Admission. Tu-Su 10AM-5:45PM, Apr-Sep; Tu-Su 10AM-5PM, Oct-Mar. 77 Rue de Varenne. Métro: Varenne. 47.05.01.34

6 Petrossian Parisians have flocked here since 1924 for caviar, smoked salmon, and foie gras. ♦ 18 Blvd de La Tour-Maubourg. Métro: La Tour-Maubourg. 45.51.59.73

6 Michel Chaudun Once chief *chocolatier* at Maison du Chocolat, Chaudun now turns out his own bonbons; particularly dangerous is the diamond-shaped mint truffle. ♦ 149 Rue de l'Université. Métro: La Tour-Maubourg. 47.53.74.40

7 Sewers The *egouts* (sewers) of Paris are always a popular underground attraction. This 1,305-mile network of tunnels was constructed during the reign of **Napoléon III** and is considered one of **Baron Haussmann's** finest achievements. If laid end to end, the tunnels would reach from Paris to Istanbul. The sewers house freshwater pipes, telephone wires, traffic-light cables, and the city's pneumatic postal network, which was shut down in 1984. The hour-long sewer tour includes a film, a photograph exhibition, and a walk through the 18-foot-high by 14-foot-wide tunnels. Ever since a notorious bank heist in which the robbers made their getaway via the sewers, underground boat cruises have not been permitted. ♦ M, W, and the last Sa of each month 2-5PM. Quai d'Orsay (Pont de l'Alma). Métro: Pont-de-l'Alma. 47.05.10.29

8 Catacombs The catacombs began as a network of quarries extending for miles beneath Paris. In 1785 several million skeletons were transported from the overcrowded **Innocents Cemetery** near Les Halles to the catacombs. Here the skulls, femurs, and tibias were stacked in a neat but rather macabre fashion. Carved near the entrance is an ominous medieval sign: "Stop. Beyond Here Is the Empire of Death." Apparently the warning deterred the occupying Nazis, because they never did discover that the secret headquarters of the French Resistance was literally under their feet. The dark reaches of the catacombs then housed radios capable of reaching London, as well as a telephone switching system handling Resistance communications for hundreds of miles around.

If you tour the catacombs, take along a flashlight and a sweater, and be sure to stay close to the group. In 1793 a Parisian took a wrong turn from his own wine cellar, wandered into the catacomb tunnels, got lost, and was not discovered until nine years later, by which time the poor fellow was quite mummified. ♦ Admission. Tu-F 2-4PM; Sa-Su 9-11AM, 2-4PM. 1 Place Denfert-Rochereau. Métro: Denfert-Rochereau. 43.22.47.63

9 Parc Montsouris Prior to the 19th century **Montsouris Park** was an abandoned granite quarry stubbled with windmills. At the turn of the century the 50-acre Montsouris was a refuge for the artists and literati of nearby Montparnasse; when **Hemingway** fled the bustling Latin Quarter, he often came here. Today, joggers run the park's half-mile perimeter, matrons feed the swans, and military brass bands play **Sousa** marches in the bandshell. Not to be missed are the gazpacho and *soupe de fruits rouge* at **Le Jardin de la Paresse** (Garden of Idleness), a Belle Epoque glass-and-iron restaurant whose outdoor terrace has accommodated a great many customers, including **Leon Trotsky** and **Jean-Paul Sartre**. ♦ Daily dawn to dusk. Le Jardin de la Paresse: daily noon-8:30PM. 20 Rue Gazan. Métro: Cité Université. Le Jardin de la Paresse restaurant: 45.88.38.52

With 53,389 people per square mile, Paris has the highest population density among advanced industrialized cities and the fourth highest (following Manila, Shanghai, and Cairo) among 105 cities around the world.

Paris ranks 42nd among 71 major cities in new housing construction.

10 Arc Majeur de 185.4° Motorists driving along **Route A6** will encounter a huge piece of geometry in the form of an incomplete circle of steel poised vertically around the road. This monumental sculpture, entitled *Arc Majeur de 185.4°*, is the brainchild of **Bernar Venet,** a French sculptor whose work often reflects a harmonious blend of mathematics and art. Six feet thick and 160 feet tall at its highest point, and more than 225 feet in diameter, it sits like an enormous broken wedding ring at the crest of a hill between the towns of Nemours and Auxerre, 140 kilometers (87 miles) southeast of Paris. At the border of the Ile-de-France and Bourgogne provinces, the arc serves as a modern gateway to the two regions for the 35 million drivers who cross the border on A6 every year. Four years in the making, the project was directed by **Johannes Schaub** and sponsored by the **Société des Autoroutes Paris-Rhin-Rhone** and the **Ministry of Culture**. Venet has already planned several arcs and angled installations for the US. ♦ Off Rte A6

11 Musée de Pain The eccentric little **Bread Museum** on the edge of Paris is certain to delight the inveterate traveler who does not hear the call of the Louvre or feel the pull of the Pompidou Center. The museum was founded by **Jacques Lorch,** who, like his father before

him, has spent his life as a miller in the service of the Parisian bakeries. In a small building that was once a dairy, Lorch has used his personal fortune to amass a collection on the art of baking as eclectic as it is passionate. You will find bread from every corner of the world; bread excavated from Egyptian tombs (2,400 BC); a display of erotic postcards whose theme is the seduction of the baker's wife; a letter from **Marie Antoinette** to her personal baker, **le Paneterie;** an exhibition of the origins of the croissant (evidence from the Byzantine Empire, seventh century); and, perhaps the most moving historical document in the collection, a Revolutionary order from the infamous minister of police **Joseph Fouche** decreeing that henceforth bakers must bake the same bread for the rich as for the poor: the French must eat the "bread of equality." ♦ Tu, Th 2-4PM; closed July-Aug. 25bis Ave Victor-Hugo in Charenton-le-Pont. Métro: Charenton-Ecoles. 43.68.43.60

12 Bois de Vincennes Only slightly smaller than the Bois de Boulogne to the west, the Bois de Vincennes acts as the second principal recreation area for the City of Paris. Like the Bois de Boulogne, Vincennes was a former royal hunting ground and was given to the city by **Napoléon III** in 1860. The major attraction of the park is its **Château de Vincennes,** a stern medieval fortress that has served variously as a royal residence, prison, porcelain factory, and arsenal. The *bois* (woods) that extend to the south of the château contain such highlights as the **Floral Garden; Daumesnil Lake;** the **Buddhist Center,** which houses the largest Buddha sculpture in Europe; and the **Zoological Park.** ♦ Floral Garden: daily 9:30AM-5PM. Château: daily 10AM-7PM. Zoological Park: daily 10AM-5:15PM. Métros: Château-de-Vincennes, Vincennes (RER). 43.73.60.49

13 Cimetière Père-Lachaise This famous graveyard named after **Louis XIV's** confessor, **Father La Chaise,** and designed by **Brongniart,** is the largest and most elite cemetery in Paris. Here lie the remains of France's most famous lovers, **Abélard** and **Héloïse,** in company with **Molière, Balzac,** and the painters **Corot, Daumier, Pissarro, David, Seurat,** and **Modigliani.** Also buried here are the 19th-century photographer **Nadar;** the city-shaping **Baron Haussmann; Jane Avril** and **Yvette Guilbert,** two cancan dancers who modeled for **Toulouse-Lautrec; Fulgence Bienvenue,** who built the Paris métro; and **Ferdinand de Lesseps,** who designed the Suez Canal.

In remembrance of things past, a single red rose may grace the black marble slab marking **Marcel Proust's** grave, and singer **Edith Piaf's** unremarkable resting place is always surrounded with flowers. Music lovers might also search out **Callas, Bizet,**

Additional Highlights

or **Poulenc. Chopin's** body is buried here (his heart is interred in Warsaw), as are the remains of **Eugène Delacroix, Prosper Mérimée,** and **Alfred de Musset,** who, like Chopin, loved **George Sand,** a great luminary of women's literature. Literati flock to **Oscar Wilde's** tomb, a stylish sphinx sculpted by **Sir Jacob Epstein** in 1909, and leftists make the pilgrimage to the grave of **Laura Marx,** daughter of **Karl. Sarah Bernhardt, Gertrude Stein,** and **Alice B. Toklas** lie here, as well as **Jim Morrison,** the Doors' rock singer who died of a drug overdose in 1971.

This lush 108-acre sanctuary in eastern Paris is as much a park as a cemetery, or, in a sense, it is a museum of French history, but far more lively than either a cemetery or a museum. Not only do some 400 cats live here, but Parisians by the hundreds come to Père-Lachaise to picnic, harvest escargots off the tombs, or neck on the benches. Chopin's tomb is used for posting love letters, and legend holds that women who kiss

or rub the statue of **Victor Noir** will marry within a year. If you're lucky you may encounter **Vincent de Langlade,** a bearded elf of a man who has spent his life studying and explaining the eligies and enigmas of Père-Lachaise. Langlade is the author of a dozen books on the necropolis. If you can't find him, make do with a detailed map available at the cemetery's entrance and begin the celebrity search. ♦ M-F 7:30AM-6PM, Sa-Su 9AM-6PM, 16 Mar-5 Nov; M-F 8AM-5:30PM, Sa-Su 9AM-5:30PM, 6 Nov-15 Mar. Blvd de Ménilmontant. Métro: Père-Lachaise

14 Musée Edith Piaf In a tiny museum filling two rooms of a private apartment near her grave in the Père-Lachaise Cemetery, the most renowned French chanteuse lives on in the adoration of her fans, who come to look at her dressing gown, shoes, the portraits of her star-crossed lovers, autographed letters, birth certificate, and photographs. Recordings of the "little sparrow" of Paris play softly in the background and the museum's devoted curator is ever present to recount the final days of the great entertainer's life. ♦ M-Th 1-6PM by appointment only. 5 Rue Crespin-du-Gast. Métro: Ménilmontant. 43.55.52.72

15 Parc des Buttes-Chaumont If you're tired of the crowds in the Luxembourg Gardens (the Central Park of Paris) and need a break from the deadly symmetry of the Tuileries, do as the French do. Buy a baguette, some ripe Brie, and a hearty Bordeaux, and head for a taste of urban wilderness in this unusual park in the northern end of Paris: Buttes-Chaumont.

The park was built in 1867 by **Baron Haussmann,** who also laid out the sewers and the city's grand boulevards for **Napoléon III.** Before Haussman, Buttes-Chaumont was a city dump. In what must count as the most inspired use of landfill in French history, a then-new material—concrete—was used to form cliffs, ravines, rivers, and an artificial lake. The grotto and waterfall were restored and reopened several years ago after having been closed since WWII because of deterioration.

Buttes-Chaumont's island is capped with a classical colonnaded temple and commands one of the city's most striking views of Montmartre and Sacré-Coeur. Travelers not inclined to mountaineering may prefer sipping a *citron pressé* on the terrace of the **Pavillon du Lac,** which serves tea and light lunches and is located on the park's west side. ♦ Daily 9AM-5PM in winter, 9AM-9:30PM in summer. Rue Botzaris. Métro: Buttes-Chaumont

Sea cures at Northern spas and thalasso-therapy centers are increasingly the Parisian solution to the wear and tear of city life. Two such spas close to Paris are the Centre Biotherm at Deauville and the Centre Thalamar in Brittany's Le Touquet, which features an indoor pool overlooking the ocean.

Restaurants/Nightlife: Red   **Hotels:** Blue
Shops/ Outdoors: Green   **Sights/Culture:** Black

16 Porte de la Villette The old slaughter-
house district, a 75-acre site in northeastern
Paris that was the last undeveloped space
in the city, was transformed into a huge
complex of buildings and parks devoted
to science and technology. The design is
united by a series of bright-red *Follies,*
whimsical structures designed by decon-
structivist architect **Bernard Tschumi** that
are uniformly plotted on a grid and serve a
variety of functions.

La Villette's centerpiece is the **Cité des
Sciences et de l'Industrie,** an 880-foot-long
$600 million research and exhibition build-
ing designed by French architect **Adrien
Fainsilber.** The gray granite, glass, and dark
steel Cité des Sciences was built around the
shell of an enormous 19th-century slaugh-
terhouse, whose lack of central pillars
created the 1.5 million square feet of usable
space. The exhibitions are organized around
general themes such as the earth and space,
matter and physics, language and communication, and life on earth. Many of these
shows are multilingual and invite public
participation. The most popular attraction
is **La Géode,** a polished-steel sphere 117
feet in diameter that houses a movie theater
where films are projected 180 degrees above
and around the audience. **La Mediathèque**
houses a thousand videodisks and 150,000
books, and a conference center for a thousand people. ♦ Hours and admission for
exhibitions vary. Cité des Sciences: Tu-Su
10AM-6PM. 211 Ave Jean-Jaurès. Métro:
Porte-de-Pantin. 42.40.27.28

17 Rue de Paradis This shabby little street
is the domain of the finest French and European tableware outlets. Nearly 50 shops selling porcelain, silver, earthenware, crystal,
and glass are crowded along its three blocks.
All the most elegant brands of tableware may
be found here (Limoges, Lalique, Christofle,
Têtard, Meissen, Rosenthal, Baccarat, and
Villeroy and Boch) and often at prices 30 to
50 percent lower than in the US. The **Musée
du Cristal** of Baccarat displays decant-
ers and glasses of its famous crystal. Some
of the pieces on display here were used by
heads of state ranging from the **Queen of
Siam** to **King Louis Philippe.** Also on view
are the Baccarat glasses commissioned
for **Henry Ford II's** yacht and **Franklin
Roosevelt's** White House in 1936. The most
dazzling exhibitions, perhaps, are the two

one-ton 79-light candelabras ordered by Russian czar **Nicholas II** for his St. Petersburg
palace. ♦ Musée du Cristal: M-F 9AM-5:30PM;
Sa 10AM-noon, 2-5PM. 30bis Rue de Paradis.
Métro: Château-d'Eau. 47.70.64.30

17 Musée de l'Affiche et da la Publicité
The **Poster and Advertising Museum**
displays more than 40,000 posters from
the 18th century to the present in a building
that provides a superb vision of Paris during
La Belle Epoque. The glass-roof building was
the headquarters of the ceramic-tile company
that at the turn of the century provided
100,000 square meters of decoration for the
first métro stations. The walls are covered
with large ceramic murals whose diverse
styles served as advertisements to prospec-
tive customers. The museum, open since
1978, offers beautiful temporary exhibitions
and has a large, reasonably priced selection
of posters. ♦ Admission. M, W-Su noon-6PM.
18 Rue de Paradis. Métro: Château-d'Eau.
42.60.26.60

18 Parc de Monceau The eccentric character
of this small park dates back to 1778, when
Philippe-Egalité, the Duke of Orléans, commissioned the painter **Carmontel** to design
a private garden on the Monceau Plain, then
outside the city limits. Carmontel indulged
the duke by creating a whimsical landscape
full of architectural follies: a pyramid, pagoda,
Roman temple, windmills, and artfully placed
ruins. The park changed hands a few times after the Revolution, but its picturesque qualities
(after the English tradition) were completed as
we see them today in 1862 by **Alphand, Baron
Haussmann's** engineer. Of particular interest
are the **Naumachie,** an oval basin with a colonnade said to have come from the unfinished
mausoleum of **Henri II** at St.-Denis, and the
round **Pavillon de Chartres,** one of four extant
barrières (tollhouses) built by **Claude-Nicho-**

las Ledoux along the old city wall in 1784.
♦ Métro: Monceau

18 Musée Cernuschi Near the east gate of the
Parc de Monceau are two small but exceptional
museums. The Cernuschi, once the mansion of
a wealthy financier, contains a fine collection of
Chinese art. ♦ Tu-Su 10AM-5:40PM. 7 Ave
Vélasquez. Métro: Villiers. 45.63.50.75

18 Musée Nissim de Camondo Around the
corner from the Cernuschi, this museum
exhibits the furniture and decorative art (including several Gobelins tapestries) of the
Count de Camondo, who once owned this
house. ♦ W-Su 10AM-noon, 2-5PM. 63 Rue
de Monceau. Métro: Velliers. 45.63.26.32

19 Grande Arche de la Défense The axis
that starts with the Carousel Arch in front of
the Louvre and runs westward through the
Tuileries Gardens to the Obelisk of Luxor,
then down the Champs-Elysées to the Arc de
Triomphe, has been extended westward with a
300,000-ton white Carrara marble monument

in the La Défense district of Paris. Designed by **Johan Otto von Spreckelsen,** who won an international competition for the commission, the arch is actually a hollow cube built on 12 pillars set 30 meters into the ground. The building houses the **Ministry of Planning and Development,** private offices as well as several cultural foundations, and the **Foundation for the Rights of Man.** Inaugurated in July 1989 as part of the 200th anniversary of the French Revolution, the building brings monumental dazzle to a sterile high-rise jungle that has become the business district of Paris. ♦ Place de La Défense. Métro: La Défense

20 Musée de la Contrefaçon The one-room **Museum of Forgeries** in the elegant 16th arrondissement might be of particular interest to the tourist who is tempted to take advantage of a fluctuating currency and do some serious shopping. It is not unusual to see the great ladies of Parisian society stopping by the museum to compare a new handbag or a Cartier watch to the near-perfect forgeries on exhibit. The museum is a veritable capitalist's cabinet of curiosities, where the *authentique* products are on display surrounded by their imitations. Ingenious copies of Louis Vuitton luggage wear counterfeit tags guaranteeing they are genuine Vuitton. Japan, Korea, Italy, Morocco, and Taiwan are said to be among the most frequent sources of fakes and forgeries. A short visit to this fascinating museum is enough to cast doubts forever on that little shop near the hotel that has a good buy on Dior key chains, Omega watches, bottles of Benedictine and Cointreau, flacons of Chanel No. 5 or Guerlain's Mitsouko, and magnums of Cordon Rouge champagne. ♦ M, W 2-4:30PM; F 9:30AM-noon. 16 Rue de la Faisanderie. Métro: Porte-Dauphine. 45.01.51.11

Additional Highlights

21 Musée Guimet The finest collection of Asian art in Paris is on view at the **Guimet Museum.** Founded by industrialist **Emile Guimet** in 1879 to house his own collection of oriental antiquities, the museum was later nationalized as the **Départment des Arts Asiatiques des Musées Nationaux.** As such, the Musée Guimet exhibits most of the Louvre's Far East collection and has steadily built up its holdings to include more than 50,000 works from China, Japan, India, Indochina, Afghanistan, and Tibet. Of particular interest are the **Rousset Collection** and the **Michel Calmann Room,** which contain Buddhist sculpture and Chinese porcelain. The museum has expanded to include a library, a research center, and an auditorium. ♦ Admission. M, W-Su 9:45AM-5:15PM. 6 Place d'Iéna. Métros: Boissière, Iéna. 47.23.61.65

22 Palais de Chaillot Perched on its hill across the Seine from the Eiffel Tower, the Palais de Chaillot serves as the Right Bank's termination for the monumental axis that sweeps up across the **Champ-de-Mars** from the **Ecole Militaire.** The white sandstone twin pavilions of the palace were built for the Paris Exhibition of 1937, replacing the earlier **Palais du Trocadéro,** a massive barrel-shaped building built for the 1878 exhibition. Although its stark forms and groups of heroic statuary uncomfortably recall the type of Fascist architecture emerging during the period in Germany and Italy, the Palais de Chaillot succeeds both as a monument and a cultural complex. Within its two curving wings (which cradle a series of descending gardens and pools) are four museums, two theaters, a library, and a restaurant. The **Théâtre National de Chaillot,** located beneath the **Palais Terrace,** was renovated and seats 1,800 people. The smaller **Théâtre Gémier** was added in 1966 as an experimental playhouse. ♦ Admission. Musée de la Marine: M, W-Su 10AM-6PM; 45.33.31.70. Musée de l'Homme: M, W-Su 9:45AM-5:15PM; 45.53.70.60. Musée des Monuments Français: M, W-Su 9AM-6PM; 47.27.35.74. Musée du Cinéma: guided tours reserved in advance; 45.53.21.86. Cinémathèque (Film library): Tu-Su 10AM-5PM; entrance on Ave Albert-de-Mun; 47.04.24.24. Métro: Trocadéro

23 Bois de Boulogne Stretching along the western flank of Paris and occupying more than 2,200 acres, this is the ultimate playground and escape for the city's population. The *bois* (woods) began as a forest in which the Merovingians hunted wild boar and wolves. It was enclosed by **Henri II** in 1556, and in the 17th century **Jean-Baptiste Colbert** transformed the park into a royal hunting domain. After **Napoléon III** gave the forest to the City of Paris, **Baron Haussmann** remodeled the landscape after London's Hyde Park and built many of the lakes, restaurants, racetracks, and paths. Haussmann designed the park so it would be entered from his own **Avenue Foch,** which leads grandly down to the **Porte Dauphine.** Once in the park, you can choose from among an infinite variety of attractions. The most notable include the **Bagatelle,** a magical park with an 18th-century villa built by the then-future **King Charles X;** the **Jardin d'Acclimatation,** an amusement park and miniature zoo; the **Auteuil** and **Longchamp** racecourses; and the **Pré Catelan,** another flower and tree garden that shelters the luxurious café/restaurant of the same name. There are numerous facilities for sport, including the nearby **Roland Garros Stadium,** where the French Open tennis tournament is held. ♦ Métros: Porte-d'Auteuil, Porte-Dauphine, Porte-Maillot. Pré Catelan restaurant: Tu-Sa noon-2:30PM, 7-10PM; Su noon-2:30PM. Route de Suresnes. Métro: Porte-Dauphine. 45.24.55.58

24 Musée Marmottan The 16th arrondissement in Paris, which stretches from the Arc de Triomphe down between the Bois de Boulogne and the Seine, is a haven for the

Proustian bourgeoisie. Out-of-town shoppers know this quarter as a place to buy old table linens, fine chocolates, and designer silk dresses, and as the location of **Omar Sharif's** private gambling club. The best-kept secret of the select 16th, however, is the 19th-century Passy town house that contains the **Marmottan Museum**. More than a hundred original paintings, pastels, and drawings by **Claude Monet** are displayed here. While tour-bus loads of noisy London schoolchildren and itinerant backpackers elbow each other in the Musée d'Orsay to glimpse Monet's *Wild Poppies,* the Marmottan, a treasure trove of the artist's work from Giverny, is relatively deserted. Avoid the crowd, catch the métro to Muette, and visit the Marmottan.

A word of advice: in touring the Marmottan, take a good look at the 300 illuminated medieval manuscripts on the ground floor, skip the two floors devoted to the cold First-Empire furniture and Flemish tapestries, and head for the basement. Here you may see the essential spirit in light and color of Monet's Giverny work: the joyous splash and swirl of poppies, tulips, irises, and apple blossoms. The exhibition culminates in a circular gallery with the artist's notebooks and palette in the center and 16 of his water-lily canvases on the walls. Stand in the middle of the room and pivot around to behold the sun's daily round as it illuminated Monet's magical pond. (In summer you can visit the actual pond and gardens at Monet's Normandy home in Giverny. For more information, see "Day Trips" on page 191.) ♦ Admission. Tu-Su 10AM-5:30PM. 2 Rue Louis-Boilly. Métro: Muette. 42.24.07.02

24 Ranelagh Gardens Directly across Avenue Raphaël from the Marmottan are the sumptuous English-style Ranelagh Gardens, home to one of the last hand-cranked merry-go-rounds in Europe. It is powered by a middle-aged woman with forearms rivaling those of Arnold Schwarzenegger. Children in ruffled pink dresses or seersucker suits and buckled shoes use one hand to hold on for dear life to the carved wooden ponies and the other to jab red sticks in the air, trying to hook the brass rings dispensed on the merry-go-round's periphery. ♦ Ave Raphaël (Rue Louis-Boilly). Métro: Muette

25 Castel Béranger French architect **Hector Guimard** established his reputation in 1898 as the country's premier Art Nouveau designer with this seven-story apartment building, which sits along a quiet residential street in the 16th arrondissement. Guimard's quasi-organic expressionism (strongly influenced by the work of **Victor Horta** in Belgium) is seen here in full glory, particularly in the curvilinear details of his ironwork, faience, and carved-wood elements, which prefigure the architect's more purely sculptural métro entrances of 1900. An inspired blend of rational planning and whimsical effusion, the building contains 36 apartments, none alike. ♦ Visits by appointment only, and unfortunately there is no telephone. 14-16 Rue La Fontaine. Métro: Jasmin

26 Foundation Le Corbusier Charles-Edouard Jeanneret, better known as **Le Corbusier** (1887-1965), was the Swiss architect who helped revolutionize today's urban environment with his passion for cubist forms. Within Paris and its suburbs stand 15 of his modular buildings, including the apartment house where he lived in 1933, a **Salvation Army** headquarters built in 1933 of glass, brick, and exposed concrete, and the famous **Swiss Dormitory** and **Brazilian Pavilion** (constructed in 1932 and 1959, respectively) at Cité Universitaire. The headquarters and research library of the **Le Corbusier Foundation** are housed in **Villa Jeanneret;** the adjoining **Villa La Roche,** also designed by the architect in 1923, contains a sparse collection of Le Corbusier's own painting, sculpture, and furniture design and is open to the public. ♦ Le Corbusier Foundation, Villa La Roche, and Villa Jeanneret: M-Th 10AM-12:30PM, 1-6PM; F 10AM-12:30PM, 1-5PM. 8-10 Square du Docteur-Blanche. Métro: Jasmin. 42.88.41.53

Restaurant Roundup

The following restaurants are not listed in the seven walks of Paris featured in the preceding chapters, but they are highly recommended and merit a visit if you're in the neighborhood:

Arpege 84 Rue de Varenne (7th arrondissement [ar.]), 45.51.47.33

Astier 44 Rue Jean-Pierre Timbaud (11th ar.), 43.57.16.35

Au Trou Gascon 40 Rue Taine (12th ar.), 43.44.34.26

Additional Highlights

Chez Philippe 106 Rue de la Folie-Méricourt (11th ar.), 43.57.33.78

Guy Savoy 18 Rue Troyon (17th ar.), 43.80.40.61

Jamin (Robuchon) 32 Rue de Longchamp (16th ar.), 47.27.12.27

L'Assiette 181 Rue du Château (14th ar.), 43.22.64.86

La Cagouille 10 Place Constantin-Brancusi (14th ar.), 43.22.09.01

La Coquille 6 Rue du Débarcadère (17th ar.), 45.72.10.73

La Maison Blanche 82 Boulevard Lefebvre (15th ar.), 48.28.38.83

La Marée 1 Rue Daru (8th ar.), 47.63.52.42

Michel Rostang 20 Rue Rennequin (17th ar.), 47.63.40.77

Ravi 214 Rue de la Croix-Nivert (15th ar.), 45.31.58.09

Vivarois 192 Avenue Victor-Hugo (16th ar.), 45.04.04.31

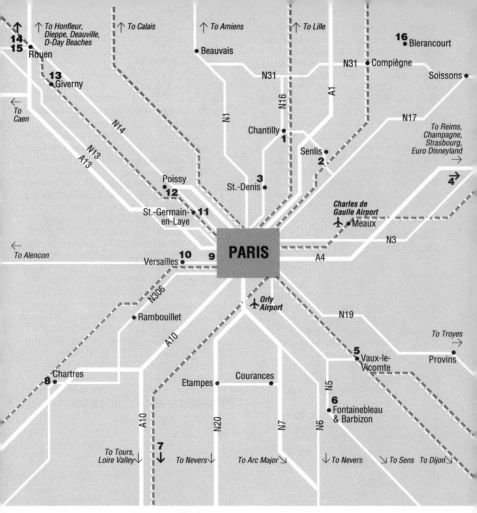

The map shows day trip destinations around Paris with numbered locations.

- 14, 15 Rouen
- To Honfleur, Dieppe, Deauville, D-Day Beaches ↑
- To Calais ↑
- To Amiens ↑
- To Lille ↑
- 16 Blerancourt
- Beauvais
- N31 Compiègne
- N31
- N16
- A1
- Soissons
- 13 Giverny
- ← To Caen
- N14
- N1
- N17
- Chantilly 1
- Senlis 2
- To Reims, Champagne, Strasbourg, Euro Disneyland →
- N13
- A13
- Poissy
- 12
- 3 St.-Denis
- 4 →
- St.-Germain- 11 en-Laye
- Charles de Gaulle Airport ✈ Meaux
- N3
- ← To Alencon
- Versailles 10 9 **PARIS**
- A4
- N306
- Orly ✈ Airport
- N19
- To Troyes →
- Rambouillet
- A10
- 5 Vaux-le-Vicomte
- Provins
- Chartres 8
- Etampes
- Courances
- N5
- 6 Fontainebleau & Barbizon
- A10
- N20
- N7
- N6
- To Tours, Loire Valley ↓
- 7 ↓
- To Nevers ↓
- To Arc Major ↘
- To Nevers ↓
- To Sens ↘ To Dijon ↘

Day Trips

1 Chantilly In 1671 **Louis de Bourbon** entertained **King Louis XIV** in his newly completed gardens at Chantilly. On that occasion, **Vatel,** the most famous chef in France, failed to deliver the fish course on time and, rather than live with the shame, promptly took his own life. Such is the tradition of excellence at Chantilly.

Rising like a mirage from a moat in the midst of a dense beech forest, the château is an artful conglomeration of the best of 16th-, 18th-, and 19th-century French architecture. During the Revolution the original château, built in the early 15th century, was razed, stone by stone, by vengeful mobs. The **Duc d'Aumale,** who was responsible for the subsequent reconstruction in 1844, showed his fine eclectic taste in other areas as well: his art collection of medieval miniatures and French, Flemish, and Italian paintings are on display in the château's **Musée Condé.** Each June the famous **Prix de Diane** horse race is run at a track on the edge of the palace grounds, and the **Grandes Ecuries,**

Chantilly's extensive stables, are in use today as part of the **Living Museum of the Horse.** The dressage exhibitions held three times daily are great entertainment for children. ♦ Trains leave from the Gare du Nord station. Paris Vision and Cityrama (see page 6) offer half-day trips on Sunday. If traveling by car, take autoroute N16, 48 km (30 miles) north of Paris.

2 Senlis The entire town of Senlis is classified as a historical monument. It is girdled by 23-foot-high, 13-foot-thick Roman walls that are punctuated by watchtowers and pierced by massive gates. The cathedral is older than Notre-Dame-de-Paris or Chartres and lofts a lacy spire considered the most beautiful in France. After visiting the cathedral, tour the ruins of the royal castle, the 28 towers of the Gallo-Roman wall, or the thousand-seat Roman amphitheater just outside of town. The streets of Senlis, such as the **Rue du Châtel** and **Rue de la Treille,** are winding, stone-paved canyonways dark with history. The best bet for exploring them is to follow the small arrows that indicate a walking route through town. ♦ Bus tours are available, or take the train from the Gare du Nord station, or follow autoroute N17 or A1, 48 km (30 miles) northeast of Paris.

3 Basilica of St.-Denis Around AD 250, Saint Denis, the first Christian evangelist to Paris, was beheaded by the Romans. Legend has it he picked up his head and carried it from Montmartre several kilometers northward, until, finally, he fell and was buried by a peasant woman. Whatever the facts, the grave of Saint Denis became a place of pilgrimage. By the 12th century pilgrims were so numerous that many were actually trampled to death in the stampede to his shrine. **Abbot Suger** (1081–1151) decreed that a new church, large and full of light, be constructed. The result was the first Gothic edifice in the world and one of the lesser-known treasures of Paris. The Basilica of St.-Denis became the starting place for the crusades and the burial place of three dynasties of French royalty. Badly neglected after the Revolution, the basilica has been restored and is now a repository of exquisite funerary sculpture. The soaring nave glows with a rainbow of light from the stained-glass windows, illuminated most brightly on winter mornings. ♦ Take métro line 13 to the destination of Basilica of St.-Denis.

4 Champagne The Champagne region is a realm of flowing hills dotted with vineyards, medieval stone towns, and châteaus. Its capital, **Reims,** was the coronation site of French kings, beginning with **Clovis** in 496. The cathedral here is stunning and definitely worth a stop. **Epernay,** the region's second city, is the home of **Moët et Chandon,** the giant among an estimated 145 champagne producers in the region. Most of the largest producers offer tours, which usually culminate in some free sampling and, be forewarned, a persuasive sales pitch once your resistance is down. Five minutes north of Epernay are two of Champagne's best restaurants: the **Royal Champagne** in Champillon, and the **Boyer.** ♦ Take a train to Reims from the Gare de l'Est, or drive east on autoroute A4, 143 km (89 miles).

4 Euro Disneyland One more American institution has come to France: Disneyland. Construction began in 1985 on a 4,806-acre site—one-fifth the size of Paris—in Marne-la-Vallée, only 32 kilometers (20 miles) east of central Paris. The \$2.5 billion vacation resort opened in April 1992 and includes a Magic Kingdom theme park similar to those in California, Florida, and Japan, as well as six hotels, a campground, and a golf course, along with office, retail, and residential development. The amusement park, which employs 12,000 people, is expected to draw 11 million visitors during its first year. It is divided into five major lands: Adventureland, Discoveryland, Fantasyland, Frontierland, and, yes, Main Street, USA. Inspired by French futurist **Jules Verne,** the Discoveryland attraction includes a 360-degree motion picture, a 3-D film, and a computer-based flight simulator created by **George *Star Wars* Lucas** that catapults passengers into "space." ♦ Drive east on autoroute A4, 32 km (20 miles). 64.74.43.06

5 Vaux-le-Vicomte Owner **Nicolas Fouquet** was superintendent of finances for **Louis XIV.** At Fouquet's housewarming party to inaugurate his newly completed château in July 1661, **Molière's** troupe was there to perform, and the guests ate from solid-gold plates. Horses, jewels, and swords were the party favors. But this excess was not generous enough. Because he neglected to offer the château itself to the seethingly jealous king, Fouquet was thrown in prison. Louis commandeered the architects who had built the château and put them to work. The outcome was the royal palace at Versailles. Vaux-le-Vicomte is generally uncrowded and beautifully restored. With a little effort it is possible to imagine living here. ♦ 58 km (36 miles) from Paris. Drive on autoroute N5 via Melun or take a Paris Vision tour bus, but avoid the train. The station in Melun is 5 km (3 miles) from the château, and the taxi drivers have a reputation for taking you for a ride. 60.66.97.09

Vaux-le-Vicomte

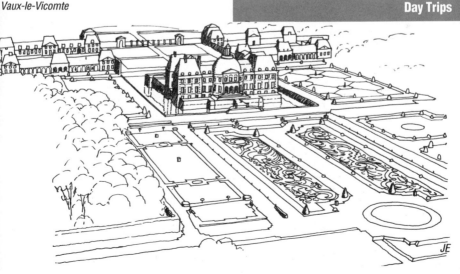

JE

6 Fontainebleau and Barbizon Newly returned from ignominious imprisonment in Spain, French **King François I** (who reigned from 1515–1547) was determined to recoup his dignity by creating a new court that would dazzle the world. He chose an old hunting lodge in the forest of Fontainebleau as its site and commanded the services of scores of Italian artists and craftsmen, who, the artist **Vasari** said, turned it into a "new Rome." Be aware that the château is the size of an entire town; to tour it even casually requires at least a couple of hours. And that doesn't count a tour of the **Fontainebleau Forest,** a magnificent 96-square-mile expanse of towering trees and dramatic promontories where you can ride, climb rocks, or simply walk. At one edge of the forest is the hamlet of **Barbizon,** once the hub of the pre-Impressionist movement of painting. **Rousseau, Millet, Daubigny,** and **Corot** painted here, and many of their houses and studios have been lovingly restored and opened to the public. ◆ Paris Vision and Cityrama offer day trips in a package tour with Versailles. Or take the train from Gare de Lyon to the Fontainebleau station and then a bus to the palace. If driving, follow autoroute A6 or N7 66 km (41 miles) southeast of Paris.

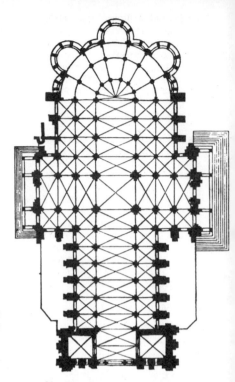

7 Loire Valley The Loire Valley would be a perfect destination for a day trip were it not for the profusion of magnificent châteaus: two weeks spent in the valley would begin to do it justice. Throughout the centuries French nobles have chosen to build their country houses along this calm river with its lush banks. Visit as many châteaus as you can. **Chambord, Chenonceaux, Cheverny, Chinon, Loches,** and **Villandry** are particularly beautiful. But take your time; each château warrants at least a morning of contemplation. (And save your afternoons for wine-tasting.) ◆ 230 km (143 miles) from Paris. Take the train to Tours or Blois and from there catch a bus to Chambord or Cheverny (two buses M, W,

Day Trips

and F). Paris Vision and Cityrama offer day tours to Amboise, Cheverny, Chenonceaux, and Chaumont. If traveling by car, follow autoroute A10 to Tours.

When Julius Caesar conquered Gaul in 57 BC, he established a local capital for the Belgic people in Champagne at Durocortorum. The locals were then called the Remi because they were thought to be descendants of Remus, the brother of Romulus, Rome's legendary founder. The appellation must have suited the population, for at the time of the collapse of the Roman Empire in the fifth century, Durocortorum was renamed Reims. After the Frankish King Clovis was baptized by Bishop Saint Remi in 496, the city became the most important in Gaul and the coronation site of all but three future French kings.

8 Chartres The cathedral at Chartres must be among the most spiritual places in the world. Though the town has changed dramatically since the building of the cathedral, you can still catch sight of the signature spire cutting into the sky above the wheat fields, a sight that for medieval pilgrims meant they had reached one of five essential holy places to visit on the path to heaven. Carved in the cathedral's celebrated portals and glowing in its stained-glass windows, the Bible unfolds with an overwhelming panoply of symbols and images. This imagery is brilliantly interpreted by **Malcolm Miller**—an English scholar who has devoted the last several decades to research and writing on the cathedral—during his morning and afternoon tours. Before or after the tour, do not fail to spend some time alone sitting in a pew and silently absorbing the majesty of Chartres. The 12th- and 13th-century stained-glass windows (the finest array in France) are so brilliant that in medieval times peasants believed they were made of ground-up gems. Modern science disproves this notion, but no one yet has explained how the medieval glassmakers at Chartres created such beauty.

After touring the cathedral, stroll around the old town in its vicinity and along the banks of the Eure River. And if you are interested in 20th-century folk art, ask about **Picassiette's House.** This is an extraordinary complex of rooms, chapels, and gardens constructed entirely from broken glass by a cemetery worker. Picassiette's House is a 30-minute walk or a five-minute taxi ride from the cathedral and is only open a few hours a week, so inquire about the schedule at the local tourist

Restaurants/Nightlife: Red   Hotels: Blue
Shops/ 🌳Outdoors: Green   Sights/Culture: Black

office before you set out. Stay overnight at **Chateau d'Esclimont,** a gorgeous 16th-century castle just 15 kilometers (9 miles) from Chartres in St.-Symphorien-Le-Château; for more information, call 37.31.15.15. ♦ 100 km (62 miles) from Paris. Trains leave from the Gare Montparnasse; Paris Vision and Cityrama offer half-day trips Tu, Th, and Sa. Cars take autoroute A11 or N10. At Chartres there are bicycles for rent at the Place Pierre-Sémard.

9 Parc de St.-Cloud For true escapists, the 1,100-acre St.-Cloud Park, landscaped by **André Le Nôtre,** is a little dream come true. Lying just outside of Paris, it's a world apart from the urban bustle. This province of leafy woods is well-traveled by bicyclists and is a delight for children. For just a few francs you can rent tandem bicycles and take a romantic ride by the park's 17th-century fountains.
♦ Métro: Boulogne-Pont-de-St.-Cloud.

10 Versailles What can you say about the palace that has everything? Pursuing a royal whim, **Louis XIV** transformed a small hunting lodge bordering a marsh into the most lavish statement of monarchic privilege that has ever existed. Owing to just such excesses, the monarchy has long since fallen, but Versailles has not. Since 1978 the French government has spent more than $19 million on the restoration of this palace, concentrating on 50 rooms in the more private family apartments. Unfortunately, the splendor at Versailles can be numbing: one grand hall begins to resemble the next very quickly. To get the most from a visit, read up on Versailles' history beforehand and reserve plenty of time for loitering. Indeed, some visitors prefer to spend the entire day just wandering in the 250 acres of gardens.

Designed by the incomparable **André Le Nôtre,** the gardens are too big to be crowded and too varied to bore. The air has a sweet smell of damp earth and is as quiet as Eden; but the precise geometry and balance of the designs betray the fact that nature, along with everything else, was forced to bow before the "Sun King." The famous fountains, **Grandes Eaux,** splash at 3:30PM on Sundays from May through September; the **Neptune Basin** floodlight and fireworks show is held four times a year. Find out when; it's worth the trip. ♦ Paris Vision and Cityrama offer both half- and full-day tours. If traveling by RER, take the C line from the Gare des Invalides or St. Michel and get off at the Versailles-Rive Gauche station. Or take the métro to Pont-de-Sèvres and transfer to bus 171. Trains leave from Gare Montparnasse. Cars should follow autoroute N10, 24 km (15 miles) southwest of Paris.

11 St.-Germain-en-Laye For **Louis XIV,** St.-Germain-en-Laye meant security. Born and bred in St.-Germain, he later took refuge here during the popular uprising in 1648–1653 known as the *Fronde*. Built in 1122 around a château that guarded the western flank of Paris, the fortress contains a replica (though it has long been without its glass) of the Ste.-

Chapelle in Paris. Today it also houses the **French National Museum of Antiquities.** The château's gardens were designed by the industrious **André Le Nôtre** before he was whisked away to landscape Versailles. In one corner of the gardens is the **Pavillon Henri IV,** where **Louis XIV,** the "Sun King," was born and **Alexandre Dumas** wrote *The Three Musketeers*. Since 1830 this historic building has also been a restaurant/hotel and a good place to lunch as you look over the Seine. ♦ Take the RER directly to the St.-Germain-en-Laye terminal or the 158 bus from La Défense. By car, it's a 19 km (12 mile) drive west on autoroute N13.

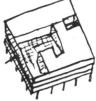

12 Villa Savoye More than seventy years after its conception, the Villa Savoye continues to be a striking and beautiful evocation of modernist architectural purity. The last of several houses built in and around Paris in the 1920s by **Le Corbusier,** this "machine for living" synthesized many of the radical ideas the great Swiss architect had produced in his book *Vers une Architecture*. Le Corbusier wished to build a new type of bourgeois suburban villa, one that would reflect the precise, controlled rationalism made possible and encouraged by modern technology. The result is an independent domestic mechanism separated from the landscape, which, in this case, it barely even touches. The Villa Savoye is essentially an L-shaped series of rooms laid into a square tray that is elevated on slender *pilotis* (columns) above the ground. As you travel on a continuous internal ramp into the villa, you experience various light-filled spaces that eventually dissolve into the open air when the

Day Trips

roof solarium is reached. The strip windows, glass walls, flat roofs, cubic forms, and grid of columns were revolutionary but by now are familiar components of the International style that Le Corbusier helped establish. For more information on Le Corbusier, see "Foundation Le Corbusier" on page 187. ♦ M-F 10AM-noon, 2-4PM. 82 Chemin de Villiers, 78300 Poissy. Trains leave from the Gare St.-Lazare. By car, take autoroute N14, 24 km (15 miles) northwest of Paris. For more information, contact La Mission des Affaires Domaniales, 42.99.44.75.

13 Giverny Anyone who's ever seen any of the well-loved **Claude Monet** water-lily paintings knows what Giverny looks like. Monet's Normandy house and gardens have been well-tended and restored, looking much as they did when the Impressionist painter lived here from

1883–1926. After the Académie des Beaux-Arts moved Monet's paintings to the Musée Marmottan (see page 186) in Paris in 1966, Giverny was neglected. Grass grew in the studio and a staircase caved in. But a renovation that was begun in 1977 and funded in part by **Lila Acheson Wallace** has awakened its former charms. Unfortunately, this is no secret, so on weekends and in warm weather, many tourists swarm to this four-acre property. Spring, before the foreign tide hits France, is the best time to visit this horticultural/artistic shrine, when the early flowers are blooming, or in autumn, when you'll be able to see all the colors of the great painter's palette but with fewer distractions. Two nice and unexpected aspects of things about Giverny: Monet's collection of Japanese prints on display in the house, and the reproductions of the blue-and-yellow plates and cups designed by Monet that are on sale in the gift shop. ◆ Admission. Tu-Su 10AM-6PM; closed Nov-Mar. 48 km (30 miles) northwest of Paris. Trains leave from Gare St.-Lazare in the direction of Rouen. Get off at Vernon, which is about four miles from Giverny, and walk or take a taxi. Cars should take the Normandy autoroute N13, and exit at Bonnieres. 32.51.28.21

14 Honfleur and Deauville Normandy, with its rugged coast, is the country of Camembert, Calvados, apple orchards, and brick-and-beam-crossed plaster houses topped by steep shingled gables. In Honfleur, one of the coast's most solidly Norman and strikingly picturesque harbors, you will be reminded that **Samuel de Champlain** departed from here in 1608 to found Québec. The old port section of Honfleur has many seafood restaurants. Don't miss the **Mariner's Museum** or the Saturday morning market bustling around the old wooden **Ste.-Catherine** church. Be aware also that just outside of town lies **La Ferme St.-Siméon,** one of Normandy's finest restaurants.

Farther west along the coast is Deauville, the summer playground of Europe's social elite. Known for its casinos, private mansions, race-

Day Trips

tracks, and an American film festival each fall, Deauville has a broad boardwalk and sandy stretch of beach that is a mere 90-minute train ride from the center of Paris. ◆ 200 km (124 miles) from Paris. Follow the Normandy autoroute A13. Then take the coastal road 513 to Honfleur and Deauville. Trains leave frequently from Gare St.-Lazare, or travel in grand style on a one hundred-passenger yacht, the *Normandie*, which leaves from the Seine in Paris and arrives in Honfleur after a seven-day trip through Normandy. For more cruise information, contact A.H.I. International, 701 Lee Street, Des Plaines, IL 60016; or in the US call 800/323.7373.

15 D-Day Beaches Before arriving at the D-Day beaches, you pass **Divessur-Mer,** the site from which **William the Conqueror** embarked in 1066 to conquer England. An impressive moment in history, but further from memory,

perhaps, than the events of 6 June 1944. Just to the west, in **Bénouville,** is the **Pegasus Bridge,** the first spot taken by the Allies in Normandy. Farther on, the D-Day beaches begin, each with its own museum, its own explanations, its own monuments. The most heartrending sight is the American cemetery at **Omaha Beach,** 10 miles short of **Point-du-Hoc,** where 9,000 of the 23,000 Americans killed in the invasion are buried. Even if you have come to experience modern history and the sorrows of the victors, it is worth visiting the town of **Bayeux** to see the magnificent 231-foot-long tapestry made in 1076 depicting William's conquests and the Norman invasion of England; it makes for a good meditation on the constancy of war. ◆ 230 km (143 miles) from Paris. Follow the Normandy autoroute A13 west via Caen and Bayeux.

16 Musée National de la Cooperation Franco-Americaine Created by a host of Vanderbilts and other Social Register Americans, French countesses, and expatriate Yank writers who supported France's role in WWI, the museum was built in the ruins of a 17th-century château by **Salomon de Brosse,** architect of the Luxembourg Palace in Paris. In 1989 it was renovated for France's bicentennial by Frenchman **Yves Lion** and Canadian **Alan Levitt**. Exhibits include hundreds of historic war photographs and memorabilia and a collection of graceful late 19th- and 20th-century paintings, drawings, and sculpture on loan from the **Musée d'Orsay**. Represented here are **Whistler, Calder,** and **Childe Hassam,** as well as French artists who worked in America. ◆ Admission. M, W-Su 10AM-1PM, 2-5PM. Gardens are always open and free. 110 km (68 miles) from Paris. 02300 Blerancourt. By car, take autoroute A1 north and exit at Compiègne, in the direction of Noyon. At Noyon, head toward Coucy-Soissons-Blerancourt. 23.39.60.16

Bests

Michel Guy
Minister of Culture 1974-1976; Director of Paris' Festival d'Automne

Favorite restaurants:

Brasserie Balzar, Brasserie Lipp, Restaurant Louis XIV on Boulevard St.-Denis, **Restaurant Louis XIV** on the Place des Victoires, **Pharamond,** and **Chez Pierrot** on Rue Etienne-Marcel.

Favorite walks and places:

Paris Opéra, Trinity Church, Gustave Moreau Museum, Plaza Athenée, St.-Vincent de Paul church, 19th-century and Art Nouveau houses along **Rue d'Abbeville, Gare du Nord, Delacroix Museum,** the two Delacroix paintings in the **St.-Sulpice church,** Monet paintings of the Walter-Guillaume collection hanging in the **Orangerie, Puvis de Chavannes** in the **Panthéon, Rue de Lappe, Rue de Charonne, Ste.-Marguerite Synagogue** by Guimard on **Rue Pavée, St.-Denis Abbey, Rodin Museum, Bourdelle Museum,** and the **Picasso Museum.**

C.K. Williams
American Poet

The park on the banks of the **Canal St.-Martin** at the level of the Rue de Marseille, where the metal footbridges cross. A good place to have some bread and cheese or a *pain au raisin* and watch the barges go through the locks.

The parks all around Notre-Dame, especially the **Square Jean XXIII** behind the apse, across from Ile St.-Louis. In the evenings, when the weather is warm, there are often musicians and singers.

The small park that's perched over the **Arènes de Lutèce** (the old Roman arena) off Rue Monge. A strange, almost spooky spot that looks out onto the empty floor of the arena.

The gardens of the **Palais Royal** or the **Place des Vosges** at dusk, when the fountains are still on, children are still playing, and the older people from the neighborhood are still chatting on their folding chairs.

The park behind the Musée de Cluny. The long, narrow stretch of land nicely separates the old museum and the ruins of the Roman baths from Boulevard St.-Germain.

The garden behind the Rodin Museum, the old palace that the great German poet Rilke found for Rodin when he was working as his secretary. This soft, melancholy garden is the most quiet spot in Paris.

The parks next to the church of St.-Germain-des-Prés. Picasso's splendid statue for Apollinaire and old Gothic ruins are here. The benches under great trees form a circle that's cozy and homey. My favorite spot in Paris.

Mark Williamson
Owner, Willi's Wine Bar, Paris

The **Palais-Royal Gardens,** which are near my backyard. Whenever I have five minutes, I pop over.

The night train to Venice in November when the tax man cometh.

The night train to Florence in March for an early taste of spring.

Watching the lights go out on **Sacré-Coeur** and the **Panthéon** at midnight while having a Wild Turkey in the **Jules Verne bar** on the second level of the **Eiffel Tower** (the bar is normally reserved for diners only; however, access may be negotiable).

A picnic of crunchy baguettes, local *chèvre,* and a cool bottle of St. Joseph in a meadow near **Giverny** before visiting Monet's gardens.

A steak in May at 3:00AM at the **Tour de Montlèry** on the Rue des Prouvairs, rubbing shoulders with the butchers who still animate the old Les Halles market. A quick cab ride will take you to the new Les Halles at Rungis to catch the tail end of the fish market at 5:30AM. Then, go to the poultry pavilion to look at rabbits, turkeys, and quails. Have a leisurely coffee at the **Café St.-Hubert** (the heart of Rungis at this time) and head off to buy fresh basil, thyme, and chives from the stalls of local farmers. Around 9AM, the cut flower market begins to bud. Finish the day with a sharpener, breakfast, or bed.

The terrace at the **Moulin de Village** in the Cité Berryer when the sun is shining.

Inside **Le Grand Véfour** when the sun isn't shining.

The **Marché aux Puces** at the **Porte de Vanves,** where one can still get lucky.

The métro.

The TGV, which makes living in Paris and lunching in Lyon possible. For longer distances, travel first class.

The **Deux Magots** on a Sunday morning when the croissants are still hot, and reading *The London Times* before the crowd arrives.

Anne-Marie Munoz
Director, Yves Saint Laurent

More than 25 years ago I arrived in Paris early on a sunny morning at the Gare d'Austerlitz. The taxi took me along the Left Bank quais, all the way to the seventh arrondissement, just before the Eiffel Tower. That is still my favorite scenery. The mixture of people and the never-ending contrasts are subtle and surprising, like French cuisine.

I like to walk the streets in different quarters. There is personality everywhere.

I often eat at the **Brasserie de l'Alma** on Avenue George V, which is near my work and frequented by movie actors who audition at the nearby casting agencies.

I love **Place de la Concorde** when it lights up at dusk.

George Lang
Restaurateur, Café des Artistes, New York

Drouant—where the Conseil des Dix meets to award the Prix Goncourt.

Dining at **Pharamond**—one of the few places left from the Les Halles area and a felicitous example of an era when the French talent for displaying food knew no limit.

Taking a break at the **Louis XIV** café, which was a 19th-century stopover for coaches.

La Closerie des Lilas where **Modigliani, Henry Miller, Oscar Wilde,** and the rest of them chewed

Day Trips

over surplus agonies and ecstasies while having a couple of Pernod drinks and endless coffees.

Bofinger—a brasserie that has enough details in its Belle Epoque interior to excite faith in this period.

Vagenende—for its glorious Art-Nouveau style. The food is standard bistro fare, but it's the perfect place for a romantic dinner.

Ismail Merchant
British Film Producer

Whenever I go to Paris, I buy mustard. The best mustard in the world is at **Fauchon** on the Place de la Madeleine. I bring back at least six bottles per trip, and the people at customs laugh when I say it's for cooking. The fact is, my cooking is as good as my movies.

T

Index

U

V

W

Y

Z

Bay *(oriel)* windows in Paris
generally date from after 1882,
when the city abolished Henri
IV's previous zoning ordi-
nance, which forbade such
projections because he feared
they would promote the spread
of fire from house to house.

Restaurants

Only restaurants with star ratings are listed below. All restaurants are listed alphabetically in the main (preceding) index. Always call in advance to ensure a restaurant has not closed, changed its hours, or booked its tables for a private party. The dollar signs reflect general price-range relationships between other restaurants; they do not represent specific rates.

★	Good
★★	Very Good
★★★	Excellent
★★★★	Extraordinary

$	The Price is Right
$$	Reasonable
$$$	Expensive
$$$$	A Month's Pay

Paris has six reservoirs, which were built during the Franco-Prussian War. Legend holds that the city keeps trout in a section of the reservoirs, rather like the practice of bringing a canary into a mine shaft. If the trout die, the water is presumed contaminated and shut off.

Features

Hotels

Bests

The first of November, All Saints' Day, is when the French make an annual pilgrimage to their favorite cemeteries to pay respects to lost loved ones and to visit other "permanent Parisians." In the Père Lachaise cemetery repose luminaries such as Chopin, Piaf, Bizet, Balzac, Jim Morrison, Colette, Proust, Victor Hugo, and Oscar Wilde. Chopin devotees even play tapes of his famous funeral march, while Morrison groupies strum bleary-eyed renditions of "Light My Fire" on 12-string guitars. Maps to the tombs are sold at the cemetery entrance for a few francs.

Writer and Researcher
Stewart McBride

Editor
Rebecca Poole Forée

Staff Editor
Lisa Zuniga

Associate Editor
Karin Mullen

Copy Editor
Margie Lee

Editorial Assistant
Daniela Sylvers

Editorial Assistant, Paris
Priscilla Buckley

Word Processing
Jerry Stanton

Art/Research Assistant
Claudia A. Goulette

Administrative Assistant
Stacee Kramer

Art Director
Cherylonda Fitzgerald

Design Coordinator
Chris Middour

Designers
Kitti Homme
M Kohnke

Map Designers
Cathy McAuliffe
Patricia Keelin

Production
Carrē Furukawa
Gerard Garbutt

Design Advisor
Stuart L. Silberman

Film Production
Digital Pre-Press International

Printing and Otabind
Webcom Limited

Cover Photo
Mark Simon

Special Thanks:
Nathalie Angles
Leslie Cook
Olivier des Clers
Ray DeMoulin and the Center for Creative Imaging
Laurie Dill
Jean-Francois, Henriette, and Matisse Gaillard
Alain and Michael Illel
David Markus
Selby McCreery
Stephanie Mills
Sally and J.U. Parker
Andrew J. Smith
Patricia and Walter Wells
Lisa Winer

ACCESS® PRESS

President
Mark Johnson

Director
Maura Carey Damacion

Project Director
Mark Goldman

Editorial Director
Rebecca Poole Forée

Place du Palais-Royal

The maps introducing each **PARIS**ACCESS® walk (from page 10 to 166) are excerpts of a remarkable map called the *Plan du Paris à Vol D'Oiseau (A Bird's-Eye View of Paris)*, created by Georges Peltier. Inspired by the famous *Turgot Map of Paris* (completed in 1739), Peltier, an artist and cartographer, began his axonometric rendering of Paris in 1920. He spent 20 years and 30,000 hours creating the map. Since he com pleted it in 1940, numerous revisions have been made to keep the map up to date. Permission to use excerpts of the *Plan du Paris* was granted by the publishers, **Blondel La Rougery.** A copy of the Paris map may be purchased by writing to: Blondel La Rougery, 268 Rue de Brémont, 93112, Rosny-Sous-Bois, France; or call 48.94.94.52.

ACCESS® PRESS does not solicit individuals, organizations, or businesses for inclusion in our books, nor do we accept payment for inclusion. We welcome, however, information from our readers, including comments, criticisms, and new listings.

Distinctive features of **ACCESS**® Travel Guides

- Organized by neighborhood, the way natives know a city and visitors experience it.

- Color-coded entries distinguish restaurants, hotels, shops, parks, architecture, and places of interest.

- Easy to use and a pleasure to read.

- Generous use of detailed maps with points of interest identified.

- Each city's flavor is conveyed by descriptions of its history, lists of the personal favorites of people who know and love the city, and trivia and lavish illustrations.

BARCELONAACCESS®
An up-to-the-minute guide to Spain's avant-garde city, home of the 1992 Summer Olympic Games. 160 pages, $17.00

BOSTONACCESS®
A guide to the many charms of America's Revolutionary capital, from historic landmarks to where to shop, walk, stay, and dine. 208 pages, $16.95

CARIBBEANACCESS®
The best of the Caribbean—from well-known resorts in the Bahamas to exotic hideaways in the US and British Virgin Islands. Includes Bermuda highlights. 208 pages, $17.00

CHICAGOACCESS®
The key to inimitable Chicago style, from its renowned architecture to its famous deep-dish pizza. 192 pages, $16.95

**FLORENCE/VENICE/
MILAN**ACCESS®
A grand tour through Northern Italy's three major cities in one comprehensive guide. 240 pages, $17.00

HAWAIIACCESS®
Organized island by island . . . what to see . . . where to stay . . . what to do. 192 pages, $17.00

LAACCESS®
The city's characteristic urban sprawl and profusion of personalities rendered accessible. 224 pages, $17.00

LONDONACCESS®
The first winner from abroad of the London Tourist Board's Guidebook of the Year Award! 224 pages, $16.95

MEXICOACCESS®
Explore Mexico—from the best Pacific coastal resorts to the archaeological highlights of the Yucatán to the pulsating center of Mexico City. 240 pages, $17.00

MIAMI & SOUTH FLORIDAACCESS®
A guide to all of sunny South Florida, including Miami, Ft. Lauderdale, Palm Beach, the Florida Keys, the Everglades, and Sanibel and Captiva islands. 224 pages, $17.00

NYCACCESS®
For natives and visitors...the ultimate guide to the city famous for everything except subtlety and understatement. 320 pages, $17.00

ORLANDO & CENTRAL FLORIDAACCESS®
A whirlwind tour of Central Florida from Orlando and Walt Disney World to the JFK Space Center, Tampa, and much more. 176 pages, $17.00

PARISACCESS®
For the first-time and the veteran visitor, a guide that opens doors to the city's magic and nuances. 208 pages, $17.00

ROMEACCESS®
An award-winning guidebook featuring favorite promenades of the Eternal City. 160 pages, $16.95

SAN DIEGOACCESS®
Discover the best of this vibrant young city, from its world-famous zoo to its sun-drenched beaches. 160 pages, $17.00

SFACCESS®
Our best-selling guide to the much-loved city includes day trips around the Bay Area. 208 pages, $17.00

SUMMER GAMES 1992 ACCESS®
A TV viewer's guide to the Summer Olympics in Barcelona, with in-depth information and colorful illustrations for all the events. 112 pages, $10.00

THE WALL STREET JOURNAL
Guide to Understanding Money & Markets
A best-selling book with details on buying stocks, bonds, and futures, spotting trends, and evaluating companies. 120 pages, $13.95

WASHINGTON DCACCESS®
A comprehensive guide to the nation's capital with descriptions of the beautiful and historic places that encircle it. 224 pages, $17.00

WINE COUNTRYACCESS®
Northern California
All the ingredients you need to create your own wine-touring vacation. Available in 1992. 208 pages, $17.00

To order these **ACCESS**®Guides, please see the other side of this page.

About **NYC**ACCESS®
At last a guidebook to Manhattan that won't put you to sleep. **NYC**ACCESS® even has a section on teaching you how to talk like a "Noo Yawker." But what's most remarkable about this lively little tome (and unusual for guidebooks) is that it not only tells you what to do, eat, and see, but in no uncertain terms tells you what to avoid.
USA Today

ACCESS® GUIDES

Order by phone, toll-free: 1-800-331-3761

Travel: Promo # RØØ111
WSJ: Promo # RØØ211

Name _____ Phone _____

Address _____

City _____ State _____ Zip _____

Please send me the following **ACCESS**®Guides:

☐ **BARCELONA**ACCESS® $17.00
0-06-277000-4

☐ **BOSTON**ACCESS® $16.95
0-06-772503-1

☐ **CARIBBEAN**ACCESS® $17.00
0-06-277042-X

☐ **CHICAGO**ACCESS® $16.95
0-06-277518-X

☐ **FLORENCE/VENICE/ MILAN**ACCESS® $17.00
0-06-277001-2

☐ **HAWAII**ACCESS® $17.00
0-06-277034-9

☐ **LA**ACCESS® $17.00
0-06-772507-4

☐ **LONDON**ACCESS® $16.95
0-06-772509-0

☐ **MEXICO**ACCESS® $17.00
0-06-277041-1

☐ **MIAMI & SOUTH FLORIDA**ACCESS® $17.00
0-06-277002-0

☐ **NYC**ACCESS® $17.00
0-06-772522-8

☐ **ORLANDO & CENTRAL FLORIDA**ACCESS® $17.00
0-06-277003-9

☐ **PARIS**ACCESS® $17.00
0-06-277038-1

☐ **ROME**ACCESS® $16.95
0-06-772510-4

☐ **SAN DIEGO**ACCESS® $17.00
0-06-277004-7

☐ **SF**ACCESS® $17.00
0-06-772511-2

☐ **SUMMER GAMES 1992** ACCESS® $10.00
0-06-277031-4

☐ **THE WALL STREET JOURNAL** Guide to Understanding Money & Markets $13.95
0-06-772516-3

☐ **WASHINGTON DC**ACCESS® $17.00
0-06-277039-X

☐ **WINE COUNTRY**ACCESS® Northern California $17.00
0-06-277006-3

Prices subject to change without notice.

Total for **ACCESS**®Guides:	$
For PA delivery, please include sales tax:	
Add $4.00 for first book S&H, $1.00 per additional book:	
Total payment:	$

☐ Check or Money Order enclosed. Offer valid in United States only.
Please make payable to HarperCollins *Publishers*

☐ Charge my credit card ☐ American Express ☐ Visa ☐ Mastercard

Card no. _____ Exp. date _____

Signature _____

Send orders to:
HarperCollins *Publishers*
P.O. Box 588
Dunmore, PA 18512-0588

Send correspondence to:
ACCESS®PRESS
10 East 53rd Street, 7th floor
New York, NY 10022

Praise for **ACCESS**® Guides

Finally, books that look at cities the way tourists do—block by block...**ACCESS**® may be the best series for the chronically lost. **USA Today**

It combines the best of the practical directories with the superior artwork of the hardcover coffee-table books at an affordable price. **New York Times**